Managing Active Directory with Windows PowerShell™: TFM®

2nd Edition

Jeffery Hicks

AF843521

SAPIEN PRESS
841 Latour Ct Ste D
Napa, CA 94558
www.SAPIENPress.com

Managing Active Directory with Windows PowerShell: TFM 2nd Edition
by
Jeffery Hicks

ISBN: 978-0-9821314-4-2
Printed in the United States of America
First printing: April 2011
10 9 8 7 6 5 4 3 2 1

Trademarks
All terms mentioned in this book that are known to be trademarks or service marks have been appropriately capitalized. SAPIEN Press cannot attest to the accuracy of this information. Use of a term in this book should not be regarded as affecting the validity of any trademark or service mark. All marks remain the property of their respective owner(s) and are used herein only for reference.

Warning and Disclaimer
Every effort has been made to make this book as complete and as accurate as possible, but no warranty or fitness is implied. The information provided is on an "as is" basis. The author(s) and the publisher shall have neither liability nor responsibility to any person or entity with respect to any loss or damages arising from the information contained in thi book.

Get More... Online!
Access downloads, technical support, and other resources for this book at www.SAPIENPress.com. Discussion forums related to this book's content may be maintained at www.ScriptingAnswers.com, or on the author(s)' private Web sites.

If You're Legal... We Thank You
If you legally purchased this book, in either electronic or print format, both the publisher and the author(s) would like to extend their sincere gratitude. Publishers and authors earn their income from the sale of their books; that income enables them to pay for their homes, feed and support their families, and remain financially solvent. By legally purchasing this book, you are encourging technical authors everywhere to continue writing books that deliver the information you need. Thank you.

Available in Print and Electronic Editions
This book is available in electronic format exclusively from www.ScriptingOutpost.com. Print editions are available from all major booksellers and from www.ScriptingOutpost.com.

Publisher & Editor-in-Chief
Ferdinand G. Rios

Copy Editor
Kevin Fansler

Indexer
Donna M. Drialo

Book Layout & Cover Design
Maricela Soria

Contents

CHAPTER 3

CHAPTER 4

CHAPTER 5

CHAPTER 12

CHAPTER 13

APPENDIX A

APPENDIX B

For Lucas and Ellena:

Who bring joy to my life and meaning to my world

For Beth:

Who makes everything possible

Acknowledgements

Writing a book is a lonely process involving many people. This is never truer than with a technical book. I am greatly indebted to my team of real-world technical reviewers who kept me on track, corrected my oversights and helped create a book that I hope you will want on your bookshelf. The success of the second edition of this book is due in large part to the efforts of Richard Siddaway, Wes Stahler, Ragnar Harper and Darrin Henshaw.

Allow me to also reiterate my appreciation for assistance on the first edition from Marco Shaw, Kirk Munro, Christopher Whitfield, Andy Bilden, Jonathon Noble, Josh Goldfarb, Richard Campos, Dominique Megard, Dmitry Sotnikov, Michel Klomp, and Dino Davis. I also received valuable advice from the PowerShell MVP community, especially Brandon Shell and Don Jones. I'd also like to thank Darren Mar-Elia of SDM Software for expanding my knowledge of all things Group Policy-related.

As always a well-earned word of thanks to my copy editor, Kevin Fansler, who makes me look great. Of course any faults in the material are entirely my own.

I would be remiss in not acknowledging all the support I get from the folks at SAPIEN. Thanks to Ferdinand, Alex, Margaret and David. An extra shout out goes to Maricela Soira for her excellent graphic art work which has graced the cover of all my books from SAPIEN Press.

I sincerely must acknowledge and thank my family, Beth, Lucas, and Ellena. Their support and love is invaluable and beyond repayment.

Finally, a long overdue thank you to all of you who read my columns, my books, attend my conference sessions and sit in my classes. I wouldn't be happily doing all that I do this if it weren't for you and your support. I am deeply humbled.

Introduction

Managing Active Directory with Windows PowerShell

When I wrote the first edition of this book, I lamented the lack of Windows PowerShell support from Microsoft for managing Active Directory. Consequently, half of the first edition's content was essentially workarounds for the missing cmdlets. How time flies in the PowerShell world. Today, Windows PowerShell 2.0 is available everywhere and Microsoft has released their PowerShell-based solution for Active Directory. The combination of the two promises to be a game changer for Windows and Active Directory administrators worldwide.

This change, by the way, ***does not*** mean you have to learn how to script. As I will show you throughout the book, you can accomplish many Active Directory administrative tasks interactively through the management console. Often these are relatively simple, one-line, PowerShell expressions that accomplish what used to take 20 lines of VBScript. Granted, you'll want to script more complex or repetitive tasks. But I'll provide plenty of examples and complete, working script that will help you get a jump start on your own administrative scripting projects.

And even though Microsoft has released a set of cmdlets, they are not the only game in town. Depending on your situation, you may not be able to take advantage of the Microsoft modules, as I explain in Chapter 1. This edition continues to include coverage (expanded and updated) of the free Active Directory cmdlets from Quest Software.

The goal of this book is to bring all the technologies, techniques, and tips into one place. Most of the products I demonstrate are free and the few commercial products I showcase are very reasonably priced. As with many Windows management tasks there are usually several ways to accomplish them. Throughout the book, I provide multiple ways to accomplish the same task. I realize that in the "real world," individuals and companies have limitations. While technique A might work for one company, it isn't possible for another. You may also find situations where one technique meets your needs better than another. My goal is to educate you about how to do something and to show you the available options.

I wrote this book for Windows administrators looking to take their skill set to the next level. I'm going to assume you have a modicum of Windows PowerShell and Active Directory experience. If some of my more advanced examples appear overwhelming, don't feel discouraged. They should just work. Of course, the more PowerShell you know the more you'll get out of the examples. If you are looking for a terrific resource to teach yourself Windows PowerShell, I hope you'll check out Windows PowerShell 2.0: TFM written by Don Jones and myself. We wrote that book to take you from ground zero to the PowerShell penthouse. Visit ScriptingOutpost.com to learn more and be sure to check out the other training material while you are there from superstar PowerShell trainer Don Jones.

Scripts

Since this *is* a Windows PowerShell book, there are many script examples. Whenever possible, I tried to base the examples in reality and make them practical. In this regard, much of the book takes a cookbook approach. Longer script examples are listed as ps1 files and are available for download at SAPIENPress.com. Creating a ps1 file was done primarily to make it easier to find a specific sample. Some of the scripts you can run outright. Others are script files with a single function or two. To use these functions, you need to copy and paste it into your PowerShell session, copy and paste the function into your PowerShell profile script or dot source the script file. Some scripts and functions may be packaged together as a PowerShell module. The download file will have complete instructions.

Setup

During the course of writing this book, I used the latest product versions I could get my hands on. I realize that by the time this book hits your desk some of these products may have released new versions; though I expect much of the material to remain relevant. If nothing else, a new release may make some tasks even easier. So please use my examples as guidelines, understanding you may need to make some minor adjustments for new versions or features.

My test environment was primarily a Windows Server 2008 R2 Active Directory domain, although I also tested with legacy domain controllers running the Active Directory Gateway Management Service. Most of my administration was done from a Microsoft Windows 7 desktop that belonged to the domain, logged on with domain administrator credentials. All appropriate updates and patches have been applied. I installed the Remote Server Administration Tools for Windows 7 primarily for the Active Directory and Group Policy roles. I'll cover this in Chapter 1.

A group of Windows administrators reviewed and tested all of the examples in their environments, which I can only assume is a mix of everything else. I have no reason to assume that the examples in the book won't work for you.

In many, if not all, of my examples, I tried to use $env:computername instead of *localhost*. Depending on the technology, such as ADSI or WMI, and what you might be trying to accomplish, sometimes *localhost* works and sometimes it produces odd results. Using $env:computername returns a real computer name that eliminates the uncertainty.

All examples are using the English-US settings. In PowerShell this is referred to as culture. You may need to modify PowerShell examples accordingly, especially with types like [DATETIME] depending on your configuration. I also used PowerShell 2.0, which is required if you wish to use the Microsoft Active Directory module. Otherwise, most everything else should work just fine with PowerShell 1.0.

I always stress this fact when speaking at conferences or training, but you must establish a non-production test environment. Please, please ***do not*** try any of my examples or anything you develop in your production domain without extensive testing. You can bring your network to its knees with PowerShell faster than you can say "Jeffrey Snover Rocks!"

Scope

Even though this book is billed as TFM (the foremost manual), there are limitations. I'm not covering the following topics, or I cover them in a very limited fashion. Although much of the material in the book could be modified to work with some of these items:

- Active Directory Application Mode (ADAM) or Active Directory Lightweight Directory Service (AD LDS)
- DNS
- DHCP
- Disaster Recovery
- Schema modifications or updates
- System.DirectoryServices.Protocols
- System.DirectoryServices.AccountManagement
- Non-Microsoft LDAP based directory services
- Exchange 2007 or Exchange 2010

Service

There are several resources you can use to learn more about PowerShell and the products discussed in the book. First, please subscribe to http://blog.SAPIEN.com. This is your one-stop shop to keep apprised of all SAPIEN-related announcements. I hope you will find time to keep up with my blog at http://jdhitsolutions.com/blog. You should also be reading the Microsoft PowerShell team blog at http://blogs.msdn.com/powershell/ and the Active Directory PowerShell blog at http://blogs.msdn.com/adpowershell/. Support for the Quest Active Directory cmdlets is at http://www.PowerGUI.org. Finally, if you have questions about any of the script samples in the book or PowerShell, I encourage you to use the forums at http://www.ScriptingAnswers.com.

Chapter 1

Managing Active Directory with Windows PowerShell Fundamentals

Although most of this book will be devoted to cmdlet-based solutions, I want you to have an understanding of what is happening "under the hood." This information might come in handy when working with the Quest or Microsoft cmdlets. Or you may have situations where you need to write your own native solution via a PowerShell script or advanced function.

I'm assuming that you already have a basic working knowledge of Windows PowerShell. If you feel you could use some additional help, I encourage you to get a copy of *Windows PowerShell 2.0: TFM* (SAPIEN Press 2010).

System.DirectoryServices

When working with Active Directory, or any directory service for that matter, Windows PowerShell relies on the directory service .NET classes. The parent namespace is System.DirectoryServices. The primary class you would use is the System.DirectoryServices.DirectoryEntry. This class will return, as the name suggests, an entry or object from a directory service. In this case, the directory service will be Active Directory, although the .NET directory service classes are designed for any LDAP-compliant directory service. In PowerShell, you use the **New-Object** cmdlet to create a directory service object. If you are running PowerShell with appropriate credentials, creating such an object is as easy as this:

```
PS C:\> New-Object DirectoryServices.DirectoryEntry "LDAP://jdhlab.local"
```

```
distinguishedName : {DC=jdhlab,DC=local}
Path              : LDAP://jdhlab.local
```

All you need to do is specify the LDAP path of a specific Active Directory object. In the example above, I'm connecting to the root of the jdhlab.local domain. You can also use the distinguished name format, as shown below:

```
PS C:\> New-Object DirectoryServices.DirectoryEntry "LDAP://dc=jdhlab,dc=local"


distinguishedName : {DC=jdhlab,DC=local}
Path              : LDAP://dc=jdhlab,dc=local
```

You need to use the distinguished name when you want to connect an organizational unit:

```
PS C:\> New-Object DirectoryServices.DirectoryEntry "LDAP://OU=Servers,DC=jdhlab,dc=local"


distinguishedName : {OU=Servers,DC=jdhlab,DC=local}
Path              : LDAP://OU=Servers,DC=jdhlab,dc=local
```

If you need to authenticate with alternate credentials, you can add them as additional constructor parameters:

```
PS C:\> $admin="jdhlab\da_jhicks"
PS C:\> $pwd=Read-Host "Enter the password for $admin"
Enter the password for jdhlab\da_jhicks: P@ssw0rd
PS C:\> New-Object DirectoryServices.DirectoryEntry "LDAP://jdhlab.local",$admin,$pwd


distinguishedName :{DC=jdhlab,DC=local}
Path              : LDAP://dc=jdhlab,dc=local
```

Don't use the **-AsSecureString** parameter with the **Read-Host** cmdlet. The password that you use in this example can't be a secure string. But don't fear—the password is not passed as clear text over the network. If you prefer, you can use a PSCredential:

```
PS C:\> $cred=get-credential jdhlab\da_jhicks
PS C:\> New-Object DirectoryServices.DirectoryEntry `
>> "LDAP://jdhlab.local",$cred.Username,$cred.GetNetworkCredential().Password
>>


distinguishedName :{DC=mycompany,DC=local}
Path              : LDAP://dc=jdhlab,dc=local
```

The $cred variable holds the PSCredential object. You can use its **Username** property to pass the string jdhlab\da_jhicks to the **New-Object** cmdlet. To get the password as a string, call the **GetNetworkCredential()** method, which returns a System.Net.NetworkCredential object. The **Password** property of this object will be a string. This technique allows you to pass strings as necessary, but not directly expose them in the console.

Case Counts

The LDAP provider is case sensitive and must be uppercase.

Now that you know how to create a directory service entry object, you can save it to a variable so you can explore it further:

```
PS C:\> $dsroot=New-Object DirectoryServices.DirectoryEntry "LDAP://jdhlab.local",
>> $cred.Username,$cred.GetnetworkCredential().Password
>>


PS C:\> $dsroot

distinguishedName :{DC=mycompany,DC=local}
Path              : LDAP://jdhlab.local
```

You can pipe $dsroot to the **Get-Member** cmdlet to discover its properties. Once informed, you can write PowerShell expressions like this to display information:

```
PS C:\> $dsroot | Select @{name="DN";Expression={$_.DistinguishedName}},
>>  @{name="Name";Expression={$_.Name}},
>>  @{name="Created";Expression={$_.WhenCreated}},
>>  @{name="Last Modified";Expression={$_.WhenChanged}},
>>  @{name="FSMO";Expression={$_.FSMORoleOwner}}
>>


DN            : DC=jdhlab,DC=local
Name          : jdhlab
Created       : 1/24/2010 8:02:31 PM
Last Modified : 7/6/2010 6:37:02 PM
FSMO          : CN=NTDS Settings,CN=COREDC01,CN=Servers,CN=Default-First-Site-Name,CN=Sites,CN...
```

In the example above, I created custom property names using associative arrays, also known in PowerShell as a hash table, to make the output more user friendly. For example, instead of displaying the property name, FSMORoleOwner, I created a custom property with a shorter name. The value is the same regardless.

Get Child Items

It is very easy to retrieve a list of child objects from a given directory services entry. Because of the way PowerShell adapts the .NET Framework classes, you don't always see every property and method. You can use the **Children** property to provide the information you are looking for:

```
PS C:\> $dsroot.children


distinguishedName : {OU=Branch Office,DC=jdhlab,DC=local}
Path              : LDAP://jdhlab.local/OU=Branch Office,DC=jdhlab,DC=local

distinguishedName : {CN=Builtin,DC=jdhlab,DC=local}
Path              : LDAP://jdhlab.local/CN=Builtin,DC=jdhlab,DC=local

distinguishedName : {CN=Computers,DC=jdhlab,DC=local}
Path              : LDAP://jdhlab.local/CN=Computers,DC=jdhlab,DC=local
```

```
distinguishedName : {OU=Contacts,DC=jdhlab,DC=local}
Path              : LDAP://jdhlab.local/OU=Contacts,DC=jdhlab,DC=local

distinguishedName : {OU=Desktops,DC=jdhlab,DC=local}
Path              : LDAP://jdhlab.local/OU=Desktops,DC=jdhlab,DC=local

distinguishedName : {OU=Domain Controllers,DC=jdhlab,DC=local}
Path              : LDAP://jdhlab.local/OU=Domain Controllers,DC=jdhlab,DC=local

distinguishedName : {OU=Employees,DC=jdhlab,DC=local}
Path              : LDAP://jdhlab.local/OU=Employees,DC=jdhlab,DC=local

...
```

The **Children** property returns a list of containers and organizational units from $dsroot.

Using DirectoryEntry objects

In the same way that you worked with a domain object, you can work with most any other Active Directory object given its distinguished name:

```
PS C:\> $roy=New-Object system.directoryservices.directoryentry `
>> "LDAP://CN=Roy G. Biv,OU=Employees,DC=jdhlab,DC=local"
>>
PS C:\> $roy


distinguishedName : {CN=Roy G. Biv,OU=Employees,DC=jdhlab,DC=local}
Path              : LDAP://CN=Roy G. Biv,OU=Employees,DC=jdhlab,DC=local
```

I have created an object that refers to the Roy G. Biv user object. Most of the properties are pretty easy to guess:

```
PS C:\> $roy | Select Name,Title,Department

Name                                Title                               Department
----                                -----                               ----------
{Roy G. Biv}                        {Manager}                           {Art}
```

For everything else, pipe the object to the **Get-Member** cmdlet or the **Select-Object** cmdlet specifying all properties:

```
PS C:\> $roy | Select *


objectClass          : {top, person, organizationalPerson, user}
cn                   : {Roy G. Biv}
sn                   : {Biv}
l                    : {Miami}
title                : {Manager}
telephoneNumber      : {200}
givenName            : {Roy}
initials             : {G}
distinguishedName    : {CN=Roy G. Biv,OU=Employees,DC=jdhlab,DC=local}
instanceType         : {4}
whenCreated          : {3/22/2010 7:04:19 PM}
whenChanged          : {7/6/2010 10:07:46 PM}
displayName          : {Roy G. Biv}
```

```
uSNCreated                : {System.__ComObject}
memberOf                  : {CN=All Managers,OU=Groups,DC=jdhlab,DC=local, CN=Sales Users,OU=Groups,
                             DC=jdhlab,DC=local}
uSNChanged                : {System.__ComObject}
department                : {Art}
company                   : {JDHLABS}
name                      : {Roy G. Biv}
objectGUID                : {247 61 90 7 202 222 234 69 185 124 177 98 231 36 72 251}
userAccountControl        : {512}
badPwdCount               : {0}
codePage                  : {0}
countryCode               : {0}
badPasswordTime           : {System.__ComObject}
lastLogoff                : {System.__ComObject}
lastLogon                 : {System.__ComObject}
pwdLastSet                : {System.__ComObject}
primaryGroupID            : {513}
objectSid                 : {1 5 0 0 0 0 0 5 21 0 0 0 163 199 225 235 194 160 23 21 139 91 10 234 125
                            4 0 0}
accountExpires            : {System.__ComObject}
logonCount                : {4}
sAMAccountName            : {roygbiv}
sAMAccountType            : {805306368}
userPrincipalName         : {roygbiv@jdhlab.local}
objectCategory            : {CN=Person,CN=Schema,CN=Configuration,DC=jdhlab,DC=local}
dSCorePropagationData     : {6/22/2010 6:51:59 PM, 1/1/1601 12:00:01 AM}
lastLogonTimestamp        : {System.__ComObject}
extensionAttribute2       : {256}
nTSecurityDescriptor      : {System.__ComObject}
AuthenticationType        : Secure
Children                  : {}
Guid                      : f73d5a07cadeea45b97cb162e72448fb
ObjectSecurity            : System.DirectoryServices.ActiveDirectorySecurity
NativeGuid                : f73d5a07cadeea45b97cb162e72448fb
NativeObject              : System.__ComObject
Parent                    : LDAP://OU=Employees,DC=jdhlab,DC=local
Password                  :
Path                      : LDAP://CN=Roy G. Biv,OU=Employees,DC=jdhlab,DC=local
Properties                : {objectClass, cn, sn, l...}
SchemaClassName           : user
SchemaEntry               : System.DirectoryServices.DirectoryEntry
UsePropertyCache          : True
Username                  :
Options                   : {}
Site                      :
Container                 :
```

One thing I hope you noticed is that many of the properties are stored as collections:

```
userPrincipalName      : {roygbiv@jdhlab.local}
```

But PowerShell is savvy enough to automatically adjust for that fact:

```
PS C:\> $roy.userprincipalname
roygbiv@jdhlab.local
```

Where it gets tricky is when you want a cleaner output or want to calculate a new property:

```
PS C:\> $roy | Select @{Name="User";Expression={$_.name.value}},
>> @{Name="Created";Expression={$_.WhenCreated.Value}},
```

```
>> @{Name="Modified";Expression={$_.WhenChanged.value}},
>> @{Name="AccountAge";Expression={(Get-Date)-$_.WhenCreated.value }}
>>

User                Created                   Modified                AccountAge
----                -------                   --------                ----------
Roy G. Biv          3/22/2010 7:04:19 PM      7/6/2010 10:07:46 PM    111.19:02:29.5636663
```

Instead of accessing the **WhenCreated** property, you need to access WhenCreated.Value.

You can also modify objects, usually by assigning a value to the property:

```
PS C:\> $roy.description="A colorful guy."
```

However, even though if I look at the property now I'll see the new value, it hasn't been written back to Active Directory. Here again, you just need to know to call the **SetInfo()** method:

```
PS C:\> $roy.SetInfo()
```

This will commit any changes you have made to the object locally back to the directory service.

The ADSI Type Adapter

Windows PowerShell is intended to be easy to use without requiring administrators to become .NET developers. One Windows PowerShell feature that meets this need is a type adapter. A type adapter is a shorthand clue that tells PowerShell: "Hey, I'm about to create something special." For Active Directory (and even local SAMAccount databases as explained in Appendix A) the [ADSI] type tells PowerShell you will be creating a System.DirectoryServices.DirectoryEntry object. So instead of using the **New-Object** cmdlet and specifying the path, you can use a short-hand approach like this:

```
PS C:\> [ADSI]$roy="LDAP://CN=Roy G. Biv,OU=Employees,DC=jdhlab,DC=local"
PS C:\> $roy


distinguishedName : {CN=Roy G. Biv,OU=Employees,DC=jdhlab,DC=local}
Path              : LDAP://CN=Roy G. Biv,OU=Employees,DC=jdhlab,DC=local
```

By the way, the type adapter is not case sensitive. You can use [ADSI], [adsi] or even [Adsi]. Regardless, the end result is an object that you can use just as I showed earlier:

```
PS C:\> $roy.WhenChanged

Monday, July 12, 2010 6:12:24 PM
PS C:\> $roy.l
Miami
PS C:\> $roy.l="Topeka"
PS C:\> $roy.setInfo()
```

The [ADSI] adapter, which is not case-sensitive, simply makes it easier to create the object reference. Appendix B offers more information on working with the "raw" .NET objects.

Using the Directory Searcher

So far I've been demonstrating how to work with individual objects. But more than likely you'll need to search Active Directory. For that, the .NET Framework provides the DirectorySearcher class. Using this class takes several steps. First, create the searcher object:

```
PS C:\> $searcher = New-Object DirectoryServices.DirectorySearcher
PS C:\> $searcher


CacheResults              : True
ClientTimeout             : -00:00:01
PropertyNamesOnly         : False
Filter                    : (objectClass=*)
PageSize                  : 0
PropertiesToLoad          : {}
ReferralChasing           : External
SearchScope               : Subtree
ServerPageTimeLimit       : -00:00:01
ServerTimeLimit           : -00:00:01
SizeLimit                 : 0
SearchRoot                : System.DirectoryServices.DirectoryEntry
Sort                      : System.DirectoryServices.SortOption
Asynchronous              : False
Tombstone                 : False
AttributeScopeQuery       :
DerefAlias                : Never
SecurityMasks             : None
ExtendedDN                : None
DirectorySynchronization :
VirtualListView           :
Site                      :
Container                 :
```

You really only need to define a few of these properties. By default, the directory searcher is configured to search for all objects:

```
Filter                    : (objectClass=*)
```

I'll show you how to change this a little later. The directory searcher begins its search from the SearchRoot:

```
SearchRoot                : System.DirectoryServices.DirectoryEntry
```

You can see this property is a DirectoryEntry object like the one used earlier. In the current example, the SearchRoot is the domain root:

```
PS C:\> $searcher.searchroot

distinguishedName : {DC=jdhlab,DC=local}
Path              : LDAP://DC=jdhlab,DC=local
```

The directory searcher has two primary methods: **FindOne()** and **FindAll()**. The first method will return the first object meeting the search criteria:

```
PS C:\> $searcher.findone()


Path                               Properties
----                               ----------
LDAP://DC=jdhlab,DC=local          {minpwdlength, dc, adspath, iscriticalsystemobject...}
```

The other method returns all objects in the Active Directory:

```
PS C:\> $searcher.findall() | Select path

Path
----
LDAP://DC=jdhlab,DC=local
LDAP://CN=Users,DC=jdhlab,DC=local
LDAP://CN=Computers,DC=jdhlab,DC=local
LDAP://OU=Domain Controllers,DC=jdhlab,DC=local
LDAP://CN=System,DC=jdhlab,DC=local
LDAP://CN=LostAndFound,DC=jdhlab,DC=local
LDAP://CN=Infrastructure,DC=jdhlab,DC=local
LDAP://CN=ForeignSecurityPrincipals,DC=jdhlab,DC=local
LDAP://CN=Program Data,DC=jdhlab,DC=local
LDAP://CN=Microsoft,CN=Program Data,DC=jdhlab,DC=local
...
```

Of course, you may want a more limited search query. You can define the **Filter** property with any LDAP query:

```
PS C:\> $searcher.filter="(objectClass=organizationalunit)"
PS C:\> $searcher.findall() | Select Path

Path
----
LDAP://OU=Domain Controllers,DC=jdhlab,DC=local
LDAP://OU=Employees,DC=jdhlab,DC=local
LDAP://OU=Servers,DC=jdhlab,DC=local
LDAP://OU=Techmentor Orlando,DC=jdhlab,DC=local
LDAP://OU=Desktops,DC=jdhlab,DC=local
LDAP://OU=Groups,DC=jdhlab,DC=local
LDAP://OU=Sales,OU=Employees,DC=jdhlab,DC=local
LDAP://OU=HR,OU=Employees,DC=jdhlab,DC=local
LDAP://OU=Customer Service,OU=Employees,DC=jdhlab,DC=local
LDAP://OU=Sales Managers,OU=Sales,OU=Employees,DC=jdhlab,DC=local
LDAP://OU=Payroll and Finance,OU=Employees,DC=jdhlab,DC=local
LDAP://OU=Operations,OU=Payroll and Finance,OU=Employees,DC=jdhlab,DC=local
LDAP://OU=Shipping,OU=Employees,DC=jdhlab,DC=local
LDAP://OU=Marketing,OU=Employees,DC=jdhlab,DC=local
LDAP://OU=IT,OU=Employees,DC=jdhlab,DC=local
LDAP://OU=Engineering,OU=Employees,DC=jdhlab,DC=local
LDAP://OU=Executive,OU=Employees,DC=jdhlab,DC=local
LDAP://OU=Test,OU=Employees,DC=jdhlab,DC=local
LDAP://OU=Microsoft Exchange Security Groups,DC=jdhlab,DC=local
LDAP://OU=Contacts,DC=jdhlab,DC=local
LDAP://OU=Branch Office,DC=jdhlab,DC=local
```

The directory searcher is looking for all organizational unit objects and PowerShell is displaying just the **Path** property. Here is a slightly more complicated example:

```
PS C:\> $searcher.Filter="(&(objectcategory=person)(objectclass=user))"
PS C:\> $searcher.findall() | Select Path

Path
----
LDAP://CN=Administrator,CN=Users,DC=jdhlab,DC=local
LDAP://CN=Guest,CN=Users,DC=jdhlab,DC=local
LDAP://CN=krbtgt,CN=Users,DC=jdhlab,DC=local
LDAP://CN=Jeff,CN=Users,DC=jdhlab,DC=local
LDAP://CN=Cassie O'Pia,OU=Employees,DC=jdhlab,DC=local
LDAP://CN=David Jaffe,OU=Branch Office,DC=jdhlab,DC=local
LDAP://CN=Chris Barry,OU=Employees,DC=jdhlab,DC=local
LDAP://CN=Daniel Roth,OU=Branch Office,DC=jdhlab,DC=local
LDAP://CN=Scott Bishop,OU=Branch Office,DC=jdhlab,DC=local
LDAP://CN=Sean Beantly,OU=Branch Office,DC=jdhlab,DC=local
...
```

In this example, the search filter is a combination that should return all user objects in your domain. The output is truncated.

The search filters can get quite complicated. In fact, you can take any LDAP query that you create using the Saved Queries feature in Active Directory Users and Computers and use it in PowerShell:

```
PS C:\>$searcher.filter=`
>>"(&(objectCategory=person)(objectClass=user)(userAccountControl:1.2.840.113556.1.4.803:=2))"
>>

PS C:\> $searcher.findall() | Select Path

Path
----
LDAP://CN=Guest,CN=Users,DC=jdhlab,DC=local
LDAP://CN=krbtgt,CN=Users,DC=jdhlab,DC=local
LDAP://CN=Daniel Roth,OU=Branch Office,DC=jdhlab,DC=local
LDAP://CN=Johnson Apacible,OU=Employees,DC=jdhlab,DC=local
LDAP://CN=Prithvi Raj,OU=Employees,DC=jdhlab,DC=local
LDAP://CN=Virginie Jean,OU=Customer Service,OU=Employees,DC=jdhlab,DC=local
LDAP://CN=John User3,OU=Branch Office,DC=jdhlab,DC=local
LDAP://CN=John User2,OU=Branch Office,DC=jdhlab,DC=local
LDAP://CN=John User1,OU=Branch Office,DC=jdhlab,DC=local
LDAP://CN=John User4,OU=Branch Office,DC=jdhlab,DC=local
LDAP://CN=John User5,OU=Branch Office,DC=jdhlab,DC=local
LDAP://CN=Jim Glynn,OU=Customer Service,OU=Employees,DC=jdhlab,DC=local
```

I've taken the LDAP query to find all disabled users and used it as my search filter. If you pipe the search results, you will see that you don't get the actual directory service entry, but rather a result object:

```
PS C:\> $disabled=$searcher.findall()
PS C:\> $disabled | Get-Member


   TypeName: System.DirectoryServices.SearchResult

Name              MemberType Definition
----              ---------- ----------
Equals            Method     bool Equals(System.Object obj)
GetDirectoryEntry Method     adsi GetDirectoryEntry()
GetHashCode       Method     int GetHashCode()
GetType           Method     type GetType()
```

```
ToString        Method      string ToString()
Path            Property    System.String Path {get;}
Properties      Property    System.DirectoryServices.ResultPropertyCollection Properties {get;}
```

This is an important distinction because if you need object specific information, or want to modify the user object, you need to take an extra step to retrieve it. Let's look at a quick example for a specific user account:

```
PS C:\> $searcher.filter="(&(objectclass=user)(samaccountname=da_jhicks))"
PS C:\> $result=$searcher.findone()
```

If I want to change the account's **Description** property, I can't simply modify $result because it doesn't connect to the user object. But I can use $result to create a new ADSI object that I can modify:

```
PS C:\> [ADSI]$user=$result.path
PS C:\> $user.description="Jeff's domain admin account"
PS C:\> $user.setInfo()
```

I can now re-run the search and see that the change has been made:

```
PS C:\> $result=$searcher.findone()
PS C:\> $result.properties.description
Jeff's domain admin account
```

LDAP Filters

I've always felt that LDAP filters belong more in the realm of systems programming as opposed to administrative scripts. Creating an effect LDAP filter can be an arcane experience and goes beyond the scope of this book. I've provided some basic examples here. If you are familiar and comfortable with LDAP filtering syntax, then by all means take advantage of it. If not, don't worry because there are plenty of other tools and techniques you'll learn throughout the book.

If you made it this far you're probably thinking that this is a lot of work. And you are right. There are better and easier ways to get to this same information and that's the purpose of this book. But I wanted you to understand what is happening "under the hood" should you feel the need to tinker. Instead, I'll be exploring two approaches that eliminate the need to use "raw" .NET objects.

Active Roles Server

Quest Software offers a free set of PowerShell cmdlets that is part of their Active Roles Server product. However, you can use these cmdlets with any Active Directory version without Quest's commercial product. Grab your copy at http://www.quest.com/powershell/activeroles-server.aspx. There are 32 and 64 bit flavors so install what is appropriate.

Nothing needs to be installed on your domain controller and I'm assuming you will manage Active Directory from the comfort of your Windows 7 desktop and your desk. You technically don't need Windows 7 or PowerShell 2.0 to run the Quest cmdlets but that's what I'm using and if you truly want to master your domain with PowerShell, this is the path to take.

Installing

The download is a standard MSI file which means you could deploy it via Group Policy or the like to all your administrators. Otherwise manually install it on your desktop. The setup will automatically register with PowerShell. Installation takes only a minute or so and doesn't require a reboot.

Loading

When you install the Active Roles Management Shell, it will add an item to your Start menu. Launching the shortcut will start a PowerShell session automatically configured with the Quest cmdlets.

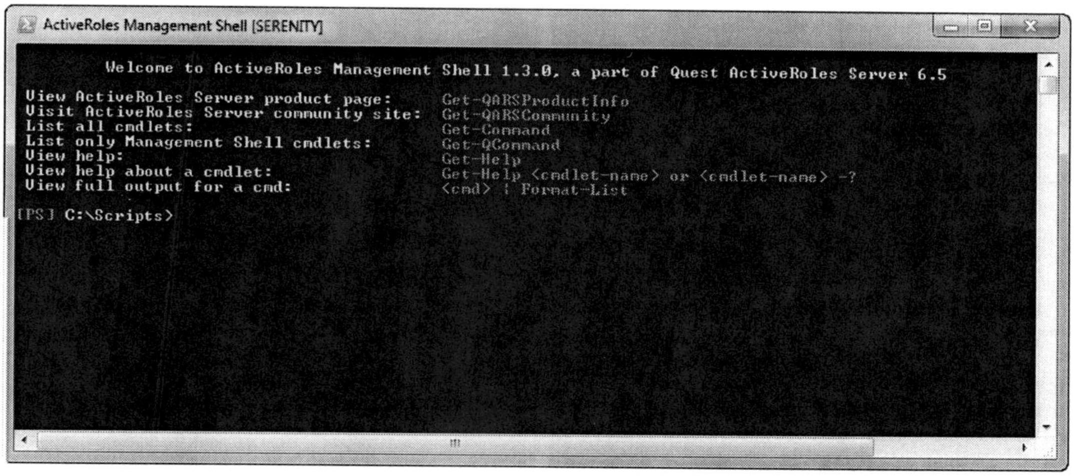

Figure 1-1 The Quest Software Active Roles Management Shell

My PowerShell profile script automatically sets my starting directory to C:\Scripts. But from here you can use the cmdlets to manage Active Directory.

However, the cmdlets are packaged as a PSSnapin, which means you can add them to any PowerShell session if you don't need their startup menu. You should be able to verify the install by checking registered snapins:

```
PS C:\> Get-PSSnapin -Registered quest.activeroles.admanagement


Name        : Quest.ActiveRoles.ADManagement
PSVersion   : 1.0
Description : This Windows PowerShell snap-in contains cmdlets to manage Active Directory and Q...
```

If you see this snapin you can add it to your current PowerShell session at any time:

```
PS C:\> Add-PSSnapin quest.activeroles.admanagement
```

Profile It

If you find yourself using the Quest cmdlets all the time, include the PSSnapin command in your PowerShell profile. Then you'll have access to the cmdlets in every PowerShell session. The snapin will also work in the PowerShell Integrated Scripting Environment (ISE).

Now let's see what goodies are packed away:

```
PS C:\> Get-Command -Module quest.activeroles.admanagement -CommandType cmdlet | Format-Wide

Add-QADGroupMember                              Add-QADMemberOf
Add-QADPasswordSettingsObjectAppliesTo          Add-QADPermission
Approve-QARSApprovalTask                        Connect-QADService
Convert-QADAttributeValue                       Deprovision-QADUser
Disable-QADComputer                             Disable-QADDiagnosticLog
Disable-QADUser                                 Disconnect-QADService
Enable-QADComputer                              Enable-QADDiagnosticLog
Enable-QADUser                                  Get-QADComputer
Get-QADDiagnosticLogStatus                      Get-QADGroup
Get-QADGroupMember                              Get-QADManagedObject
Get-QADMemberOf                                 Get-QADObject
Get-QADObjectSecurity                           Get-QADPasswordSettingsObject
Get-QADPasswordSettingsObjectAppliesTo          Get-QADPermission
Get-QADPSSnapinSettings                         Get-QADRootDSE
Get-QADUser                                     Get-QARSAccessTemplate
Get-QARSAccessTemplateLink                      Get-QARSApprovalTask
Get-QARSLastOperation                           Get-QARSOperation
Get-QARSWorkflowDefinition                      Get-QARSWorkflowInstance
Move-QADObject                                  New-QADComputer
New-QADGroup                                    New-QADObject
New-QADPasswordSettingsObject                   New-QADUser
New-QARSAccessTemplateLink                      Publish-QARSGroup
Reject-QARSApprovalTask                         Remove-QADGroupMember
Remove-QADMemberOf                              Remove-QADObject
Remove-QADPasswordSettingsObjectAppliesTo       Remove-QADPermission
Remove-QARSAccessTemplateLink                   Rename-QADObject
Reset-QADComputer                               Restore-QADDeletedObject
Set-QADComputer                                 Set-QADGroup
Set-QADObject                                   Set-QADObjectSecurity
Set-QADPSSnapinSettings                         Set-QADUser
Set-QARSAccessTemplateLink                      Unlock-QADUser
Unpublish-QARSGroup
```

The first thing I hope you'll notice is that the cmdlet nouns all have a prefix of either QAD or QARS. This is to prevent name collisions with other cmdlets, say from Microsoft. Some of these cmdlets only apply to Quest's commercial product but I will be explaining many of these throughout the book.

All of the cmdlets have complete help and examples.

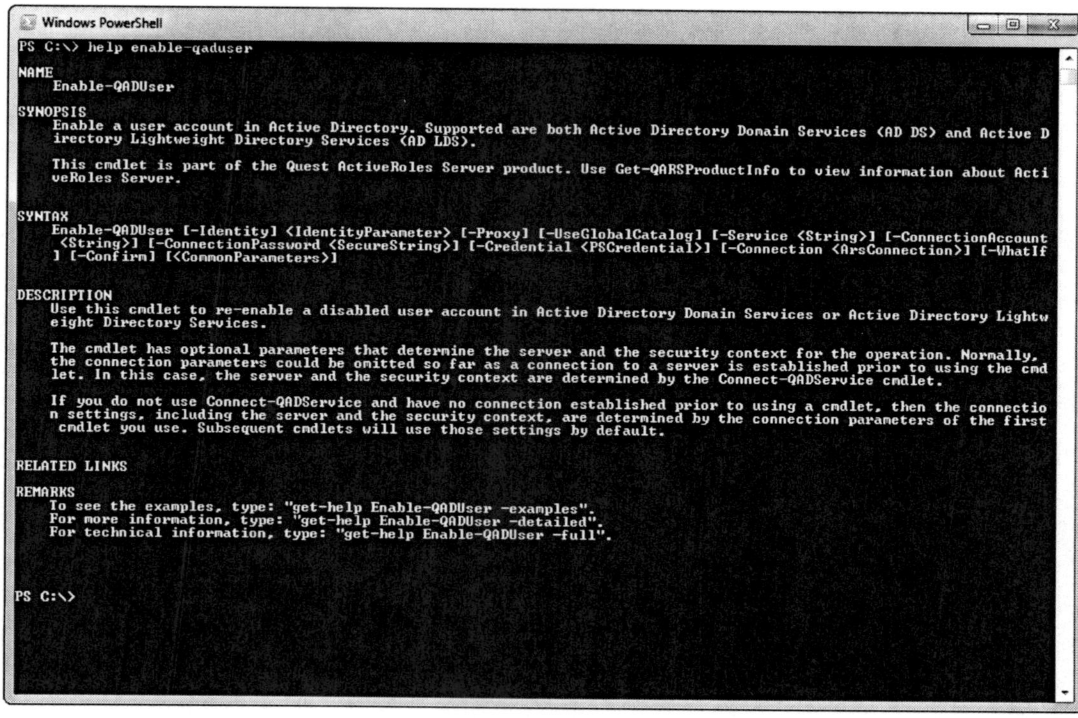

Figure 1-2 Getting Help

These cmdlets provide a friendly "wrapper" for the underlying .NET Framework System.DirectoryServices.DirectoryEntry class. The cmdlets perform a lot of abstracting and re-formatting of data so that you end up with a very admin-friendly experience. The Quest cmdlets take a traditional, LDAP-oriented approach meaning they use port 389 to connect to a domain controller. This is a tried-and-true approach that should work for just about any organization. Although you'll have the best success if you have access to a domain controller in the same Active Directory site as your management desktop.

Microsoft Active Directory Web Service

The release of Windows Server 2008 R2 ushered in an entirely new way to manage Active Directory leveraging Windows PowerShell 2.0. Instead of relying on the traditional LDAP approach, Microsoft introduced a new web-based service called the Microsoft Active Directory Web Service. It is "web-based" but doesn't require an installation of IIS. By default the service listens on port 9389 but you can modify this setting through Group Policy.

This service is automatically available when you install the Active Directory Domain Services or Lightweight Directory Services role on a Windows Server 2008 R2 platform (Standard, Enterprise, or Datacenter). Windows PowerShell 2.0 is not required. This service listens for requests from the new cmdlets in the Active Directory module, which I'll cover in bit. This service does not replace the more traditional LDAP-oriented approach for managing Active Directory. If you have 2008 R2 domain controllers, there's nothing else you need to do for the purposes of this book.

You can read much more about this service at Microsoft TechNet by visiting http://tinyurl.com/2v87so8.

Microsoft Active Directory Management Gateway Service

Because many organizations aren't jumping immediately to Microsoft's latest offering, Microsoft also released the Active Directory Management Gateway Service. This service offers the same functionality as the R2 AD Web Service. You can install this service on domain controllers running the following operating systems:

- Windows Server® 2003 R2 with Service Pack 2 (SP2)
- Windows Server 2003 SP2
- Windows Server 2008
- Windows Server 2008 SP2

It should not matter what domain or forest functional level you are running. To get started you'll need to download the appropriate install file from http://tinyurl.com/yzubo3l. But before you get too carried away, there are a few requirements you'll need to attend to first.

Requirements

First, you'll need to have the .NET Framework 3.5 SP1 installed. Domain controllers running any version Windows Server 2003 or Windows Server 2008 will need to download the hotfix referenced in Knowledge Base article 969166 (http://tinyurl.com/33t7af9). Next, if you are running Windows Server 2003 R2 SP2 or Windows Server 2003 SP2, you will need the hotfix described in Knowledge Base article 969429 (http://tinyurl.com/344mdr3). Domain controllers running Windows Server 2008 will need the hotfix from Knowledge Base article 967574 (http://tinyurl.com/3828rsw). If you are running Windows Server 2008 SP2, you don't need anything else. These installs will almost always certainly require a reboot or two.

Installing

Installing the operating system specific update is pretty straightforward and only takes a minute or two. Double-click the setup file and follow the few prompts. Windows PowerShell 2.0 is not required on the domain controller. Installing the service also does not mean you have modified your domain in any way. All you've done is add a service that responds to management requests and modifies the underlying directory service accordingly.

Remember, you only need to go through these steps if you do not have a Windows Server 2008 R2 domain controller.

Configuring Windows 7

You must load the Active Directory module in a Windows PowerShell 2.0 session. Personally I think this is best done from a Windows 7 client that is a domain member. Here's what you will need to do.

First, download and install the Remote Server Administration Tools for Windows 7 from Microsoft at http://tinyurl.com/qru5en. You'll find 32 and 64 bit versions. If you have any previous version of Remote Server Administration Tools, uninstall them. To install, double-click the .MSU file and follow the setup wizard.

To configure the necessary tools go to Control Panel—Programs—Programs and Features. Click the "Turn Windows Features On or Off" link in the left side panel. Scroll down to Remote Server Administration Tools and expand Role Administration Tools. Expand the nodes under AD DS and LDS Tools.

You will want to check at least these boxes:

- Active Directory Module for Windows PowerShell
- AD DS Snapins and Command Line Tools
- Active Directory Administrative Center.

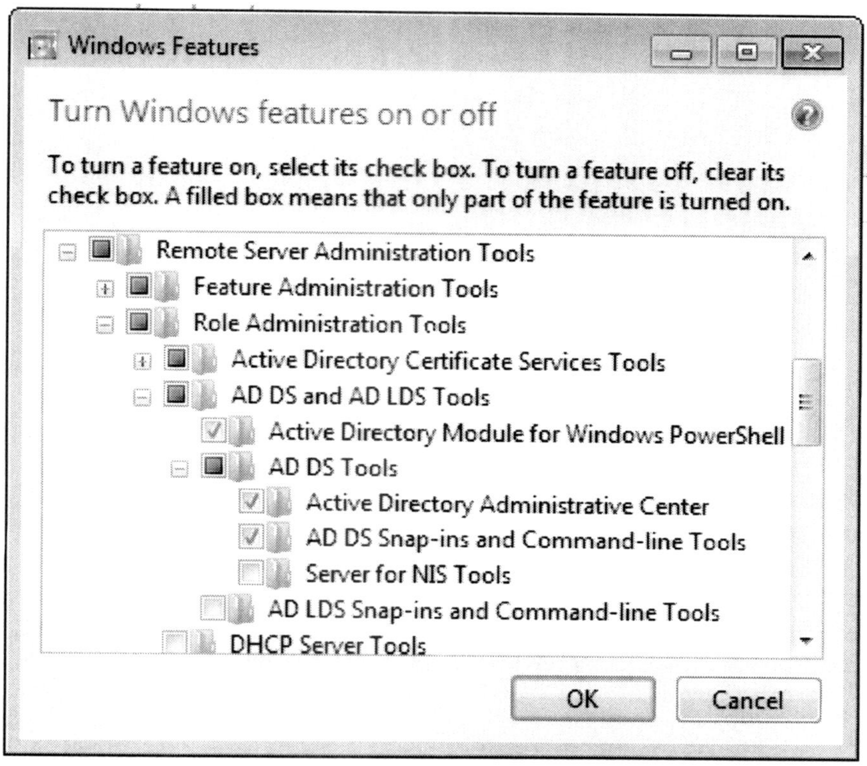

Figure 1-3 Configuring Active Directory Tools

While you're here, go ahead and expand Feature Administration Tools and select Group Policy Management Tools. You'll need this later in the book.

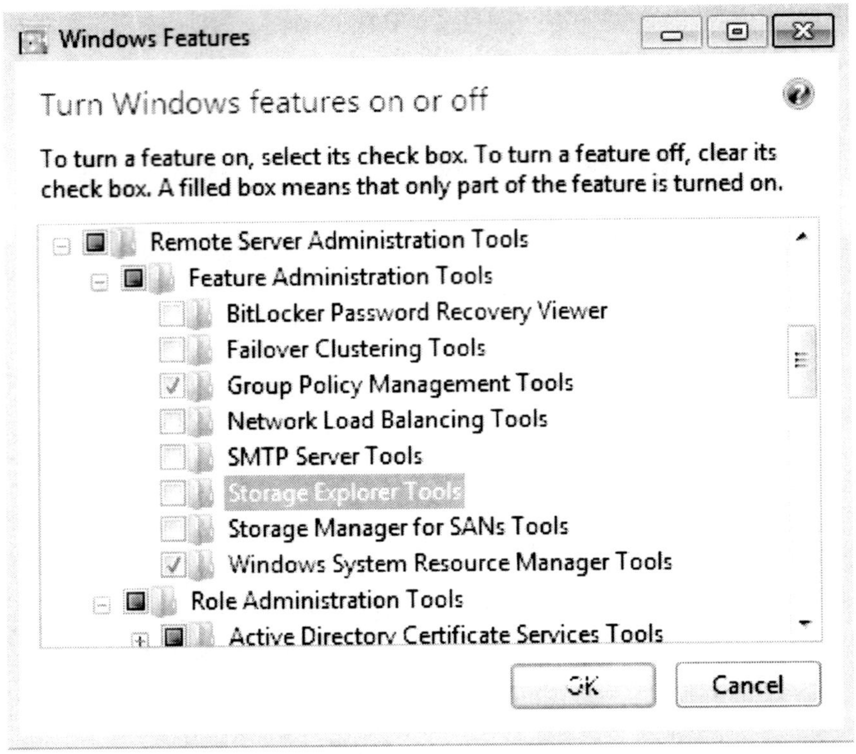

Figure 1-4 Installing Group Policy Management Tools

Feel free to add whatever other tools you feel you need. When finished, open a Windows PowerShell 2.0 session and verify you have the ActiveDirectory and GroupPolicy modules:

```
PS C:\> Get-Module GroupPolicy,ActiveDirectory -ListAvailable

ModuleType Name                          ExportedCommands
---------- ----                          ----------------
Manifest   ActiveDirectory               {}
Manifest   GroupPolicy                   {}
```

Now, you haven't actually loaded the module and its cmdlets into your Windows PowerShell session. Before you can do anything, you must import the module:

```
PS C:\> import-module ActiveDirectory
```

As with the Quest snapin, you can use the **Get-Command** cmdlet to view the module contents:

```
PS C:\> get-command -module ActiveDirectory | Select Name | Format-Wide

Add-ADComputerServiceAccount               Add-ADDomainControllerPasswordReplicationPolicy
Add-ADFineGrainedPasswordPolicySubject     Add-ADGroupMember
Add-ADPrincipalGroupMembership             Clear-ADAccountExpiration
Disable-ADAccount                          Disable-ADOptionalFeature
Enable-ADAccount                           Enable-ADOptionalFeature
Get-ADAccountAuthorizationGroup            Get-ADAccountResultantPasswordRepli...
```

```
Get-ADComputer                                  Get-ADComputerServiceAccount
Get-ADDefaultDomainPasswordPolicy               Get-ADDomain
Get-ADDomainController                          Get-ADDomainControllerPasswordRepli...
Get-ADDomainControllerPasswordReplication...    Get-ADFineGrainedPasswordPolicy
Get-ADFineGrainedPasswordPolicySubject          Get-ADForest
Get-ADGroup                                     Get-ADGroupMember
Get-ADObject                                    Get-ADOptionalFeature
Get-ADOrganizationalUnit                        Get-ADPrincipalGroupMembership
Get-ADRootDSE                                   Get-ADServiceAccount
Get-ADUser                                      Get-ADUserResultantPasswordPolicy
Install-ADServiceAccount                        Move-ADDirectoryServer
Move-ADDirectoryServerOperationMasterRole       Move-ADObject
New-ADComputer                                  New-ADFineGrainedPasswordPolicy
New-ADGroup                                     New-ADObject
New-ADOrganizationalUnit                        New-ADServiceAccount
New-ADUser                                      Remove-ADComputer
Remove-ADComputerServiceAccount                 Remove-ADDomainControllerPasswordRe...
Remove-ADFineGrainedPasswordPolicy              Remove-ADFineGrainedPasswordPolicy...
Remove-ADGroup                                  Remove-ADGroupMember
Remove-ADObject                                 Remove-ADOrganizationalUnit
Remove-ADPrincipalGroupMembership               Remove-ADServiceAccount
Remove-ADUser                                   Rename-ADObject
Reset-ADServiceAccountPassword                  Restore-ADObject
Search-ADAccount                                Set-ADAccountControl
Set-ADAccountExpiration                         Set-ADAccountPassword
Set-ADComputer                                  Set-ADDefaultDomainPasswordPolicy
Set-ADDomain                                    Set-ADDomainMode
Set-ADFineGrainedPasswordPolicy                 Set-ADForest
Set-ADForestMode                                Set-ADGroup
Set-ADObject                                    Set-ADOrganizationalUnit
Set-ADServiceAccount                            Set-ADUser
Uninstall-ADServiceAccount                      Unlock-ADAccount
```

If you see this, you're ready to roll. Just remember to import the module whenever you want to use any of these cmdlets. If you always want to have these commands available, add the **Import-Module** cmdlet to your Windows PowerShell profile.

Working with Active Directory

Search Sizes

Before you get too far in the book, I want to discuss a few general principals regarding Active Directory and these tool sets in particular. First off, by design Active Directory has limits in place that controls how many objects are returned when querying Active Directory. The default is 1000. For many organizations this is not an issue. You can use a cmdlet like **Get-QADGroup** and, unless you have more than 1000 groups, you'll get all of them back. If you happen to have 1001 groups, then PowerShell will tell you that only the first 1000 were returned. With the Quest cmdlets you can control how many objects are returned with the **-SizeLimit** parameter. Just about all the cmdlets from Quest support this parameter.

You can set it to any value:

```
PS C:\> Get-QADGroup -SizeLimit 3
```

```
Name                              Type          DN
----                              ----          --
Administrators                    group         CN=Administrators,CN=Builtin,DC=jdhlab,DC=local
Users                             group         CN=Users,CN=Builtin,DC=jdhlab,DC=local
Guests                            group         CN=Guests,CN=Builtin,DC=jdhlab,DC=local
WARNING: This search was configured to retrieve only the first 3 results. To retrieve more
results, increase the size
limit using the -SizeLimit parameter or set the default size limit using Set-
QADPSSnapinSettings with the
-DefaultSizeLimit parameter. Use 0 as the value of size limit to retrieve all possible search
results.
```

If you set the parameter to 0, then all matching objects are returned. If you know you always want the search size set at a specific size, then use this command:

```
PS C:\> Set-QADPSSnapinSettings -DefaultSizeLimit 0
```

This is a per-PowerShell-session setting so if you always want this value, add the line to your PowerShell profile after you've added the snapin.

When using the Microsoft cmdlets look for the **-ResultSetSize** parameter:

```
PS C:\> Get-ADGroup -ResultSetSize 3 -filter * | Select distinguishedname

distinguishedname
-----------------
CN=Administrators,CN=Builtin,DC=jdhlab,DC=local
CN=Users,CN=Builtin,DC=jdhlab,DC=local
CN=Guests,CN=Builtin,DC=jdhlab,DC=local
```

Scope

By default the cmdlets you'll be exploring all work from the domain root for the current user. If your domain isn't too large this is generally not an issue. However, you can often improve performance by limiting cmdlets to a specific container or organizational unit. Many of the Microsoft cmdlets will have a **-SearchBase** parameter where you can specify a distinguished name:

```
PS C:\> Get-ADUser -SearchBase "OU=Employees,DC=jdhlab,DC=local" -filter * | Measure-Object


Count    : 1124
Average  :
Sum      :
Maximum  :
Minimum  :
Property :
```

The Quest cmdlets use the **-SearchRoot** parameter. The effect is the same:

```
PS C:\> Get-QADUser -Searchroot "OU=Branch Office,DC=jdhlab,DC=local" -title "Training Manager"

Name                              Type          DN
----                              ----          --
Daniel Roth                       user          CN=Daniel Roth,OU=Branch Office,DC=jdhlab,DC=local
Sean Beantly                      user          CN=Sean Beantly,OU=Branch Office,DC=jdhlab,DC=local
```

There are other ways to import search performance as well using filtering parameters. As you begin to work with these cmdlets be sure to read the full help and examples and look for parameters like **-Filter** and **-LDAPFilter**. Syntax will vary but the help examples should get you started.

Credentials

```
PS C:\> Get-ADComputer -filter * -credential "jdhlab\jshortz"
```

```
PS C:\> $admin=Get-Credential "jdhlab\administrator"
PS C:\> Get-QADGroup -Identity "AlphaGroup" -Credential $admin

Name                          Type          DN
----                          ----          --
AlphaGroup                    group         CN=AlphaGroup,OU=Groups,DC=jdhlab,DC=local
```

Which Should I Use?

Actually, this doesn't have to be an either or proposition. If you have a 2008 R2 domain controller or running the Active Directory Management Gateway service you can use the Active Directory module or the Quest cmdlets. Which you use might depend on the situation and task at hand. Personally, I find the Quest cmdlets a little more administrator friendly but the Active Directory module more powerful for administrators with LDAP and ADSI experience.

If you have a legacy domain, then the Quest cmdlets are your only option. But because they will work with newer domains as well you aren't wasting any resources. Any investment you make in using the Quest cmdlets can continue when your domain is upgraded.

The only other influential factor, and this probably applies only to larger, distributed enterprises, is network connectivity. If you have to manage domain controllers across a wide area network, your networking configuration may dictate your management tool. The Quest tools require the traditional LDAP port, 389, and the Microsoft Active Directory Web Service requires 9389, although that is configurable.

What I hope is that by the end of the book you'll have a solid understanding of both approaches and will use whichever is the right tool for the job at hand.

Get Help

Throughout the rest of the book I'll be introducing many new Windows PowerShell cmdlets. I'll be demonstrating how to use the most common features to solve typical management challenges. However, there is plenty of good information in the help documentation for each cmdlet. Whenever I introduce a new cmdlet, I hope you'll take a few minutes to look at full help for the cmdlet, including examples, before continuing in the chapter.

```
PS C:\> Get-Help New-ADUser -full
```

It will help put my examples in context and get you comfortable with PowerShell's help system.

Let's get started.

Chapter 2
Managing Active Directory Users

It is probably safe to say that the most managed object in Active Directory, or at least the most critical, is a user object. In this chapter I'll demonstrate how to accomplish common management tasks with Windows PowerShell. In many cases you'll see some similarities between the Microsoft and Quest cmdlets.

Finding User Accounts

Often you need to find user accounts that meet particular criteria so you can do something specific with them. When using PowerShell to manage Active Directory users, you can use the **Get-ADUser** cmdlet from Microsoft class or Quest Software's **Get-QADUser** cmdlet. You'll find many similarities and a few critical differences.

Using Get-ADUser

Let's get started by first importing the Active Directory module:

```
PS C:\> Import-Module activedirectory
```

I'll Assume...

From this point forward, whenever I'm talking about using cmdlets from the Active Directory module, I'll assume you've run the **Import-Module** command prior to trying any examples from the book. Remember that even though I'll write about the "Active Directory" module, the module name has no spaces as in the example above.

If you know the SAMAccountname of an individual user, you can use it as a positional value for the **-Identity** parameter with the **Get-ADUser** cmdlet:

```
PS C:\> Get-ADUser jeff


DistinguishedName : CN=Jeff,CN=Users,DC=jdhlab,DC=local
Enabled           : True
GivenName         : Jeffery
Name              : Jeff
ObjectClass       : user
ObjectGUID        : 7d160a6e-49b1-45dd-8101-d9a48c9ac0a2
SamAccountName    : Jeff
SID               : S-1-5-21-3957442467-353870018-3926547339-1103
Surname           : Hicks
UserPrincipalName : Jeff@jdhlab.com
```

You can also use a distinguished name or an object's SID:

```
PS C:\> Get-ADUser "CN=Jeff,CN=Users,DC=jdhlab,DC=local"


DistinguishedName : CN=Jeff,CN=Users,DC=jdhlab,DC=local
Enabled           : True
GivenName         : Jeffery
Name              : Jeff
ObjectClass       : user
ObjectGUID        : 7d160a6e-49b1-45dd-8101-d9a48c9ac0a2
SamAccountName    : Jeff
SID               : S-1-5-21-3957442467-353870018-3926547339-1103
Surname           : Hicks
UserPrincipalName : Jeff@jdhlab.com
```

If you want to use the user's Active Directory name, then you'll need a filter, which I'll cover shortly.

As I hope you can tell, there is not a lot of information here. Even piping the object to the **Select-Object** cmdlet and selecting all properties doesn't offer much more:

```
PS C:\> Get-ADUser jeff | Select -Property *


DistinguishedName : CN=Jeff,CN=Users,DC=jdhlab,DC=local
Enabled           : True
GivenName         : Jeffery
Name              : Jeff
ObjectClass       : user
ObjectGUID        : 7d160a6e-49b1-45dd-8101-d9a48c9ac0a2
SamAccountName    : Jeff
SID               : S-1-5-21-3957442467-353870018-3926547339-1103
Surname           : Hicks
UserPrincipalName : Jeff@jdhlab.com
PropertyNames     : {DistinguishedName, Enabled, GivenName, Name...}
PropertyCount     : 10
```

That's because by default and design, only a subset of user properties are returned. If you tried a command like this, it will fail because the properties are not returned from Active Directory:

```
PS C:\> Get-ADUser jeff | Select Name,Title,Department,Description

Name                Title               Department          Description
----                -----               ----------          -----------
Jeff
```

Instead, you need to tell the **Get-ADUser** cmdlet to include these properties using the **-Properties** parameter:

```
PS C:\> Get-ADUser jeff -Properties Title,Department,Description |
>> Select Name,Title,Department,Description
>>

Name                Title               Department          Description
---                 -----               ----------          -----------
Jeff                Admin               IT                  alternate admin
```

The parameter also accepts a wildcard to include all properties. This is helpful when you may want to work with multiple different properties:

```
PS C:\> $jeff=Get-ADUser jeff -Properties *
```

I've saved the full user object to the variable $jeff. Now I can easily access different properties:

```
PS C:\> $jeff.passwordlastset

Wednesday, March 10, 2010 10:37:08 AM


PS C:\> $jeff | Select when*

whenChanged                             whenCreated
-----------                             -----------
7/20/2010 1:51:44 PM                    1/26/2010 7:24:54 PM
```

This is also a great way of discovering the property names:

```
PS C:\> $jeff | Get-Member -MemberType Property | Format-Wide -Column 3


AccountExpirationDate          accountExpires                 AccountLockoutTime
AccountNotDelegated            adminCount                     AllowReversiblePass...
BadLogonCount                  badPasswordTime                badPwdCount
CannotChangePassword           CanonicalName                  Certificates
City                           CN                             codePage
Company                        Country                        countryCode
Created                        createTimeStamp                Deleted
Department                     Description                    DisplayName
DistinguishedName              Division                       DoesNotRequirePreAuth
dSCorePropagationData          EmailAddress                   EmployeeID
EmployeeNumber                 Enabled                        Fax
GivenName                      HomeDirectory                  HomedirRequired
HomeDrive                      HomePage                       HomePhone
Initials                       instanceType                   isDeleted
LastBadPasswordAttempt         LastKnownParent                lastLogoff
lastLogon                      LastLogonDate                  lastLogonTimestamp
LockedOut                      logonCount                     LogonWorkstations
Manager                        MemberOf                       MNSLogonAccount
```

```
MobilePhone                        Modified                          modifyTimeStamp
msDS-SupportedEncryptionTypes      msDS-User-Account-Control-Computed Name
nTSecurityDescriptor               ObjectCategory                    ObjectClass
ObjectGUID                         objectSid                         Office
OfficePhone                        Organization                      OtherName
PasswordExpired                    PasswordLastSet                   PasswordNeverExpires
PasswordNotRequired                POBox                             PostalCode
PrimaryGroup                       primaryGroupID                    ProfilePath
ProtectedFromAccidentalDeletion    pwdLastSet                        SamAccountName
sAMAccountType                     ScriptPath                        sDRightsEffective
ServicePrincipalNames              SID                               SIDHistory
SmartcardLogonRequired             sn                                State
StreetAddress                      Surname                           Title
TrustedForDelegation               TrustedToAuthForDelegation        UseDESKeyOnly
userAccountControl                 userCertificate                   UserPrincipalName
uSNChanged                         uSNCreated                        whenChanged
whenCreated
```

Some of these properties are read-only. Here's a command you can run to see which properties you can modify, which will come in handy later in the chapter:

```
PS C:\> $jeff | Get-Member -MemberType Property | Where {$_.definition -match "set"} |
>> Format-Wide -Column 3
>>

AccountExpirationDate              accountExpires                    AccountLockoutTime
AccountNotDelegated                adminCount                        AllowReversiblePass...
badPasswordTime                    badPwdCount                       CannotChangePassword
Certificates                       City                              codePage
Company                            Country                           countryCode
Department                         Description                       DisplayName
DistinguishedName                  Division                          DoesNotRequirePreAuth
EmailAddress                       EmployeeID                        EmployeeNumber
Enabled                            Fax                               GivenName
HomeDirectory                      HomedirRequired                   HomeDrive
HomePage                           HomePhone                         Initials
lastLogoff                         lastLogon                         lastLogonTimestamp
LockedOut                          logonCount                        LogonWorkstations
Manager                            MNSLogonAccount                   MobilePhone
msDS-SupportedEncryptionTypes      nTSecurityDescriptor              ObjectClass
ObjectGUID                         Office                            OfficePhone
Organization                       OtherName                         PasswordExpired
PasswordLastSet                    PasswordNeverExpires              PasswordNotRequired
POBox                              PostalCode                        primaryGroupID
ProfilePath                        ProtectedFromAccidentalDeletion   pwdLastSet
SamAccountName                     sAMAccountType                    ScriptPath
ServicePrincipalNames              SID                               SmartcardLogonRequired
sn                                 State                             StreetAddress
Surname                            Title                             TrustedForDelegation
TrustedToAuthForDelegation         UseDESKeyOnly                     userAccountControl
userCertificate                    UserPrincipalName
```

When getting more than one user, or if you want to find a user by their Active Directory name, you'll need a search filter. The **Get-ADUser** cmdlet permits filtering using either the **-Filter** or **-LDAPFilter** parameters. The former utilizes syntax that you might use in a **Where-Object** expression:

```
PS C:\> Get-ADUser -filter "name -eq 'Jack Sprat'" | Select *Name
```

```
DistinguishedName : CN=Jack Sprat,OU=Shipping,OU=Employees,DC=jdhlab,DC=local
GivenName         : Jack
Name              : Jack Sprat
SamAccountName    : jsprat
Surname           : Sprat
UserPrincipalName : jsprat@jdhlab.local
```

In this example, I'm filtering to return a specific user object and display a few properties. Usually you'll want to find multiple user accounts that meet some criteria:

```
PS C:\> Get-ADUser -Filter "name -like 'je*'" | Select -Property name -first 3

name
----
Jean Drumwright
Jeff
Jefferey Harn
```

In this expression I found all users with a name that starts with "je" and selected the first three. You can use a wildcard with the **-Filter** parameter, which will return ALL user objects:

```
PS C:\> Get-ADUser -filter * | Measure-Object


Count    : 2660
Average  :
Sum      :
Maximum  :
Minimum  :
Property :
```

The end result is that I see I have 2660 user accounts in my domain. If you are more comfortable constructing LDAP filters, then you can use the **-LDAPFilter** parameter. Here's an LDAP filter version of an earlier filter:

```
PS C:\> Get-ADUser -LDAPFilter "(name=Je*)" | Select -Property Name -First 3

Name
----
Jean Drumwright
Jeff
Jefferey Harn
```

Complete coverage of LDAP filter syntax is beyond the scope of this book. Your best bet is to search MSDN or try http://tinyurl.com/2gy2ucj.

By default, both filtering techniques start at the domain root. You can limit your search to a particular container by using the **-SearchBase** parameter:

```
PS C:\> Get-ADUser -filter * -SearchBase "OU=Employees,DC=jdhlab,DC=local" | Measure-Object


Count    : 1131
Average  :
Sum      :
```

```
Maximum  :
Minimum  :
Property :
```

This is the same command I ran earlier to count the total number of user objects in my domain. Except this time, I only searched for user accounts in the Employees organizational unit (OU). Using **-SearchBase** is a great technique to make sure accounts are getting in the proper container.

You can refine your searching further using the **-SearchScope** parameter, which can be one of three values:

- Base
- OneLevel
- SubTree

The default is SubTree, which recursively searches from the starting container. A value of OneLevel will search for immediate children of the starting container:

```
PS C:\> Get-ADUser -filter * -SearchBase "OU=Employees,DC=jdhlab,DC=local" `
>> -searchscope one-level |  Measure-Object
>>


Count    : 10
Average  :
Sum      :
Maximum  :
Minimum  :
Property :
```

A **-SearchScope** value of Base means the search will only be at the container level:

```
PS C:\> Get-ADUser -filter * -SearchBase "OU=Employees,DC=jdhlab,DC=local" -searchscope base |
>> Measure-Object
>>


Count    : 0
Average  :
Sum      :
Maximum  :
Minimum  :
Property :
```

I rarely find a practical use for this value.

Don't forget that the returned object only has a small set of properties. Even if you construct a filter using a property, if you want to see that property you need to include it:

```
PS C:\> Get-ADUser -filter "(department -eq 'HR')" `
>> -SearchBase "ou=Employees,DC=jdhlab,DC=local" -properties Title,Department |
>> Select name,title,Department
>>

name                                    title                                   Department
----                                    -----                                   ----------
John Rodman                             Benefits Administrator                  HR
```

```
Ann Beebe                          Benefits Manager              HR
Phil Gibbins                       Benefits Clerk                HR
Kari Furse                         Benefits Clerk                HR
```

In the example above, I'm searching for any user in the Employees organizational until that has a department property value of HR. I then want to display the user's name, title, and department. If I had not used the **-Properties** parameter to specify the additional properties, my report would have been blank save for the user name. This is true regardless of whether you use the **-Filter** or **-LDAPFilter** parameters.

Let's wrap up this section with a common task such as finding disabled user accounts:

```
PS C:\> Get-ADUser -filter "Enabled -eq '$false'" `
>> -SearchBase "OU=Employees,DC=jdhlab,DC=local" -properties Description |
>> Select DistinguishedName,Name,Description
>>

DistinguishedName                         Name                    Description
-----------------                         ----                    -----------
CN=Johnson Apacible,OU=Employees,DC=...   Johnson Apacible        temp account
CN=Prithvi Raj,OU=Employees,DC=jdhla...   Prithvi Raj             temp account
CN=Virginie Jean,OU=Customer Service...   Virginie Jean
CN=Jim Glynn,OU=Customer Service,OU=...   Jim Glynn
```

My filter is pretty simple, looking for accounts with the **Enabled** property set to $False in the Employees organizational unit. I also want to include the **Description** property so I can select the user's name, distinguished name, and description.

Using Get-QADUser

The Quest approach is similar, but in many ways easier to use. Here's what you can expect:

```
PS C:\> Get-QADUser rbiv

Name                          Type           DN
----                          ----           --
Roy G. Biv                    user           CN=Roy G. Biv,OU=Employees,DC=jdhlab,DC=local
```

You can use the SAMAccountname as I've done here. The Active Directory name:

```
PS C:\> Get-QADUser "Roy G. Biv"
```

Or the UserPrincipalName:

```
PS C:\> Get-QADUser "rbiv@jdhlab.com"
```

The resulting object still only contains a subset of user properties, but it is a much larger subset and contains properties you most likely want to use:

```
PS C:\> Get-QADUser rbiv | Select Name,Title,Department,Office

Name                        Title                       Department                Office
----                        -----                       ----------                ------
Roy G. Biv                  Manager                     Art                       SW777
```

You can use the cmdlet to search by name with wildcards. For example, here are the user accounts in my domain that contain "roy" in the name:

```
PS C:\> Get-QADUser roy*

Name                          Type       DN
----                          ----       --
Roy Antebi                    user       CN=Roy Antebi,OU=Sales,OU=Employees,DC=jdhlab,DC...
Roy G. Biv                    user       CN=Roy G. Biv,OU=Employees,DC=jdhlab,DC=local
Roy Hemish                    user       CN=Roy Hemish,OU=Test,OU=Employees,DC=jdhlab,DC=...
Royal Ratulowski              user       CN=Royal Ratulowski,OU=Test,OU=Employees,DC=jdhl...
Royce Bacchi                  user       CN=Royce Bacchi,OU=Test,OU=Employees,DC=jdhlab,D...
Royce Greenough               user       CN=Royce Greenough,OU=Test,OU=Employees,DC=jdhla...
Royce Halmes                  user       CN=Royce Halmes,OU=Test,OU=Employees,DC=jdhlab,D...
Royce Lohnes                  user       CN=Royce Lohnes,OU=Test,OU=Employees,DC=jdhlab,D...
Kieth Royall                  user       CN=Kieth Royall,OU=Test,OU=Employees,DC=jdhlab,D...
```

Or you can get users based on some property such as **LastName** or **Department**. Many common properties have been "parameterized".

Table 2-1 Get-QADUser Common Property Parameters

AccountExpiresAfter	AccountExpiresBefore	AccountNeverExpires
Company	Connection	City
CreatedOn	CreatedAfter	CreatedBefore
Description	Disabled	Department
Enabled	HomeDirectory	DisplayName
FirstName	Identity	Email
HomePhone	IndirectMemberOf	Fax
LastChangedAfter	LastChangedBefore	HomeDrive
LastKnownParent	LastName	Initials
Locked	LogonScript	LastChangedOn
MemberOf	Notes	NotIndirectMemberOf
Name	Manager	Office
MobilePhone	Pager	PasswordNeverExpires
PostOfficeBox	PhoneNumber	NotMemberOf
Recycled	ProfilePath	PostalCode
SAMAccountName	StateOrProvince	StreetAddress
Title	UserPrincipalName	WebPage

Let me find users by last name:

```
PS C:\> Get-QADUser -LastName smith

Name                          Type       DN
----                          ----       --
Ben Smith                     user       CN=Ben Smith,OU=Sales,OU=Employees,DC=jdhlab,DC=local
```

Turns out I only have one "Smith" in my domain. What about by department?

```
PS C:\> Get-QADUser -department shipping -SearchRoot "Employees"

Name                     Type       DN
----                     ----       --
Mark Twain               user       CN=Mark Twain,OU=Shipping,OU=Employees,DC=jdhlab,DC=local
```

I'm limiting my search here to the Employees organizational unit with the **-SearchRoot** parameter. There is also a **-SearchScope** parameter with the same values as **Get-ADUser**: Base, OneLevel and SubTree, which is the default.

The **Get-QADUser** cmdlet can also combine parameters to return user accounts that meet a combination of requirements:

```
PS C:\> Get-QADUser -city Atlanta -title *Manager | Select Name,Title,Department

Name                                    Title                                   Department
----                                    -----                                   ----------
Daniel Roth                             Training Manager                        Training
Sean Beantly                            Training Manager                        Training
```

Here are all the Training Managers in Atlanta. You're probably thinking: What can I do with something like this? I'll get to it later in this chapter and in future chapters.

What I like about the Quest cmdlets is that I can return some pretty deep information with almost no effort. As an example, the **Get-QADUser** cmdlet has a **-Manager** parameter, which I could use to find all users who report to one person:

```
PS C:\> Get-QADUser -manager "Bradley Marek" | Select Name,Title,Department

Name                                    Title                                   Department
----                                    -----                                   ----------
Warren Lynaugh                          IT Intern                               IT
Stephan Knilands                        IT Intern                               IT
Frankie Buchauer                        IT Intern                               IT
Marc Boscarino                          IT Intern                               IT
Darrin Ferry                            IT Intern                               IT
Bettina Tamburri                        IT Intern                               IT
```

With one simple command I discovered all the users who report to Bradley Marek. I can also turn this around because the user object has a **DirectReports** property:

```
PS C:\> Get-QADUser "Bradley Marek" -IncludedProperties DirectReports |
>> Select -expandproperty DirectReports
>>

CN=Bettina Tamburri,OU=IT,OU=Employees,DC=jdhlab,DC=local
CN=Darrin Ferry,OU=IT,OU=Employees,DC=jdhlab,DC=local
CN=Marc Boscarino,OU=IT,OU=Employees,DC=jdhlab,DC=local
CN=Frankie Buchauer,OU=IT,OU=Employees,DC=jdhlab,DC=local
CN=Stephan Knilands,OU=IT,OU=Employees,DC=jdhlab,DC=local
CN=Warren Lynaugh,OU=IT,OU=Employees,DC=jdhlab,DC=local
```

The **DirectReports** property is not included by default, so I have to specifically request it using the **-IncludedProperties** parameter. An alternative, which is easy to use but not necessarily a best practice, is to use the **-IncludeAllProperties** parameter. In any event, because the property value is stored as an array I use the **-ExpandProperty** parameter with the **Select-Object** cmdlet to provide the final result.

Which technique you use will most likely depend on the size of your domain. The first technique has to look at every user object and filter from there. The second technique simply grabs the individual account and checks the manager links. In my testing, the latter approach was slightly faster by a few milliseconds. Your mileage will vary.

But suppose you want the same level of detail that I had in the first example? You can get it by taking advantage of the pipeline:

```
PS C:\> (Get-QADUser "Bradley Marek" -IncludedProperties DirectReports).DirectReports |
>> Get-QADUser | Select Name,Title,Department
>>

Name                                    Title                                   Department
----                                    -----                                   ----------
Bettina Tamburri                        IT Intern                               IT
Darrin Ferry                            IT Intern                               IT
Marc Boscarino                          IT Intern                               IT
Frankie Buchauer                        IT Intern                               IT
Stephan Knilands                        IT Intern                               IT
Warren Lynaugh                          IT Intern                               IT
```

I'm taking a shortcut in the first part of the expression by accessing the **DirectReports** property directly. This will be the same collection of distinguished names. Each name is then piped to the **Get-QADuser** cmdlet, and then on to the **Select-Object** cmdlet to display the necessary information.

But what if you need to find user accounts where there isn't an available parameter? In those situations you can also use the **-SearchAttributes** parameter for a custom search. Use a hash table with the property name and value you wish to search for. In this example I'm getting a head count of all users in the Operations division. Don't forget with the Quest cmdlets a **-SizeLimit** parameter value of 0 indicates to return all users, not just the default first 1000:

```
PS C:\> Get-QADUser -SearchAttributes @{division="Operations"} -sizelimit 0 | Measure-Object


Count    : 458
Average  :
Sum      :
Maximum  :
Minimum  :
Property :
```

You can search for multiple properties, separated by a semicolon:

```
PS C:\> Get-QADUser -SearchAttributes @{division="Operations";department="engineering"} `
>> -sizelimit 0 | Measure-Object
>>


Count    : 176
Average  :
Sum      :
Maximum  :
Minimum  :
Property :
```

Finally, if none of the cmdlet's parameters are sufficient, you can specify a custom LDAP filter:

```
PS C:\> $f = "(&(&(&(objectCategory=person)(objectClass=user)(!name=Guest)
(!Name=Administrator)(objectCategory=person)(objectClass=user)
(userAccountControl:1.2.840.113556.1.4.803:=65536))))"
PS C:\> Get-QADUser -LdapFilter $f -enabled

Name                          Type       DN
----                          ----       --
Jeff                          user       CN=Jeff,CN=Users,DC=jdhlab,DC=local
Sherwood McNeal               user       CN=Sherwood McNeal,OU=Executive,OU=Employees,DC=...
Aldo Shebby                   user       CN=Aldo Shebby,OU=IT,OU=Employees,DC=jdhlab,DC=l...
DA_Hicks                      user       CN=DA_Hicks,OU=Employees,DC=jdhlab,DC=local
```

The filter is a bit long and must be entered as one line. It is looking for all user accounts with non-expiring passwords, except for the Guest and Administrator accounts. I'm combining the LDAP filter with the **-Enabled** parameter to only return enabled accounts.

By the way, if you want to get all disabled accounts, use the handy **-Disabled** parameter:

```
PS C:\> Get-QADUser -Disabled -SearchRoot "Employees"

Name                          Type       DN
----                          ----       --
Vincenzo Ziesman              user       CN=Vincenzo Ziesman,OU=Executive,OU=Employees,DC...
Teodoro Ewings                user       CN=Teodoro Ewings,OU=Executive,OU=Employees,DC=j...
Ulysses Wiatrowski            user       CN=Ulysses Wiatrowski,OU=Executive,OU=Employees,...
Stewart Sider                 user       CN=Stewart Sider,OU=Executive,OU=Employees,DC=jd...
Johnson Apacible              user       CN=Johnson Apacible,OU=Employees,DC=jdhlab,DC=local
Prithvi Raj                   user       CN=Prithvi Raj,OU=Employees,DC=jdhlab,DC=local
Virginie Jean                 user       CN=Virginie Jean,OU=Customer Service,OU=Employee...
Jim Glynn                     user       CN=Jim Glynn,OU=Customer Service,OU=Employees,DC...
```

With a very simple command I was able to retrieve all disabled user accounts in the Employees organizational unit hierarchy.

Finally, I can also use this cmdlet to export user objects to a CSV or XML file:

```
PS C:\> Get-QADUser -Disabled -SearchRoot "Employees" |
>> Export-Csv c:\work\disabled.csv -NoTypeInformation
```

This exports all common and default user properties for the disabled user accounts under Employees to a CSV file. The **-NoTypeInformation** parameter strips off the extra type definition so that I can open the file in something like Microsoft Excel:

Creating User Accounts

Using the Active Directory Module

Creating any type of object in Active Directory first requires a connection to the parent container. This can be an organizational unit (OU) or a built-in container like Users. You need to specify the ADSI path accordingly. For example, to create a new object in the Employees organizational unit you might pass a path like this:

```
OU=Employees,DC=jdhlab,DC=com
```

Or maybe you want to use the default Users container:

```
CN=Users,DC=jdhlab,DC=com
```

A common error is to use OU=Users when you are actually referring to a non-organizational unit container. Containers like Users and Computers must be referenced like CN=Users. This is important because when creating new Active Directory objects you almost always need to specify the correct path to the parent container.

You'll be using the **New-ADUser** cmdlet to create new user accounts. At a minimum you'll need to specify the Active Directory name and SAMAccountname:

```
PS C:\> New-ADUser -name "Margo Rida" -samaccountname "mrida"
```

This will create the account in the default container for users. Also, from a practical point, the account also doesn't have a user principal name (UPN). Let's try again and put the account in the Sales organizational unit:

```
PS C:\> New-ADUser -Name "Margo Rida" -SamAccountName "mrida" `
>> -userprincipalname mrida@jdhlab.local -Path "OU=Sales,OU=Employees,DC=jdhlab,DC=local"
```

But you know, you're still missing a few things. For example, what is Margo's initial password? Does she need to change it at first logon? What about basic information like her first and last names? The **New-ADUser** cmdlet has many parameters to handle the most common properties.

Table 2-2 New-ADUser Parameters

AccountExpirationDate	AccountNotDelegated	AccountPassword
AllowReversiblePasswordEncryption	AuthType	CannotChangePassword
Certificates	ChangePasswordAtLogon	City
Company	Country	Credential
Department	Description	DisplayName
Division	EmailAddress	EmployeeID
EmployeeNumber	Enabled	Fax
GivenName	HomeDirectory	HomeDrive
HomePage	HomePhone	Initials
Instance	LogonWorkstations	Manager
MobilePhone	Name	Office
OfficePhone	Organization	OtherAttributes
OtherName	PassThru	PasswordNeverExpires
PasswordNotRequired	Path	POBox
PostalCode	ProfilePath	SAMAccountName
ScriptPath	Server	ServicePrincipalNames
SmartcardLogonRequired	State	StreetAddress

Surname	Title	TrustedForDelegation
Type	UserPrincipalName	

Many of these parameters take string values. Let's re-create the account for Margo, but this time as a much more fleshed out account.

The first thing you need to do is provide an initial password. The **New-ADUser** cmdlet expects a secure string:

```
PS C:\> $password=Read-Host "enter a new password" -AsSecureString
enter a new password: ********
```

With this secure string in hand, you can use this code to create the account:

```
PS C:\> New-ADUser -Name "Margo Rida" -SamAccountName "mrida" `
>>  -userprincipalname mrida@jdhlab.local -Path "OU=Sales,OU=Employees,DC=jdhlab,DC=local" `
>>  -givenName "Margo" -surname "Rida" -description "laptop user" `
>>  -title "Southwest Sales Manager" -mobilephone "555-9876" -accountpassword $password `
>>  -DisplayName "Margo Rida" -Office "AUS344" -enabled $True  -ChangePasswordAtLogon $True
>>
```

The account is enabled, and Margo must change her password at next logon. Unlike other cmdlets you may have used, parameters like **-Enabled** and **-ChangePasswordAtLogon**, which are essentially switches, must have a specific Boolean value such as $True or $False. The account will be created Disabled unless you specify otherwise.

Password Requirements
The **New-ADUser** cmdlet will throw an exception if the password doesn't meet domain requirements. The cmdlet has no way of knowing the password is sufficient until it tries to use it. If you are developing scripted solutions and want to validate the password, you'll need to create your own functions, most likely using regular expressions.

If you ran this command, or something like it, you probably noticed nothing was written to the pipeline. You can force the cmdlet to do so by including the **-Passthru** parameter:

```
PS C:\> New-ADUser -Name "Margo Rida" -SamAccountName "mrida" `
>>  -userprincipalname mrida@jdhlab.local -Path "OU=Sales,OU=Employees,DC=jdhlab,DC=local" `
>>  -givenName "Margo" -surname "Rida2" -description "laptop user" `
>>  -title "Southwest Sales Manager" -mobilephone "555-9876" -accountpassword $password `
>>  -DisplayName "Margo Rida" -Office "AUS344" -enabled $True  -ChangePasswordAtLogon $True `
>>  -passthru
>>


DistinguishedName : CN=Margo Rida,OU=Sales,OU=Employees,DC=jdhlab,DC=local
Enabled           : True
GivenName         : Margo
Name              : Margo Rida
ObjectClass       : user
ObjectGUID        : 07fb507a-6655-46c8-afc1-4b5f2b64e6b0
```

```
SamAccountName    : mrida
SID               : S-1-5-21-3957442467-353870018-3926547339-5041
Surname           : Rida2
UserPrincipalName : mrida@jdhlab.local
```

Granted, that's a lot to type every time you want to create a new user. But I'm betting that when creating a new user many properties are standardized or can be calculated. You might be better off creating a function to create a new user. Here's one version that should get you started in the right direction:

New-MyADUser.ps1

```
Function New-MyADUser {

[cmdletbinding()]

Param(
[Parameter(Position=0,Mandatory=$True,HelpMessage="Enter the new user name")]
[string]$name,
[Parameter(Position=1,Mandatory=$True,HelpMessage="Enter the new password as a secure
string.")]
[security.securestring]$pass,
[Parameter(Position=2)]
[string]$path="OU=Employees,DC=jdhlab,DC=local",
[string]$title,
[string]$description="Created $(get-date)",
[string]$department,
[string]$office="Corp",
[string]$company="JDH Labs"
)

#load Active Directory module if not already running
if (-not (Get-Module ActiveDirectory)) {
    Import-Module ActiveDirectory
}

#define some values based on the name
$split=$name.split()
$firstname=$split[0]
$lastname=$split[1]
$sam="{0}{1}" -f $firstname.substring(0,1),$lastname
$upn="{0}@jdhlabs.com" -f $sam

New-ADUser -Name $name -SamAccountName $sam `
 -userprincipalname $upn -Path $path `
 -givenName $firstname -surname $lastname -description $description `
 -title $title -department $department -accountpassword $password `
 -DisplayName $name -Office $office -enabled $True  -ChangePasswordAtLogon $True `
 -company $company -passthru

} #end function
```

The **New-MyADUser** function will create a new user account based on the user name. All accounts will be created in the Employees organizational unit, unless otherwise specified. You can also specify properties such as title, department, office, and description. Some properties, like description, have a default value in case you don't specify anything. My function takes the user name and splits it in two so I can get the first and last name. From those values I construct a SAMAccountname that is the first initial of the first name and the last name. I also construct a user principal name:

```
$split=$name.split()
$firstname=$split[0]
$lastname=$split[1]
$sam="{0}{1}" -f $firstname.substring(0,1),$lastname
$upn="{0}@jdhlabs.com" -f $sam
```

Once all my values are set, I call the **New-ADUser** cmdlet. In my domain I'm creating the accounts as Enabled and forcing the user to change password at next logon. To use the cmdlet, I define my initial password as a secure string:

```
PS C:\>$password=Read-Host "enter a new password" -AsSecureString
```

Then I run the function:

```
PS C:\> New-Myaduser "Francis Drake" $password -title "Sr. Engineer" -department "IT" `
>> -office "5-South-233"
>>


DistinguishedName : CN=Francis Drake,OU=Employees,DC=jdhlab,DC=local
Enabled           : True
GivenName         : Francis
Name              : Francis Drake
ObjectClass       : user
ObjectGUID        : 058c0fc3-0dc6-425c-a291-b793e35c38ad
SamAccountName    : FDrake
SID               : S-1-5-21-3957442467-353870018-3926547339-5047
Surname           : Drake
UserPrincipalName : FDrake@jdhlabs.com
```

Test and Revise

While this script works, you'll need to tweak the script for your environment. It also lacks any error handling, logging, or other features you may require. It also isn't written to handle a user name like Rip van Winkle. Because everybody has a slightly different set of requirements, please consider all of my script samples as starting points for your own script development. You will need to test, revise, and extend as needed.

Other Attributes

For the vast majority of administrators I think the cmdlet's parameters should meet your needs. But should you need to set a value for a property that lacks a parameter, you can use the **-OtherAttributes** parameter. This parameter accepts a hash table that consists of the LDAP property name and the value. You can use a tool like ADSIEdit to discover property names. Here's an example of how you might use it.

I need to create a temporary account for Sunny Day who will be sitting in as a receptionist. I want the account to expire in 30 days and I don't want her to be able to change her password. But I also want to add a comment, which has an LDAP property name of "Info":

```
PS C:\> New-aduser -name "Sunny Day" -path "OU=Temp,OU=Employees,DC=jdhlab,DC=local" `
>> -AccountPassword $password -description "Temp account" -title "Reception" `
>> -samaccountname "sday" -userprincipalname "sday@jdhlab.com" -givenname "Sunny" `
>> -surname "Day" -officePhone "0001" -displayname "Sunny Day - TEMP" `
>> -accountexpirationDate (Get-Date).AddDays(30) -CannotChangePassword $True `
>> -enabled $True -OtherAttributes @{Info="created per JDH $(get-date)"} -passthru
>>


DistinguishedName : CN=Sunny Day,OU=Temp,OU=Employees,DC=jdhlab,DC=local
Enabled           : True
GivenName         : Sunny
Name              : Sunny Day
ObjectClass       : user
ObjectGUID        : 87ccee7c-21e0-4f49-af83-c3a6b7a7046c
SamAccountName    : sday
SID               : S-1-5-21-3957442467-353870018-3926547339-5050
Surname           : Day
UserPrincipalName : sday@jdhlab.com
```

You can see the result in Figure 2-1.

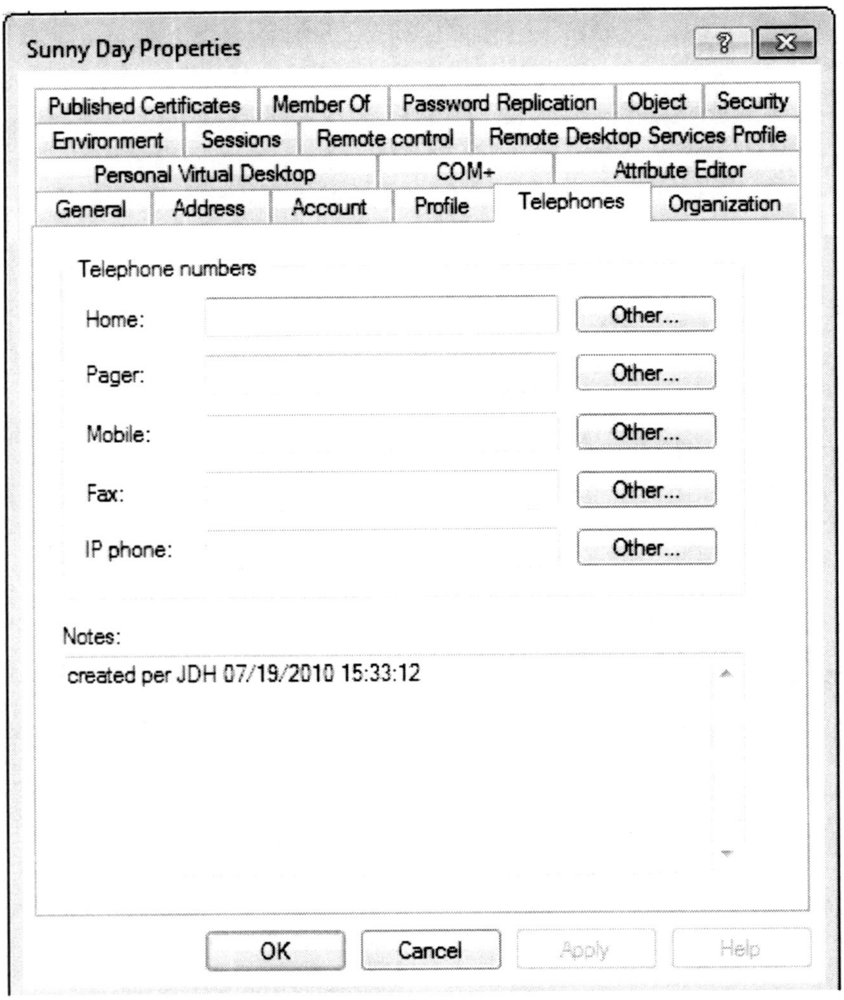

Figure 2-1 New User with Info Field Populated

Another approach is to create a new user based on an existing user or template. This is a common practice when using the GUI that can also be done with Windows PowerShell. In fact, setting some properties like restricted hours are easier to define if you can copy them from another object. Let's recreate the Sunny Day account by copying values from a template account, restrictedbizhours.

The account has a few properties I want to copy such as logonhours, description, and a few password settings:

```
PS C:\> Get-ADUser restrictedbizhours -properties Description,PasswordNeverExpires, `
>> CannotChangePassword,LogonHours,Company |
>> Select description,PasswordNeverExpires,CannotChangePassword,logonhours,Company


Description          : restricted hours
PasswordNeverExpires : True
CannotChangePassword : True
logonhours           : {0, 0, 0, 0...}
Company              : JDHLab
```

Here's a script that shows how I might accomplish this, Copy-User.ps1:

Copy-User.ps1

```
#requires -version 2.0

Import-Module ActiveDirectory
$password=Read-Host "Enter a default password" -AsSecureString

#the name of the template account
$template="restrictedbizhours"

#get the template user account
$copy=Get-ADUser -Identity "restrictedbizhours" `
-properties Description,PasswordNeverExpires,CannotChangePassword,LogonHours,Company

#define where to create the new account
$parent="OU=Temp,OU=Employees,DC=jdhlab,DC=local"

New-ADUser -name "Sunny Day" -path $parent -PasswordNeverExpires $copy.PasswordNeverExpires`
-AccountPassword $password -description $copy.description -title "Reception" `
-company $copy.company -department "Customer Service" -samaccountname "sday" `
-userprincipalname "sday@jdhlab.com" -givenname "Sunny" -surname "Day" -officePhone "0001" `
-displayname "Sunny Day - TEMP" -accountexpirationDate (Get-Date).AddDays(30) `
-CannotChangePassword $copy.CannotChangePassword -LogonWorkstations "RECP01,RECP02" `
-office "Front01" -enabled $True -OtherAttributes @{Info="created per JDH $(get-date)";
otherTelePhone="0022","0023";logonhours=$copy.logonhours} -passthru
```

Much of this script is similar to what I've used previously. The primary difference is that I get the template user account and save it to a variable. Specifying the additional properties I'll need:

```
#the name of the template account
$template="restrictedbizhours"

#get the template user account
$copy=Get-ADUser -Identity "restrictedbizhours" `
-properties Description,PasswordNeverExpires,CannotChangePassword,LogonHours,Company
```

Then in the **New-ADUser** command I use the values from the template account where necessary. I've highlighted them in the code. Certainly, you could take this concept and run pretty far with it. I'll cover copying group memberships later.

Using New-QADUser

On the Quest Software side, let's take a look at the **New-QADUser** cmdlet, for creating new Active Directory user accounts:

```
PS C:\> get-help New-QADUser

NAME
    New-QADUser

SYNOPSIS
    Create a new user account in Active Directory. Supported are both Active Directory Domain
Services (AD DS) and Active Directory Lightweight Directory Services (AD LDS).

    This cmdlet is part of the Quest ActiveRoles Server product. Use Get-QARSProductInfo to
view information about ActiveRoles Server.


SYNTAX
    New-QADUser -ParentContainer <IdentityParameter> [-Name] <String> [-UserPassword <String>]
[-City <String>] [-Company <String>] [-Department <String>] [-Email <String>] [-Fax <String>]
[-FirstName <String>] [-HomeDirectory <String>] [-HomeDrive <String>] [-HomePhone <String>]
[-Initials <String>] [-LastName <String>] [-LogonScript <String>]
[-Manager <IdentityParameter>] [-MobilePhone <String>] [-Notes <String>] [-Office <String>]
[-Pager <String>] [-PhoneNumber <String>] [-PostalCode <String>] [-PostOfficeBox <String>]
[-ProfilePath <String>]
[-SamAccountName <String>] [-StateOrProvince <String>] [-StreetAddress <String>]
[-Title <String>] [-UserPrincipalName <String>] [-WebPage <String>]
[-ObjectAttributes <ObjectAttributesParameter>] [-Description <String>]
[-DisplayName <String>] [-ExcludedProperties <String[]>]
[-IncludedProperties <String[]>] [-DeserializeValues] [-UseDefaultExcludedProperties [<Boolean>]]
[-Proxy] [-UseGlobalCatalog] [-Service <String>] [-ConnectionAccount <String>]
[-ConnectionPassword <SecureString>] [-Credential <PSCredential>] [-Connection <ArsConnection>]
[-WhatIf] [-Confirm] [<CommonParameters>]
...
```

I'm Overwhelmed!

You're probably looking at the preceding help excerpt and feeling a little overwhelmed. And this is just one cmdlet! Quest has done an outstanding job in provided very complete cmdlets for most everything you need to accomplish. There is a great deal of flexibility with all the Quest cmdlets and I can't possibly cover every parameter of every cmdlet in great detail. Yet I will show you how to use the cmdlets in a way that should meet the majority of your needs. Should you need additional help or information on these cmdlets, you can look at full help in PowerShell, use the support forums at PowerGUI.org, or download the Management Shell for Active Directory–Administrator's guide from http://www.quest.com/activeroles-server/arms.aspx.

Here's how to create a new user. First you need to load the snapin:

```
PS C:\> add-pssnapin Quest.ActiveRoles.ADManagement
```

Then you can run the **New-QADuser** cmdlet, saving the result to a variable:

```
PS C:\> $user=New-QADUser -parent "OU=HR,OU=Employees,DC=jdhlab,dc=local" `
>>  -name "Sam Apple" -First "Sam" -Last "Apple" `
>>  -userprincipal "sapple@jdhlab.com" `
>>  -userpassword "P@ssw0rd" `
>>  -Display "Sam Apple" `
>>  -samAccountName "sapple"
>>
PS C:\> $user

Name                           Type       DN
----                           ----       --
Sam Apple                      user       CN=Sam Apple,OU=HR,OU=Employees,DC=jdhlab,dc=local
```

I used the **New-QADUser** cmdlet with only a few parameters to create user Sam Apple in the HR organizational unit. The first, last, and display names parameters aren't required but I like having a few properties defined for the user. Also, even though Active Directory doesn't require it, I prefer to specify a user principal name as I did when using the **New-ADUser** cmdlet. In fact, I'm sure you noticed a number of parameter similarities. One main difference is that the user password can be passed as a simple string with the **New-QADUser** cmdlet. It's still secure over the wire. By default, new accounts are Enabled. I'll show you later how to change that should you wish to create Disabled accounts. For now, let's take a look at the new user's default properties:

```
PS C:\> $user | Select *


City                          :
Company                       :
Department                    :
Email                         :
Fax                           :
FirstName                     : Sam
HomePhone                     :
Initials                      :
LastName                      : Apple
LogonName                     : sapple
Manager                       :
MobilePhone                   :
Office                        :
Pager                         :
PhoneNumber                   :
PostalCode                    :
PostOfficeBox                 :
PrimaryGroupId                : 513
StateOrProvince               :
StreetAddress                 :
Title                         :
WebPage                       :
HomeDirectory                 :
HomeDrive                     :
ProfilePath                   :
LogonScript                   :
UserPrincipalName             : sapple@jdhlab.com
TsProfilePath                 :
TsHomeDirectory               :
TsHomeDrive                   :
TsAllowLogon                  :
```

```
TsRemoteControl            :
TsMaxDisconnectionTime     :
TsMaxConnectionTime        :
TsMaxIdleTime              :
TsReconnectionAction       :
TsBrokenConnectionAction   :
TsConnectClientDrives      :
TsConnectPrinterDrives     :
TsDefaultToMainPrinter     :
TsWorkDirectory            :
TsInitialProgram           :
AccountExpires             :
PasswordLastSet            : 7/19/2010 3:10:23 PM
PasswordAge                : 00:05:11.4163387
PasswordExpires            : 8/30/2010 3:10:23 PM
LastLogonTimestamp         :
LastLogon                  :
LastLogoff                 :
AccountIsDisabled          : False
AccountIsLockedOut         : False
PasswordNeverExpires       : False
UserMustChangePassword     : False
AccountIsExpired           : False
PasswordIsExpired          : False
AccountExpirationStatus    : Never
PasswordStatus             : Expires at: Monday, August 30, 2010
NTAccountName              : JDHLAB\sapple
SamAccountName             : sapple
Security                   : Quest.ActiveRoles.ArsPowerShellSnapIn.UI.SecurityDescriptor
Domain                     : JDHLAB\
LastKnownParent            :
MemberOf                   : {}
NestedMemberOf             : {}
Notes                      :
AllMemberOf                : {}
Keywords                   : {}
Path                       : LDAP://COREDC01.jdhlab.local/CN=Sam Apple,OU=HR,OU=Employees,DC=jdhl...
DN                         : CN=Sam Apple,OU=HR,OU=Employees,DC=jdhlab,dc=local
CanonicalName              : jdhlab.local/Employees/HR/Sam Apple
CreationDate               : 7/19/2010 3:10:23 PM
ModificationDate           : 7/19/2010 3:10:23 PM
ParentContainer            : jdhlab.local/Employees/HR
ParentContainerDN          : OU=HR,OU=Employees,DC=jdhlab,dc=local
Name                       : Sam Apple
ClassName                  : user
Type                       : user
Guid                       : d3099762-3da8-4c82-b881-6d1906f6ee28
Sid                        : S-1-5-21-3957442467-353870018-3926547339-5048
Description                :
DisplayName                : Sam Apple
OperationID                :
OperationStatus            : Unknown
Cache                      : Quest.ActiveRoles.ArsPowerShellSnapIn.BusinessLogic.ObjectCache
Connection                 : Quest.ActiveRoles.ArsPowerShellSnapIn.Data.ArsADConnection
DirectoryEntry             : System.DirectoryServices.DirectoryEntry
```

Notice that there this is a System.DirectoryServices.DirectoryEntry:

```
DirectoryEntry             : System.DirectoryServices.DirectoryEntry
```

The Quest cmdlets do a terrific job of abstracting a great deal, making them easy to use for administrators. But if you ever need access to the "raw" underlying .NET object, here it is:

```
PS C:\> $user.DirectoryEntry | Select *


objectClass           : {top, person, organizationalPerson, user}
cn                    : {Sam Apple}
sn                    : {Apple}
givenName             : {Sam}
distinguishedName     : {CN=Sam Apple,OU=HR,OU=Employees,DC=jdhlab,DC=local}
instanceType          : {4}
whenCreated           : {7/19/2010 7:10:23 PM}
whenChanged           : {7/19/2010 7:10:23 PM}
displayName           : {Sam Apple}
uSNCreated            : {System.__ComObject}
uSNChanged            : {System.__ComObject}
name                  : {Sam Apple}
objectGUID            : {98 151 9 211 168 61 130 76 184 129 109 25 6 246 238 40}
userAccountControl    : {544}
badPwdCount           : {0}
codePage              : {0}
countryCode           : {0}
badPasswordTime       : {System.__ComObject}
lastLogoff            : {System.__ComObject}
lastLogon             : {System.__ComObject}
pwdLastSet            : {System.__ComObject}
primaryGroupID        : {513}
objectSid             : {1 5 0 0 0 0 0 5 21 0 0 0 163 199 225 235 194 160 23 21 139 91 10...
accountExpires        : {System.__ComObject}
logonCount            : {0}
sAMAccountName        : {sapple}
sAMAccountType        : {805306368}
userPrincipalName     : {sapple@jdhlab.com}
objectCategory        : {CN=Person,CN=Schema,CN=Configuration,DC=jdhlab,DC=local}
dSCorePropagationData : {1/1/1601 12:00:00 AM}
nTSecurityDescriptor  : {System.__ComObject}
AuthenticationType    : Secure, Signing, Sealing, ServerBind
Children              : {}
Guid                  : 629709d3a83d824cb8816d1906f6ee28
ObjectSecurity        : System.DirectoryServices.ActiveDirectorySecurity
NativeGuid            : 629709d3a83d824cb8816d1906f6ee28
NativeObject          : System.__ComObject
Parent                : LDAP://COREDC01.jdhlab.local/OU=HR,OU=Employees,DC=jdhlab,dc=local
Password              :
Path                  : LDAP://COREDC01.jdhlab.local/CN=Sam Apple,OU=HR,OU=Employees,...
Properties            : {objectClass, cn, sn, givenName...}
SchemaClassName       : user
SchemaEntry           : System.DirectoryServices.DirectoryEntry
UsePropertyCache      : True
Username              :
Options               : {}
Site                  :
Container             :
```

Aren't you glad you don't have to work with this every day?

Because you have objects, it is much easier to accomplish basic tasks. As an example, when I create a new user account with the **New-QADUser** cmdlet, it is enabled by default. The cmdlet doesn't have a parameter for changing this. However, I can use the **Disable-QADUser** cmdlet:

```
PS C:\> $user | Disable-QADUser
```

I simply pipe the $user object to the **Disable-QADUser** cmdlet and it is disabled. By the way, there is also an **Enable-QADUser** cmdlet. Knowing this, let's revisit the command for creating Sam Apple and create a Disabled account:

```
PS C:\> $user=New-QADUser -parent "OU=HR,OU=Employees,DC=jdhlab,dc=local" `
>>   -name "Sam Apple" -First "Sam" -Last "Apple" `
>>   -userprincipal "sapple@jdhlab.com" `
>>   -userpassword "P@ssw0rd" `
>>   -Display "Sam Apple" `
>>   -samAccountName "sapple" | Disable-QADuser
>>
PS C:\> $user

Name                          Type         DN
----                          ----         --
Sam Apple                     user         CN=Sam Apple,OU=HR,OU=Employees,DC=jdhlab,dc=local


PS C:\> $user.AccountIsDisabled
True
```

The only difference from what I did earlier is that I piped the new object to the **Disable-QADUser** cmdlet.

Before you leave Sam's account, I want to briefly cover something that beginners might find confusing. When I invoked the **New-QADuser** cmdlet, the cmdlet has a **-Title** parameter, but I didn't use it. The cmdlet results were saved as **$user**, so you might think I can simply set the **Title** property:

```
PS C:\> $user.title="Technical Recruiter"
PS C:\> $user.title
Technical Recruiter
```

It looks like it worked because there is no error message. However, if you check the object in Active Directory, you'll see it hasn't changed. **$User** is a static object holding the properties of the user object in Active Directory when it was created. Because $user is not the actual or live Active Directory object, it cannot be changed directly. Instead, you'll use another Quest cmdlet, **Set-QADUser**, to effect the change:

```
PS C:\> $user | Set-QADUser -title "Technical Recruiter"

Name                 Type                DN
----                 ----                --
Sam Apple            user                CN=Sam Apple,OU=HR,OU=Employees,DC=jdhlab,dc=local
```

Piping the $user object to the **Set-QADuser** cmdlet sets the user's title property.

If you go back and compare the syntax between the **New-ADUser** and **New-QADUser** cmdlets, you'll notice the latter is lacking parameters to set an account expiration date, force a password change, or create the account with a non-expiring password. The way you work around this apparent limitation is to pipe the new user object to the **Set-QADUser** cmdlet as it is created:

```
PS C:\> New-Qaduser -ParentContainer "OU=HR,OU=Employees,dc=jdhlab,dc=local" `
>>  -Name "Penny Lane" -SamAccountName "plane" `
>>  -UserPrincipalName "plane@jdhlab.com" -UserPassword "P@ssw0rd" `
>>  -FirstName "Penny" -LastName "Lane" `
```

```
>>  -Description "Seasonal hire"  -DisplayName "Penny Lane" `
>>  -Department "HR" -Manager "Sam Apple" -Title "Recruiting Assistant" `
>>  -phonenumber "x787" -Company "JDH Labs" `
>>  -info "created $(get-date) by $env:username" |
>>  Set-QADUser -UserMustChangePassword $True -AccountExpires (get-date).AddDays(90)
>>

Name                              Type       DN
----                              ----       --
Penny Lane                        user       CN=Penny Lane,OU=HR,OU=Employees,dc=jdhlab,dc=local
```

You've seen most of the code for the **New-QADUser** cmdlet before. What's different is that the object the cmdlet sends to the pipeline is piped to the **Set-QADUser** cmdlet, where I configure the password change and account expiration date:

```
>>  -info "created $(get-date) by $env:username" |
>>  Set-QADUser -UserMustChangePassword $True -AccountExpires (get-date).AddDays(90)
```

I'll cover the **Set-QADUser** cmdlet in more detail later in the chapter.

There's no doubt that PowerShell requires a lot of typing, especially with a cmdlet like **New-QADUser**. So to make life easier, I created a script that prompts you for the most commonly used and necessary parameters for **New-QADuser**:

Prompt-QADUser.ps1

```
#requires -version 2.0
#requires -pssnapin Quest.ActiveRoles.ADManagement

#add Quest snapin if not already loaded
if (-not (Get-PSSnapin Quest.ActiveRoles.ADManagement)) {
   Add-PSSnapin Quest.ActiveRoles.ADManagement
}

#define the cmdlet to run"
$cmd="New-Qaduser"

#a list of typically used  new user parameters
$parameters ="ParentContainer","Name","SamAccountName","UserPrincipalName","UserPassword", `
"FirstName","Initials","LastName","Description","DisplayName","Department","Title", `
"PhoneNumber","Office","Company","StreetAddress","PostOfficeBox","City","StateOrProvince", `
"PostalCode","HomePhone","Manager","MobilePhone","Notes","ObjectAttributes"

Write-Host "When prompted to enter a parameter value, enclose it in quotes, `r`
EXCEPT for ObjectAttributes which you should enter as a hash table. `r`
Press Enter to leave the parameter blank, type Done to stop prompts or `r`
Abort to quit completely.`n" -foregroundcolor Green

#go through each parameter and build a command string
foreach ($item in $parameters) {
    $value=Read-Host "Enter a value for $item "
    Switch -regex ($value) {
        "done" {$done=$True;Break}
        "abort" {$abort=$True;Break}
        #only build a command for something entered
        "\S+" {$cmd = $cmd + " -$item " + $value}
    }
    if ($abort) {
        exit
        }
```

```
        elseif ($done) {
            break
            }
} #close foreach

$rc=Read-Host "Do you want to this account to be DISABLED? [YN]"
if ($rc -match "Y") {$cmd=$cmd + " | Disable-QADuser"}

Write-Host `n$cmd`n -ForegroundColor cyan

$rc=Read-Host "Do you want to run this command? [YN]"
if ($rc -match "Y") {Invoke-Expression $cmd}
```

The **Prompt-QADUser** script requires the Quest cmdlets and loads the snapin if not already running:

```
#requires -pssnapin Quest.ActiveRoles.ADManagement

#add Quest snapin if not already loaded
if (-not (Get-PSSnapin Quest.ActiveRoles.ADManagement)) {
   Add-PSSnapin Quest.ActiveRoles.ADManagement
}
```

Within the script I define a variable, $parameters, that contains all the most commonly used parameter names:

```
$parameters ="ParentContainer","Name","SamAccountName","UserPrincipalName","UserPassword", `
"FirstName","Initials","LastName","Description","DisplayName","Department","Title", `
"PhoneNumber","Office","Company","StreetAddress","PostOfficeBox","City","StateOrProvince", `
"PostalCode","HomePhone","Manager","MobilePhone","Notes","ObjectAttributes"
```

The script goes through each parameter, prompting you for a value. If you enter a value other than "Done" or "Abort", it is added to the command expression:

```
        #only build a command for something entered
        "\S+" {$cmd = $cmd + " -$item " + $value}
```

A value of "Abort" will exit the script and a value of "Done" will break the **ForEach** loop and jump to the next line. Assuming you've entered your values, the script prompts if you want to disable the account. If so, the command string is revised:

```
$rc=Read-Host "Do you want to this account to be DISABLED? [YN]"
if ($rc -match "Y") {$cmd=$cmd + " | Disable-QADuser"}
```

Finally, the script displays the final command and asks if you wish to execute it:

```
Write-Host `n$cmd`n -ForegroundColor cyan

$rc=Read-Host "Do you want to run this command? [YN]"
if ($rc -match "Y") {Invoke-Expression $cmd}
```

Here's an example of this script in action with the output piped to the **Set-QADuser** cmdlet to force the user to change password at next logon:

```
PS C:\> c:\scripts\Prompt-QADUser.ps1 | Set-QADuser -UserMustChangePassword $True
When prompted to enter a parameter value, enclose it in quotes,
EXCEPT for ObjectAttributes which you should enter as a hash table.
Press Enter to leave the parameter blank, type Done to stop prompts or
Abort to quit completely.

Enter a value for ParentContainer : "OU=HR,OU=Employees,dc=jdhlab,dc=local"
Enter a value for Name : "Sandy Bottom"
Enter a value for SamAccountName : sbottom
Enter a value for UserPrincipalName : sbottom@jdhlab.com
Enter a value for UserPassword : "P@ssw0rd"
Enter a value for FirstName : "Sandy"
Enter a value for Initials :
Enter a value for LastName : "Bottom"
Enter a value for Description : "Project Omega"
Enter a value for DisplayName : "Sandy Botton"
Enter a value for Department : "Benefits"
Enter a value for Title : "Benefits Administrator"
Enter a value for PhoneNumber : "x567"
Enter a value for Office :
Enter a value for Company : "JDH Labs"
Enter a value for StreetAddress :
Enter a value for PostOfficeBox :
Enter a value for City :
Enter a value for StateOrProvince :
Enter a value for PostalCode :
Enter a value for HomePhone :
Enter a value for Manager : "Ann Beebe"
Enter a value for MobilePhone :
Enter a value for Notes : "Created $(get-date) by $env:username"
Enter a value for ObjectAttributes : @{Division="Employee Operations"}
Do you want to this account to be DISABLED? [YN]: N

New-Qaduser -ParentContainer "OU=HR,OU=Employees,dc=jdhlab,dc=local" -Name "Sandy Bottom"
-SamAccountName sbottom -UserPrincipalName sbottom@jdhlab.com -UserPassword "P@ssw0rd"
-FirstName "Sandy" -LastName "Bottom" -Description "Project Omega" -DisplayName "Sandy Botton"
-Department "Benefits" -Title "Benefits Administrator" -PhoneNumber "x567" -Company "JDH Labs"
-Manager "Ann Beebe" -Notes "Created $(get-date) by $env:username" -ObjectAttributes @
{Division="Employee Operations"}

Do you want to run this command? [YN]: Y

Name                          Type        DN
----                          ----        --
Sandy Bottom                  user        CN=Sandy Bottom,OU=HR,OU=Employees,dc=jdhlab,dc=...
```

What If and Confirm

Since the **New-QADUser** and **New-ADUser** cmdlets are making a change to Active Directory, they support the common **-WhatIf** parameter. If you include **-WhatIf** to your expression, PowerShell shows you what it would have done, but the command isn't actually carried out:

```
PS C:\> New-QADUser -parent $ou -name "Edgar Allen Poe" -first "Edgar" -initial "A" `
>> -last "Poe" -sam "eapoe" -userprincipal "poe@Jdhlab.com" -pass "P@ssw0rd" -whatif
>>

What if: Creating user named 'Edgar Allen Poe' in OU=Temp,OU=Employees,DC=jdhlab,DC=local.
```

This is a great sanity check. You can also use the common **-Confirm** parameter for most of the Quest and Microsoft cmdlets:

```
PS C:\> $ou= "OU=Temp,OU=Employees,DC=jdhlab,DC=local"
PS C:\> New-QADUser -parent $ou -name "Edgar Allen Poe" -first "Edgar" -initial "A" `
>> -last "Poe" -sam "eapoe" -userprincipal "poe@Jdhlab.com" -pass "P@ssw0rd" -confirm
>>

Confirm
Are you sure you want to perform this action?
Creating user named 'Edgar Allen Poe' in OU=Temp,OU=Employees,DC=jdhlab,DC=local.
[Y] Yes  [A] Yes to All  [N] No  [L] No to All  [S] Suspend  [?] Help (default is "Y"): y

Name                Type            DN
----                ----            --
Edgar Allen Poe     user            CN=Edgar Allen Poe,OU=Temp,OU=Employees,DC=jdhlab,DC=local
```

You should find most cmdlets that create, delete, or modify objects in Active Directory support both of these parameters.

Modifying User Accounts

Life would be easier if you never had to touch a user account after it was created, but this isn't likely to happen. If you have a simple need, using the Active Directory Users and Computers management console should suffice. For more complicated tasks or for the sake of efficiency, use Windows PowerShell and the appropriate cmdlet from either Microsoft or Quest Software.

Using Set-ADUser

The **Set-ADUser** cmdlet requires an identity, usually a SAMAccountname, and then one or more parameters that indicate what new value you wish to set. Most of the common user properties can be modified with one of the parameters in Table 2-3.

Table 2-3 Set-ADUser Parameters

Name	Type
AccountExpirationDate	System.Nullable`1[System.DateTime]
AccountNotDelegated	System.Nullable`1[System.Boolean]
AllowReversiblePasswordEncryption	System.Nullable`1[System.Boolean]
CannotChangePassword	System.Nullable`1[System.Boolean]
Certificates	System.Collections.Hashtable
ChangePasswordAtLogon	System.Nullable`1[System.Boolean]
City	System.String
Company	System.String
Country	System.String
Department	System.String
Description	System.String
DisplayName	System.String
Division	System.String
EmailAddress	System.String
EmployeeID	System.String
EmployeeNumber	System.String
Enabled	System.Nullable`1[System.Boolean]

Fax	System.String
GivenName	System.String
HomeDirectory	System.String
HomeDrive	System.String
HomePage	System.String
HomePhone	System.String
Identity	Microsoft.ActiveDirectory.Management.ADUser
Initials	System.String
Instance	Microsoft.ActiveDirectory.Management.ADUser
LogonWorkstations	System.String
Manager	Microsoft.ActiveDirectory.Management.ADUser
MobilePhone	System.String
Office	System.String
OfficePhone	System.String
Organization	System.String
OtherName	System.String
PasswordNeverExpires	System.Nullable`1[System.Boolean]
PasswordNotRequired	System.Nullable`1[System.Boolean]
POBox	System.String
PostalCode	System.String
ProfilePath	System.String
SAMAccountName	System.String
ScriptPath	System.String
SmartcardLogonRequired	System.Nullable`1[System.Boolean]
State	System.String
StreetAddress	System.String
Surname	System.String
Title	System.String
TrustedForDelegation	System.Nullable`1[System.Boolean]
UserPrincipalName	System.String

Let's take the Penny Lane account created earlier and change her office, city, and state:

```
PS C:\> Set-ADUser "plane" -Office "NW981" -city "Seattle" -State "WA"
```

The cmdlet doesn't write anything to the pipeline unless you specified the **-Passthru** parameter. But the properties were in fact set:

```
PS C:\> Get-ADUser "plane" -Properties City,State,Office | Select City,State,Office

City                                    State                                   Office
----                                    -----                                   ------
Seattle                                 WA                                      NW981
```

If a property already has a value, it will be overwritten. To clear a property value that can be set with a parameter using the **Set-ADUser** cmdlet, simply set the value to $null:

```
PS C:\> Set-ADUser "sday" -Description $null

Name                          Type     DN
----                          ----     --
Sunny Day                     user     CN=Sunny Day,OU=Temp,OU=Employees,DC=jdhlab,DC=...
```

For all other properties you can add, remove, replace, or clear these values with the corresponding parameter. Specify the property and value in a hash table:

```
PS C:\> Set-ADUser "plane" -Add @{otherTelephone="246-1230"}
```

I can replace a value:

```
PS C:\> Set-ADUser "plane" -Replace @{otherTelephone="246-1230","246-0321"}
```

This does not replace 246-1230 with 246-0321. Instead it is replacing the current property value to a new multi-value property because the **OtherTelephone** property supports multiple values.

I can remove a property value just as easily:

```
PS C:\> Set-ADUser "plane"-Remove @{otherTelephone="246-0321"}
```

In a multi-value property like **OtherTelephone** no other values are touched. In a single value property this has the effect of clearing the property. Or I can explicitly clear everything:

```
PS C:\> Set-ADUser "plane" -clear "otherTelephone"
```

It doesn't matter if the property is single or multi-valued, everything will be cleared.

When you use the **-Add**, **-Remove**, **-Replace**, and **-Clear** parameters together, be aware that the operations will take place in the order: Remove, Add, Replace, and lastly Clear.

Unlocking an Account

I'll assume that most of the time when you need to unlock an account, you will know the account name. With that, it is almost trivial to use the **Unlock-ADAccount** cmdlet:

```
PS C:\> Unlock-ADAccount jshortz
```

But to find locked out accounts, you'll need a filtering query to check the **LockoutTime** property. If an account is locked, this property will have a value greater than 0:

```
PS C:\> Get-ADUser -filter "lockouttime -gt 0"  -properties lockouttime |
>> Select distinguishedname,LockoutTime
>>
```

```
distinguishedname                                        LockoutTime
-----------------                                        -----------
CN=Jim Shortz,OU=Employees,DC=jdhlab,DC=local            129246309886531730
CN=Francis Drake,OU=Employees,DC=jdhlab,DC=local         129246310266007794
```

The **LockoutTime** value is the number of clock ticks since the beginning of time. Well, actually since January 1, 1601. Given that, it only takes an extra step to convert this value to a more admin-friendly date time:

```
PS C:\> [datetime]$utc="1/1/1601"
PS C:\> $utc.AddTicks(129246309886531730)

Monday, July 26, 2010 3:16:28 PM
```

The date time value is in GMT. But I can get the current time zone from WMI and adjust it locally:

```
PS C:\> $os=Get-WmiObject win32_operatingsystem
PS C:\> $utc.AddTicks(129246309886531730).AddMinutes($os.currentTimeZone)

Monday, July 26, 2010 11:16:28 AM
```

I can incorporate this logic into my original PowerShell expression and display the raw and friendly formats:

```
PS C:\> Get-ADUser -filter "lockouttime -gt 0"  -properties lockouttime |
>> Select distinguishedname,LockoutTime,@{Name="Locked";Expression={
>> [datetime]$utc="1/1/1601"
>> $os=Get-WmiObject -class win32_operatingsystem
>> $utc.AddTicks($_.lockouttime).AddMinutes($os.currentTimeZone)
>> }}
>>

distinguishedname                                    LockoutTime         Locked
-----------------                                    -----------         ------
CN=Jim Shortz,OU=Employees,DC=jdhlab,DC=local        129246309886531730  7/26/2010 11:16:28 AM
CN=Francis Drake,OU=Employees,DC=jdhlab,DC=local     129246310266007794  7/26/2010 11:17:06 AM
```

Since I have several locked accounts, I can take advantage of the pipeline and handle them all at once:

```
PS C:\> Get-ADUser -filter "lockouttime -gt 0" | Unlock-ADAccount -whatif
What if: Performing operation "Set" on Target "CN=Jim Shortz,OU=Employees,DC=jdhlab,DC=local".
What if: Performing operation "Set" on Target "CN=Francis Drake,OU=Employees,DC=jdhlab,...
```

Remove the **-WhatIf** parameter and the accounts will be unlocked.

Using Set-QADUser

The **Set-QADUser** cmdlet makes it very easy to modify Active Directory user accounts. All you need to do is specify the name of the object and one or more attributes to modify:

```
PS C:\> Set-QADUser jdhlab\jeff -title "Sr. System Architect"
```

You can specify the user object using the down-level name, or as shown in the examples below:

```
PS C:\> Set-QADUser jeff@Jdhlab.com -description "Scripting Guru"

Name                Type            DN
----                ----            --
Jeff                user            CN=Jeff,CN=Users,DC=jdhlab,DC=local

PS C:\> Set-QADUser "CN=Jeff,CN=Users,DC=jdhlab,DC=local" -city Miami -state FL


Name                Type            DN
----                ----            --
Jeff                user            CN=Jeff,CN=Users,DC=jdhlab,DC=local

PS C:\> Set-QADUser "Jdhlab.local/Users/Jeff" -objectAttributes @{"PreferredLanguage"="English"}


Name                Type            DN
----                ----            --
Jeff                user            CN=Jeff,CN=Users,DC=jdhlab,DC=local
```

In the last example, I'm setting a property value for a parameter that isn't part of the regular cmdlet. I'm setting the PreferredLanguage attribute to "English". In addition to the examples here, you can also specify the user account by SID or GUID.

Clearing Property Values

To clear a property value, simply specify the appropriate parameter for the **Set-QADUser** cmdlet, and then set the value to $Null:

```
PS C:\> Set-QADUser jeff@Jdhlab.com -description $null
```

Managing Multi-value Properties

Some user properties, such as **OtherTelephone**, are multi-value. Setting them using the **Set-QADUser** cmdlet only requires that you specify the parameter values as a hash table:

```
PS C:\> Set-QADUser "jeff" -objectattributes @{"othertelephone"="555-0202","555-0303"}
```

This expression will modify the **OtherTelephone** user property to display these two telephone numbers.

Yet, what about if you want to keep the existing values and add a new telephone number? This takes a little extra work and can be confusing at first. You still need to use the **-ObjectAttributes** parameter and specify the property name. But the value will be a special type of hash table with a keyword that tells the cmdlet what to do:

```
PS C:\> Set-QADUser "jeff" -ObjectAttributes @{othertelephone=@{Append="555-9999"}}
```

With this command I've appended a new phone number to the account. Or I can delete a number:

```
PS C:\> Set-QADUser "jeff" -ObjectAttributes @{othertelephone=@{Delete="555-9999"}}
```

Unlocking an Account

If a user has been locked out of their account, you can easily use PowerShell and the **Unlock-QADUser** cmdlet:

```
PS C:\ Unlock-QADUser jdhlab\rgbiv
```

You can safely run this command whether or not the account is locked out. If it isn't, it won't affect the object.

To find locked-out accounts search for user objects, simply use the **-Locked** parameter:

```
PS C:\> Get-QADUser -locked

Name                          Type       DN
----                          ----       --
Roy G. Biv                    user       CN=Roy G. Biv,OU=Employees,DC=jdhlab,DC=local
Penny Lane                    user       CN=Penny Lane,OU=HR,OU=Employees,DC=jdhlab,DC=local
```

Unlike the Microsoft cmdlet, the Quest cmdlet will automatically convert the lockout time to a friendlier format. Just remember to include the **LockoutTime** property:

```
PS C:\> Get-QADUser -locked -IncludedProperties LockoutTime |
>> Select DN,Name,Lockouttime
>>

DN                                                   Name         lockoutTime
--                                                   ----         -----------
CN=Roy G. Biv,OU=Employees,DC=jdhlab,DC=local        Roy G. Biv   7/26/2010 5:08:02 PM
CN=Penny Lane,OU=HR,OU=Employees,DC=jdhlab,DC=local  Penny Lane   7/26/2010 5:10:16 PM
```

If I know the SAMAccountname, unlocking is pretty simple with the **Unlock-QADUser** cmdlet:

```
PS C:\> Unlock-QADUser "jshortz"-confirm

Confirm
Are you sure you want to perform this action?
Modify object 'CN=Jim Shortz,OU=Employees,DC=jdhlab,DC=local'.
[Y] Yes  [A] Yes to All  [N] No  [L] No to All  [S] Suspend  [?] Help (default is "Y"): Y

Name                          Type          DN
----                          ----          --
Jim Shortz                    user          CN=Jim Shortz,OU=Employees,DC=jdhlab,DC=local
```

This expression takes the result of the **Get-QADUser** cmdlet and pipes it to the **Unlock-QADUser** cmdlet. I use the **-Confirm** parameter to make sure I only unlock accounts I want to unlock. Or I can leverage the pipeline and unlock all locked accounts:

```
PS C:\> Get-QADUser -locked | Unlock-QADUser

Name                          Type       DN
----                          ----       --
Roy G. Biv                    user       CN=Roy G. Biv,OU=Employees,DC=jdhlab,DC=local
Penny Lane                    user       CN=Penny Lane,OU=HR,OU=Employees,DC=jdhlab,DC=local
```

Using Disable-QADUser

Need to disable a user account? It's as simple as this:

```
PS C:\> Disable-QADUser sapple
```

You can also specify the user account by its userprincipal, distinguished, or down-level names.

Using Enable-QADUser

To enable a user account, you can use the same approach as shown for disabling an account:

```
PS C:\> Enable-QADUser "l.butler"

Name                Type                DN
----                ----                --
Lois Butler         user                CN=Lois Butler,OU=Temp,OU=Employees,DC=jdhlab,DC=local
```

Both the **Disable-QADUser** and **Enable-QADUser** cmdlets support the **-WhatIf** and **-Confirm** parameters, so you can avoid making mistakes:

```
PS C:\> Get-QADUser k.cruz | Enable-QADUser -confirm

Confirm
Are you sure you want to perform this action?
Modify Object 'CN=Kim Cruz,OU=Payroll,OU=Employees,DC=jdhlab,DC=local'.
[Y] Yes  [A] Yes to All  [N] No  [L] No to All  [S] Suspend  [?] Help (default is "Y"): y

Name                Type                DN
----                ----                --
Kim Cruz            user                CN=Kim Cruz,OU=Payroll,OU=Employees,DC=jdhlab,DC=local
```

Renaming User Accounts

Occasionally you will need to rename a user account. There are a few ways you can do this. In this example, the user Jane Smith has gotten married and wishes to change her name to Jane Jones.

Using Microsoft Cmdlets

Renaming a user object only involves a few property names and the **Rename-ADObject** cmdlet. When you first look at this cmdlet, an expression like this succeeds:

```
PS C:\> Rename-ADObject -Identity `
>> "CN=Jane Smith,OU=Operations,OU=Payroll,OU=employees,DC=jdhlab,DC=local" -new "Jane Jones"
```

There are no errors and if you look in Active Directory Users and Computers you will see that Jane is now "Jane Jones". However, you haven't change the rest of her user object like SAMAccountname and UPN. You can change these items with the **Set-ADUser** cmdlet, but you need an object. For that, tell the **Rename-ADObject** cmdlet to pass its object onto the pipeline with the **-Passthru** parameter:

```
PS C:\> Rename-ADObject -Identity `
>> "CN=Jane Smith,OU=Operations,OU=Payroll,OU=employees,DC=jdhlab,DC=local" `
>> -new "Jane Jones" -passthru |
>> Set-ADUser -SamAccountName "jjones" -UserPrincipalName "jjones@jdhlab.com" `
>> -DisplayName "Jane Jones" -Surname "Jones" -passthru
>>


DistinguishedName : CN=Jane Jones,OU=Operations,OU=Payroll,OU=Employees,DC=jdhlab,DC=local
Enabled           : True
GivenName         : Jane
Name              : Jane Jones
ObjectClass       : user
ObjectGUID        : cd0cd86b-2e69-4761-98f2-34bd1ffc6cff
SamAccountName    : jjones
SID               : S-1-5-21-3957442467-353870018-3926547339-5086
Surname           : Jones
UserPrincipalName : jjones@jdhlab.com
```

Using Rename-QADObject

Or you can use Quest's **Rename-QADObject** cmdlet, which will get part of the job done. You can use an expression like this:

```
PS C:\> Rename-QADObject -identity "jdhlab\jsmith" -newname "Jane Jones"

Name                Type          DN
----                ----          --
Jane Jones          user          cn=Jane Jones,OU=Operations,OU=Payroll,OU=Employees,DC=jd...
```

This will rename the Active Directory user object like you did with the **Rename-ADObject** cmdlet, but you still to need change her SAMAccountname and user principal name. A slightly more complex expression is needed to take care of everything:

```
PS C:\> Rename-QADObject jdhlab\jsmith -newname "Jane Jones" |
>> Set-QADUser -samaccount "jjones" -userprincipal "jjones@Jdhlab.com" -display "Jane Jones" `
>> -LastName "Jones"
>>

Name                                Type        DN
----                                ----        --
Jane Jones                          user        cn=Jane Jones,OU=Operations,OU=Payroll,OU=Employ...
```

This expression does the initial rename of the Active Directory object and pipes its output object to the **Set-QADUser** cmdlet, which changes all the other properties including her new last name.

I created a function that streamlines much of this process. It will rename the user account assuming that only the last name has changed:

Rename-User.ps1

```
Function Rename-User {
#requires -pssnapin Quest.ActiveRoles.ADManagement

[cmdletbinding(SupportsShouldProcess=$True,ConfirmImpact="High")]

Param(
```

```
[Parameter(Position=0,Mandatory=$True,HelpMessage="Enter a user's current SAMAccountname")]
[ValidateNotNullorEmpty()]
[string]$SAMAccountname,
[Parameter(Position=1,Mandatory=$True,HelpMessage="Enter the NEW SAMAccountname")]
[ValidateNotNullorEmpty()]
[string]$newSAMAccountname,
[Parameter(Position=2,Mandatory=$True,HelpMessage="Enter the NEW Active Directory
accountname")]
[ValidateNotNullorEmpty()]
[string]$newAccountname,
[Parameter(Mandatory=$False,HelpMessage="Enter the NEW UserPrincipalname")]
[ValidateNotNullorEmpty()]
[string]$userprincipalname,
[Parameter(Mandatory=$False,HelpMessage="Enter the NEW first name")]
[ValidateNotNullorEmpty()]
[string]$firstname,
[Parameter(Mandatory=$False,HelpMessage="Enter the NEW last name")]
[ValidateNotNullorEmpty()]
[string]$lastname

)

#verify account exists
$user=Get-QADUser -Identity $samaccountname
if ($user) {
     Write-Verbose "Renaming $samaccountname"

#define an expression
$command="Rename-QADObject -Identity '$samaccountname' -NewName '$newAccountname' |
Set-QADuser -SamAccountName '$newSAMAccountname' -DisplayName '$newAccountname'"

#check for optional settings
Write-Verbose "Checking for optional parameters"
"userprincipalname","firstname","lastname" | Foreach {
 if ($PSBoundParameters.ContainsKey($_)) {
     Write-Verbose "Adding $_ $($PSBoundParameters.Item($_))"
    $command=$command + " -$_ '" + $PSBoundParameters.Item($_) +"'"
 }
}

Write-Verbose "Executing $command"
 #WhatIf
 if ($pscmdlet.ShouldProcess($user.dn)) {
   Invoke-Expression $command
 }

}
else {
    Write-Warning "Failed to find user $samaccountname"
 }

} #end Function
```

The **Rename-User** function relies on the Quest cmdlets and assumes that when you change a user account you also want to change other properties. As written, the function uses the user's SAMAccountname to locate the account. The other required parameters are the user's new SAMAccountname and the new Active Directory name. The function is essentially a wizard to build a proper Windows PowerShell expression. This is the starting point:

```
$command="Rename-QADObject -Identity '$samaccountname' -NewName '$newAccountname' |
Set-QADuser -SamAccountName '$newSAMAccountname' -DisplayName '$newAccountname'"
```

The remaining parameters are optional but if specified will be added to the command:

```
Write-Verbose "Checking for optional parameters"
"userprincipalname","firstname","lastname" | Foreach {
 if ($PSBoundParameters.ContainsKey($_)) {
     Write-Verbose "Adding $_ $($PSBoundParameters.Item($_))"
    $command=$command + " -$_ '" + $PSBoundParameters.Item($_) +"'"
 }
}
```

Because renaming an account has implications, the function supports the **-WhatIf** parameter:

```
#WhatIf
 if ($pscmdlet.ShouldProcess($user.dn)) {
   Invoke-Expression $command
 }
```

If you don't specify **-WhatIf**, then the **Invoke-Expression** cmdlet is executed. I've also set the impact to high so that you will always be prompted if you want to rename the account:

```
[cmdletbinding(SupportsShouldProcess=$True,ConfirmImpact="High")]
```

You can also use the **-Confirm** parameter, and every cmdlet within the function will ask for confirmation. Let me show you this in action:

```
PS C:\> Rename-User "jsmith" -newSamaccountname "jjones" -newaccountname "Jane Jones" `
>> -userprincipalname "jjones@jdhlab.com" -lastname "Jones" -confirm
>>

Confirm
Are you sure you want to perform this action?
Performing operation "Rename-User" on Target "CN=Jane
Smith,OU=Operations,OU=Payroll,OU=Employees,DC=jdhlab,DC=local".
[Y] Yes  [A] Yes to All  [N] No  [L] No to All  [S] Suspend  [?] Help (default is "Y"):

Confirm
Are you sure you want to perform this action?
Renaming user named 'Jane Smith' in OU=Operations,OU=Payroll,OU=Employees,DC=jdhlab,DC=local
to
 Jane Jones.
[Y] Yes  [A] Yes to All  [N] No  [L] No to All  [S] Suspend  [?] Help (default is "Y"):

Confirm
Are you sure you want to perform this action?
Modify object 'cn=Jane Jones,OU=Operations,OU=Payroll,OU=Employees,DC=jdhlab,DC=local'.
[Y] Yes  [A] Yes to All  [N] No  [L] No to All  [S] Suspend  [?] Help (default is "Y"):

Name                          Type      DN
----                          ----      --
Jane Jones                    user      cn=Jane Jones,OU=Operations,OU=Payroll,OU=Employ...
```

Moving User Accounts

If there's one constant about Active Directory, it's that it is never static. Users get hired, fired, promoted, and transferred. Often this means moving a user object from one organizational unit to another.

Using Move-ADObject

Moving a user object with the Microsoft cmdlet, **Move-ADObject**, is very straightforward. As the name implies, the cmdlet can be used to move any object. All you need is to specify the object identity and the target path:

```
PS C:\> Move-ADObject "CN=Jack Frost,OU=Temp,OU=Employees,DC=jdhlab,DC=local" `
>> -TargetPath "OU=Payroll,OU=Employees,DC=jdhlab,DC=local"
```

The most challenging aspect here is that you need to specify the user's distinguished name. But that involves a lot of typing and effort on your part, so let's have PowerShell do the work for us. Here's a revised and simpler approach:

```
PS C:\> Get-ADUser "jfrost" | Move-ADObject `
>> -TargetPath "OU=Payroll,OU=Employees,DC=jdhlab,DC=local"
```

This is also a great way for moving multiple users based on some filter or search criteria. In this example I'm going to find all users somewhere in the Employees organizational unit that are in the Research department and move them to the IT organizational unit:

```
PS C:\> Get-ADUser -filter "department -eq 'Research'" `
>> -SearchBase >> "OU=Employees,DC=jdhlab,DC=local" |
>> Move-ADObject -TargetPath "OU=IT,OU=Employees,DC=jdhlab,DC=local" -passthru
>>

DistinguishedName                Name                 ObjectClass   ObjectGUID
-----------------                ----                 -----------   ----------
CN=Ashley Metallo,OU=IT,OU...    Ashley Metallo       user          0c0dbf95-9e4e-434e-9c17-87...
CN=Anibal Dillahunt,OU=IT,...    Anibal Dillahunt     user          7ea6d15e-fb8d-4c63-b024-ce...
CN=Alden Larzazs,OU=IT,OU=...    Alden Larzazs        user          96eb1b5a-e9a5-41e7-ae45-67...
CN=Barrett Mcghin,OU=IT,OU...    Barrett Mcghin       user          037b01ff-fdd3-41cf-a0a6-5c...
CN=Benedict Gerthung,OU=IT...    Benedict Gerthung    user          80b09be8-628c-41ab-a4cc-52...
```

I included the **-Passthru** parameter to force the **Move-ADObject** cmdlet to write objects to the pipeline. This would be useful if I wanted to log information about the moved accounts.

Using the Active Directory PSDrive

When you import the Microsoft Active Directory module, you should also get a PSDrive called AD:. This drive allows you to navigate Active Directory as if it were a file system. Let me change drives and see what I have:

```
PS C:\> cd AD:
PS AD:\> dir

Name                 ObjectClass          DistinguishedName
----                 -----------          -----------------
jdhlab               domainDNS            DC=jdhlab,DC=local
Configuration        configuration        CN=Configuration,DC=jdhlab,DC=local
Schema               dMD                  CN=Schema,CN=Configuration,DC=jdhlab,DC=local
DomainDnsZones       domainDNS            DC=DomainDnsZones,DC=jdhlab,DC=local
ForestDnsZones       domainDNS            DC=ForestDnsZones,DC=jdhlab,DC=local
```

To change "directories" you need to use the distinguished name:

```
PS AD:\> cd "dc=jdhlab,dc=local"
PS AD:\dc=jdhlab,dc=local> dir

Name                  ObjectClass           DistinguishedName
----                  -----------           -----------------
asample146            user                  CN=asample146,DC=jdhlab,DC=local
asample147            user                  CN=asample147,DC=jdhlab,DC=local
asample148            user                  CN=asample148,DC=jdhlab,DC=local
asample149            user                  CN=asample149,DC=jdhlab,DC=local
Branch Office         organizationalUnit    OU=Branch Office,DC=jdhlab,DC=local
Builtin               builtinDomain         CN=Builtin,DC=jdhlab,DC=local
Computers             container             CN=Computers,DC=jdhlab,DC=local
Contacts              organizationalUnit    OU=Contacts,DC=jdhlab,DC=local
Desktops              organizationalUnit    OU=Desktops,DC=jdhlab,DC=local
Domain Controllers    organizationalUnit    OU=Domain Controllers,DC=jdhlab,DC=local
Employees             organizationalUnit    OU=Employees,DC=jdhlab,DC=local
ForeignSecurityPr... container             CN=ForeignSecurityPrincipals,DC=jdhlab,DC=local
Groups                organizationalUnit    OU=Groups,DC=jdhlab,DC=local
Infrastructure        infrastructureUpdate CN=Infrastructure,DC=jdhlab,DC=local
LostAndFound          lostAndFound          CN=LostAndFound,DC=jdhlab,DC=local
Managed Service A... container             CN=Managed Service Accounts,DC=jdhlab,DC=local
Microsoft Exchang... organizationalUnit    OU=Microsoft Exchange Security Groups,DC=jdhlab,DC=local
Microsoft Exchang... msExchSystemObjec... CN=Microsoft Exchange System Objects,DC=jdhlab,DC=local
NTDS Quotas           msDS-QuotaContainer   CN=NTDS Quotas,DC=jdhlab,DC=local
Program Data          container             CN=Program Data,DC=jdhlab,DC=local
Servers               organizationalUnit    OU=Servers,DC=jdhlab,DC=local
System                container             CN=System,DC=jdhlab,DC=local
Templates             organizationalUnit    OU=Templates,DC=jdhlab,DC=local
Users                 container             CN=Users,DC=jdhlab,DC=local
```

You can continue to change directories by using distinguished names:

```
PS AD:\dc=jdhlab,dc=local> cd "OU=Temp,OU=Employees"
PS AD:\OU=Temp,OU=Employees,dc=jdhlab,dc=local> dir

Name                  ObjectClass       DistinguishedName
----                  -----------       -----------------
Dennis Chilo          user              CN=Dennis Chilo,OU=Temp,OU=Employees,DC=jdhlab,DC=local
Eugene Sillas         user              CN=Eugene Sillas,OU=Temp,OU=Employees,DC=jdhlab,DC=local
Hans Panetta          user              CN=Hans Panetta,OU=Temp,OU=Employees,DC=jdhlab,DC=local
Sunny Day             user              CN=Sunny Day,OU=Temp,OU=Employees,DC=jdhlab,DC=local
```

To move a user, you should specify the target's distinguished name in the PSDrive:

```
PS AD:\OU=Temp,OU=Employees,dc=jdhlab,dc=local> Move-Item "CN=Sunny Day" `
>> -Destination "AD:\OU=Customer Service,OU=Employees,DC=jdhlab,DC=local" -passthru
>>

Name                  ObjectClass     DistinguishedName
----                  -----------     -----------------
Sunny Day             user            CN=Sunny Day,OU=Customer Service,OU=Employees,DC=jdhl...
```

The PSDrive provider understands how to translate the **Move-Item** cmdlet in this context. I've now moved the Sunny Day user account to the Customer Service organizational unit which I can verify by the distinguished name above.

You can use relative paths, but be careful:

```
PS AD:\OU=Temp,OU=Employees,dc=jdhlab,dc=local> Move-Item "CN=Dennis Chilo" `
>>-Destination "..\OU=Engineering" -passthru
>>

Name                ObjectClass     DistinguishedName
----                -----------     -----------------
Dennis Chilo        user            CN=Dennis Chilo,OU=Engineering,OU=Employees,dc=jdhlab...
```

You'll run into fewer problems if you use a complete destination path.

You can also use wildcards to move more than one object with the PSDrive:

```
PS AD:\OU=Temp,OU=Employees,dc=jdhlab,dc=local> Move-Item * `
>> -Destination "..\OU=Shipping" -passthru
>>

Name                ObjectClass     DistinguishedName
----                -----------     -----------------
Eugene Sillas       user            CN=Eugene Sillas,OU=Shipping,OU=Employees,dc=jdhlab,d...
Hans Panetta        user            CN=Hans Panetta,OU=Shipping,OU=Employees,dc=jdhlab,dc...
```

Using Move-QADObject

The **Move-QADObject** cmdlet is just as easy to use:

```
PS C:\> Move-QADObject "jdhlab\jfrost" -newparentcontainer "Jdhlab.local/Employees/Payroll"
```

All you need to do is specify the user's name; it can be a down-level name like this, or its SAMAccountname, distinguished name, or user principal name, and the canonical or distinguished name of the target organizational unit or container.

Because of the implications surrounding moving an object, I strongly encourage you to use the **-WhatIf** and **-Confirm** parameters:

```
PS C:\> Move-QADObject "jfrost" -newparentcontainer `
>> "OU=Payroll,OU=Employees,DC=jdhlab,DC=local"-confirm
>>

Confirm
Are you sure you want to perform this action?
Moving user named 'Jack Frost' from OU=Temp,OU=Employees,DC=jdhlab,DC=local to
OU=Payroll,OU=Employees,DC=jdhlab,DC=local.
[Y] Yes  [A] Yes to All  [N] No  [L] No to All  [S] Suspend  [?] Help (default is "Y"): y

Name                          Type       DN
----                          ----       --
Jack Frost                    user       CN=Jack Frost,OU=Payroll,OU=Employees,DC=jdhlab,...
```

The result of using the **Get-QADUser** cmdlet is piped to the **Move-QADObject** cmdlet, and then the object is moved to the new parent container. These cmdlets also lend themselves to moving a lot of accounts:

```
PS C:\> Get-QADUser -Department "Finance" -SearchRoot "OU=Employees,DC=jdhlab,DC=local" |
>> Move-QADObject -NewParentContainer "OU=Finance,OU=Employees,DC=jdhlab,DC=local"
>>
```

```
Name                  Type    DN
----                  ----    --
Jamal Pingrey         user    CN=Jamal Pingrey,OU=Finance,OU=Employees,DC=jdhl...
Neil Dickmann         user    CN=Neil Dickmann,OU=Finance,OU=Employees,DC=jdhl...
Lester Yoeckel        user    CN=Lester Yoeckel,OU=Finance,OU=Employees,DC=jdh...
Lenard Machin         user    CN=Lenard Machin,OU=Finance,OU=Employees,DC=jdhl...
Cary Calcaterra       user    CN=Cary Calcaterra,OU=Finance,OU=Employees,DC=jd...
Will Cambia           user    CN=Will Cambia,OU=Finance,OU=Employees,DC=jdhlab...
Dean Arseneault       user    CN=Dean Arseneault,OU=Finance,OU=Employees,DC=ja...
Wilbert Fredricksen   user    CN=Wilbert Fredricksen,OU=Finance,OU=Employees,D...
Wilfred Boilard       user    CN=Wilfred Boilard,OU=Finance,OU=Employees,DC=jd...
Wilmer Derossett      user    CN=Wilmer Derossett,OU=Finance,OU=Employees,DC=j...
Norman Preist         user    CN=Norman Preist,OU=Finance,OU=Employees,DC=jdhl...
```

With a one-line command I found all user accounts in the Finance department and moved them to the Finance OU. If the accounts were already in the OU, the **Move-QADObject** cmdlet still processes the account, but nothing is changed.

Deleting User Accounts

Using Remove-ADUser

Deleting a user account using the **Remove-ADUser** cmdlet is very direct. Specify the account name and it is gone. Although I encourage you to use the **-Confirm** parameter:

```
PS C:\> Remove-ADUser -Identity "a.rottner" -confirm

Confirm
Are you sure you want to perform this action?
Performing operation "Remove" on Target "CN=Alvin Rottner,OU=Finance,OU=Employees,DC=jdhlab,D
C=local".
[Y] Yes  [A] Yes to All  [N] No  [L] No to All  [S] Suspend  [?] Help (default is "Y"):
```

This cmdlet also makes it handy to delete multiple accounts at once:

```
PS C:\> Get-ADUser -filter * -SearchBase "OU=Obsolete,DC=jdhlab,DC=local" | Remove-ADUser -whatif
What if: Performing operation "Remove" on Target "CN=Emmitt Cotney,OU=Obsolete,DC=jdhlab,DC=l....
What if: Performing operation "Remove" on Target "CN=Erika Laity,OU=Obsolete,DC=jdhlab,DC=local".
What if: Performing operation "Remove" on Target "CN=Enrique Rohner,OU=Obsolete,DC=jdhlab,DC=l....
What if: Performing operation "Remove" on Target "CN=Herma Toher,OU=Obsolete,DC=jdhlab,DC=local".
What if: Performing operation "Remove" on Target "CN=Hans Lerwill,OU=Obsolete,DC=jdhlab,DC=local".
What if: Performing operation "Remove" on Target "CN=Isidro Cipolloni,OU=Obsolete,DC=jdhlab,DC....
What if: Performing operation "Remove" on Target "CN=Hal Araujo,OU=Obsolete,DC=jdhlab,DC=local".
What if: Performing operation "Remove" on Target "CN=Hunter Tallerico,OU=Obsolete,DC=jdhlab,DC....
What if: Performing operation "Remove" on Target "CN=Geraldo Pullom,OU=Obsolete,DC=jdhlab,DC=l....
```

If I had not used the **-WhatIf** parameter, then all user accounts in the Obsolete organizational unit would have been removed.

Using the Active Directory PSDrive

As you saw earlier when moving Active Directory objects, it is also extremely easy, perhaps even dangerously so, to delete user accounts:

```
PS C:\> cd "AD:\OU=Obsolete,DC=jdhlab,DC=local"
PS AD:\OU=Obsolete,DC=jdhlab,DC=local> dir

Name                  ObjectClass          DistinguishedName
----                  -----------          -----------------
Micah Brisbois        user                 CN=Micah Brisbois,OU=Obsolete,DC=jdhlab,DC=local
Monroe Demonbreun     user                 CN=Monroe Demonbreun,OU=Obsolete,DC=jdhlab,DC=local
Nolan Zbell           user                 CN=Nolan Zbell,OU=Obsolete,DC=jdhlab,DC=local
Otto Nejaime          user                 CN=Otto Nejaime,OU=Obsolete,DC=jdhlab,DC=local
Porter Aleman         user                 CN=Porter Aleman,OU=Obsolete,DC=jdhlab,DC=local

PS AD:\OU=Obsolete,DC=jdhlab,DC=local> del "CN=nolan zbell" -whatif
What if: Performing operation "Remove" on Target "CN=nolan zbell,OU=Obsolete,DC=jdhlab,DC=lo
cal".
```

I've navigated to the Obsolete OU and you can see I have several user objects. The DEL command is an alias for the **Remove-Item** cmdlet, which supports the **-WhatIf** and **-Confirm** parameters. Allow me to actually delete the user and verify it is gone:

```
PS AD:\OU=Obsolete,DC=jdhlab,DC=local> del "CN=nolan zbell"

Are you sure you want to remove?
CN=nolan zbell,OU=Obsolete,DC=jdhlab,DC=local
[Y] Yes  [N] No  [S] Suspend  [?] Help (default is "Y"): y
PS AD:\OU=Obsolete,DC=jdhlab,DC=local> dir

Name                  ObjectClass          DistinguishedName
----                  -----------          -----------------
Micah Brisbois        user                 CN=Micah Brisbois,OU=Obsolete,DC=jdhlab,DC=local
Monroe Demonbreun     user                 CN=Monroe Demonbreun,OU=Obsolete,DC=jdhlab,DC=local
Otto Nejaime          user                 CN=Otto Nejaime,OU=Obsolete,DC=jdhlab,DC=local
Porter Aleman         user                 CN=Porter Aleman,OU=Obsolete,DC=jdhlab,DC=local
```

Wild cards can also be used to delete users:

```
PS AD:\OU=Obsolete,DC=jdhlab,DC=local> del * -whatif
What if: Performing operation "Remove" on Target "CN=Micah Brisbois,OU=Obsolete,DC=jdhlab,DC=l....
What if: Performing operation "Remove" on Target "CN=Monroe Demonbreun,OU=Obsolete,DC=jdhlab,D....
What if: Performing operation "Remove" on Target "CN=Otto Nejaime,OU=Obsolete,DC=jdhlab,DC=local".
What if: Performing operation "Remove" on Target "CN=Porter Aleman,OU=Obsolete,DC=jdhlab,DC=lo....
```

Fortunately when you do it for real, the cmdlet prompts for confirmation.

Using Remove-QADObject

There is no specific Quest cmdlet for removing user objects. Instead, you can use the more generic **Remove-QADObject** cmdlet. The "hard" way to use this cmdlet is to specify the user's distinguished name. Doing that requires that you first know the name and then you have to type it out. I prefer to use the account's down-level name:

```
PS C:\> Remove-QADObject "djones" -confirm

Confirm
Are you sure you want to perform this action?
Performing operation "Remove-QADObject" on Target "CN=Don Jones,OU=Temp,OU=Employees,DC=jdhla
b,DC=local".
[Y] Yes  [A] Yes to All  [N] No  [L] No to All  [S] Suspend  [?] Help (default is "Y"): n
```

```
PS C:\>
```

In this example, it doesn't matter which organizational unit or container the "Don Jones" user object resides in. The cmdlet will find it. Or I can leverage the pipeline and remove many users at once:

```
PS C:\> Get-QADUser -searchroot "Jdhlab.local/Employees/Temp" | Remove-QADObject -whatif

What if: Performing operation "Remove-QADObject" on Target "CN=Albert
Einstein,OU=Temp,OU=Empl....
What if: Performing operation "Remove-QADObject" on Target "CN=Don
Jones,OU=Temp,OU=Employees,....
```

This expression will search the Temp organizational unit for all user accounts and pipe them to the **Remove-QADObject** cmdlet. I used the **-WhatIf** parameter so I can see what accounts would be deleted if I decided to run the expression without it. By the way, I'm using the container's canonical name, but you can use the distinguished name if you prefer. All the Quest cmdlets that require an OU can be specified using either format.

Bulk User Management

If you only manage one or two users at a time, the graphical tools are appropriate. However, when you have a more complicated task or need to manage a number of users, you need PowerShell. You can accomplish bulk user management with the Microsoft or the Quest cmdlets. One thing to remember: if you can accomplish something for a single user you can accomplish it for 10 or 10,000 users.

Creating, Deleting, and Moving

A common bulk management task is creating new accounts. Perhaps your company hires 10 new employees once a month; or you are an educational organization that needs to create 1000 new accounts every semester. Here are a couple of approaches to using automation.

One typical scenario is to take a CSV file of new user information, import it, and then create the corresponding user accounts. The biggest hurdle is getting your CSV file in the right format, but once you do, creating 1000 user objects with a single command is very exciting.

First, I have a PowerShell script that imports a comma-separated list of new users with a number of properties defined. I'll be using the **Import-CSV** cmdlet, which will create a custom object like this:

```
PS C:\work> Import-Csv .\hrusers-simple.csv | Select -first 1


Name                  : John Rodman
SamAccountName        : JRodman
Title                 : Benefits Administrator
Department            : HR
givenname             : John
surname               : Rodman
userprincipalname     : JRodman@jdhlab.com
displayname           : John Rodman
Path                  : OU=Benefits,OU=HR,OU=Employees,DC=jdhlab,DC=local
AccountExpirationDate :
```

The property names come from the CSV header line and, if you are paying attention you'll notice, the property names are identical to the parameter names of the **New-ADUser** cmdlet. This is no accident. Because the cmdlet is designed to take pipelined input by property name, I can use properties to pipe my imported objects directly to the **New-ADUser** cmdlet. I can use the other cmdlet parameters to further configure the new accounts. For example, I'm going to need an initial password:

```
PS C:\work> $pass=Read-Host "Enter an initial password" -AsSecureString
Enter an initial password: ********
```

Now I can import the CSV file and pipe it to the **New-ADUser** cmdlet:

```
PS C:\work> Import-Csv .\hrusers-simple.csv | New-ADUser -AccountPassword $pass -Enabled $True `
>>  -ChangePasswordAtLogon $True -OtherAttributes @{Info="Created $(get-date) by
$env:userdomain\$env:username"} -passthru | Select DistinguishedName


DistinguishedName
-----------------
CN=John Rodman,OU=Benefits,OU=HR,OU=Employees,DC=jdhlab,DC=local
CN=Ann Beebe,OU=Benefits,OU=HR,OU=Employees,DC=jdhlab,DC=local
CN=Phil Gibbins,OU=Benefits,OU=HR,OU=Employees,DC=jdhlab,DC=local
CN=Kari Furse,OU=Benefits,OU=HR,OU=Employees,DC=jdhlab,DC=local
CN=Sally Sweet,OU=Temp,OU=Employees,DC=jdhlab,DC=local
```

All of the parameters, such as **-Enabled,** apply to all the imported accounts.

There's no requirement that the CSV file use the identical property names. Even if your CSV file uses different names, you can still use PowerShell but you'll need a slightly more complex expression:

```
Import-Csv .\new-users.csv | Foreach {
New-ADUser -name $_.user -path $_.ou -accountpassword $pass `
-givenname $_.first -surname $_.last -displayname "$($_.first) $($_.last)" `
-samaccountname $_.sam -userprincipalname "$($_.sam)@jdhlab.com" `
-ChangePasswordAtLogon $True
}
```

In this example, the CSV has headings like user, ou, first, last, and sam. The **New-ADUser** cmdlet takes the incoming object (**$_**) and grabs the appropriate value for each parameter.

These examples work just fine with strings and dates. But if you wanted to add an entry for something like the **-ChangePasswordAtLogon** parameter, it's a little trickier. This parameter requires a Boolean value like **$**True or an integer it can treat as a Boolean like 1. However, when you use either of these values in the CSV file, the **Import-Csv** cmdlet treats them as strings, which when passed to the **New-ADUser** cmdlet don't provide the results you would expect. But I have a workaround.

First, in your CSV file use 1 for True and 0 for False. The hack is to intercept the new object from the **Import-Csv** cmdlet and re-define the Boolean property with a Boolean value. I have another CSV file with column headings for the **-ChangePasswordAtLogon**, **-CannotChangePassword** and **-PasswordNeverExpires** parameters so that different accounts can have different settings. Each new and imported user is piped to the **ForEach-Object** construct. Within this construct I specifically cast these properties as Booleans. However, I also have to take an extra step to first treat the current string value as an integer so that PowerShell can properly convert it. Each update object is then passed on in the pipeline to the **New-ADUser** cmdlet:

```
PS C:\work> Import-Csv .\hrusers.csv | Foreach {
>>   [boolean]$_.enabled=$_.enabled -as [int]
>>   [boolean]$_.ChangePasswordAtLogon=$_.ChangePasswordAtLogon -as [int]
>>   [boolean]$_.CannotChangePassword=$_.CannotChangePassword -as [int]
>>   [boolean]$_.PasswordNeverExpires=$_.PasswordNeverExpires -as [int]
>>   $_
>> } | New-ADUser -accountpassword $pass -passthru -company "JDH Lab" `
>> -otherattributes @{Info="Created $(get-date) by $env:userdomain\$env:username"} |
>> Select DistinguishedName


DistinguishedName
-----------------
CN=John Rodman,OU=Benefits,OU=HR,OU=Employees,DC=jdhlab,DC=local
CN=Ann Beebe,OU=Benefits,OU=HR,OU=Employees,DC=jdhlab,DC=local
CN=Phil Gibbins,OU=Benefits,OU=HR,OU=Employees,DC=jdhlab,DC=local
CN=Kari Furse,OU=Benefits,OU=HR,OU=Employees,DC=jdhlab,DC=local
CN=Sally Sweet,OU=Temp,OU=Employees,DC=jdhlab,DC=local
```

I admit it's a little wonky but it works. Again, you only need this hack if you are trying to set Boolean values in your CSV file.

You can also use the **New-QADUser** cmdlet to create users in bulk. Again, if you have a CSV file with new user data this isn't too difficult. However, even though it seems like it should work and even if your CSV headings correspond to the cmdlet parameters, you can't simply pipe the import objects. This will fail:

```
PS C:\> Import-Csv "s:\newhires.csv" | New-QADUser -userpassword "P@ssw0rd"
```

Instead you need to pipe the imported objects to the **ForEach-Object** construct:

```
PS C:\> Import-Csv S:\NewHires.csv | Foreach {New-QADUser -ParentContainer $_.parentcontainer `
>>  -name $_.Name -samaccountname $_.SamAccountname -userprincipalname $_.userprincipalname `
>>  -firstname $_.firstname -lastname $_.lastname -title $_.title -department $_.department `
>>  -city $_.city -phonenumber $_.phonenumber -userpassword "P@ssw0rd" -displayname $_.name `
>>  -company "JDH Lab" -objectattributes @{Info="Created $(get-date) by $env:userdomain\$env:
username"}} |
>>  Set-QADUser -UserMustChangePassword $True
>>

Name                          Type      DN
----                          ----      --
Skip Towne                    user      CN=Skip Towne,OU=Sales,OU=Employees,DC=jdhlab,DC...
Terry Kloth                   user      CN=Terry Kloth,OU=Sales,OU=Employees,DC=jdhlab,D...
Bill Freely                   user      CN=Bill Freely,OU=Finance,OU=Employees,DC=jdhlab...
John Plumber                  user      CN=John Plumber,OU=Employees,DC=jdhlab,DC=local
Chip Shotz                    user      CN=Chip Shotz,OU=IT,OU=Employees,DC=jdhlab,DC=local
```

Again, the property names for each imported object, such as $_.samaccountname, come from the CSV heading. Because you have to explicitly define each parameter, you can use whatever property names you want. In my case I made them the same simply for the sake of convenience so I wouldn't have to remember how the CSV was structured.

If you want to adopt a process like this in your environment I strongly encourage you to adopt a CSV standard. Then you can take the entire import expression like I have above and put it in a PowerShell script. Then all you need to do is run the script. Here's my version using the basic expression above:

Import-QADUser.ps1

```
#requires -version 2.0
#requires -pssnapin Quest.ActiveRoles.ADManagement

[cmdletbinding(SupportsShouldProcess=$True)]

Param(
[Parameter(Position=0,Mandatory=$True,HelpMessage="Enter the file name and path to the CSV
file.")]
[string]$file,
[Parameter(Position=1,Mandatory=$False)]
[string]$password="P@ssw0rd"

)

Try {
    Write-Verbose "Importing $file"
    $users=Import-Csv -Path $file -ErrorAction "Stop"
    $count=($users | Measure-Object).count
    #pipe imported data
    Write-Verbose "Creating $count new user accounts"
    $users | Foreach {
       New-QADUser -ParentContainer $_.parentcontainer -name $_.Name `
       -samaccountname $_.SamAccountname -userprincipalname $_.userprincipalname `
       -firstname $_.firstname -lastname $_.lastname -title $_.title `
       -department $_.department -city $_.city -phonenumber $_.phonenumber `
       -userpassword $password -displayname $_.name -company "JDH Lab" `
      -objectattributes @{Info="Created $(get-date) by $env:userdomain\$env:username"}
      } |  Set-QADUser -UserMustChangePassword $True
     Write-Verbose "Finished"
} #try

Catch {
    Write-Warning "Failed to find $file"
}
```

The main part of the script should look familiar. The only thing I've done is add some parameters to the script so you can specify a CSV file and initial password. The Try Catch block handles the error you might get if you type a bad CSV file name. The script also supports the **-WhatIf** parameter. Otherwise, it's as easy to run as this:

```
PS C:\> c:\scripts\import-qaduser s:\newhires.csv -password "H3ll0W()rld"

Name                          Type    DN
----                          ----    --
Skip Towne                    user    CN=Skip Towne,OU=Sales,OU=Employees,DC=jdhlab,DC...
Terry Kloth                   user    CN=Terry Kloth,OU=Sales,OU=Employees,DC=jdhlab,D...
Bill Freely                   user    CN=Bill Freely,OU=Finance,OU=Employees,DC=jdhlab...
John Plumber                  user    CN=John Plumber,OU=Employees,DC=jdhlab,DC=local
Chip Shotz                    user    CN=Chip Shotz,OU=IT,OU=Employees,DC=jdhlab,DC=local
```

Earlier in the chapter, I showed you how to move a single account. Here's an example of how you can move multiple user objects. The scenario is that you'd like to find all disabled user accounts and move them to a particular organizational unit. Using the **Get-ADUser** cmdlet requires a simple filter to find the disable accounts, which are then piped to the **Move-ADObject** cmdlet:

```
PS C:\> Get-ADUser -Filter "Enabled -eq '$False'" -SearchBase "OU=Employees,DC=jdhlab,DC=local" |
>> Move-ADObject -TargetPath "OU=Disabled Users,DC=jdhlab,DC=local" -whatif
>>
What if: Performing operation "Move" on Target "CN=Vincenzo Ziesman,OU=Executive,OU=Employees,....
What if: Performing operation "Move" on Target "CN=Teodoro Ewings,OU=Executive,OU=Employees,DC....
What if: Performing operation "Move" on Target "CN=Ulysses Wiatrowski,OU=Executive,OU=Employee....
What if: Performing operation "Move" on Target "CN=Stewart Sider,OU=Executive,OU=Employees,DC=....
What if: Performing operation "Move" on Target "CN=Warren Lynaugh,OU=IT,OU=Employees,DC=jdhlab....
...
```

I'm using a search base because I don't want to include accounts like krbtgt, which is disabled by default. When you perform the actual move, nothing is written to the pipeline unless you use the **-Passthru** parameter.

I like to take this a step further by documenting the move. Wouldn't it be nice to know what OU the user was originally in? I like to put that information in the Info field as a comment. Here's one approach you might take:

Move-DisabledUser.ps1

```
$destination="OU=Disabled Users,DC=JDHLab,DC=Local"
$search="OU=Employees,DC=jdhlab,DC=local"
Get-ADUser -Filter "Enabled -eq '$False'" -SearchBase $search -properties "Info"|
Foreach {
 #get the object's current parent
 $parent=$_.distinguishedname.Substring($_.distinguishedname.IndexOf(",")+1)
 #get the user's current Info property if found
 if ($_.info) {
     $info=$_.info+"'r'nMoved from $parent on $(Get-date) by $env:userdomain\$env:username"
 }
 else {
    $info="Moved from $parent on $(Get-date) by $env:userdomain\$env:username"
 }
 Write-Host "Moving $($_.name) from $parent" -foregroundcolor Yellow
 Move-ADObject -identity $_ -TargetPath $destination -passthru | Set-ADUser -Replace @
{Info=$info}
}
```

The **Get-ADUser** cmdlet portion of the command hopefully looks familiar by now. Each user object is then piped to the **ForEach-Object** construct. I parse out the parent container from the user's distinguished path using the **Substring()** method. Everything after the first comma is returned as the parent path:

```
$parent=$_.distinguishedname.Substring($_.distinguishedname.IndexOf(",")+1)
```

Thus if a user's distinguished name is OU=Vito Risler,OU=Executive,OU=Employees,DC=jdhlab, DC=local, the $parent value will be OU=Executive,OU=Employees,DC=jdhlab,DC=local.

Because the **Info** property might already have a value, and it is not a multi-value property, I want to save the existing data and append my new information. The `r`n will add a line return. If Info is not defined, then I simply specify what I want. I like to indicate where the object came from and who made the move:

```
if ($_.info) {
     $info=$_.info+"'r'nMoved from $parent on $(Get-date) by $env:userdomain\$env:username"
 }
 else {
```

```
    $info="Moved from $parent on $(Get-date) by $env:userdomain\$env:username"
 }
```

Each object is then moved to the destination organizational unit. I use the **-Passthru** parameter so an object will be written to the pipeline. This allows me to use the **Set-ADUser** cmdlet to update the account:

```
Move-ADObject -identity $_ -TargetPath $destination -passthru | Set-ADUser -Replace @
{Info=$info}
```

Let's repeat the task, this time using the Quest cmdlets. If you don't care about excluding any accounts, this is as simple as this:

```
PS C:\> Get-QADUser -disabled -searchroot " OU=Employees,DC=jdhlab,DC=local" -sizelimit 0 |
>> Move-QADObject -newparent "OU=Disabled Users,DC=jdhlab,DC=local" -whatIf
```

The syntax is very similar to the Microsoft solution. In fact, there's not much difference in my advanced technique of updating the **Info** property, except that I don't have to parse out the parent name. The Quest cmdlet defines a property called **ParentContainerDN** that I can use. You could also use the **ParentContainer** property if you wanted the canonical name instead:

Move-DisabledQADUser.ps1

```
$destination="OU=Disabled Users,DC=JDHLab,DC=Local"
$search="OU=Employees,DC=jdhlab,DC=local"
Get-QADUser -disabled -Searchroot $search -Includedproperties "Info" -sizelimit 0 |
foreach {
 #get the user's current Info property if found
 if ($_.info) {
     $info=$_.info+"'r'nMoved from $($_.parentContainerDN) on $(Get-date) by
$env:userdomain\$env:username"
  }
  else {
    $info="Moved from $($_.parentContainerDN) on $(Get-date) by $env:userdomain\$env:username"
  }
 Write-Host "Moving $($_.name) from $($_.parentContainerDN)" -foregroundcolor Yellow
 Move-QADObject -identity $_ -NewParentContainer $destination | Set-QADUser -ObjectAttributes
@{Info=$info}
}
```

The only thing I really had to do was modify a few cmdlet and parameter names.

Or perhaps you are reorganizing accounts and your organizational unit structure. You might want to find all users that work in Los Angeles and move them to a new OU. This can be accomplished with a one-line command:

```
PS C:\> Get-QADUser -city "Los Angeles" -enabled | Move-QADObject -newparent `
>> "OU=LA,OU=Divisions,DC=jdhlab,DC=local"
```

The **Get-QADUser** cmdlet returns all enabled user objects with a city property of Los Angeles, and then moves them to the LA organizational unit.

Bulk deletions are just as easy. Suppose that the Los Angeles office is closing and you need to delete any user accounts from that office:

```
PS C:\> Get-QADUser -city "Los Angeles" | Move-QADObjectRemove-QADObject
```

Every user object with a city property of Los Angeles will be removed from Active Directory by the **Remove-QADObject** cmdlet.

Here's how you would accomplish the same task using the Microsoft cmdlets. Moving the users:

```
PS C:\> Get-ADUser -filter "City -eq 'Los Angeles'" |
>> move-adobject -TargetPath "OU=LA,OU=Divisions,DC=jdhlab,DC=local"
```

And removing the users:

```
PS C:\> Get-ADUser -filter "City -eq 'Los Angeles'" | Remove-ADObject
```

Here's one more typical administrative task. Suppose I want to delete all enabled user accounts that haven't changed their password in at least 180 days. To me, this is a pretty good indication that the user account is obsolete. You could do anything you want with these accounts, but I'll delete them.

When using the **Get-ADUser** cmdlet, you can check the **PasswordLastSet** property:

```
PS C:\> Get-ADUser "jfrost" -Properties PassWordLastSet | Select Name,Enabled,PasswordLastSet

Name       Enabled PasswordLastSet
----       ------- ---------------
Jack Frost    True 7/26/2010 3:37:14 PM
```

If an account is new and the password hasn't been set yet, this value will be 1/1/1601. With this information I can create a search filter to find disabled accounts with a password age of 180 days from today. Oh…I should also filter out accounts with non-expiring passwords:

```
PS C:\> $search="OU=Employees,DC=jdhlab,DC=local"
PS C:\> $filter="PasswordNeverExpires -eq '$False' -AND `
>> enabled -eq '$True' -AND `
>> PassWordLastSet -lt '$((get-date).AddDays(-180))' -AND `
>> PasswordLastSet -gt '1/1/1601'"
>> Get-ADUser  -filter $filter -SearchBase $search `
>> -properties PasswordLastSet,PasswordNeverExpires |
>> Sort PasswordLastSet | Select Name,PasswordLastSet,PasswordNeverExpires,Enabled
>>

Name                 PasswordLastSet                PasswordNeverExpires        Enabled
----                 ---------------                --------------------        -------
Lisa Andrews         3/4/2010 1:24:40 PM            False                       True
Cassie O'Pia         3/10/2010 10:37:08 AM          False                       True
Chris Barry          3/10/2010 10:37:09 AM          False                       True
Roy Antebi           3/10/2010 10:37:09 AM          False                       True
Darcy Jayne          3/10/2010 10:37:10 AM          False                       True
Jacek Jelitto        3/10/2010 10:37:10 AM          False                       True
Don Richardson       3/10/2010 10:37:10 AM          False                       True
William Flash        3/10/2010 10:37:11 AM          False                       True
Toby Nixon           3/10/2010 10:37:11 AM          False                       True
Zac Woodall          3/10/2010 10:37:11 AM          False                       True
```

I don't really need the last two properties, but I wanted to verify. Once I'm satisfied I can re-run the query and pipe the results to the **Remove-ADObject** cmdlet:

```
PS C:\> Get-ADUser  -filter $filter -SearchBase `
>> $search -properties PasswordLastSet,PasswordNeverExpires |
>> Remove-ADObject -Whatif
>>
What if: Performing operation "Remove" on Target "CN=Cassie O'Pia,OU=Employees,DC=jdhlab,DC=lo....
What if: Performing operation "Remove" on Target "CN=Chris Barry,OU=Employees,DC=jdhlab,DC=local".
What if: Performing operation "Remove" on Target "CN=William Flash,OU=Employees,DC=jdhlab,DC=j....
What if: Performing operation "Remove" on Target "CN=Toby Nixon,OU=Employees,DC=jdhlab,DC=local".
What if: Performing operation "Remove" on Target "CN=Lisa Andrews,OU=Sales,OU=Employees,DC=jdh....
What if: Performing operation "Remove" on Target "CN=Roy Antebi,OU=Sales,OU=Employees,DC=jdhlo....
What if: Performing operation "Remove" on Target "CN=Don Richardson,OU=Sales,OU=Employees,DC=j....
What if: Performing operation "Remove" on Target "CN=Darcy Jayne,OU=Customer Service,OU=Employ....
What if: Performing operation "Remove" on Target "CN=Jacek Jelitto,OU=Customer Service,OU=Empl....
What if: Performing operation "Remove" on Target "CN=Zac Woodall,OU=Customer Service,OU=Employ....
```

You can accomplish the same task with the Quest cmdlets, and in some ways it is a little easier:

```
PS C:\> Get-QADUser -Enabled -SearchRoot $search -sizelimit 0 -PasswordNotChangedFor 180 |
>> Sort PasswordLastSet | Select Name,PasswordAge,PasswordLastSet
>>

Name                                PasswordAge                        PasswordLastSet
----                               -----------                        ---------------
Lisa Andrews                        196.01:04:08.7033632               3/4/2010 1:24:40 PM
Cassie O'Pia                        190.03:51:40.0391081               3/10/2010 10:37:08 AM
Chris Barry                         190.03:51:39.8047331               3/10/2010 10:37:09 AM
Roy Antebi                          190.03:51:39.0547331               3/10/2010 10:37:09 AM
Darcy Jayne                         190.03:51:38.6484831               3/10/2010 10:37:10 AM
Jacek Jelitto                       190.03:51:38.3672331               3/10/2010 10:37:10 AM
Don Richardson                      190.03:51:38.2266081               3/10/2010 10:37:10 AM
William Flash                       190.03:51:37.9141081               3/10/2010 10:37:11 AM
Toby Nixon                          190.03:51:37.8047331               3/10/2010 10:37:11 AM
Zac Woodall                         190.03:51:37.6641081               3/10/2010 10:37:11 AM
```

The **Get-QADuser** cmdlet includes a parameter called **-PasswordNotChangedFor**. The value is the number of days since the password was last set. In addition, the cmdlet automatic ally converts values and lets you easily see the date the password was last set as well as its age. Again, once I'm satisfied it is dangerously easy to remove the user accounts:

```
PS C:\> Get-QADUser -Enabled -SearchRoot $search -sizelimit 0 -PasswordNotChangedFor 90 |
>> Move-QADObjectRemove-QADObject -whatif
What if: Performing operation "Remove-QADObject" on Target "CN=Cassie O'Pia,OU=Employees,DC=jd....
What if: Performing operation "Remove-QADObject" on Target "CN=Chris Barry,OU=Employees,DC=jdh....
What if: Performing operation "Remove-QADObject" on Target "CN=William Flash,OU=Employees,DC=j....
What if: Performing operation "Remove-QADObject" on Target "CN=Toby Nixon,OU=Employees,DC=jdhl....
What if: Performing operation "Remove-QADObject" on Target "CN=Lisa Andrews,OU=Sales,OU=Employ....
What if: Performing operation "Remove-QADObject" on Target "CN=Roy Antebi,OU=Sales,OU=Employee....
What if: Performing operation "Remove-QADObject" on Target "CN=Don Richardson,OU=Sales,OU=Empl....
What if: Performing operation "Remove-QADObject" on Target "CN=Darcy Jayne,OU=Customer Service....
What if: Performing operation "Remove-QADObject" on Target "CN=Jacek Jelitto,OU=Customer Servi....
What if: Performing operation "Remove-QADObject" on Target "CN=Zac Woodall,OU=Customer Service....
```

This cmdlet also has a parameter called **-InactiveFor**. It takes a value for the number of days since any of these conditions are met:

- The number of days the account has been expired
- The number of days since the password was last changed
- The number of days since the account was used for a logon.

You need to be careful with this to make sure you are getting just the accounts you really are interested in. For example, when I use 180 for the value, the **Get-QADuser** cmdlet should return all accounts that expired 180 days ago (or more), a password age of at least 180 days, or no logon activity for at least 180 days. I can fine tune this a bit by querying only for enabled accounts and those with passwords that can expire:

```
PS C:\> Get-QADUser -Enabled -SearchRoot $search -sizelimit 0 -Inactivefor 180 `
>>-PasswordNeverExpires:$false | Select DN

DN
--
CN=Cassie O'Pia,OU=Employees,DC=jdhlab,DC=local
CN=Chris Barry,OU=Employees,DC=jdhlab,DC=local
CN=William Flash,OU=Employees,DC=jdhlab,DC=local
CN=Toby Nixon,OU=Employees,DC=jdhlab,DC=local
CN=Lisa Andrews,OU=Sales,OU=Employees,DC=jdhlab,DC=local
CN=Roy Antebi,OU=Sales,OU=Employees,DC=jdhlab,DC=local
CN=Don Richardson,OU=Sales,OU=Employees,DC=jdhlab,DC=local
CN=Ben Smith,OU=Sales,OU=Employees,DC=jdhlab,DC=local
CN=Darcy Jayne,OU=Customer Service,OU=Employees,DC=jdhlab,DC=local
CN=Jacek Jelitto,OU=Customer Service,OU=Employees,DC=jdhlab,DC=local
CN=Zac Woodall,OU=Customer Service,OU=Employees,DC=jdhlab,DC=local
CN=Belinda Newman,OU=Customer Service,OU=Employees,DC=jdhlab,DC=local
```

Depending on what you're looking for you'll need to refine the expression, but fortunately the **Get-QADuser** cmdlet has plenty of parameters to make this a little easier.

Property Updates

You might also want to update multiple users to normalize data, find blank properties, or add new information. Here are some examples, first with a solution using the Microsoft **Set-ADUser** cmdlet and then one using Quest's **Set-QADUser** cmdlet. You should be able to use these examples as templates or examples for your own management needs.

First, suppose users in the Atlanta manufacturing department have a new manager and you want to modify their Active Directory accounts accordingly:

```
PS C:\> Get-ADUser -filter "city -eq 'Atlanta' -AND department -eq 'Manufacturing'" |
>> Set-ADUser -Manager "L.Puzio"
```

With this one-line command, I found all users with a City property of Atlanta who work in the Manufacturing department, and then changed the Manager property to Lou Puzio. In this example I used Lou's SAMAccountname. But let's say you didn't have it handy. No problem:

```
PS C:\> Get-ADUser -filter "city -eq 'Atlanta' -AND department -eq 'Manufacturing'" |
>> Set-ADUser -Manager (Get-ADUser -filter "name -eq 'Lou Puzio'") -passthru |  select name
>>

Name
----
Cassie O'Pia
Henrik Jensen
Kevin Kennedy
Lou Puzio
```

The value for the **-Manager** parameter will come from the result of the nested **Get-ADUser** cmdlet. But there is one more thing you should tweak. Since Lou Puzio is also in Atlanta and apparently in the Manufacturing department, his manager property was set to himself. Probably not what you really intended. All you need is a slight adjustment. Since the filter is getting a little long, I created a variable for it:

```
PS C:\> $filter="city -eq 'Atlanta' -AND department -eq 'Manufacturing' -and name -ne 'Lou
Puzio'"
PS C:\> Get-ADUser -filter $filter | Set-ADUser -Manager "L.Puzio" -PassThru | Select Name

Name
----
Cassie O'Pia
Henrik Jensen
Kevin Kennedy
```

Here's how to achieve the same result using the Quest cmdlets:

```
PS C:\> Get-QADUser -City "Atlanta" -Department "Manufacturing" |
>> Set-QADUser -Manager "Lou Puzio" -whatif
>>
What if: Modify object 'CN=Cassie O'Pia,OU=Employees,DC=jdhlab,DC=local'.
What if: Modify object 'CN=Henrik Jensen,OU=Branch Office,DC=jdhlab,DC=local'.
What if: Modify object 'CN=Kevin Kennedy,OU=Branch Office,DC=jdhlab,DC=local'.
What if: Modify object 'CN=Lou Puzio,OU=Executive,OU=Employees,DC=jdhlab,DC=local'.
```

Run the command without the **-WhatIf** parameter and it's done. Although you still have the issue of making Lou his own manager. I would handle it this way:

```
PS C:\> Get-QADUser -City "Atlanta" -Department "Manufacturing" |
>> where {$_.name -notmatch "Lou Puzio"} | Set-QADUser -manager "Lou Puzio" | Select Name
>>

Name
----
Cassie O'Pia
Henrik Jensen
Kevin Kennedy
```

Because I'm not expecting an extraordinary number of Atlanta Manufacturing users, I can filter the results with the **Where-Object** cmdlet to drop Lou's account. The rest of the expression after that is unchanged.

As often happens when Active Directory is administered by more than one person, you may end up with inconsistent entries. For example, my organization's name is JDH Lab. However in the company field it has been entered as jdhlab, Jdhlabs.com or any number of other variations. Wouldn't it be nice to have a standard value?

```
PS C:\> Get-ADUser -filter "company -ne 'JDH Lab'" -searchbase $search  |
>> Set-ADUser -Company "JDH Lab"
```

This expression will find all user objects in my search path (the one I've been using for most of the chapter) where the company doesn't equal "JDH Lab" and will set the company property accordingly. I used this filter to speed up the command so PowerShell wouldn't try to get users with a correct Company property. However, be aware that you can't use regular expressions here and the comparison is case-insensitive. This means that an account with a Company property like "jdh lab" won't get changed. Of course, you can simply get all users and make the change universal:

```
PS C:\> Get-ADUser -filter * -searchbase $search -properties Company |
>> Set-ADUser -Company "JDH Lab"
```

Using the Quest cmdlets is just as easy:

```
PS C:\> Get-QADUser -searchroot $search -sizelimit 0 | Set-QADUser -company "JDH Lab"
```

You could just as easily set multiple properties at the same time. Remember to set the **-SizeLimit** parameter to 0 if you have more than 1000 users, otherwise only the first 1000 will be modified.

Finally, here's another likely scenario. Your Active Directory displayname property should be the user's first and last name, but some administrators forget to set it. No problem. You can use PowerShell to fix it.

Using the Microsoft cmdlets, I simply need to get the user account and pipe it to the **Set-ADUser** cmdlet in a **ForEach-Object** construct so that I can use the first and last name properties:

```
PS C:\> Get-ADUser -filter "*" -searchbase $search -properties "DisplayName" | Foreach {
>> $display="$($_.givenname) $($_.surname)"
>> write-Host "Updating $display" -foregroundcolor Green
>> Set-ADUser -identity $_ -displayname $display
>> }
>>
Updating Columbus Suglia
Updating Marshall Korpal
Updating Lawrence Aridas
Updating Abdul Cheshire
Updating Daryl Vadasy
...
```

For the sake of clarity I've defined a variable, $display, and then used it in the **Write-Host** message as well as the **Set-ADuser** cmdlet. Of course, this assumes the first and last names have been defined. Using the Quest cmdlets, this is a PowerShell one-liner:

```
PS C:\> Get-QADUser -firstname * -lastname * -searchroot $search -sizelimit 0 | Foreach {
>> Set-QADUser -identity $_ -displayname "$($_.firstname) $($_.lastname)"}
```

Again, I'm using the **Get-QADuser** cmdlet to find users with a populated first and last name. The **Set-QADUser** cmdlet modifies the displayname with the first and last name values of the piped in user object.

I will wrap up this chapter with one last example. The scenario is that your company wants to begin using the employee ID number to Active Directory. It is supported even though you can't easily access it in the Active Directory Users and Computers management console. You have a CSV file with the user's distinguished name and employee ID. Your goal is to update each user with their employee ID. You've already seen how easy it is to import data using PowerShell. This isn't much different:

```
PS C:\> Import-Csv r:\ids.csv | Foreach {
>> Set-ADUser -Identity $_.dn -EmployeeID $_.employeeid -verbose
>>}
```

```
VERBOSE: Performing operation "Set" on Target "CN=Columbus Suglia,OU=Executive,OU=Employees,DC....
VERBOSE: Performing operation "Set" on Target "CN=Marshall Korpal,OU=Executive,OU=Employees,D....
VERBOSE: Performing operation "Set" on Target "CN=Lawrence Aridas,OU=Executive,OU=Employees,DC...
VERBOSE: Performing operation "Set" on Target "CN=Abdul Cheshire,OU=Executive,OU=Employees,DC....
VERBOSE: Performing operation "Set" on Target "CN=Daryl Vadasy,OU=Executive,OU=Employees,DC=j....
VERBOSE: Performing operation "Set" on Target "CN=Reuben Persampieri,OU=Executive,OU=Employee....

...
```

The CSV file has headings called DN and EmployeeID. Using the **Import-Csv** cmdlet, PowerShell creates new objects and pipes them to the **ForEach-Object** construct, which then modifies the corresponding user account using the **Set-ADUser** cmdlet. Since **Set-ADUser** doesn't write to the pipeline, unless you use the -**Passthru** parameter, I decided to use the common -**Verbose** parameter so I could monitor progress.

Using the Quest cmdlets to achieve the same result takes an almost identical approach:

```
PS C:\> Import-Csv r:\ids.csv | Foreach {
>> Set-QADUser $_.dn -objectattributes @{employeeID= $_.employeeID}
>> }
>>

Name                              Type       DN
----                              ----       --
Columbus Suglia                   user       CN=Columbus Suglia,OU=Executive,OU=Employees,DC=...
Marshall Korpal                   user       CN=Marshall Korpal,OU=Executive,OU=Employees,DC=...
Lawrence Aridas                   user       CN=Lawrence Aridas,OU=Executive,OU=Employees,DC=...
...
```

Again, the **Import-CSV** cmdlet imports the user objects from ids.csv and pipes each one to the **ForEach** cmdlet. I then call the **Set-QADUser** cmdlet to modify the current object in the pipeline. The cmdlet sets the **EmployeeID** property to the **EmployeeID** property from the corresponding object in the pipeline.

Finally, here's how you verify the update:

```
PS C:\> Get-QADUser -ObjectAttributes @{employeeID='*'} | Select Name,Department,EmployeeID

Name                                    Department                              employeeID
----                                    ----------                              ----------
Reuben Persampieri                      Executive                               1006
Ernie Lamontagna                        Executive                               1018
Lou Puzio                               Manufacturing                           1026
Coleman Vanderbeek                      Executive                               1027
...
```

Managing Active Directory user accounts with PowerShell is not especially difficult with either the Microsoft or Quest cmdlets and, as you saw, the differences between the two are often minor. Upcoming chapters will cover password management and group membership.

Chapter 3
Active Directory Password Management

Probably no other area of Active Directory management is more important than user passwords. Passwords must be secure to protest network assets and if a user can't log on, they usually can't get their job done. This is especially serious when the user is your manager!

Password Properties

Let's start by documenting your current domain password policies. I'll cover password policy settings introduced in Windows Server 2008 at the end of the chapter.

Domain Properties

To discover or perhaps document your domain password policy settings, you can use the **Get-ADDefaultDomainPasswordPolicy** cmdlet from the Microsoft Active Directory module:

```
PS C:\> Get-ADDefaultDomainPasswordPolicy


ComplexityEnabled           : True
DistinguishedName           : DC=jdhlab,DC=local
LockoutDuration             : 00:30:00
LockoutObservationWindow    : 00:30:00
LockoutThreshold            : 5
MaxPasswordAge              : 42.00:00:00
MinPasswordAge              : 1.00:00:00
MinPasswordLength           : 7
objectClass                 : {domainDNS}
```

```
objectGuid                  : 9db48ea5-9dea-43c9-9301-f2262b244ce2
PasswordHistoryCount        : 24
ReversibleEncryptionEnabled : False
```

This cmdlet defaults to the current domain. However you can specify a different domain and even a specific domain controller:

```
PS C:\> Get-ADDefaultDomainPasswordPolicy -Identity "jdhitsolutions.local" -server
"jdhit-dc01"


ComplexityEnabled           : True
DistinguishedName           : DC=jdhitsolutions,DC=local
LockoutDuration             : 00:10:00
LockoutObservationWindow    : 00:02:00
LockoutThreshold            : 7
MaxPasswordAge              : 60.00:00:00
MinPasswordAge              : 30.00:00:00
MinPasswordLength           : 7
objectClass                 : {domainDNS}
objectGuid                  : debe5394-56d0-4fbe-9000-9bd4081b69da
PasswordHistoryCount        : 24
ReversibleEncryptionEnabled : False
```

I was logged on with an account that had permissions in the other domain but I also could have used the **-Credential** parameter and a PSCredential object.

Because the **-Identity** parameter accepts pipelined input, you can document all domains in your forest with a relatively simple one-line command:

```
PS C:\> (Get-ADForest).domains | Foreach {
>> $dc=(Get-ADDomain -Identity $_).pdcemulator
>> Get-ADDefaultDomainPasswordPolicy -Identity $_ -Server $dc
>> }
>>


ComplexityEnabled           : True
DistinguishedName           : DC=MYCOMPANY,DC=LOCAL
LockoutDuration             : 00:30:00
LockoutObservationWindow    : 00:30:00
LockoutThreshold            : 5
MaxPasswordAge              : 60.00:00:00
MinPasswordAge              : 1.00:00:00
MinPasswordLength           : 7
objectClass                 : {domainDNS}
objectGuid                  : 2132219a-da45-49b9-88a3-5c0dbb7d51c3
PasswordHistoryCount        : 24
ReversibleEncryptionEnabled : True
ComplexityEnabled           : True
DistinguishedName           : DC=RESEARCH,DC=MYCOMPANY,DC=LOCAL
LockoutDuration             : 00:30:00
LockoutObservationWindow    : 00:30:00
LockoutThreshold            : 0
MaxPasswordAge              : 42.00:00:00
MinPasswordAge              : 1.00:00:00
MinPasswordLength           : 7
objectClass                 : {domainDNS}
objectGuid                  : c95dc716-ed1b-465d-9c7d-a89b63f8f2f2
PasswordHistoryCount        : 24
ReversibleEncryptionEnabled : False
```

I used the **Get-ADForest** cmdlet to return the current forest. This object has a property called **Domains**. Each value in this property is piped to a **ForEach-Object** loop, which in turn passes the domain name to the **Get-ADDefaultDomainPasswordPolicy** cmdlet, which displays the results. In this example I'm writing results to the console but you could just as easily export to a CSV or XML file.

Multiple Domains

In the example above, because my forest included multiple domains, I found I had to specify a domain controller in each domain in order to find password policy settings. To accomplish that, I used the **Get-ADDomain** cmdlet to find the PDCEmulator and use that server. This may simply be the result of an unidentified misconfiguration in my DNS setup.

If you have a single domain, single forest you can get by with a command like this:

```
PS C:\> (Get-ADForest).domains | Get-ADDefaultDomainPasswordPolicy
```

If by chance your computer and user accounts are in separate domains, you can use this cmdlet to retrieve either domain using the **-Current** parameter. The logged on user policy is most likely going to be the same as the current domain:

```
PS C:\> Get-ADDefaultDomainPasswordPolicy -Current LoggedOnUser
```

Or to get the computer account domain, use this:

```
PS C:\> Get-ADDefaultDomainPasswordPolicy -Current LocalComputer
```

While I doubt you'll modify your domain's default password policy often enough to warrant some type of automation, it can be done with the **Set-ADDefaultDomainPasswordPolicy** cmdlet. You can change any policy setting you might want to modify using the corresponding parameter as shown in Table 3.1.

Table 3-1 Set-ADDefaultDomainPasswordPolicy Parameters

Parameter Name	Parameter Value Type
ComplexityEnabled	System.Boolean
LockoutDuration	System.TimeSpan
LockoutObservationWindow	System.TimeSpan
LockoutThreshold	System.Int32
MaxPasswordAge	System.TimeSpan
MinPasswordAge	System.TimeSpan
MinPasswordLength	System.Int32
PasswordHistoryCount	System.Int32
ReversibleEncryptionEnabled	System.Boolean

I've decided I want to change my current policy so that the maximum password age is 50 days, the number of remembered passwords is 12, and the lockout threshold will be increased to 7:

```
PS C:\> Set-ADDefaultDomainPasswordPolicy -identity "jdhlab.local" -MaxPasswordAge 50.00:00:00 `
>>  -PasswordHistoryCount 12 -LockoutThreshold 7 -passthru
>>


ComplexityEnabled           : True
DistinguishedName           : DC=jdhlab,DC=local
LockoutDuration             : 00:30:00
LockoutObservationWindow    : 00:30:00
LockoutThreshold            : 7
MaxPasswordAge              : 50.00:00:00
MinPasswordAge              : 1.00:00:00
MinPasswordLength           : 7
objectClass                 : {domainDNS}
objectGuid                  : 9db48ea5-9dea-43c9-9301-f2262b244ce2
PasswordHistoryCount        : 12
ReversibleEncryptionEnabled : False
```

Using the **Set-ADDefaultDomainPasswordPolicy** cmdlet, all I need to do is specify the domain, jdhlab.local, and the new values. By default the cmdlet doesn't write anything to the pipeline so I used the **-Passthru** parameter to force it to do so.

You can achieve similar results using the Quest cmdlets, although it is not as elegant. There is no dedicated cmdlet, but you can use **Get-QADObject** cmdlet to get the domain root. This cmdlet has properties that reflect almost all of the domain password settings. Unfortunately, most of the properties are not included by default, so I find it easiest to define a variable with all the properties I'm going to need:

```
PS C:\> $Properties=@("LockOutThreshold","LockoutObservationWindow","LockoutDuration",`
>> "ResetLockoutCounterAfter","MaxPwdAge","MinPwdAge","MinPwdLength","PwdHistoryLength")
```

Then I can use the cmdlet, instructing it to include all of the properties. To keep it nice and neat I pipe this resulting object to the **Select-Object** cmdlet to display just those properties:

```
PS C:\> Get-QADObject -identity "dc=jdhlab,dc=local" -includedProperties $properties |
>> select -Property $properties
>>


lockoutThreshold         : 7
lockOutObservationWindow : 00:30:00
LockoutDuration          : 00:30:00
ResetLockoutCounterAfter : 00:30:00
maxPwdAge                : 50.00:00:00
minPwdAge                : 1.00:00:00
minPwdLength             : 7
pwdHistoryLength         : 12
```

What's missing is information about the complex password requirement and whether reversible encryption is enabled. However, you can use my **Get-DomainPWDProperties** function:

Get-DomainPWDProperties.ps1

```
#requires -version 2.0

Function Get-PWDProperty {

[cmdletbinding()]
    Param(
    [Parameter(Position=0,Mandatory=$True,ValueFromPipeline=$True,
    HelpMessage="Enter a property flag value")]
    [ValidateNotNullorEmpty()]
    [int]$flag
    )
Begin {
    # constant values for pwdProperties bitmask flag
    New-Variable DOMAIN_PASSWORD_COMPLEX 1 -option constant
    New-Variable DOMAIN_PASSWORD_NO_ANON_CHANGE 2 -option constant
    New-Variable DOMAIN_PASSWORD_NO_CLEAR_CHANGE 4 -option constant
    New-Variable DOMAIN_LOCKOUT_ADMINS 8 -option constant
    New-Variable DOMAIN_PASSWORD_STORE_CLEARTEXT 16 -option constant
    New-Variable DOMAIN_REFUSE_PASSWORD_CHANGE 32 -option constant

}

Process {

    #set default values
    $Complex=$False
    $Anonymous=$False
    $NoClearChange=$False
    $AdminLockout=$False
    $Reversible=$False
    $Refuse=$False
    Write-Verbose "Parsing $flag"

    if ($flag -band $DOMAIN_PASSWORD_COMPLEX) {
         Write-Verbose "Complex passwords required"
         $Complex=$True
        }

    if ($flag -band $DOMAIN_PASSWORD_NO_ANON_CHANGE) {
         Write-Verbose "Anonymous change not allowed"
         $Anonymous=$True
        }

    if ($flag -band $DOMAIN_PASSWORD_NO_CLEAR_CHANGE) {
         Write-Verbose "No clear change allowed"
         $NoClearChange=$True
        }

    if ($flag -band $DOMAIN_LOCKOUT_ADMINS) {
         Write-Verbose "Admin lockout allowed"
         $AdminLockout=$True
        }

    if ($flag -band $DOMAIN_PASSWORD_STORE_CLEARTEXT) {
         Write-Verbose "Reversible encryption enabled"
         $Reversible=$True
        }

    if ($flag -band $DOMAIN_REFUSE_PASSWORD_CHANGE) {
         Write-Verbose "Refuse domain password change"
         $Refuse=$True
```

```
        }
    Write-Verbose "Creating object"
    #create a custom object with the password property values
    New-Object -TypeName PSObject -Property @{
        ComplexPasswords=$complex
        NoAnonymousChange=$anonymous
        NoClearChangeAllowed=$NoClearChange
        AdminLockout=$AdminLockout
        ReversibleEncryption=$Reversible
        RefusePasswordChange=$Refuse
    }
  }
 End {
  #this is not used
  }
} #end of function
```

You can calculate password properties, such as whether reversible encryption is enabled or complex passwords are required, by performing a bitwise comparison of certain values with the **pwdProperties** property of the domain object. My function performs these calculations and creates a custom password property object. You can retrieve the value for the **pwdProperties** property by using the **Get-QADObject** cmdlet:

```
PS C:\> $jdhlab=get-QADObject -Identity "dc=jdhlab,dc=local" -include pwdproperties
PS C:\> $jdhlab.pwdproperties
1
```

Passing this value to my function shows me the domain password properties:

```
PS C:\> get-pwdproperty 1


ReversibleEncryption : False
NoAnonymousChange    : False
ComplexPasswords     : True
NoClearChangeAllowed : False
AdminLockout         : False
RefusePasswordChange : False
```

While you can make some modifications using the **Set-QADObject** cmdlet:

```
PS C:\> Set-QADobject -Identity "dc=jdhlab,dc=local" -otherattributes @{minPwdLength=5}
```

Unfortunately, some properties can't be set because of the way the underlying property is stored:

```
PS C:\> Set-QADObject -Identity "dc=jdhlab,dc=local" -objectattributes @{lockoutduration=900}
Set-QADObject : A device attached to the system is not functioning.
At line:1 char:14
+ Set-QADObject <<<<  -Identity "dc=jdhlab,dc=local" -objectattributes @{lockoutduration=900}
    + CategoryInfo          : NotSpecified: (:) [Set-QADObject], DirectoryServicesCOMException
    + FullyQualifiedErrorId : System.DirectoryServices.DirectoryServicesCOMException,Quest.
ActiveRoles.ArsPowerShellSn
   apIn.Powershell.Cmdlets.SetObjectCmdlet
```

Although I have to admit this doesn't concern me much. Changing domain password policy settings is not an everyday task, and certainly one that doesn't benefit from command-line automation.

Managing User Password Properties

One password management task you may occasionally require is configuring a user account so that the user cannot change their password. This is accomplished by adjusting the security permissions on the user account object. When you check the appropriate box for the user account in Active Directory Users and Computers, what is really happening behind the scenes is a permission modification. You can also accomplish the same thing with PowerShell. First, let's look at a user account where the user can still change her own password:

```
PS C:\> Get-ADUser ssweet -Properties CannotChangePassword


CannotChangePassword : False
DistinguishedName    : CN=Sally Sweet,OU=Temp,OU=Employees,DC=jdhlab,DC=local
Enabled              : True
GivenName            : Sally
Name                 : Sally Sweet
ObjectClass          : user
ObjectGUID           : def0004f-3680-4c8e-8fc7-9c7bd2e77a0b
SamAccountName       : ssweet
SID                  : S-1-5-21-3957442467-353870018-3926547339-5158
Surname              : Sweet
UserPrincipalName    : ssweet@jdhlab.com
```

But Sally Sweet, nice as she is, can't be trusted. I want to configure her account so that she can't change her password. I can easily make this change with the Microsoft **Set-ADAccountControl** cmdlet:

```
PS C:\> Set-ADAccountControl -Identity ssweet -CannotChangePassword $True
```

That's all it takes. You'll find this very handy when you need to configure many user accounts:

```
PS C:\> Get-ADUser -filter * -SearchBase "OU=Temp,Ou=Employees,DC=jdhlab,DC=local" |
>> Set-ADAccountControl -CannotChangePassword $True -passthru | Select distinguishedname
>>

distinguishedname
-----------------
CN=Lester Tigert,OU=Temp,OU=Employees,DC=jdhlab,DC=local
CN=Jonathon Litchmore,OU=Temp,OU=Employees,DC=jdhlab,DC=local
CN=Maxwell Haub,OU=Temp,OU=Employees,DC=jdhlab,DC=local
CN=Mervin Abdelal,OU=Temp,OU=Employees,DC=jdhlab,DC=local
CN=Jefferey Harn,OU=Temp,OU=Employees,DC=jdhlab,DC=local
CN=Luigi Sienko,OU=Temp,OU=Employees,DC=jdhlab,DC=local
CN=Luke Evanoski,OU=Temp,OU=Employees,DC=jdhlab,DC=local
CN=Sally Sweet,OU=Temp,OU=Employees,DC=jdhlab,DC=local
CN=Merlin Sayasane,OU=Temp,OU=Employees,DC=jdhlab,DC=local
```

Using the **Get-ADUser** cmdlet I retrieved all user accounts in the TEMP organizational unit and passed each one to the **Set-ADAccountControl** cmdlet, which removed their right to change their own password. The cmdlet doesn't write to the pipeline by default so I used the **-Passthru** parameter so I could see what objects were modified. If I want to change them back I can run the same command and specify $False for the **-CannotChangePassword** parameter.

There is a Windows PowerShell cmdlet called the **Get-ACL** cmdlet, but it isn't designed to work with Active Directory objects. However, if you have the Quest cmdlets, the **Get-QADPermission** cmdlet is very easy to use:

```
PS C:\> Get-QADPermission -Identity ssweet
Permissions for: jdhlab.local/Employees/Temp/Sally Sweet


Ctrl   Account              Rights                        Source           AppliesTo
----   -------              ------                        ------           ---------
Deny   Everyone             Change Password               Not inherited    This object only
Deny   NT AUTHORITY\SELF    Change Password               Not inherited    This object only
```

I will cover the permission cmdlets in greater detail in a later chapter, but let me briefly explain what's happening here. The cmdlet is looking at the Sally Sweet user object and checking permissions. As you can see, SELF and EVERYONE are denied the Change Password right. Let me remove the permission, and then I'll add it back.

There is a **Remove-QADPermission** cmdlet, and the easiest way to use it is to pipe an ACL object to it using the **Get-QADPermission** cmdlet:

```
PS C:\> Get-QADPermission -Identity ssweet -Account "self","Everyone" -Deny `
>> -ExtendedRight "User-Change-Password" | remove-qadpermission
>>
Permissions for: jdhlab.local/Employees/Temp/Sally Sweet

Ctrl   Account              Rights                        Source           AppliesTo
----   -------              ------                        ------           ---------
Deny   Everyone             Change Password               Not inherited    This object only
Deny   NT AUTHORITY\SELF    Change Password               Not inherited    This object only
WARNING: Only explicit permissions were displayed. To display inherited and AD default
permissions
use-Inherited and -SchemaDefault switches respectively.
```

I used some additional parameters with the **Get-QADPermission** cmdlet to make sure I only returned permissions related to the change password right. To add the permission, I bet you can guess what cmdlet you need:

```
PS C:\> Add-QADPermission -Identity ssweet -Account "self","Everyone" -Deny `
>> -ExtendedRight "User-Change-Password"
```

I hope you guessed the **Add-QADPermission** cmdlet.

What about finding all users who can't change their own password?

```
PS C:\> $nochange=Get-QADUser -enabled -sizelimit 0 | Get-QADPermission -account self -deny `
>> -right ExtendedRight -extendedright "User-Change-Password" | Select TargetObject
>>

PS C:\> $nochange.count
10
PS C:\> $nochange

TargetObject
------------
JDHLAB\M.Sayasane
JDHLAB\M.Haub
JDHLAB\J.Harn
JDHLAB\L.Evanoski
JDHLAB\L.Tigert
JDHLAB\J.Litchmore
```

```
JDHLAB\M.Abdelal
JDHLAB\L.Sienko
JDHLAB\sday
JDHLAB\ssweet
```

I've truncated the output you get when running the command. I also saved the results to a variable; otherwise, it's next to impossible to see the results. If you run the expression yourself, you'll see what I'm referring to.

This task is much easier to accomplish with the Microsoft **Get-ADUser** cmdlet:

```
PS C:\> Get-ADUser -filter * -Properties CannotChangePassword |
>> where {$_.CannotChangePassword} | Select Distinguishedname
>>

Distinguishedname
-----------------
CN=Guest,CN=Users,DC=jdhlab,DC=local
CN=Merlin Sayasane,OU=Temp,OU=Employees,DC=jdhlab,DC=local
CN=Maxwell Haub,OU=Temp,OU=Employees,DC=jdhlab,DC=local
CN=Jefferey Harn,OU=Temp,OU=Employees,DC=jdhlab,DC=local
CN=Luke Evanoski,OU=Temp,OU=Employees,DC=jdhlab,DC=local
CN=Lester Tigert,OU=Temp,OU=Employees,DC=jdhlab,DC=local
CN=Jonathon Litchmore,OU=Temp,OU=Employees,DC=jdhlab,DC=local
CN=Mervin Abdelal,OU=Temp,OU=Employees,DC=jdhlab,DC=local
CN=Luigi Sienko,OU=Temp,OU=Employees,DC=jdhlab,DC=local
CN=Restricted BusinessHours,OU=Templates,DC=jdhlab,DC=local
CN=Sales Template,OU=Templates,DC=jdhlab,DC=local
CN=Sunny Day,OU=Customer Service,OU=Employees,DC=jdhlab,DC=local
CN=Sally Sweet,OU=Temp,OU=Employees,DC=jdhlab,DC=local
```

Unfortunately, you can't filter on an extended attribute with the **Get-ADUser** cmdlet, so you need to pipe all user objects to the **Where-Object** cmdlet to return only those where the user cannot change their own password.

There are other password properties for a domain user account, such as whether the password can expire, if it can be stored in reversible encryption, or if the user is not allowed to change their password. These settings are stored in the **UserAccountControl** property. You can evaluate this bitmask value with a binary AND against values that represent the different settings. I used this technique earlier in the chapter. Fortunately, the **Get-ADUser** cmdlet handles the calculations. All you need to do is specify a property set since most of these properties are not returned by default:

```
$properties=@("PasswordNeverExpires",
"PasswordNotRequired",
"PasswordExpired"
"AllowReversiblePasswordEncryption",
"CannotChangePassword",
"SmartCardLogonRequired")
```

With this it is very easy then to see all password-related properties for a given account:

```
PS C:\> Get-ADUser jshortz -properties $properties | Select $properties


PasswordNeverExpires              : True
PasswordNotRequired               : True
PasswordExpired                   : False
AllowReversiblePasswordEncryption : True
```

```
CannotChangePassword              : True
SmartCardLogonRequired            : False
```

It is very easy to modify any of these values using the **Set-ADUser** cmdlet:

```
PS C:\> Set-ADUser -Identity jshortz -AllowReversiblePasswordEncryption $false `
>> -CannotChangePassword $false -PasswordNeverExpires $True -PasswordNotRequired $False `
>> -SmartcardLogonRequired $False
```

You rarely will modify all settings at once, but I wanted to demonstrate the parameters you would use. Specify either $True or $False to enable or disable accordingly. The cmdlet handles all the bit-wise manipulation. I'll get the properties again and verify the change:

```
PS C:\> Get-ADUser jshortz -properties $properties | Select $properties


PasswordNeverExpires              : True
PasswordNotRequired               : False
PasswordExpired                   : False
AllowReversiblePasswordEncryption : False
CannotChangePassword              : False
SmartCardLogonRequired            : False
```

Unfortunately, getting the same information with the equivalent **Get-QADUser** cmdlet is not as easy, since it doesn't decode all of the user account control flags. However, you can use the cmdlet to get the value, and then parse the value using my **Get-PasswordProperty** function:

Get-PasswordProperty.ps1

```
Function Get-PasswordProperty {

    [cmdletbinding()]

    Param(
    [Parameter(Position=0,Mandatory=$True,ValueFromPipeline=$True,
    HelpMessage="Enter a property flag value")]
    [ValidateNotNullorEmpty()]
    [int]$flag
    )

Begin {
    Write-Verbose "Defining flag constants"
    New-Variable ADS_UF_PASSWD_NOTREQD 0x0020 -Option Constant
    New-Variable ADS_UF_ENCRYPTED_TEXT_PASSWORD_ALLOWED 0x0080 -Option Constant
    New-Variable ADS_UF_DONT_EXPIRE_PASSWD 0x10000 -Option Constant
    New-Variable ADS_UF_SMARTCARD_REQUIRED 0x40000 -Option Constant
    New-Variable ADS_UF_PASSWD_EXPIRED 0x800000 -Option Constant
 }

 Process {
        Write-Verbose "Parsing $flag"

        #set default values
        $DoNotExpire=$False
        $PwdNotRequired=$False
        $EncryptedTextPwdAllowed=$False
        $SmartCardRequired=$False
        $PwdExpired=$False
```

```
        if ($flag -band $ADS_UF_DONT_EXPIRE_PASSWD ) { $DoNotExpire=$True }
        if ($flag -band $ADS_UF_PASSWD_NOTREQD )     { $PwdNotRequired=$True }
        if ($flag -band $ADS_UF_ENCRYPTED_TEXT_PASSWORD_ALLOWED) {$EncryptedTextPwdAllowed=$True }
        if ($flag -band $ADS_UF_SMARTCARD_REQUIRED ) { $SmartCardRequired=$True }
        if ($flag -band $ADS_UF_PASSWD_EXPIRED ) { $PwdExpired=$True }

        New-Object -TypeName PSObject -Property @{
            PasswordDoesNotExpire=$DoNotExpire
            PasswordNotRequired=$PwdNotRequired
            ReversibleEncryptionAllowed=$EncryptedTextPwdAllowed
            SmartCardRequired=$SmartCardRequired
            PasswordExpired=$PwdExpired
        }
    } #process

  End {
     #not used
   }
} #function
```

Once loaded into your PowerShell session, the function will "decode" the UserAccountControl value:

```
PS C:\> $account= Get-QADUser da_jhicks -include useraccountcontrol
PS C:\> Get-PasswordProperty $account.useraccountcontrol


PasswordExpired             : False
SmartCardRequired           : True
PasswordNotRequired         : False
ReversibleEncryptionAllowed : False
PasswordDoesNotExpire       : True
```

You can use the **Set-QADUser** cmdlet to modify the account so that the password never expires:

```
PS C:\> Set-QADUser -Identity ssweet -PasswordNeverExpires $true

Name                        Type      DN
----                        ----      --
Sally Sweet                 user      CN=Sally Sweet,OU=Temp,OU=Employees,DC=jdhlab,DC=local
```

This is very useful when you have a number of accounts to modify:

```
PS C:\> Get-QADUser -title "*Administrator" | Set-QADUser -PasswordNeverExpires $true
```

Any user account with Administrator in the title, presumably domain administrator accounts, is passed to the **Set-QADUser** cmdlet, which changes the **PasswordExpires** property. Unfortunately, for changing password properties, like allowing reversible encryption or requiring smartcards, you'll need to calculate an appropriate user account control flag and apply it to the user account.

A normal user account has a user account control flag of 512. To calculate a new value, perform a bitwise OR operation with any of the following values:

- Password Not Required = 32
- Reversible Encryption Allowed = 128

- Don't Expire Password = 65536
- Smartcard required for logon = 262144

So suppose I want to configure one or more accounts to have a non-expiring password and require smartcards for logon. The first step is to calculate a new user account control value:

```
PS C:\> 512 -bor 65536 -bor 262144
328192
```

Then I can use the **Set-QADUser** cmdlet to apply the new value:

```
PS C:\> Set-QADUser -Identity "Sandy Bottom" -ObjectAttributes @{useraccountcontrol=328192}

Name                          Type       DN
----                          ----       --
Sandy Bottom                  user       CN=Sandy Bottom,OU=HR,OU=Employees,DC=jdhlab,DC=local
```

Given everything I've covered thus far, wouldn't it be nice to have a password property report for all your user accounts? Using the **Get-ADUser** cmdlet as you did earlier in the chapter is probably the easiest way. Here's an example:

Get-ADUserPasswordProperty.ps1

```
#requires -version 2.0

Import-Module ActiveDirectory

$search="OU=Employees,DC=jdhlab,DC=local"

$properties=@(
"Name",
"DistinguishedName",
"PasswordNeverExpires",
"PasswordNotRequired",
"PasswordExpired"
"AllowReversiblePasswordEncryption",
"CannotChangePassword",
"SmartCardLogonRequired")

Get-ADUser -filter * -searchBase $search -properties $properties | Select $properties
```

Most of this script is what I used earlier. All I've done is add some properties and a default search base. When executed, I get an object like this for each user account:

```
Name                              : Roy G. Biv
DistinguishedName                 : CN=Roy G. Biv,OU=Employees,DC=jdhlab,DC=local
PasswordNeverExpires              : True
PasswordNotRequired               : False
PasswordExpired                   : False
AllowReversiblePasswordEncryption : False
CannotChangePassword              : False
SmartCardLogonRequired            : False
```

I would probably use this to document current account settings; perhaps exporting the results to a CSV file:

```
PS C:\> R:\Get-ADUserPasswordProperty.ps1 | Export-Csv -Path c:\work\passwordprop.csv
```

Accomplishing the same with the Quest cmdlets is a little more involved since you have to pull information from several sources. Here's a script I use:

Get-QADPasswordProperty.ps1

```
#requires -version 2.0
#requires -pssnapin Quest.ActiveRoles.ADManagement

#dot source the password property
. .\get-passwordproperty.ps1

#define a function to check permissions to see if user can change password
Function Test-PasswordChange {
#requires -version 2.0
#requires -pssnapin Quest.ActiveRoles.ADManagement

    Param(
    [Parameter(Position=0,Mandatory=$True,
    HelpMessage="Enter a user identity such as a user name or distinguishedname",
    ValueFromPipeline=$True)]
    [ValidateNotNullorEmpty()]
    [string]$identity
    )
    #turn off the warning pipeline to minimize the output from Get-QADPermission
    $WarningPreference="silentlycontinue"

    $perm=Get-QADPermission -Identity $identity -Account "Self","Everyone" -Deny
    if ($perm) {
        $True
    }
    else {
        $False
    }


} #end function

$search="OU=Employees,DC=jdhlab,DC=local"

Get-QADUser -SearchRoot $search -SizeLimit 0 -includedProperties UserAccountControl |
Foreach {
    $obj=get-passwordproperty $_.useraccountcontrol
    #add some user properties
    $obj | Add-Member -MemberType Noteproperty -Name "CannotChangePassword" -Value (Test-
PasswordChange $_.dn)
    $obj | Add-Member -MemberType Noteproperty -Name "Name" -Value $_.name
    $obj | Add-Member -MemberType Noteproperty -Name "DN" -Value $_.dn -passthru
}
```

The script assumes the **Get-PasswordProperty** function from earlier in the chapter is in the same folder. I've also written a nested function to check if the account's permissions are configured to deny the user the change-password right. If so, the function returns **$True**. With these tools I can get every user account in my search path and, for each one, decode the **useraccountcontrol** property, saving that as a variable:

```
Get-QADUser -SearchRoot $search -SizeLimit 0 -includedProperties UserAccountControl |
Foreach {
    $obj=get-passwordproperty $_.useraccountcontrol
```

Using this as my starting point, I can add some additional properties, such as whether the user can change their password and some name values:

```
    $obj | Add-Member -MemberType Noteproperty -Name "Name" -Value $_.name
    $obj | Add-Member -MemberType Noteproperty -Name "DN" -Value $_.dn -passthru
```

As with the Microsoft-based script, I find it easier to save the results to a variable:

```
PS C:\> $qusers=.\Get-QADPasswordProperty.ps1
```

Then I can analyze the results, such as finding all accounts that require smart cards:

```
PS C:\> $qusers | where {$_.SmartCardRequired} | Select dn

DN
--
CN=DA_Hicks,OU=Employees,DC=jdhlab,DC=local
CN=Sandy Bottom,OU=HR,OU=Employees,DC=jdhlab,DC=local
```

Or export the results; maybe this time to an XML file:

```
PS C:\> $qusers | Export-Clixml c:\work\quserprop.xml
```

Password Age

On a related topic, you might also want to find how old a user's password is. A couple chapters ago I showed you how easy this is. This is easily accomplished with the Microsoft **Get-ADUser** cmdlet:

```
PS C:\> Get-ADUser -Identity "da_jhicks" -Properties PasswordLastSet,PasswordNeverExpires |
>> Select DistinguishedName,Name,Password*,@{Name="PasswordAge";Expression={
>> (get-date) -$_.passwordlastset}  }
>>

DistinguishedName     : CN=DA_Hicks,OU=Employees,DC=jdhlab,DC=local
Name                  : DA_Hicks
PasswordLastSet       : 7/12/2010 1:30:09 PM
PasswordNeverExpires  : True
PasswordAge           : 35.03:41:00.9764654
```

The only thing I've really done here is define a new property called PasswordAge that returns a time span object from when the password was last set to the current date. It's not much harder to extend this to every user in the domain, creating a report. Again, I like saving results to a variable first:

```
PS C:\> $data=Get-ADUser -filter * -searchbase "OU=Employees,DC=jdhlab,DC=local" `
>> -Properties PasswordLastSet,PasswordNeverExpires |
>> Select DistinguishedName,Password*,@{Name="PasswordAge";Expression={
>> (get-date) -$_.passwordlastset}  }
```

Now I can slice and dice. For example, let me find the 10 accounts with the oldest password age:

```
PS C:\> $data | Sort PasswordAge -descending | Select -first 10

DistinguishedName                PasswordLastSet         PasswordNeverExpires PasswordAge
-----------------                ---------------         -------------------- -----------
CN=Lisa Andrews,OU=Sales,O... 3/4/2010 1:24:40 PM     False                165.03:50:16.7702876
CN=Cassie O'Pia,OU=Employe... 3/10/2010 10:37:08 AM  False                159.06:37:48.0747825
CN=Roy Antebi,OU=Sales,OU=... 3/10/2010 10:37:09 AM  False                159.06:37:47.1060325
CN=Johnson Apacible,OU=Emp... 3/10/2010 10:37:10 AM  False                159.06:37:46.9497825
CN=Prithvi Raj,OU=Employee... 3/10/2010 10:37:10 AM  False                159.06:37:46.8091575
CN=Darcy Jayne,OU=Customer... 3/10/2010 10:37:10 AM  False                159.06:37:46.7154075
CN=Virginie Jean,OU=Custom... 3/10/2010 10:37:10 AM  False                159.06:37:46.5747825
CN=Jacek Jelitto,OU=Custom... 3/10/2010 10:37:10 AM  False                159.06:37:46.4341575
CN=Don Richardson,OU=Sales... 3/10/2010 10:37:10 AM  False                159.06:37:46.2779075
CN=William Flash,OU=Employ... 3/10/2010 10:37:11 AM  False                159.06:37:45.9497825
```

Once I'm done, I can save the result. Maybe this time to a text file:

```
PS C:\> $data | Format-List | out-file "c:\work\pwdreport.txt"
```

To avoid truncating the distinguished names in the output, I added an intermediate step to force PowerShell to treat the output as a list before sending it to the file.

Want to use the **Get-QADUser** cmdlet? Using this cmdlet is even easier to get the same information and you don't need the function:

```
PS C:\> Get-QADUser -searchroot "OU=employees,DC=jdhlab,DC=local" -includedProperties "Pass*" `
>> -Sizelimit 0 | Select DN,Name,PasswordAge,PasswordLastSet,
>> PasswordStatus,PasswordIsExpired |
>> Export-Csv c:\work\userpwdreport.csv -notypeinformation
```

Using the **Get-QADUser** cmdlet, I'm searching my **Employees** organizational unit for all user accounts, including all password-related properties. Each object is then piped to the **Select-Object** cmdlet to return a subset of properties, all of which are then exported to a CSV file.

Using **Get-QADUser** I can also find accounts that have not had a password change in X number of days:

```
PS C:\> Get-QADUser -SearchRoot "OU=Employees,DC=jdhlab,DC=local" -passwordNeverExpires:$false `
>> -passwordNotChangedFor 90 | Select dn,pass*
>>


DN                   : CN=Cassie O'Pia,OU=Employees,DC=jdhlab,DC=local
PasswordLastSet      : 3/10/2010 10:37:08 AM
PasswordAge          : 159.07:04:18.5071777
PasswordExpires      : 4/29/2010 10:37:08 AM
PasswordNeverExpires : False
PasswordIsExpired    : True
PasswordStatus       : Expired

DN                   : CN=Johnson Apacible,OU=Employees,DC=jdhlab,DC=local
PasswordLastSet      : 3/10/2010 10:37:10 AM
PasswordAge          : 159.07:04:17.4134277
PasswordExpires      : 4/29/2010 10:37:10 AM
PasswordNeverExpires : False
```

```
PasswordIsExpired     : True
PasswordStatus        : Expired
...
```

In this expression I'm also using the **-PasswordNeverExpires** parameter to only return user accounts with passwords that can expire. Otherwise the "password not changed" value is meaningless.

Changing Passwords

Certainly one of the most frequent password management tasks you will have is for changing a user's password.

Reset a Password

You can reset a domain user's password with either the Microsoft or Quest cmdlets. The Microsoft **Set-ADAccountPassword** cmdlet is pretty straightforward, with one "gotcha." You must specify the password as a secure string:

```
PS C:\> $newpass=Read-Host "Enter the new password" -AsSecureString
Enter the new password: *******
```

With this, you can invoke the cmdlet specifying an Active Directory user account. You can use just about anything that will identify the account. I happen to prefer the SAMAccountname:

```
PS C:\> Set-ADAccountPassword -Identity "ssweet" -NewPassword $newpass
```

If you don't know the SAMAccountname off hand you can use the **Get-ADUser** cmdlet and pipe the object to the **Set-ADAccountPassword** cmdlet:

```
PS C:\> Get-ADUser -filter "name -eq 'Lester Tigert'" |
>> Set-ADAccountPassword -NewPassword $newpass
```

If you would like to avoid the extra step in entering the secure string password, you can nest the **ConvertTo-SecureString** cmdlet:

```
PS C:\> Set-ADAccountPassword -Identity "sbottom" `
>> -NewPassword (ConvertTo-SecureString -asPlainText -string "P@$$w0rd!23" -force)
```

The conversion cmdlet needs a little prodding when converting plain text strings so you need to use the parameters as I've done here. But there's no need for prompting; although, if you prefer an interactive approach, you don't have to specify password parameter values:

```
PS C:\> Set-ADAccountPassword -Identity "sapple" -reset
Please enter the desired password for 'CN=Sam Apple,OU=HR,OU=Employees,DC=jdhlab,DC=local'
Password: ***********
Repeat Password: ***********
```

In this scenario I'm prompted to enter the new password AND repeat it. You must use the **-Reset** parameter; otherwise, you will also be prompted for the user's old password, which you likely don't know.

The one potential drawback to this cmdlet is that there is no provision to force the user to change password at next logon. But you can accomplish that using the **Set-ADUser** cmdlet. Here's a command sequence you might use:

```
Get-ADUser -filter "name -eq 'Terry Kloth'" |
Set-ADAccountPassword -newPassword $newPass  -passthru |
Set-ADuser -ChangePasswordAtLogon $True -passthru
```

Well...It Should

According to cmdlet help, the above expression should work. However in my testing, using a variety of clients and domains it does not. The **-Passthru** parameter for the **Set-ADAccountPassword** cmdlet does not appear to work. The password will get set but because it won't write an object to the pipeline the **Set-ADUser** cmdlet will fail. The workaround is to simply use two steps:

```
PS C:\> Get-ADUser -filter "name -eq 'Terry Kloth'" |
>> Set-ADAccountPassword -newPassword $newPass
PS C:\> Get-ADUser -filter "name -eq 'Terry Kloth'" |
>> Set-ADuser -ChangePasswordAtLogon $True
```

I'm hoping that at some point the pipelined expression above will work as that's the whole point about Windows PowerShell, which is why I'm still including it here.

This task is also easy to do with the **Set-QADUser** cmdlet:

```
PS C:\> Set-QADUser jdhlab\jfrost -password "P@ssw0rd"

Name                    Type       DN
----                    ----       --
Jack Frost              user       CN=Jack Frost,OU=Payroll,OU=Employees,DC=jdhlab,DC=local
```

Simply specify the user account name and the new password. In this example I'm using the canonical name. There's no need to create a secure string. But don't worry. Nothing is ever passed in clear text over the wire.

To force the user to also change their password at next logon, simply append the **-UserMustChangePassword** parameter with a value of $True:

```
PS C:\> Set-QADUser jdhlab\jfrost -Userpassword "P@ssw0rd" -UserMustChangePassword $True

Name                    Type       DN
----                    ----       --
Jack Frost              user       CN=Jack Frost,OU=Payroll,OU=Employees,DC=jdhlab,DC=local
```

If you can change the password for one you can change it for many. Let's say I need to change passwords for everyone in the branch office:

```
PS C:\> Get-QADUser -enabled -SearchRoot "OU=Branch Office,DC=jdhlab,DC=local" |
>> Set-QADUser -UserPassword "N3wP@$$" -UserMustChangePassword $True
>>
```

```
Name                  Type     DN
----                  ----     --
David Jaffe           user     CN=David Jaffe,OU=Branch Office,DC=jdhlab,DC=local
Scott Bishop          user     CN=Scott Bishop,OU=Branch Office,DC=jdhlab,DC=local
Sean Beantly          user     CN=Sean Beantly,OU=Branch Office,DC=jdhlab,DC=local
Henrik Jensen         user     CN=Henrik Jensen,OU=Branch Office,DC=jdhlab,DC=local
Kevin Kennedy         user     CN=Kevin Kennedy,OU=Branch Office,DC=jdhlab,DC=local
Dennis Saylor         user     CN=Dennis Saylor,OU=Branch Office,DC=jdhlab,DC=local
```

The drawback is that everyone is configured to use the same password. One solution is to create a new password for each user. I've put together a version in the **New-QADPassword** script:

New-QADPassword.ps1

```
Add-PSSnapin Quest.ActiveRoles.ADManagement

#define a substitution hash table
$hash=@{"a"="2";"e"="3";"i"="1";"o"="0";"u"="%";"y"="7"}
#define an array of random characters to insert at the end"
$arr=@(")","(","*",",&","^","%","$","#","[","]","<",">")
#define a file to save new password results
$file="c:\work\newpass.txt"

Set-Content -Path $file -Value "New Passwords"

#get minimum domain password length
$minLength=(Get-QADObject -Identity "DC=jdhlab,DC=local" -includedProperties minPwdLength).
minPwdLength

Get-QADUser -SearchRoot "OU=Branch Office,DC=jdhlab,DC=local" | Foreach {
    #get user's last name and perform character substitution
    $newpass=$_.lastname
    Foreach ($key in $hash.keys) {
        if ($newpass.Contains($key)) {
            $newpass=$newpass.Replace($key,$hash.item($key))
        }
    }
    #pad newpass if it is less than domain minimum length
    if ($newpass.length -lt $minLength) {
        While ($newpass.length -lt $minLength) {
            #get a random character from the array and append it
            $newPass+=$arr[(get-random -min 0 -max ($arr.count))]
        }
    }
    #verify newpass has at least one symbol
    if ($newpass -notmatch "\W") {
        $newPass+=$arr[(get-random -min 0 -max ($arr.count))]
    }
    #save new passwords to the file
    Add-Content -Path $file -value "$($_.dn) = $newpass"
    #implement the change
    Set-QADUser -Identity $_.DN -UserPassword $newpass -UserMustChangePassword $False

} #foreach
```

The premise is very simple. For every user account that you want to set, take the user's last name and perform a few simple character substitutions. Make sure the length of the new password meets the domain password requirement and finally make sure the password has at least one non-word character. The new password is then used with the **Set-QADUser** cmdlet. My code also creates a text file with the user's distinguished name and their new password with the assumption that you'll be communicating the new password to them. My code also assumes you are using complex passwords.

Force User to Change

As I just discussed in the previous section, very often after changing a user's password, you want to force the user to change their password again at next logon. But there may be times when you simply want to force a password change alone. I'll use the same cmdlets. When using the Microsoft module, use the **Set-ADUser** cmdlet:

```
PS C:\> Set-ADUser -identity "l.andrews" -ChangePasswordatLogon $True
```

As I showed you earlier if you need to force this change for a group of users, get the user objects and pass them to the **Set-ADUser** cmdlet:

```
PS C:\> Get-ADUser -filter * -searchBase "OU=Legal,OU=Employees,DC=jdhlab,DC=local" |
>> Set-ADUser  -ChangePasswordatLogon $True -passthru | Select DistinguishedName
```

The Quest cmdlets work the same way. Use the **-UserMustChangePassword** parameter and specify a Boolean value:

```
PS C:\> Set-QADUser "s.wells" -usermustchangepassword $True

Name              Type          DN
----              ----          --
Sheila Wells      user          CN=Sheila Wells,OU=Executive,OU=Employees,DC=jdhlab,DC=local
```

Managing Fine-grained Password Policies

Windows Server 2008 supports fine-grained and multiple password policies which allow you to specify different password settings for different users or groups. Windows Server 2008 extends the Active Directory schema to include the new object class **msDS-PasswordSettings**.

Using the Active Directory Module

The Active Directory module includes a number of cmdlets for managing Password Settings Objects, or PSOs:

```
PS C:\> Get-Command -noun "ADFine*" | Select name

Name
----
Add-ADFineGrainedPasswordPolicySubject
Get-ADFineGrainedPasswordPolicy
Get-ADFineGrainedPasswordPolicySubject
New-ADFineGrainedPasswordPolicy
Remove-ADFineGrainedPasswordPolicy
Remove-ADFineGrainedPasswordPolicySubject
Set-ADFineGrainedPasswordPolicy
```

Creating a Policy

To create a new PSO, you'll use the **New-ADFineGrainedPasswordPolicy** cmdlet. Table 3-2 shows you the parameters you are likely to use.

Table 3-2 New-ADFineGrainedPasswordPolicy Parameters

Name	Type
ComplexityEnabled	System.Boolean
Description	System.String
DisplayName	System.String
Instance	Microsoft.ActiveDirectory.Management. ADFineGrainedPasswordPolicy
LockoutDuration	System.TimeSpan
LockoutObservationWindow	System.TimeSpan
LockoutThreshold	System.Int32
MaxPasswordAge	System.TimeSpan
MinPasswordAge	System.TimeSpan
MinPasswordLength	System.Int32
Name	System.String
OtherAttributes	System.Collections.Hashtable
PasswordHistoryCount	System.Int32
Precedence	System.Int32
ProtectedFromAccidentalDeletion	System.Boolean
ReversibleEncryptionEnabled	System.Boolean

The **-Name** and **-Precedence** parameters are required. The latter is a numeric value that is used when multiple policies might apply to a given user. The policy with the lower precedence value "wins." Typically this value is set in multiples of 10 or 100. Each PSO must have a unique Precedence value. Otherwise the cmdlet will throw an exception.

I want to create a new policy for members of the Legal group. Remember, you can only link a policy to a group, not an organizational unit:

```
PS C:\> New-ADFineGrainedPasswordPolicy -Name "LegalPSO" -Precedence 100 `
>> -DisplayName "Legal PSO" `
>> -Description "PSO for legal department users" `
>> -MinPasswordLength 10 `
>> -MaxPasswordAge "30.00:00:00" `
>> -LockoutDuration "0.01:00:00" `
>> -LockoutThreshold 4 `
>> -LockoutObservationWindow "0.01:00:00" `
>> -ReversibleEncryptionEnabled $False `
>> -ComplexityEnabled $True `
>> -passthru
>>

AppliesTo                     : {}
ComplexityEnabled             : True
```

```
DistinguishedName            : CN=LegalPSO,CN=Password Settings Container,CN=System,DC=...
LockoutDuration              : 01:00:00
LockoutObservationWindow     : 01:00:00
LockoutThreshold             : 4
MaxPasswordAge               : 30.00:00:00
MinPasswordAge               : 1.00:00:00
MinPasswordLength            : 10
Name                         : LegalPSO
ObjectClass                  : msDS-PasswordSettings
ObjectGUID                   : 97d2161d-d6d5-4b46-bdbf-8c65b2feed26
PasswordHistoryCount         : 24
Precedence                   : 100
ReversibleEncryptionEnabled  : False
```

Values for parameters such as **-LockoutDuration** and **-MaxPasswordAge** are specified as time spans. Thus the LockoutDuration on this PSO is 1 hour and the MaxPasswordAge is 30 days. By default the cmdlet does not write anything to the pipeline, which is why I used the **-Passthru** parameter.

However, now that I have a PSO I can also use the **Get-ADFineGrainedPasswordPolicy** cmdlet to retrieve it:

```
PS C:\> Get-ADFineGrainedPasswordPolicy -filter *


AppliesTo                    : {}
ComplexityEnabled            : True
DistinguishedName            : CN=LegalPSO,CN=Password Settings Container,CN=System,DC=...
LockoutDuration              : 01:00:00
LockoutObservationWindow     : 01:00:00
LockoutThreshold             : 4
MaxPasswordAge               : 30.00:00:00
MinPasswordAge               : 1.00:00:00
MinPasswordLength            : 10
Name                         : LegalPSO
ObjectClass                  : msDS-PasswordSettings
ObjectGUID                   : 97d2161d-d6d5-4b46-bdbf-8c65b2feed26
PasswordHistoryCount         : 24
Precedence                   : 100
ReversibleEncryptionEnabled  : False
```

The filter tells the cmdlet to return all PSOs. Otherwise you should be able to filter on most any PSO property:

```
PS C:\> Get-ADFineGrainedPasswordPolicy -filter "lockoutthreshold -le 5" |
>> Select Name,AppliesTo,Lockout*


Name                     : LegalPSO
AppliesTo                : {}
LockoutDuration          : 01:00:00
LockoutObservationWindow : 01:00:00
LockoutThreshold         : 4
```

Of course I only have a single PSO right now, but I hope you get the idea.

Modifying a Policy

But let's say I need to modify this PSO. For that you can use the **Set-ADFineGrainedPasswordPolicy cmdlet.** Table 3-3 displays the commonly used parameters.

Table 3-3 Set-ADFineGrainedPassword Policy Parameters

Name	Type
ComplexityEnabled	System.Boolean
Description	System.String
DisplayName	System.String
Identity	Microsoft.ActiveDirectory.Management. ADFineGrainedPasswordPolicy
LockoutDuration	System.TimeSpan
LockoutObservationWindow	System.TimeSpan
LockoutThreshold	System.Int32
MaxPasswordAge	System.TimeSpan
MinPasswordAge	System.TimeSpan
MinPasswordLength	System.Int32
PasswordHistoryCount	System.Int32
Precedence	System.Int32
ProtectedFromAccidentalDeletion	System.Boolean
ReversibleEncryptionEnabled	System.Boolean

Let's say I need to raise the lockout window to 90 minutes. Here's how I can accomplish this:

```
PS C:\> Set-ADFineGrainedPasswordPolicy -Identity "LegalPSO" -LockoutDuration "01:30:00" `
>> -LockoutObservationWindow "-1:30:00" -passthru | Select Name,Lockout*
>>

Name                LockoutDuration      LockoutObservationWindow      LockoutThreshold
----                ---------------      ------------------------      ----------------
LegalPSO            01:30:00             01:30:00                                     4
```

Adding a Policy Subject

Now that I have a PSO I need to link to something. For that I'll use the **Add-ADFineGrainedPasswordPolicySubject** cmdlet. The syntax is pretty simple: Specify the PSO and the group name:

```
PS C:\> Add-ADFineGrainedPasswordPolicySubject -Identity "LegalPSO" -Subjects "Legal" -PassThru


AppliesTo                   : {CN=Legal,OU=Groups,DC=jdhlab,DC=local}
ComplexityEnabled           : True
DistinguishedName           : CN=LegalPSO,CN=Password Settings Container,CN=System,DC=...
LockoutDuration             : 01:30:00
LockoutObservationWindow    : 01:30:00
LockoutThreshold            : 4
MaxPasswordAge              : 30.00:00:00
```

```
MinPasswordAge              : 1.00:00:00
MinPasswordLength           : 10
Name                        : LegalPSO
ObjectClass                 : msDS-PasswordSettings
ObjectGUID                  : 97d2161d-d6d5-4b46-bdbf-8c65b2feed26
PasswordHistoryCount        : 24
Precedence                  : 100
ReversibleEncryptionEnabled : False
```

As with the other password policy cmdlets, nothing is written to the pipeline unless you use the **-Passthru** parameter. But as you can see, I've now linked this PSO to the Legal global group. You can also specify multiple subjects, separated by commas. You'll need to use the group's pre-Windows2000 name:

```
PS C:\> Add-ADFineGrainedPasswordPolicySubject -Identity "LegalPSO" `
>> -Subjects "Legal","HRUsers" -PassThru | Select AppliesTo
>>

AppliesTo
---------
{CN=Legal,OU=Groups,DC=jdhlab,DC=local, CN=HR Users,OU=Groups,DC=jdhlab,DC=local}
```

Although if you don't know the name to use, you can use the **Get-ADGroup** cmdlet and pipe the group to the **Add-ADFineGrainedPasswordPolicy** cmdlet:

```
PS C:\> Get-ADGroup -filter "Name -eq 'HR Users'" |
>> Add-ADFineGrainedPasswordPolicySubject -Identity "LegalPSO"
```

Technically Speaking

Technically, you can also apply a PSO to an individual user account. But from a practical perspective I try to link to groups only. In my opinion a user-specific PSO should be for special-case situations and thus the exception rather than the rule.

Managing Policy Subjects

Creating reports of all your PSO settings is not that difficult. What policies do I have and who do they apply to?

```
PS C:\> Get-ADFineGrainedPasswordPolicy -filter * | Select Name,AppliesTo

Name                AppliesTo
----                ---------
LegalPSO            {CN=Legal,OU=Groups,DC=jdhlab,DC=local, CN=HR Users,OU=Groups,DC=jdhlab,DC=l...
TestDomainUsersPSO {CN=AlphaGroup,OU=Groups,DC=jdhlab,DC=local}
HighSecurityPSO     {CN=IT Admins,OU=Groups,DC=jdhlab,DC=local}
```

Or perhaps you need to document PSOs for your security audit. Because you may have multiple subjects, an XML format is the best choice:

```
PS C:\> $xml=Get-ADFineGrainedPasswordPolicy -filter * `
>> -Properties WhenCreated,WhenChanged,ProtectedFromAccidentalDeletion | ConvertTo-XML
PS C:\> $xml.Save("C:\work\PSOReport.xml")
```

In this example I'm retrieving all password objects, including some additional properties. The collection of password objects is converted to an XML object, which is then saved to a file. I could have used the **Export-Clixml** cmdlet, but I wanted a more portable XML file.

A likely task, especially when troubleshooting a problem, is to figure out what policy applies to a given user. This is especially needed when more than one PSO might apply to a user. Frankly, the easiest solution is a non-PowerShell one using the command line CMD) utility, **DSGet.exe**:

```
C:\>dsget user "CN=Jim Shortz,OU=Legal,OU=Employees,DC=Jdhlab,DC=local" -effectivePSO
  effectivepso

  "CN=HighSecurityPSO,CN=Password Settings Container,CN=System,DC=jdhlab,DC=local"
dsget succeeded
```

But since this is a PowerShell book let's see what else you can do. One tool you can use is the **Get-ADFineGrainedPasswordPolicySubject** cmdlet:

```
PS C:\> Get-ADFineGrainedPasswordPolicySubject -Identity LegalPSO


DistinguishedName : CN=HR Users,OU=Groups,DC=jdhlab,DC=local
Name              : HR Users
ObjectClass       : group
ObjectGUID        : f03dc03c-a0f7-424b-86d7-a6d4c7add842
SamAccountName    : HRUsers
SID               : S-1-5-21-3957442467-353870018-3926547339-1144
DistinguishedName : CN=Legal,OU=Groups,DC=jdhlab,DC=local
Name              : Legal
ObjectClass       : group
ObjectGUID        : 58d08c6c-479f-4d50-88bf-3a6a2bb4f0f0
SamAccountName    : Legal
SID               : S-1-5-21-3957442467-353870018-3926547339-5490
```

This cmdlet is handy because it returns the actual group objects (in this case) for each PSO subject. You can take this a step further and use the **Get-ADGroupMember** cmdlet to return group membership:

```
PS C:\> Get-ADFineGrainedPasswordPolicySubject -Identity LegalPSO  | Foreach {
>> Get-ADGroupMember -identity $_ } | Select Distinguishedname
>>

Distinguishedname
-----------------
CN=Benefits Users,OU=Groups,DC=jdhlab,DC=local
CN=Chris Barry,OU=Employees,DC=jdhlab,DC=local
CN=Scott Bishop,OU=Branch Office,DC=jdhlab,DC=local
CN=Sean Beantly,OU=Branch Office,DC=jdhlab,DC=local
CN=Belinda Newman,OU=Customer Service,OU=Employees,DC=jdhlab,DC=local
CN=Jim Shortz,OU=Legal,OU=Employees,DC=jdhlab,DC=local
CN=Al Broady,OU=Legal,OU=Employees,DC=jdhlab,DC=local
```

Now I have a list of all users that should be affected by this policy. If you are using nested groups, as I am here, then you'll most likely want to use the **-Recursive** parameter with the **Get-ADGroupMember** cmdlet:

```
PS C:\> Get-ADFineGrainedPasswordPolicySubject -Identity LegalPSO  | Foreach {
>> Get-ADGroupMember -identity $_ -recursive} | Select Distinguishedname
```

Finding the effective PSO for a user means you have to turn this around on its head. You need to search the subjects for each policy, looking for the user account. The PSO with the lowest precedence value of all matching policies is the winner. The best way to determine this is by using the **Get-ADUserResultantPasswordPolicy** cmdlet:

```
PS C:\> Get-ADUserResultant. PasswordPolicy jshortz


AppliesTo                   : {CN=AD Admins,OU=Groups,DC=jdhlab,DC=local, CN=IT Admins,OU=...
ComplexityEnabled           : True
DistinguishedName           : CN=HighSecurityPSO,CN=Password Settings Container,CN=System,DC...
LockoutDuration             : 01:00:00
LockoutObservationWindow    : 00:30:00
LockoutThreshold            : 3
MaxPasswordAge              : 5.00:00:00
MinPasswordAge              : 1.00:00:00
MinPasswordLength           : 12
Name                        : HighSecurityPSO
ObjectClass                 : msDS-PasswordSettings
ObjectGUID                  : b4701bb7-7b7e-456d-97e7-4e9eef17be90
PasswordHistoryCount        : 36
Precedence                  : 50
ReversibleEncryptionEnabled : False
```

The cmdlet's output tells me that for Jim Shortz, the final password policy to be applied was HighSecurityPSO:

```
Name                        : HighSecurityPSO
```

The remaining properties describe the user's password properties.

Removing a Policy Subject

If you decide you need to remove a subject you'll use the **Remove-ADFineGrainedPasswordPolicySubject** cmdlet:

```
PS C:\> Remove-ADFineGrainedPasswordPolicySubject -Identity "LegalPSO" -Subjects "HRUsers"

Confirm
Are you sure you want to perform this action?
Performing operation "Set" on Target "CN=LegalPSO,CN=Password Settings Container,CN=System,DC=
jdhlab,DC=local".
[Y] Yes  [A] Yes to All  [N] No  [L] No to All  [S] Suspend  [?] Help (default is "Y"):
```

Now the LegalPSO object no longer applies to members of HRUsers.

Removing a Policy

If you decide you no longer need a PSO, you don't necessarily have to delete it. Personally, I'd simply remove all the subjects and leave the PSO alone. If there are no subjects, the PSO has no effect. But you might want to use it later or as a template for future PSOs. Given all of that, if you still want to delete the policy, use the **Remove-ADFineGrainedPassowordPolicy** cmdlet:

```
PS C:\> Remove-ADFineGrainedPasswordPolicy -Identity "LegalPSO" -whatif
What if: Performing operation "Remove" on Target "CN=LegalPSO,CN=Password Settings Container,
CN=System,DC=jdhlab,DC=local".
```

I didn't really want to delete this policy so I used the **-WhatIf** parameter.

Using Quest Active Directory Cmdlets

On the Quest side of the house, there are a number of cmdlets you can use:

```
PS C:\> Get-Command -noun "QADPass*" | Select name

Name
----
Add-QADPasswordSettingsObjectAppliesTo
Get-QADPasswordSettingsObject
Get-QADPasswordSettingsObjectAppliesTo
New-QADPasswordSettingsObject
Remove-QADPasswordSettingsObjectAppliesTo
```

Creating a Policy

To create a new object from PowerShell, use the **New-QADPasswordSettingsObject** cmdlet. The parameters you are most likely to use are in Table 3-4.

Table-3-4 New-QADPasswordSettingsObject Parameters

Name	Type
AppliesTo	Quest.ActiveRoles.ArsPowerShellSnapIn.Data.IdentityParameter[]
Description	System.String
DisplayName	System.String
LockoutDuration	Quest.ActiveRoles.ArsPowerShellSnapIn.BusinessLogic.Parameters.TimeSpanAndMinutesParameter
LockoutThreshold	System.Int32
MaximumPasswordAge	Quest.ActiveRoles.ArsPowerShellSnapIn.BusinessLogic.Parameters.TimeSpanAndDaysParameter
MinimumPasswordAge	Quest.ActiveRoles.ArsPowerShellSnapIn.BusinessLogic.Parameters.TimeSpanAndDaysParameter
MinimumPasswordLength	System.Int32
Name	System.String
ObjectAttributes	Quest.ActiveRoles.ArsPowerShellSnapIn.Data.ObjectAttributesParameter
ParentContainer	Quest.ActiveRoles.ArsPowerShellSnapIn.Data.IdentityParameter
PasswordComplexityEnabled	System.Boolean
PasswordHistoryLength	System.Int32
Precedence	System.Int32
ResetLockoutCounterAfter	Quest.ActiveRoles.ArsPowerShellSnapIn.BusinessLogic.Parameters.TimeSpanAndMinutesParameter
ReversibleEncryptionEnabled	System.Boolean

The cmdlet takes care of all the hard work of translating values to the appropriate type. As with the Microsoft cmdlet you must specify a unique precedence value:

```
PS C:\> New-QADPasswordSettingsObject -Name "Customer-Service-Password-Settings" `
>> -passwordhistorylength 12 `
>> -passwordcomplexityenabled $True `
>> -minimumpasswordlength 9 `
>> -minimumpasswordage 1 `
>> -maximumpasswordage 30 `
>> -lockoutThreshold 7 `
>> -appliesTo 'jdhlab\CustomerServiceUsers' `
>> -precedence 400
>>

Name                          Type              DN
----                          ----              --
Customer-Service-Password-S... msDS-Passwor...  CN=Customer-Service-Password-Settings,CN=Password..
```

You'll notice I also specified a group name that will be subjected by this policy. This is purely optional but if you know what groups you wish to control, you can save some typing by doing everything with one command. Specify multiple group names by commas. Otherwise, I'll show you in a moment how to handle policy subjects.

Modifying a Policy

Unfortunately, there is not a Quest cmdlet that is equivalent to Microsoft's **Set-ADFineGrainedPasswordPolicy** cmdlet. If you need to modify a PSO from PowerShell without the Microsoft Active Directory module, you'll need to use the more generic **Set-QADObject** cmdlet. The downside is that you need to use the LDAP property names:

```
PS C:\> Get-QADPasswordSettingsObject -Name "HighSecurityPSO" |
>> Set-QADObject -ObjectAttributes @{"msDS-PasswordReversibleEncryptionEnabled"=$False;
>> "msDS-PasswordHistoryLength"=36}
>>

Name                     Type              DN
----                     ----              --
HighSecurityPSO          msDS-Passwor...   CN=HighSecurityPSO,CN=Password Settings Containe...
```

You'll find it easier to use the **Get-QADPasswordSettingsObject** cmdlet to retrieve the PSO and pipe it to the **Set-QADObject** cmdlet, where you can modify it. I've turned off reversible encryption and set the password history length to 36.

Let's take a look at the password settings objects in my domain:

```
PS C:\> Get-QADPasswordSettingsObject | Select name

Name
----
LegalPSO
TestDomainUsersPSO
HighSecurityPSO
Customer-Service-Password-Settings
```

You can also select a single password setting object by its name, as I have done earlier. Like any other Active Directory object, there are many more properties than that you see by default:

```
PS C:\> Get-QADPasswordSettingsObject "Customer-service-password-settings" | Select *


objectClass                               : {top, msDS-PasswordSettings}
msDS-LockoutDuration                      : 00:30:00
objectGUID                                : E4BEE511CF956443BCFE48C1E4DD824A
msDS-LockoutThreshold                     : 7
whenCreated                               : 8/18/2010 5:24:12 PM
msDS-MinimumPasswordAge                   : 1.00:00:00
msDS-PSOAppliesTo                         : CN=Customer Service Users,OU=Groups,DC=jdhlab,DC=...
whenChanged                               : 8/18/2010 5:24:12 PM
msDS-PasswordSettingsPrecedence           : 400
msDS-PasswordComplexityEnabled            : True
msDS-PasswordReversibleEncryptionEnabled : False
msDS-MaximumPasswordAge                   : 30.00:00:00
msDS-MinimumPasswordLength                : 9
msDS-PasswordHistoryLength                : 12
msDS-LockoutObservationWindow             : 00:30:00
objectSid                                 :
edsvaNamingContextDN                      :
AppliesTo                                 : {CN=Customer Service Users,OU=Groups,DC=jdhlab,...
LockoutDuration                           : 00:30:00
LockoutThreshold                          : 7
MaximumPasswordAge                        : 30.00:00:00
MinimumPasswordAge                        : 1.00:00:00
MinimumPasswordLength                     : 9
PasswordComplexityEnabled                 : True
PasswordHistoryLength                     : 12
Precedence                                : 400
ResetLockoutCounterAfter                  : 00:30:00
ReversibleEncryptionEnabled               : False
Security                                  : Quest.ActiveRoles.ArsPowerShellSnapIn.
UI.SecurityDe...
Domain                                    : JDHLAB\
LastKnownParent                           :
MemberOf                                  : {}
NestedMemberOf                            : {}
Notes                                     :
AllMemberOf                               : {}
Keywords                                  : {}
ProxyAddresses                            : {}
PrimarySMTPAddress                        :
PrimarySMTPAddressPrefix                  :
PrimarySMTPAddressSuffix                  :
PrimaryX400Address                        :
PrimaryMSMailAddress                      :
PrimaryCCMailAddress                      :
PrimaryMacMailAddress                     :
PrimaryLotusNotesAddress                  :
PrimaryGroupWiseAddress                   :
EmailAddressPolicyEnabled                 : False
Path                                      : LDAP://COREDC01.jdhlab.local/ CN=Customer-...
DN                                        : CN=Customer-Service-Password-Settings,CN=...
CanonicalName                             : jdhlab.local/System/Password Settings Container/...
CreationDate                              : 8/18/2010 5:24:12 PM
ModificationDate                          : 8/18/2010 5:24:12 PM
ParentContainer                           : jdhlab.local/System/Password Settings Container
ParentContainerDN                         : CN=Password Settings Container,CN=System,DC=...
Name                                      : Customer-Service-Password-Settings
ClassName                                 : msDS-PasswordSettings
Type                                      : msDS-PasswordSettings
Guid                                      : 11e5bee4-95cf-4364-bcfe-48c1e4dd824a
Sid                                       :
Description                               :
```

```
DisplayName                              :
OperationID                              :
OperationStatus                          : Unknown
Cache                                    : Quest.ActiveRoles.ArsPowerShellSnapIn.Business...
Connection                               : Quest.ActiveRoles.ArsPowerShellSnapIn.Data....
DirectoryEntry                           : System.DirectoryServices.DirectoryEntry
```

Once you know all the property names, you can build reports like this:

```
PS C:\> Get-QADPasswordSettingsObject | Select Name,Description,PasswordComplexityEnabled,
>> MinimumPasswordAge,MaximumPasswordAge,LockoutDuration,LockoutThreshold,
>> PasswordHistoryLength,WhenCreated,WhenChanged
>>


Name                      : LegalPSO
Description               : PSO for legal department users
PasswordComplexityEnabled : True
MinimumPasswordAge        : 1.00:00:00
MaximumPasswordAge        : 30.00:00:00
LockoutDuration           : 01:30:00
LockoutThreshold          : 4
PasswordHistoryLength     : 24
whenCreated               : 8/18/2010 11:54:34 AM
whenChanged               : 8/18/2010 2:46:38 PM

Name                      : TestDomainUsersPSO
Description               : Test Domain Users Password Policy
PasswordComplexityEnabled : True
MinimumPasswordAge        : 1.00:00:00
MaximumPasswordAge        : 42.00:00:00
LockoutDuration           : 12:00:00
LockoutThreshold          : 10
PasswordHistoryLength     : 24
whenCreated               : 8/18/2010 1:39:04 PM
whenChanged               : 8/18/2010 1:45:41 PM

Name                      : HighSecurityPSO
Description               : High Security Password Policy
PasswordComplexityEnabled : True
MinimumPasswordAge        : 1.00:00:00
MaximumPasswordAge        : 5.00:00:00
LockoutDuration           : 01:00:00
LockoutThreshold          : 3
PasswordHistoryLength     : 36
whenCreated               : 8/18/2010 1:42:23 PM
whenChanged               : 8/18/2010 5:42:31 PM

Name                      : Customer-Service-Password-Settings
Description               :
PasswordComplexityEnabled : True
MinimumPasswordAge        : 1.00:00:00
MaximumPasswordAge        : 30.00:00:00
LockoutDuration           : 00:30:00
LockoutThreshold          : 7
PasswordHistoryLength     : 12
whenCreated               : 8/18/2010 5:24:12 PM
whenChanged               : 8/18/2010 5:24:12 PM
```

You could save this to a text file or export it to an XML or CSV file.

Adding a Policy Subject

You don't have to specify the security principle affected by a PSO when creating the object. You can specify a user or group later using the **Add-QADPasswordSettingsObjectAppliesTo** cmdlet:

```
PS C:\> Add-QADPasswordSettingsObjectAppliesTo -Identity "HighSecurityPSO" `
>> -AppliesTo "AD Admins"
>>

Name                          Type           DN
----                          ----           --
AD Admins                     group          CN=AD Admins,OU=Groups,DC=jdhlab,DC=local
```

You can either use the security principal's distinguished name, object name, SAMAccountname, or canonical name. Specify multiple users or groups separated by commas.

Managing a Policy Subject

As I covered with the Microsoft cmdlets, wouldn't it be nice to see who is affected by your policies? First, let's look at this from the PSO's perspective using the **Get-QADPasswordSettingsObject** cmdlet:

```
PS C:\> Get-QADPasswordSettingsObject -Identity "HighSecurityPSO" |
>> Select -expandproperty AppliesTo
>>

CN=AD Admins,OU=Groups,DC=jdhlab,DC=local
CN=IT Admins,OU=Groups,DC=jdhlab,DC=local
```

The **AppliesTo** property stores the policy subjects as a collection, so I'm using the **-ExpandProperty** parameter with the **Select-Object** cmdlet to present the members as a list. Doing this for all PSOs takes a little extra finesse using the **Format-Table** cmdlet:

```
PS C:\> Get-QADPasswordSettingsObject |
>> Format-Table -GroupBy Name -Property Description,
>> @{Name="Subjects";Expression={$_.appliesto | out-string}} -wrap
>>


   Name: LegalPSO

Description                                      Subjects
-----------                                      --------
PSO for legal department users                   CN=Legal,OU=Groups,DC=jdhlab,DC=local
                                                 CN=Roy G. Biv,OU=Employees,DC=jdhlab,DC=local
                                                 CN=HR Users,OU=Groups,DC=jdhlab,DC=local



   Name: TestDomainUsersPSO

Description                                      Subjects
-----------                                      --------
Test Domain Users Password Policy                CN=AlphaGroup,OU=Groups,DC=jdhlab,DC=local
```

```
   Name: HighSecurityPSO

Description                                  Subjects
-----------                                  --------
High Security Password Policy                CN=AD Admins,OU=Groups,DC=jdhlab,DC=local
                                             CN=IT Admins,OU=Groups,DC=jdhlab,DC=local


   Name: Customer-Service-Password-Settings

Description                                  Subjects
-----------                                  --------
                                             CN=Customer Service Users,OU=Groups,DC=jdhl...
```

This is fine for viewing or printing, but if you need to archive this information, an XML document would work best using similar steps like you did with the Microsoft cmdlets:

```
PS C:\> $xml=Get-QADPasswordSettingsObject | ConvertTo-XML
PS C:\> $xml.Save("c:\work\qadpso.xml")
```

Another way to discover who is subjected to a PSO using the Quest cmdlets is with the **Get-QADPasswordSettingsObjectAppliesTo** cmdlet:

```
PS C:\> Get-QADPasswordSettingsObjectAppliesTo  -identity LegalPSO

Name                           Type            DN
----                           ----            --
Legal                          group           CN=Legal,OU=Groups,DC=jdhlab,DC=local
Roy G. Biv                     user            CN=Roy G. Biv,OU=Employees,DC=jdhlab,DC=local
HR Users                       group           CN=HR Users,OU=Groups,DC=jdhlab,DC=local
```

The default is to show all subjects. But you can filter with the **-Type** parameter, specifying either user or group:

```
PS C:\> Get-QADPasswordSettingsObjectAppliesTo  -Identity "LegalPSO" -Type User

Name                           Type            DN
----                           ----            --
Roy G. Biv                     user            CN=Roy G. Biv,OU=Employees,DC=jdhlab,DC=local
```

Unfortunately there's no parameter to search for a user who might be affected via group membership. But, you can put the PowerShell pipeline to work. The **Get-QADPasswordSettingsObjectAppliesTo** cmdlet can write group objects to the pipeline. Which means you can use the **Get-QADGroupMember** cmdlet to display all users, even in nested groups:

```
PS C:\> Get-QADPasswordSettingsObjectAppliesTo  -Identity "LegalPSO" -Type group |
>> Get-QADGroupMember -Indirect -Type User
>>

Name                           Type      DN
----                           ----      --
Al Broady                      user      CN=Al Broady,OU=Legal,OU=Employees,DC=jdhlab,DC=...
Jim Shortz                     user      CN=Jim Shortz,OU=Legal,OU=Employees,DC=jdhlab,DC...
Luigi Sienko                   user      CN=Luigi Sienko,OU=Benefits,OU=HR,OU=Employees,D...
Mervin Abdelal                 user      CN=Mervin Abdelal,OU=Benefits,OU=HR,OU=Employees...
Jonathon Litchmore             user      CN=Jonathon Litchmore,OU=Benefits,OU=HR,OU=Emplo...
```

```
Alden Larzazs                 user       CN=Alden Larzazs,OU=IT,OU=Employees,DC=jdhlab,DC...
Lester Tigert                 user       CN=Lester Tigert,OU=Benefits,OU=HR,OU=Employees,...
Domingo Olmedo                user       CN=Domingo Olmedo,OU=Finance,OU=Employees,DC=jdh...
Luke Evanoski                 user       CN=Luke Evanoski,OU=Benefits,OU=HR,OU=Employees,...
Jefferey Harn                 user       CN=Jefferey Harn,OU=Benefits,OU=HR,OU=Employees,...
Maxwell Haub                  user       CN=Maxwell Haub,OU=Benefits,OU=HR,OU=Employees,D...
Merlin Sayasane               user       CN=Merlin Sayasane,OU=Benefits,OU=HR,OU=Employe...
Belinda Newman                user       CN=Belinda Newman,OU=Customer Service,OU=Employe...
Sean Beantly                  user       CN=Sean Beantly,OU=Branch Office,DC=jdhlab,DC=local
Scott Bishop                  user       CN=Scott Bishop,OU=Branch Office,DC=jdhlab,DC=local
Chris Barry                   user       CN=Chris Barry,OU=Employees,DC=jdhlab,DC=local
```

This is also a handy way to find if a user is affected by a PSO: Add a filtering expression:

```
PS C:\> Get-QADPasswordSettingsObjectAppliesTo  -Identity "LegalPSO" -Type group |
>> Get-QADGroupMember -Indirect -Type User | where {$_.name -match "Chris Barry"}
>>

Name                          Type            DN
----                          ----            --
Chris Barry                   user            CN=Chris Barry,OU=Employees,DC=jdhlab,DC=local
```

The last challenge is looking at this from the user's perspective and determining the effective password setting object. I took my function I created for the Microsoft cmdlets and came up with a variation using the Quest cmdlets:

Get-QADEffectivePSO.ps1

```
#requires -version 2.0

Function Get-QADEffectivePSO {

[cmdletBinding()]

Param(
[Parameter(Position=0,Mandatory=$True,
HelpMessage="Enter a user's SAMAccountname",
ValueFromPipeline=$True,ValueFromPipelineByPropertyName=$True)]
[ValidateNotNullorEmpty()]
[string[]]$samAccountname
)

Begin {
    Write-Verbose "Starting function"
    if (-Not (Get-PSSnapin "Quest.ActiveRoles.ADManagement")) {
        Write-Verbose "Loading Quest snapin if necessary"
        Add-PSSnapin "Quest.ActiveRoles.ADManagement"
    }
    #Get all fine grained password policy objects
    Write-Verbose "Getting PSOs"
    $policies=Get-QADPasswordSettingsObject
    Write-Verbose "Found $($policies.count) policies"
    #get all users subjected to the policy and add them as a custom property
    foreach ($policy in $policies) {
        Write-Verbose "Getting subjects for $($policy.name)"
        #initialize a variable
        $s=@()
        #get direct users
        Get-QADPasswordSettingsObjectAppliesTo -Identity $policy -Type User |
         foreach {$s+=$_}
```

```
        #get users from all groups
        Get-QADPasswordSettingsObjectAppliesTo -Identity $policy -Type Group |
         Get-QADGroupMember -Indirect -Type User |
          foreach {$s+=$_}
        Write-Verbose "Found $($s.count) users"
        #add this is as new property to the PSO
        $policy | Add-Member -MemberType Noteproperty -Name "Subjects" -Value $s
    }

} #close begin

Process {
    Foreach ($sam in $samaccountname) {
        #initialize a variable to hold matching policies
        $match=@()
        Write-Verbose "Looking for $sam"
        #get the subject for each policy
        foreach ($policy in $policies) {
            Write-Verbose "Searching $($policy.name) subjects"
          if ($policy.subjects | where {$_.samaccountname -match $sam}) {
            Write-Verbose "Found a match"
            $match+=$policy
          }

        } #foreach $policy

         if ($match) {
           #write the highest policy found, if any
           $pso=$match | Sort -Property Precedence -descending | Select -last 1
           #create a custom object
           New-Object -TypeName PSObject -Property @{
            SamAccountname=$sam
            EffectivePSO=$pso
            }
          }
          else {
            Write-Warning "No effective policy found for $sam"
           }

    } #foreach $sam

} #close process

End {
    Write-Verbose "Finished"
 } #close end
} #function
```

The primary difference is that I collect all policy subjects up front and save them to a variable:

```
$s=@()
#get direct users
Get-QADPasswordSettingsObjectAppliesTo -Identity $policy -Type User |
 foreach {$s+=$_}
#get users from all groups
Get-QADPasswordSettingsObjectAppliesTo -Identity $policy -Type Group |
 Get-QADGroupMember -Indirect -Type User |
  foreach {$s+=$_}
```

The function then adds this variable as a new property to the policy object:

```
$policy | Add-Member -MemberType Noteproperty -Name "Subjects" -Value $s
```

With this, all the function needs to do is search each policy's **Subjects** property for the matching SAMAccountname. If found, the policy is added to an array:

```
foreach ($policy in $policies) {
    Write-Verbose "Searching $($policy.name) subjects"
  if ($policy.subjects | where {$_.samaccountname -match $sam}) {
    Write-Verbose "Found a match"
    $match+=$policy
  }
```

Assuming the user was found, the $match will have one or more PSOs. The function sorts them by precedence and selects the one with the lowest value:

```
$pso=$match | Sort -Property Precedence -descending | Select -last 1
```

At this point, I could just write the policy to the pipeline to get the effective PSO. But I designed the function to accept pipelined input and process multiple user names. If I just wrote the policy to the pipeline there would be no way of knowing which user it is referring to. To get around this I create a simple custom object:

```
New-Object -TypeName PSObject -Property @{
 SamAccountname=$sam
 EffectivePSO=$pso
 }
```

Here's the function in action:

```
PS C:\> "rbiv","jshortz" | Get-QADEffectivePSO

SamAccountname                                  EffectivePSO
--------------                                  ------------
rbiv                                            CN=LegalPSO,CN=Password Settings Co...
jshortz                                         CN=HighSecurityPSO,CN=Password Sett...
```

The **EffectivePSO** property is the nested policy object from the **Get-QADPasswordSettingsObject** cmdlet. This means you can tweak this output with the **Select-Object** cmdlet and a few custom hash tables:

```
PS C:\> Get-QADEffectivePSO -samAccountname "rbiv","jshortz" | Select Samaccountname,
>> @{Name="PSO";Expression={$_.EffectivePSO.Name}},
>> @{Name="Description";Expression={$_.EffectivePSO.Description}},
>> @{Name="Precedence";Expression={$_.EffectivePSO.Precedence}}
>>

SamAccountname       PSO                  Description                       Precedence
--------------       ---                  -----------                       ----------
rbiv                 LegalPSO             PSO for legal department u...            100
jshortz              HighSecurityPSO      High Security Password Policy             50
```

Removing a Policy Subject

To remove a user or a group from the policy, use the **Remove-QADPasswordSettingsObjectAppliesTo** cmdlet. Specify the PSO and the user or group to remove:

```
PS C:\> Remove-QADPasswordSettingsObjectAppliesTo -Identity "LegalPSO" -AppliesTo "rbiv"

Name                           Type         DN
----                           ----         --
Roy G. Biv                     user         CN=Roy G. Biv,OU=Employees,DC=jdhlab,DC=local
```

The cmdlet writes the user or group to the pipeline, although nothing is actually done to it. The PSO is the object that is actually modified.

Removing a Policy

Finally, to remove a policy altogether, you'll need a combination of cmdlets since the Quest snapin doesn't offer a dedicated tool. The PSO is merely another object in Active Directory, so once you know its distinguished name, you can delete it with the **Remove-QADObject** cmdlet:

```
PS C:\> Get-QADPasswordSettingsObject -Identity "TestDomainUsersPSO" | Remove-QADObject

Warning!
Are you sure you want to delete this object: CN=TestDomainUsersPSO,CN=Password Settings
Container,CN=System,DC=jdhlab,DC=local?
[Y] Yes  [A] Yes to All  [N] No  [L] No to All  [S] Suspend  [?] Help (default is "Y"):
```

Fine-grained Alternatives

In addition to the PowerShell options I've demonstrated in this chapter, there are other alternatives, although not necessarily PowerShell specific. You could use ADSIEdit as one of the book's technical reviewers is fond of. You might also take a look at the password solution from SpecOps.

I assume managing fine-grained password policies is not going to be an everyday task where command-line automation is a benefit. However, when it comes to documenting or troubleshooting, such as finding a user's effective policy, PowerShell will definitely be worth your time.

Chapter 4
Managing Active Directory Contacts

An Active Directory contact is a special type of object often used in Exchange organizations. If you are running Exchange 2007 or Exchange 2010, you have a number of contact related cmdlets to use. In this chapter I'll focus on using the Microsoft Active Directory and the Quest Active Directory cmdlets.

Using the Active Directory Module

The Active Directory module doesn't have any cmdlets specifically designed for contacts. But a contact is simply another object type, which means you can use the **Get-ADObject** cmdlet:

```
PS C:\> Get-ADObject -filter "name -eq 'Jeff Hicks'"

DistinguishedName                           Name       ObjectClass ObjectGUID
-----------------                           ----       ----------- ----------
CN=Jeff Hicks,OU=Contacts,DC=jdhlab,DC=local Jeff Hicks contact     894a750c-71c6-4477-a023-a60...
```

In this example, I've retrieved a specific contact by its identity. As you saw with the **Get-ADUser** cmdlet, only a few common properties are returned unless you specify otherwise:

```
PS C:\> Get-ADObject -filter "name -eq 'Jeff Hicks'" -properties "Title","Description","Company"


Company           : JDH Information Technology Solutions
Description       : PowerShell Consultant
DistinguishedName : CN=Jeff Hicks,OU=Contacts,DC=jdhlab,DC=local
```

```
Name              : Jeff Hicks
ObjectClass       : contact
ObjectGUID        : 894a750c-71c6-4477-a023-a60dda39d6e4
Title             : Principal Consultant
```

These examples assumed you already knew the contact name. But what if you are looking for a list of all contacts? All you need to do is slightly modify the filter. Did you notice the **ObjectClass** property in the previous example? Here's how to use it:

```
PS C:\> Get-ADObject -filter "objectclass -eq 'contact'" `
>> -properties "Title","Description","Company"
>>


Company           : JDH Information Technology Solutions
Description       : PowerShell Consultant
DistinguishedName : CN=Jeff Hicks,OU=Contacts,DC=jdhlab,DC=local
Name              : Jeff Hicks
ObjectClass       : contact
ObjectGUID        : 894a750c-71c6-4477-a023-a60dda39d6e4
Title             : Principal Consultant

Company           : SAPIEN Technologies
Description       : SAPIEN Technologies
DistinguishedName : CN=Ferdinand Rios,OU=Contacts,DC=jdhlab,DC=local
Name              : Ferdinand Rios
ObjectClass       : contact
ObjectGUID        : cea840e5-9ad8-4b7c-bf86-347d1241e1d0

Company           : Microsoft
Description       : Windows PowerShell Architect
DistinguishedName : CN=Jeffrey Snover,OU=Contacts,DC=jdhlab,DC=local
Name              : Jeffrey Snover
ObjectClass       : contact
ObjectGUID        : ff208958-a63a-4d09-9fdc-7740a81af0bb
Title             : Distinguished Engineer
```

If you need to be even more selective, revise your filter string:

```
PS C:\> Get-ADObject -filter "objectclass -eq 'contact' -AND company -like 'SAPIEN*'" `
>> -properties "Title","Description","Company"
>>


Company           : SAPIEN Technologies
Description       : SAPIEN Technologies
DistinguishedName : CN=Ferdinand Rios,OU=Contacts,DC=jdhlab,DC=local
Name              : Ferdinand Rios
ObjectClass       : contact
ObjectGUID        : cea840e5-9ad8-4b7c-bf86-347d1241e1d0E
```

Even though I specified the **Title** property, it doesn't display because it is not defined for this particular contact.

I only have a few contacts but I've modified my filter to retrieve all contacts where the company property also starts with "SAPIEN". As with the other Get cmdlets in the Active Directory module, you can also use an LDAP filter:

```
PS C:\> Get-ADObject -ldapfilter "(&(objectclass=contact)(company=SAPIEN*))" `
>> -properties "Title","Description","Company"
>>


Company           : SAPIEN Technologies
Description       : SAPIEN Technologies
DistinguishedName : CN=Ferdinand Rios,OU=Contacts,DC=jdhlab,DC=local
Name              : Ferdinand Rios
ObjectClass       : contact
ObjectGUID        : cea840e5-9ad8-4b7c-bf86-347d1241e1d0
```

Deciding when to use the **-Filter** or **-LDAPFilter** parameters is a matter of comfort and experience.

Using Get-QADObject

Like the Active Directory module, there are no cmdlets from Quest Software specifically for contact objects. Instead, like the previous discussion, you can use the generic **Get-QADObject** cmdlet and specify the name of the contact:

```
PS C:\> Get-QADObject -Identity "Jeff Hicks" | Select *


objectGUID         : 0C754A89C6717744A023A60DDA39D6E4
whenChanged        : 7/5/2010 11:14:28 AM
objectClass        : {top, person, organizationalPerson, contact}
whenCreated        : 7/5/2010 11:13:20 AM
objectSid          :
Security           : Quest.ActiveRoles.ArsPowerShellSnapIn.UI.SecurityDescriptor
Domain             : JDHLAB\
LastKnownParent    :
MemberOf           : {}
NestedMemberOf     : {}
Notes              :
AllMemberOf        : {}
Keywords           : {}
Path               : LDAP://COREDC01.jdhlab.local/CN=Jeff Hicks,OU=Contacts,DC=jdhlab,DC=local
DN                 : CN=Jeff Hicks,OU=Contacts,DC=jdhlab,DC=local
CanonicalName      : jdhlab.local/Contacts/Jeff Hicks
CreationDate       : 7/5/2010 11:13:20 AM
ModificationDate   : 7/5/2010 11:14:28 AM
ParentContainer    : jdhlab.local/Contacts
ParentContainerDN  : OU=Contacts,DC=jdhlab,DC=local
Name               : Jeff Hicks
ClassName          : contact
Type               : contact
Guid               : 894a750c-71c6-4477-a023-a60dda39d6e4
Sid                :
Description        : PowerShell Consultant
DisplayName        : Jeff Hicks
OperationID        :
OperationStatus    : Unknown
Cache              : Quest.ActiveRoles.ArsPowerShellSnapIn.BusinessLogic.ObjectCache
Connection         : Quest.ActiveRoles.ArsPowerShellSnapIn.Data.ArsADConnection
DirectoryEntry     : System.DirectoryServices.DirectoryEntry
```

More than likely all you need is a subset of this information:

```
PS C:\> Get-QADObject -Identity "Jeff Hicks" -includedproperties `
>> "Company","TelephoneNumber","Mail" | Select Name,Description,TelephoneNumber,Mail,Company
>>


Name            : Jeff Hicks
Description     : PowerShell Consultant
telephoneNumber : 315-555-7023
mail            : jhicks@jdhitsolutions.com
company         : JDH Information Technology Solutions
```

By default and design not every property is automatically returned by the **Get-QADObject** cmdlet. I had to specifically request the **Company, TelephoneNumber**, and **Mail** properties. You need to take this step whether you are listing one contact or all of them:

```
PS C:\> Get-QADObject -type "contact" -includedproperties "Company","wwwHomePage" |
>> select Name,Description,wwwHomePage,Company
>>

Name            Description                 wWWHomePage                     company
----            -----------                 -----------                     -------
Jeff Hicks      PowerShell Consultant       http://jdhitsolutions.com/blog  JDH Information Te...
Ferdinand Rios  SAPIEN Technologies         http://www.SAPIEN.com           SAPIEN Technologie...
Jeffrey Snover  Microsoft Distinguished E... http://blogs.msdn.com/powershell Microsoft
...
```

Creating Contacts

Creating a contact object is essentially no different than creating a user object. In fact, it is a little easier because it is not a security principal.

Using the Active Directory module

To create a contact you'll use the **New-ADObject** cmdlet. At a minimum you need to specify the name, object type, and a path for the new object:

```
PS C:\> New-ADObject -Name "Jack Frost" -Type "Contact" `
>> -Path "OU=contacts,DC=jdhlab,dc=local"
>> -otherattributes @{givenname="Jack";sn="Frost";telephonenumber="555-COLD";
>> Company="Frost Industries";Title="Sales Manager"} -DisplayName="Jack Frost"-passthru
>>

DistinguishedName              Name              ObjectClass    ObjectGUID
-----------------              ----              -----------    ----------
cn=Jack Frost,OU=contacts,...  Jack Frost        contact        8da9da4b-973b-4efe-8e...
```

Use the **-OtherAttributes** parameter to define other properties for the contact. In this example I have a hash table of all the values I want to set. The tricky part is that you need to use the LDAP property name and not necessarily the name you see in the GUI. For example, it's "sn" not "lastname". Some of this knowledge will come with experience. Or use a tool like ADSIEdit to discover the actual property names. By default the **New-ADObject** cmdlet doesn't write to the pipeline, which is why I used the **-Passthru** parameter so I could see the results.

Although the cmdlet doesn't direct pipeline input, it is still possible to use it to create many contacts at once. Here's a short CSV file with new contacts that I want to import into Active Directory:

```
Name,firstname,lastname,Title,Company,Telephonenumber,Description,email
John Q. Public,John,Public,CPA,Public Accounting LLC,555-1040,auditor,john@jqp.biz
Adam Blast,Adam,Blast,Security Consultant,Black Ops Security,555-7777,$null,blast@black.pro
Betsy Baker,Betsy,Baker,President,Baker Farms,555-4000,board member,betsy.baker@bakerfarms.net
```

It doesn't matter if there are 3 or 300 contacts, the process is the same. To import these contacts, I'll use the code shown in Import-Contacts.ps1:

Import-Contacts.ps1

```
import-Csv c:\work\newcontacts.csv | Foreach {
 New-ADObject -type "Contact" -path "OU=Contacts,DC=jdhlab,DC=local" -name $_.name `
 -displayname $_.name -otherAttributes @{
  Givenname=$_.firstname;
  sn=$_.lastname;
  title=$_.title;
  company=$_.company;
  mail=$_.email;
  telephonenumber=$_.telephonenumber;
  description=$_.description} -passthru} |
Get-Adobject -properties Mail,Title,Company | Select -property Name,Mail,Title,Company
```

I use PowerShell's **Import-CSV** cmdlet to import the CSV file. Each "object" is then piped to the **ForEach-Object** cmdlet. Each imported contact object is "processed" by the **New-ADObject** cmdlet using the syntax I employed previously. Because I want to see my results I tell the **New-ADObject** cmdlet to pass on its objects to the pipeline. In order to see the non-default properties like **Mail** and **Title**, I need to pipe it to the **Get-ADObject** cmdlet and specify the properties. Finally I can pipe everything to the **Select-Object** cmdlet, which gives me a result like this:

```
Name                Mail                        Title                Company
----                ----                        -----                -------
John Q. Public      john@jqp.biz                CPA                  Public Accounti...
Adam Blast          blast@black.pro             Security Consultant  Black Ops Security
Betsy Baker         betsy.baker@bakerfarms.net  President            Baker Farms
```

One important note here is that when defining attributes, the **New-ADObject** cmdlet doesn't like blank values. If you look back at my CSV file you'll see that Adam Blast doesn't have a Description value. I've had to set it to $Null. Usually an empty value is no problem, but in this situation you need to change blanks to $Null.

Using the New-QADObject cmdlet

With the Quest cmdlets you follow a similar approach, using the **New-QADObject** cmdlet to create a contact object:

```
PS C:\> $contact=New-QADObject -type contact -parent "OU=Contacts,DC=jdhlab,DC=local" `
>> -name "John Steinbeck"
```

You'll need to specify the object type, the parent container, and the new contact name. If you prefer to specify additional properties at creation, use the **-ObjectAttributes** parameter:

```
PS C:\work> New-QADObject -type contact -parent "OU=Contacts,DC=jdhlab,DC=local" `
>>  -name "John Steinbeck" -displayname "John Steinbeck" -ObjectAttributes @{
>>  givenname="John";
>>  sn="Steinbeck"; `
>>  mail="steinbeck@canneryrow.com";
>>  telephonenumber="555-3409"; `
>>  company="Grapes Unlimited";
>>  title="President"
>>  }
>>

Name                          Type           DN
----                          ----           --
John Steinbeck                contact        cn=John Steinbeck,OU=Contacts,DC=jdhlab,DC=local
```

As you can see the cmdlet is very similar to the Microsoft cmdlet. I just created a contact for John Steinbeck with a number of properties. Because the two cmdlets are so similar, it's easy to make a mistake, especially with the **-OtherAttributes** vs **-ObjectAttributes** parameters.

Modifying Contacts

You may periodically need to modify contact information, or even add additional information you forgot to include when creating the contact.

Using the Active Directory module

Since you've used the **Get-ADObject** cmdlet and the **New-ADObject** cmdlet, did you guess you'll be using the **Set-ADObject** cmdlet? Assuming you know the contact's distinguishedname, modifying a contact is as easy as this:

```
PS C:\> set-adobject -Identity "CN=Jack Frost,OU=Contacts,DC=jdhlab,DC=local" `
>> -DisplayName "Jack R. Frost" -description "Seasonal consultant"
```

With this one line command I've updated the DisplayName and description properties for Jack Frost. To change other attributes depends on whether they have a value. If there is no existing value you use **-Add** parameter. If you need to update an existing value, use the **-Replace** parameter; to erase a value, use the **-Clear** parameter:

```
PS C:\> Get-ADObject -filter "name -eq 'Jack Frost'" |
>> set-adobject -Add @{mail="jfrost@frostco.biz"} -replace @{Title="Account Manager"} '
>> -clear "Department"}
```

In this example I'm taking advantage of the PowerShell pipeline so that I don't have to know the contact's distinguished name. The contact is then piped to the **Set-ADObject** cmdlet, which adds an email address, replaces the title, and clears the department. If you have a multi-value property and want to remove one of the values, then use the **-Remove** parameter and a hash table of the property:

```
PS C:\> Get-ADObject -filter "name -eq 'Jack Frost'" |
>> set-adobject -Remove @{OtherTelephone="555-9999"}
```

This will remove 555-9999 from other telephone numbers but leave any other entries.

It is possible to combine these parameters to update the same property. The cmdlet processes the parameters in this order:

- Remove
- Add
- Replace
- Clear

```
PS C:\> Get-ADObject -filter "name -eq 'Jack Frost'" |
>> set-adobject -remove @{otherTelephone="555-9999"} `
>> -Add @{otherTelephone="555-9876"}
```

In this variation I've removed the 555-9999 phone number leaving any other phone numbers intact, and then added a new phone number of 555-9876.

Using the Set-QADObject cmdlet

Use the **Set-QADObject** cmdlet to modify an existing contact. The cmdlet has a few properties you can set directly, but for the most part you need to use the **ObjectAttributes** property as I've done here to set the phone number, address, ZIP code and locality, or city:

```
PS C:\> Set-QADObject "Betsy Baker" -displayname "Betsy K. Baker" `
>> -description "board of directors"-objectAttributes @{
>> telephonenumber="555-1225";
>> streetaddress="123 Dodge Street";
>> l="Omaha";
>> st="Nebraska";
>> postalcode=68104}
>>

Name                           Type            DN
----                           ----            --
Betsy Baker                    contact         CN=Betsy Baker,OU=Contacts,DC=jdhlab,DC=local
```

To remove a property, use this same approach and set the value to $Null:

```
PS C:\> Set-QADObject "Betsy Baker" -description $null
```

Group Membership

I'll cover group management in Chapter 5, which will also apply to contacts. I don't want to repeat too much material, so I'll just give you some quick examples.

Using the Active Directory Module

Normally I would use the **Add-ADGroupMember** cmdlet. Unfortunately, this cmdlet does not support adding a contact to any type of group. So while you can add a contact manually to a group through Active Directory Users and Computers, as well as with the Quest cmdlet, it cannot be done with the cmdlet you would expect.

However, you can still use the **Set-ADObject** cmdlet and modify the **Member** property:

```
PS C:\> Set-ADObject -Identity "CN=Board of Directors,OU=Groups,DC=jdhlab,DC=local" `
>> -add @{member="cn=Jeff Hicks,OU=Contacts,DC=jdhlab,DC=local"}
```

It is not very pretty or elegant, but with this example I've added my contact to the Board of Directors group. The tricky part is getting the distinguished name of the member to add.

I have an All Contacts distribution list and I want all my contacts to belong to this group. I know I can use the **Set-ADObject** cmdlet, but I need a collection of names. First, I'll initialize an empty array:

```
PSS C:\> $members=@()
```

This array will hold the distinguished names of all contacts. I'll use the **Get-ADObject** cmdlet to populate the array:

```
PS C:\> Get-ADObject -filter "objectclass -eq 'contact'" | Foreach {
>> $members+=$_.distinguishedname}
```

All that remains is to set the member property on the group:

```
PS C:\> Set-ADObject -Identity "CN=All Contacts,OU=Groups,DC=jdhlab,DC=local" `
>> -add @{member=$members}
```

You would follow a similar process to remove a contact from a group by modifying the member property with the **-Remove** parameter.

Even using the **Get-ADGroupMember** cmdlet to enumerate a group will fail to display any contacts. But you can fall back to the **Get-ADObject** cmdlet and expand the **Member** property:

```
PS C:\> Get-ADObject -Filter "name -eq 'All Contacts'" -Properties Member |
>> select -ExpandProperty Member
>>

CN=Sales,OU=Contacts,DC=jdhlab,DC=local
CN=John Steinbeck,OU=Contacts,DC=jdhlab,DC=local
CN=Betsy Baker,OU=Contacts,DC=jdhlab,DC=local
CN=Adam Blast,OU=Contacts,DC=jdhlab,DC=local
CN=John Q. Public,OU=Contacts,DC=jdhlab,DC=local
CN=Jack Frost,OU=Contacts,DC=jdhlab,DC=local
CN=Jeffrey Snover,OU=Contacts,DC=jdhlab,DC=local
CN=Ferdinand Rios,OU=Contacts,DC=jdhlab,DC=local
CN=Jeff Hicks,OU=Contacts,DC=jdhlab,DC=local
```

Using the Add-QADGroupMember cmdlet

Using the Quest cmdlets is easier because you can take advantage of the pipeline and the membership cmdlets don't mind working with contacts:

```
PS C:\> Get-QADObject "Betsy Baker" | Add-QADGroupmember -identity "Board of Directors"
```

```
Name                            Type          DN
----                            ----          --
Betsy Baker                     contact       CN=Betsy Baker,OU=Contacts,DC=jdhlab,DC=local
```

Instead of having to type the contact's distinguished name, I'll pass it from the **Get-QADObject** cmdlet to the **Add-QADGroupMember** cmdlet. The contact is added to the Board of Directors group. Removing a contact is just as easy:

```
PS C:\> Get-QADObject "Betsy Baker" | Remove-QADGroupmember "Board of Directors"
```

If you want to manage contacts in bulk, these cmdlets will save you a great deal of time:

```
PS C:\> Get-QADObject -type contact -includedproperties Company |
>> where {$_.company -match "SAPIEN"} | Add-QADGroupmember -Identity "SAPIEN"
>>

Name                            Type        DN
----                            ----        --
Ferdinand Rios                  contact     CN=Ferdinand Rios,OU=Contacts,DC=jdhlab,DC=local
Sales                           contact     CN=Sales,OU=Contacts,DC=jdhlab,DC=local
```

The first part of this expression finds all contact objects where the company name matches "SAPIEN". Each object is then piped to the **Add-QADGroupMember** cmdlet, which adds the contact to the "SAPIEN" distribution list.

Deleting Contacts

Deleting contacts is no different than deleting a user object.

Using the Active Directory Module

Because you have a cmdlet to use that supports the **-WhatIf** and **-Confirm** parameters, I encourage you to use them until you are more comfortable. The **Remove-ADObject** cmdlet is the cmdlet of choice here:

```
PS C:\> Get-ADObject -Filter "name -eq 'Jack B. Gone'" | Remove-ADObject -whatif
What if: Performing operation "Remove" on Target "CN=Jack B. Gone,OU=Contacts,DC=jdhlab,DC=lo
cal".
```

I like using a pipelined expression like this because otherwise I have to know, and type, the full distinguished name when using the **Remove-ADObject** cmdlet alone.

I'll go ahead and remove this contact:

```
PS C:\> Get-ADObject -Filter "name -eq 'Jack B. Gone'" | Remove-ADObject -confirm

Confirm
Are you sure you want to perform this action?
Performing operation "Remove" on Target "CN=Jack B. Gone,OU=Contacts,DC=jdhlab,DC=local".
[Y] Yes  [A] Yes to All  [N] No  [L] No to All  [S] Suspend  [?] Help (default is "Y"):
```

Using the Remove-QADObject cmdlet

Using the Quest **Remove-QADObject** cmdlet is also dangerously easy. As with the Active Directory module, I recommend using the **-WhatIf** or **-Confirm** parameters:

```
PS C:\> Remove-QADObject "test contact1" -whatif
What if: Performing operation "Remove-QADObject" on Target "CN=Test Contact1,OU=Contacts,Dc=j
dhlab,DC=local".
```

In fact, if you use the **-Confirm** parameter, the cmdlet will take extra steps to protect you from making a mistake:

```
PS C:\> Remove-QADObject "test contact1" -confirm

Confirm
Are you sure you want to perform this action?
Performing operation "Remove-QADObject" on Target "CN=Test Contact1,OU=Contacts,Dc=jdhlab,DC=
local".
[Y] Yes  [A] Yes to All  [N] No  [L] No to All  [S] Suspend  [?] Help (default is "Y"): y

Warning!
Are you sure you want to delete this object: CN=Test Contact1,OU=Contacts,Dc=jdhlab,DC=local?
[Y] Yes  [A] Yes to All  [N] No  [L] No to All  [S] Suspend  [?] Help (default is "Y"):
PS C:\>
```

Remember, PowerShell is all about the pipeline and passing objects from one cmdlet to another.

Suppose I needed to delete all contacts that worked for SAPIEN Technologies:

```
PS C:\> Get-QADObject -Type "contact" -SearchAttributes @{company="SAPIEN Technologies"} |
>> Remove-QADObject -whatif
>>

What if: Performing operation "Remove-QADObject" on Target "CN=Ferdinand Rios,OU=Contacts,DC=j
dhlab,DC=local".
What if: Performing operation "Remove-QADObject" on Target "CN=Sales,OU=Contacts,DC=jdhlab,DC
=local".>>
PS C:\>
```

The first part of the expression gets all contact objects where the company name is exactly SAPIEN Technologies:

```
PS C:\> Get-QADObject -type contact  SearchAttributes @{company="SAPIEN Technologies"}
```

This output is then piped to the **Remove-QADObject** cmdlet, which would remove the object if I let it.

But what if contacts were created and the company name wasn't consistent? I want to find any contact with SAPIEN in the company name. I think an LDAP filter should do the trick:

```
PS C:\> Get-QADObject -LdapFilter "(&(objectclass=contact)(company=SAPIEN*))" |
>> Remove-QADObject -whatif
>>
What if: Performing operation "Remove-QADObject" on Target "CN=training@sapien.com,OU=Contacts
,DC=jdhlab,DC=local".
What if: Performing operation "Remove-QADObject" on Target "CN=Ferdinand Rios,OU=Contacts,DC=j
```

```
dhlab,DC=local".
What if: Performing operation "Remove-QADObject" on Target "CN=Sales,OU=Contacts,DC=jdhlab,DC
=local".
```

With an LDAP filter I found another contact that had SAPIEN as part of the company name. If I wanted to delete them for real I could re-run the command and omit the **-WhatIf** parameter.

I suspect that if you are running Exchange 2007 or Exchange 2010, you'll likely use appropriate Exchange cmdlets. But if you are still running Exchange 2003 or have other contact needs, you can use the techniques from this chapter. Contact management doesn't have to be a complicated task when using Windows PowerShell.

Chapter 5

Managing Active Directory Groups

Managing Active Directory groups and group membership can be a full-time job for some organizations. Hopefully, PowerShell will allow you to become more efficient. In this chapter, I will talk about creating both security-enabled and distribution groups. However, I won't discuss mail-enabled groups or other Microsoft Exchange tasks related to groups and distribution lists. I will focus on managing Active Directory groups independent of Microsoft Exchange.

Creating Groups

Using the Active Directory Module

Creating a new group with the Active Directory module is a relatively straightforward process using the **New-ADGroup** cmdlet. At a minimum you need to specify an Active Directory name and a group scope (i.e., Universal, Global, or DomainLocal):

```
PS C:\> New-ADGroup -Name "Accounting Managers" -GroupScope "Global"
```

This cmdlet created a new global security group called "Accounting Manager", with a SAMAccountname of the name value in the default container. The **New-ADGroup** cmdlet does not write anything to the pipeline unless you use the **-Passthru** parameter. Let's create another group with a little more detail:

```
PS C:\> New-ADGroup -Name "Mfg Staff" -GroupScope "Universal" -SamAccountName "MfgStaff" `
>> -Description "Corp. manufacturing division users" -Path "OU=Groups,DC=jdhlab,DC=local" `
```

```
>> -DisplayName "Mfg Staff" -ManagedBy "L.Puzio" -PassThru
>>


DistinguishedName : CN=Mfg Staff,OU=Groups,DC=jdhlab,DC=local
GroupCategory     : Security
GroupScope        : Universal
Name              : Mfg Staff
ObjectClass       : group
ObjectGUID        : c09cde4a-a2a9-4e68-ade9-311b76d549f0
SamAccountName    : MfgStaff
SID               : S-1-5-21-3957442467-353870018-3926547339-5501
```

I just created a universal security group in the Groups organizational unit for the manufacturing staff, managed by Lou Puzio (L.Puzio). I'll cover adding members to the group in a little bit. By the way, if you want to create a distribution group, use the **-GroupCategory** parameter and specify a value of "Distribution".

Using New-QADGroup

The Quest **New-QADGroup** cmdlet is also an easy solution for creating new groups. By defaults it creates global security groups. All you need to do is specify a parent container and some names:

```
PS C:\> New-QADGroup -parent "OU=Groups,DC=jdhlab,DC=local" -name "Mobile Users" `
>> -samAccountname "Mobile Users"
>>

Name              Type              DN
----              ----              --
Mobile Users      group             CN=Mobile Users,OU=Groups,DC=jdhlab,DC=local
```

Unlike the **New-ADGroup** cmdlet, you should specify the SAMAccountname. Otherwise Active Directory will create one like $0C5000-5BHSCDTFSBDH.

You can create other group types by specifying a combination of the **-GroupType** and **-GroupScope** parameters:

```
PS C:\> New-QADgroup -parent "OU=Groups,DC=jdhlab,DC=local" -name "UG Finance" `
>> -samaccountname "UG Finance" -groupscope "Universal" `
>> -description "Universal group for all Finance Users" -ManagedBy "A.Ventola"
>>

Name                          Type           DN
----                          ----           --
UG Finance                    group          CN=UG Finance,OU=Groups,DC=jdhlab,DC=local
```

This creates a universal security group. It is just as easy to create a distribution group by specifying a group type:

```
PS C:\> New-QADGroup -parent "OU=Groups,DC=jdhlab,DC=local" -name "DL Human Resources" `
>> -samaccountname "DL Human Resources" -groupscope "global" -grouptype "distribution" `
>> - description "Distribution group for all HR Staff" `
>> -objectattributes @{"info"="Created $(Get-Date) by $env:userdomain\$env:username"}
>>
```

```
Name                 Type                 DN
----                 ----                 --
DL Human Resources group                CN=DL Human Resources,OU=Groups,DC=jdhlab,DC=local
```

Here, I've created a global distribution group for Human Resources. I've also used the **-ObjectAttributes** parameter to define the **Info** property, which you see as a Note when looking at the group in Active Directory Users and Computers.

Managing Groups

Using the Active Directory Module

To find one or more groups using the Active Directory module will require the **Get-ADGroup** cmdlet. Like the cmdlets for users and computers, you can find one or more groups by identity, a PowerShell filter, or an LDAP filter. Let's get the Mobile Users group I just created using each of these techniques:

```
PS C:\> Get-ADGroup -Identity "Mobile Users"


DistinguishedName : CN=Mobile Users,OU=Groups,DC=jdhlab,DC=local
GroupCategory     : Security
GroupScope        : Global
Name              : Mobile Users
ObjectClass       : group
ObjectGUID        : 353a9dd3-9dbb-4e3d-b532-9babab53ea17
SamAccountName    : Mobile Users
SID               : S-1-5-21-3957442467-353870018-3926547339-5505

PS C:\> Get-ADGroup -filter "name -eq 'Mobile Users'"


DistinguishedName : CN=Mobile Users,OU=Groups,DC=jdhlab,DC=local
GroupCategory     : Security
GroupScope        : Global
Name              : Mobile Users
ObjectClass       : group
ObjectGUID        : 353a9dd3-9dbb-4e3d-b532-9babab53ea17
SamAccountName    : Mobile Users
SID               : S-1-5-21-3957442467-353870018-3926547339-5505

PS C:\> Get-ADGroup -ldapfilter "(&(name=Mobile Users))"


DistinguishedName : CN=Mobile Users,OU=Groups,DC=jdhlab,DC=local
GroupCategory     : Security
GroupScope        : Global
Name              : Mobile Users
ObjectClass       : group
ObjectGUID        : 353a9dd3-9dbb-4e3d-b532-9babab53ea17
SamAccountName    : Mobile Users
SID               : S-1-5-21-3957442467-353870018-3926547339-5505
```

Use whichever technique is most comfortable. Although the easiest way to find all groups is to use the **-Filter** parameter:

```
PS C:\> Get-ADGroup -filter * -SearchBase "OU=Groups,DC=jdhlab,DC=local" | Measure-Object


Count    : 39
Average  :
Sum      :
Maximum  :
Minimum  :
Property :
```

By default, the **Get-ADGroup** cmdlet searches the entire domain. But in this example I limited my search to a single organizational unit and piped results to the **Measure-Object** cmdlet, which shows that I have 39 groups in this OU.

As with the other Microsoft cmdlets, only a subset of properties is returned by default. You'll have to explicitly request other information:

```
PS C:\> Get-ADGroup -filter * -SearchBase "OU=Groups,DC=jdhlab,DC=local" `
>> -properties "Description" | Sort Name | Select Name,GroupScope,GroupCategory,Description
>>

Name                        GroupScope    GroupCategory   Description
----                        ----------    -------------   -----------
AD Admins                   Universal     Security
All Contacts                Universal     Distribution
All Executives              Universal     Security
All Managers                Universal     Security
AlphaGroup                  Universal     Security
Atlanta Sales               Global        Security
Benefits Users              Universal     Security
Board of Directors          Universal     Distribution    Mailing list for board
Customer Service Users      Global        Security
Desktop Support             Global        Security
DL Human Resources          Global        Distribution    Distribution group for all HR Staff
DL_Demo                     Universal     Distribution
DL_Demo2                    Universal     Distribution
dl_IT                       Universal     Distribution
DL_Mfg Staff                Universal     Distribution    mailing list for Corp. manufacturin...
DL_Sales                    Universal     Distribution
Finance Users               Universal     Security
Group-1                     Universal     Distribution
Group-10                    Universal     Distribution
Group-2                     Universal     Distribution
Group-3                     Universal     Distribution
Group-4                     Universal     Distribution
Group-5                     Universal     Distribution
Group-6                     Universal     Distribution
Group-7                     Universal     Distribution
Group-8                     Universal     Distribution
Group-9                     Universal     Distribution
Help Desk                   Universal     Security
HR Users                    Universal     Security
IT Admins                   Global        Security
Legal                       Global        Security
Local Admins                Universal     Security
Marketing Staff             Global        Security
Mfg Staff                   Universal     Security        Corp. manufacturing division users
Mobile Users                Global        Security
PHXUsers                    Universal     Distribution
Sales Users                 Global        Security
SAPIEN                      Universal     Distribution
UG Finance                  Universal     Security        Universal group for all Finance Users
```

If you are looking for certain group scopes or types, your best bet is to use a filter:

```
PS C:\> Get-ADGroup -filter "groupscope -eq 'global' -AND groupcategory -eq 'security'" `
>> -SearchBase "OU=Groups,DC=jdhlab,DC=local" | Select Name
>>

Name
----
IT Admins
Legal
Marketing Staff
Mobile Users
Atlanta Sales
Customer Service Users
Sales Users
Desktop Support
```

This expression returns all global security groups in my Groups organizational unit and displays the group name only.

To modify a group, use the **Set-ADGroup** cmdlet:

```
PS C:\> Set-ADGroup  -identity "Legal" -Description "Legal Dept. Staff" `
>> -DisplayName "Legal Users" -ManagedBy (Get-ADUser -filter "name -eq 'Al Broady'")
```

Because I didn't know Al Broady's SAMAccountname, I nested a **Get-ADUser** expression to return the user object. The **Set-ADGroup** cmdlet handled the rest. The cmdlet does not write anything to the pipeline by default, but you can see that these properties have been set:

```
PS C:\> Get-ADGroup -identity "Legal" -Properties * | Select Distinguishedname,Displayname,
>> SAMAccountname,Name,Description,ManagedBy,GroupCategory,GroupScope,When*
>>


Distinguishedname : CN=Legal,OU=Groups,DC=jdhlab,DC=local
Displayname       : Legal Users
SAMAccountname    : Legal
Name              : Legal
Description       : Legal Dept. Staff
ManagedBy         : CN=Al Broady,OU=Legal,OU=Employees,DC=jdhlab,DC=local
GroupCategory     : Security
GroupScope        : Global
whenChanged       : 8/23/2010 3:38:19 PM
whenCreated       : 8/18/2010 10:44:50 AM
```

Using the Quest Cmdlets

I think you'll find using Quest's **Get-QADGroup** cmdlet is just as easy for getting group objects:

```
PS C:\> Get-QADGroup -sizelimit 0

Name                Type                DN
----                ----                --
Administrators      group               CN=Administrators,CN=Builtin,Dc=jdhlab,DC=local
Users               group               CN=Users,CN=Builtin,Dc=jdhlab,DC=local
```

```
Guests              group            CN=Guests,CN=Builtin,Dc=jdhlab,DC=local
Print Operators     group            CN=Print Operators,CN=Builtin,Dc=jdhlab,DC=local
Backup Operators    group            CN=Backup Operators,CN=Builtin,Dc=jdhlab,DC=local
Replicator          group            CN=Replicator,CN=Builtin,Dc=jdhlab,DC=local
Remote Desktop ... group            CN=Remote Desktop Users,CN=Builtin,Dc=jdhlab,DC=local
...
```

As you can tell from the output, without any parameters, the cmdlet searches the entire domain. If your groups are all under a different path, you can search it:

```
PS C:\> Get-QADGroup -SearchRoot "OU=Groups,DC=jdhlab,DC=local" -SizeLimit 0 | Measure-Object


Count    : 39
Average  :
Sum      :
Maximum  :
Minimum  :
Property :
```

Now I have 39 groups in my Groups OU. Of course, I can retrieve a single group as well using its SAMAccountname or **Name** property:

```
PS C:\> Get-QADGroup "All Executives" | Select DN,Name,SamAccountname,GroupScope,GroupType


DN             : CN=All Executives,OU=Groups,DC=jdhlab,DC=local
Name           : All Executives
SamAccountName : AllExecutives
GroupScope     : Universal
GroupType      : Security
```

Since the cmdlet is outputting objects, it is very easy to create a report like this:

```
PS C:\> Get-QADGroup -sizelimit 0 | Where {$_.ParentContainerDN -notMatch "BuiltIn"  } |
>> Sort CreationDate -descending | Sort GroupScope,GroupType |
>> Select Name,GroupScope,GroupType,CreationDate
>>
Name                                      GroupScope   GroupType CreationDate
----                                      ----------   --------- ------------
Exchange Servers                           Universal    Security 6/22/2010 2:51:50 PM
Exchange Recipient Administrators          Universal    Security 6/22/2010 2:51:50 PM
Exchange Public Folder Administrators      Universal    Security 6/22/2010 2:51:50 PM
Exchange Organization Administrators       Universal    Security 6/22/2010 2:51:50 PM
Enterprise Read-only Domain Controllers    Universal    Security 1/24/2010 3:04:51 PM
Exchange Trusted Subsystem                 Universal    Security 6/22/2010 2:51:51 PM
ExchangeLegacyInterop                      Universal    Security 6/22/2010 2:51:51 PM
Exchange View-Only Administrators          Universal    Security 6/22/2010 2:51:50 PM
Local Admins                               Universal    Security 3/3/2010 10:02:58 AM
Help Desk                                  Universal    Security 3/2/2010 11:11:38 AM
HR Users                                   Universal    Security 3/1/2010 9:42:15 PM
...
```

With this expression, I've returned all groups in my domain, except those in the BuiltIn container. The groups are then sorted by CreationDate in descending order so the newest groups are at the top of the list. Groups are then sorted by scope and type, and then finally I select a subset of properties.

You can also limit your search to specific group scopes and types:

```
PS C:\> Get-QADGroup -grouptype Distribution

Name                          Type        DN
----                          ----        --
Group-1                       group       CN=Group-1,OU=Groups,DC=jdhlab,DC=local
Group-2                       group       CN=Group-2,OU=Groups,DC=jdhlab,DC=local
Group-3                       group       CN=Group-3,OU=Groups,DC=jdhlab,DC=local
Group-4                       group       CN=Group-4,OU=Groups,DC=jdhlab,DC=local
Group-5                       group       CN=Group-5,OU=Groups,DC=jdhlab,DC=local
Group-6                       group       CN=Group-6,OU=Groups,DC=jdhlab,DC=local
Group-7                       group       CN=Group-7,OU=Groups,DC=jdhlab,DC=local
Group-8                       group       CN=Group-8,OU=Groups,DC=jdhlab,DC=local
Group-9                       group       CN=Group-9,OU=Groups,DC=jdhlab,DC=local
Group-10                      group       CN=Group-10,OU=Groups,DC=jdhlab,DC=local
DL_Sales                      group       CN=DL_Sales,OU=Groups,DC=jdhlab,DC=local
dl_IT                         group       CN=dl_IT,OU=Groups,DC=jdhlab,DC=local
DL_Demo                       group       CN=DL_Demo,OU=Groups,DC=jdhlab,DC=local
DL_Demo2                      group       CN=DL_Demo2,OU=Groups,DC=jdhlab,DC=local
PHXUsers                      group       CN=PHXUsers,OU=Groups,DC=jdhlab,DC=local
Board of Directors            group       CN=Board of Directors,OU=Groups,DC=jdhlab,DC=local
All Contacts                  group       CN=All Contacts,OU=Groups,DC=jdhlab,DC=local
SAPIEN                        group       CN=SAPIEN,OU=Groups,DC=jdhlab,DC=local
DL_Mfg Staff                  group       CN=DL_Mfg Staff,OU=Groups,DC=jdhlab,DC=local
DL Human Resources            group       CN=DL Human Resources,OU=Groups,DC=jdhlab,DC=local

PS C:\> Get-QADGroup -grouptype security -groupscope universal `
>> -SearchRoot "OU=Groups,DC=jdhlab,DC=local"
>>

Name                          Type        DN
----                          ----        --
Finance Users                 group       CN=Finance Users,OU=Groups,DC=jdhlab,DC=local
Benefits Users                group       CN=Benefits Users,OU=Groups,DC=jdhlab,DC=local
All Managers                  group       CN=All Managers,OU=Groups,DC=jdhlab,DC=local
All Executives                group       CN=All Executives,OU=Groups,DC=jdhlab,DC=local
AD Admins                     group       CN=AD Admins,OU=Groups,DC=jdhlab,DC=local
Mfg Staff                     group       CN=Mfg Staff,OU=Groups,DC=jdhlab,DC=local
UG Finance                    group       CN=UG Finance,OU=Groups,DC=jdhlab,DC=local
HR Users                      group       CN=HR Users,OU=Groups,DC=jdhlab,DC=local
Help Desk                     group       CN=Help Desk,OU=Groups,DC=jdhlab,DC=local
Local Admins                  group       CN=Local Admins,OU=Groups,DC=jdhlab,DC=local
AlphaGroup                    group       CN=AlphaGroup,OU=Groups,DC=jdhlab,DC=local
```

If you want to modify a group's properties, you need to use the **Set-QADGroup** parameter:

```
PS C:\> Set-QADGroup "IT Admins" -description "IT staff with admin rights" `
>> -ManagedBy "Aldo Shebby" -displayname "IT Admins" `
>> -objectattributes @{"info"=(Get-QADGroup 'IT Admins' -properties Info).info + `
>> "'r'nUpdated $(Get-Date) by $env:userdomain\$env:username"}
>>

Name                          Type            DN
----                          ----            --
IT Admins                     group           CN=IT Admins,OU=Groups,DC=jdhlab,DC=local
```

With this expression, I updated the **Description** and **ManagedBy** properties and an object attribute property, **Info**. I don't want to overwrite any existing documentation, so first I get the current **Info** property value, and then concatenate the new information:

```
>> -objectattributes @{"info"=(Get-QADGroup 'IT Admins' -properties Info).info + `
>> "'r'nUpdated $(Get-Date) by $env:userdomain\$env:username"}
```

The `r`n inserts a return and line feed between the old value and the new text.

Changing Scope

On rare occasions, you may find yourself needing to modify a group's scope and/or type. You might originally have created a global security group, but now you want to make it a universal security group. Be aware that there are implications whenever you change group type or scope, and PowerShell will not warn you. PowerShell assumes you know what you are doing.

Using Set-ADGroup

To change a group's scope and/or type all you need to do is use the **Set-ADGroup** parameter and specify the new value. Remember, by default the cmdlet doesn't write anything to the pipeline unless you use the **-Passthru** parameter:

```
PS C:\> Set-ADGroup -Identity "Mobile Users" -GroupScope "Universal" -passthru


DistinguishedName : CN=Mobile Users,OU=Groups,DC=jdhlab,DC=local
GroupCategory     : Security
GroupScope        : Universal
Name              : Mobile Users
ObjectClass       : group
ObjectGUID        : 353a9dd3-9dbb-4e3d-b532-9babab53ea17
SamAccountName    : Mobile Users
SID               : S-1-5-21-3957442467-353870018-3926547339-5505
```

The identity I used, "Mobile Users" is actually the SAMAccountname for the group. But I could have used the group's distinguished name or a filtering query. With one quick expression I changed the global security group to a universal security group. Changing a group type is just as easy. The Microsoft cmdlet refers to the group type as a group category:

```
PS C:\> Set-ADGroup -Identity "AllManagers" -GroupCategory "distribution" `
>> -groupscope "Universal" -passthru
>>


DistinguishedName : CN=All Managers,OU=Groups,DC=jdhlab,DC=local
GroupCategory     : Distribution
GroupScope        : Universal
Name              : All Managers
ObjectClass       : group
ObjectGUID        : d9b875ab-aece-40f7-a2cb-a896b0cbf859
SamAccountName    : AllManagers
SID               : S-1-5-21-3957442467-353870018-3926547339-5001
```

Here, not only did I turn the All Managers group into a distribution list, I also changed its scope to universal.

Using Set-QADGroup

The **Set-QADGroup** cmdlet works essentially the same way. Let's say this distribution list now needs to be a security group:

```
PS C:\> Get-QADGroup "PHXUsers" | Select Name,Group*

Name                          GroupName               GroupType          GroupScope
----                          ---------               ---------          ----------
PHXUsers                      PHXUsers                Distribution       Global
```

Now let's modify it:

```
PS C:\> Set-QADGroup "PHXUsers" -groupType "Security" | Select Name,Group*

Name                          GroupName               GroupType          GroupScope
----                          ---------               ---------          ----------
PHXUsers                      PHXUsers                Security           Global
```

The **Set-QADGroup** cmdlet by default writes the object to the pipeline, so I simply selected a few properties to reflect the change. I can also change a group's scope. Let's also make this group a universal group:

```
PS C:\> Set-QADGroup "PHXUsers" -groupscope "Universal" | Select Name,Group*

Name                          GroupName               GroupType          GroupScope
----                          ---------               ---------          ----------
PHXUsers                      PHXUsers                Security           Universal
```

Of course, I could have combined these two parameters in one expression, but I wanted to make sure you understood them separately. Here's one more demonstration:

```
PS C:\> Get-QADGroup "Test Users" | Format-List GroupType,GroupScope


GroupType  : Security
GroupScope : Global
```

I want to change the group's scope to domainlocal:

```
PS C:\> Set-QADGroup "test users" -groupscope "domainlocal"
Set-QADGroup : Changing group scope from 'Domain local' straight to 'Global' is not supported
by Active Directory. Try
to change group scope to 'Universal' first.
At line:1 char:13
+ Set-QADGroup <<<<  "test users" -groupscope "domainlocal"
    + CategoryInfo          : NotSpecified: (:) [Set-QADGroup], ConstraintViolationException
    + FullyQualifiedErrorId : Quest.ActiveRoles.ArsPowerShellSnapIn.BusinessLogic.ConstraintVio
lationException,Quest.A
   ctiveRoles.ArsPowerShellSnapIn.Powershell.Cmdlets.SetGroupCmdlet
```

Oh…that didn't work. You shouldn't be surprised because you should know you can't directly change between a global and domain local group. You first have to change the scope to universal, and then you can change it to either global or domainlocal. You can easily accomplish this with the PowerShell pipeline:

```
PS C:\> Set-QADGroup "Test Users" -groupscope "Universal" |
>> Set-QADGroup -groupscope "domainlocal" | Select Name,DN,GroupScope,GroupType
>>

Name                       DN                                 GroupScope          GroupType
----                       --                                 ----------          ---------
Test Users                 CN=Test Users,OU=Groups,DC...      DomainLocal         Security
```

The first **Set-QADGroup** cmdlet changes the group scope to universal and the output is piped to the same cmdlet, this time setting the group scope to domainlocal.

Renaming Groups

To rename a group typically involves two changes. You usually need to change the group's canonical name as well as its SAMAccountname.

Using the Active Directory Module

There is no cmdlet specifically intended for renaming groups. Instead you will use the more generic, **Rename-ADObject** cmdlet. You can use this cmdlet to change the Active Directory name, but if you also need to change the SAMAccountname, which will most likely be the case, you also need to use the **Set-ADGroup** cmdlet. Fortunately, PowerShell makes it easy to put this all together into a single pipelined expression:

```
PS C:\> Get-ADGroup -identity "Group-9" | Rename-ADObject -NewName "Omega Mail" -PassThru |
>> Set-ADGroup -SamAccountName "Omega Mail" -passthru | Select Name,GroupCategory,GroupScope
>>

Name                             GroupCategory                    GroupScope
----                             -------------                    ----------
Omega Mail                       Distribution                     Universal
```

In my domain I had a distribution group called Group-9 that I wanted to continue to use, but with a new name. The **Rename-ADObject** cmdlet prefers a distinguished name as an identity. But I didn't want to take the time to look it up and type it so I used the **Get-ADGroup** cmdlet to retrieve it and pipe it to the **Rename-ADObject** cmdlet. This cmdlet does the actual object renaming and pipes the new object (via the **-Passthru** parameter) to the **Set-ADGroup** cmdlet, so that I can modify the SAMAccountname. Finally, to verify the change, I pass this object to the **Select-Object** cmdlet and pick a few properties.

Using the Quest Cmdlets

The Quest PSSnapin follows the same design. There is no group specific cmdlet or parameter from Quest, so you will use the **Rename-QADObject** cmdlet:

```
PS C:\> Get-QADGroup "IT Programmers" | rename-qadobject -newname "IT Developers" |
>> Set-QADGroup -samaccountname "IT Developers" -displayname "IT Developers" |
>> Format-List Name,samaccountname,DisplayName,DN
>>


Name           : IT Developers
SamAccountName : IT Developers
DisplayName    : IT Developers
DN             : CN=IT Developers,OU=Groups,Dc=jdhlab,DC=local
```

In this example, I use the **Get-QADGroup** cmdlet to retrieve the "IT Programmers" group. I need to rename it to "IT Developers" and change the SAMAccountname as well. This will take a few steps, but they can all be part of the same pipelined expression. First, use the **Rename-QADObject** cmdlet to rename the Active Directory object:

```
Rename-QADObject -newname "IT Developers" |
```

To change the SAMAccountname, the object is then passed to the **Set-QADGroup** cmdlet, which changes this property, as well as the display name:

```
Set-QADGroup -samaccountname "IT Developers" -displayname "IT Developers" |
```

The result is then piped to the **Format-List** cmdlet to show the new changes.

Managing Group Membership

By far the biggest group management task is group membership. Is the user in the right groups? What groups does the user belong to? If I'm using nested groups, how can I find all the groups a user belongs to directly and indirectly?

Using the Active Directory Module

In the Active Directory module, all the membership cmdlets have a noun of ADGroupMember:

- **Add-ADGroupMember**
- **Get-ADGroupMember**
- **Remove-ADGroupMember**

These cmdlets all operate from the group's perspective. That is to say, you get the group, and then you do something with its membership list.

Add a Member

Adding a member to a group is as simple as identifying the group and supplying the member's SAMAccountname:

```
PS C:\> Add-ADGroupMember -Identity "Omega Mail" -Members "rbiv"
```

You can specify a comma-separated list of members, or leverage the pipeline. I want to get all users in the Project Omega organizational unit and add them to the Omega Mail distribution list:

```
PS C:\> Add-ADGroupMember -Identity "Omega Mail" `
>> -members (Get-ADUser -filter * -searchbase "OU=Project Omega,DC=jdhlab,DC=local") `
>> -PassThru
>>


DistinguishedName : CN=Omega Mail,OU=Groups,DC=jdhlab,DC=local
GroupCategory     : Distribution
GroupScope        : Universal
Name              : Omega Mail
ObjectClass       : group
```

```
ObjectGUID        : 77a90f38-2a17-4e02-ac95-af21c3a424c7
SamAccountName    : Omega Mail
SID               : S-1-5-21-3957442467-353870018-3926547339-1159
```

Because the **Get-ADUser** expression is in parentheses, it is evaluated and the resulting user objects are passed to the **-Members** parameter. By the way, the **Add-ADGroupMember** cmdlet doesn't write to the pipeline unless you use the **-Passthru** parameter. Even then, it just writes the group, not the members.

Another way to leverage the pipeline is to add a user to multiple groups. The Finance department has a new hire, Bill Freely. He needs to be added to all groups that start with "Finance":

```
PS C:\> Get-ADGroup -filter "name -like 'Finance*'" | Add-ADGroupMember -Members "BFreely" `
>> -passthru | Select Name
>>

Name
----
Finance Database
Finance Group
Finance Mail
Finance Users
```

The **Get-ADGroup** expression finds all groups that start with "Finance". Each group is then piped to the **Add-ADGroupMember** cmdlet, which uses the piped-in group's identity to add the BFreely user account. I included the **-Passthru** parameter so I could see which groups he was added to.

You can also tackle this from the user side using the **Add-ADPrincipalGroupMembership** cmdlet:

```
PS C:\>  Add-ADPrincipalGroupMembership -Identity "jshortz" -MemberOf Group-4 -PassThru


DistinguishedName : CN=Jim Shortz,OU=Legal,OU=Employees,DC=jdhlab,DC=local
Name              : Jim Shortz
ObjectClass       : user
ObjectGUID        : 7401d440-34e0-4a93-a525-343b3cd5d1a5
SamAccountName    : jshortz
SID               : S-1-5-21-3957442467-353870018-3926547339-1171
```

The cmdlet doesn't write anything to the pipeline unless you use the **-Passthru** parameter. You can also add a user to multiple groups with a single cmdlet:

```
PS C:\> Add-ADPrincipalGroupMembership -Identity "sapple" `
>> -MemberOf "DL Human Resources","Omega Mail","AlphaGroup"
```

I just added Sam Apple to three groups.

Enumerating Membership

To retrieve group members, use the **Get-ADGroupMember** cmdlet:

```
PS C:\> Get-ADGroupMember -Identity "AtlantaSales"


distinguishedName : CN=Lisa Andrews,OU=Sales,OU=Employees,DC=jdhlab,DC=local
name              : Lisa Andrews
```

```
objectClass       : user
objectGUID        : 1019ec03-09be-4f08-96e0-10716a2e291f
SamAccountName    : L.Andrews
SID               : S-1-5-21-3957442467-353870018-3926547339-1115

distinguishedName : CN=Roy Antebi,OU=Sales,OU=Employees,DC=jdhlab,DC=local
name              : Roy Antebi
objectClass       : user
objectGUID        : bae6dcd3-4c26-4a34-8436-17484fcf083e
SamAccountName    : R.Antebi
SID               : S-1-5-21-3957442467-353870018-3926547339-1116
```

The identity parameter can be either the group's SAMAccountname, as I've done here, or the group's distinguished name. The cmdlet's output is an object representing each group member. In this example, I can see two users in the Atlanta Sales group. If I want a little more information, I can extend my pipeline:

```
PS C:\> Get-ADGroupMember -Identity "AtlantaSales" |
>> Get-ADUser -Properties Title,Department |
>> Select Name,Title,Department
>>

Name                                   Title                                  Department
----                                   -----                                  ----------
Lisa Andrews                           Account Representative                 Sales
Roy Antebi                             Account Representative                 Sales
```

The output from the **Get-ADGroupMember** cmdlet can't provide this information, but I can pipe the objects to the **Get-ADUser** cmdlet to retrieve it.

Enumerating Nested Membership

A commonly used task, especially for your help desk, is to enumerate nested group membership. This is easily accomplished using the **-Recursive** parameter with the **Get-ADGroupMember** cmdlet. I have a rollup group, All Managers, whose immediate members are other groups:

```
PS C:\> Get-ADGroupmember -id "AllManagers"


distinguishedName : CN=Sales Managers,OU=Sales,OU=Employees,DC=jdhlab,DC=local
name              : Sales Managers
objectClass       : group
objectGUID        : b919a7ff-2159-488d-8740-9d49eac75f4c
SamAccountName    : Sales Managers
SID               : S-1-5-21-3957442467-353870018-3926547339-5516

distinguishedName : CN=Engineering Managers,OU=Engineering,OU=Employees,DC=jdhlab,DC=local
name              : Engineering Managers
objectClass       : group
objectGUID        : 5788f0b0-a082-421b-8ca8-a07b62c9e6a5
SamAccountName    : Engineering Managers
SID               : S-1-5-21-3957442467-353870018-3926547339-5514

distinguishedName : CN=Finance Managers,OU=Finance,OU=Employees,DC=jdhlab,DC=local
name              : Finance Managers
objectClass       : group
objectGUID        : a47e1f97-eb3c-4883-bd7d-22783f18f013
SamAccountName    : Finance Managers
SID               : S-1-5-21-3957442467-353870018-3926547339-5513
```

If I want to find all the users in these groups, I merely tell the cmdlet to recursively get all members:

```
PS C:\> Get-ADGroupmember -id "AllManagers" -Recursive | Select distinguishedname

distinguishedname
-----------------
CN=Skip Towne,OU=Sales,OU=Employees,DC=jdhlab,DC=local
CN=Margo Rida,OU=Sales,OU=Employees,DC=jdhlab,DC=local
CN=Andrea Dunker,OU=Sales,OU=Employees,DC=jdhlab,DC=local
CN=Don Richardson,OU=Sales,OU=Employees,DC=jdhlab,DC=local
CN=Joye Calle,OU=Engineering,OU=Employees,DC=jdhlab,DC=local
CN=Myron Seith,OU=Engineering,OU=Employees,DC=jdhlab,DC=local
CN=Jared Fiely,OU=Engineering,OU=Employees,DC=jdhlab,DC=local
CN=Dora Witsell,OU=Finance,OU=Employees,DC=jdhlab,DC=local
CN=Danny Bary,OU=Finance,OU=Employees,DC=jdhlab,DC=local
CN=Bryan Bashara,OU=Finance,OU=Employees,DC=jdhlab,DC=local
```

Again, the output is not the full user object. Think of it more as a pointer. But you can extend our expression as you did above to display even more information:

```
PS C:\> Get-ADGroupmember -id "AllManagers" -Recursive |
>>  Get-ADUser -properties title,department,office | Select name,title,department,office
>>

name                          title                      department              office
----                          -----                      ----------              ------
Skip Towne                    Regional Sales Manager     Sales                   BLD345
Margo Rida                    Southwest Sales Manager                            AUS344
Andrea Dunker                 Western Sales Manager      Sales                   DEN870
Don Richardson                Eastern Sales Manager      Sales                   NYC444
Joye Calle                    Manager                    Engineering             CP134
Myron Seith                   Manager                    Engineering             CP136
Jared Fiely                   Manager                    Engineering             CP167
Dora Witsell                  Manager                    Finance                 CP260
Danny Bary                    Manager                    Finance                 HM909
Bryan Bashara                 Manager                    Finance                 KM763
```

MemberOf

What about looking at this from the user's perspective? Each user object has a property, **MemberOf**, which contains a collection of all groups the user immediately belongs to. Although you have to tell PowerShell to return it:

```
PS C:\> Get-ADUser "rbiv" -Properties memberof | Select -ExpandProperty MemberOf
CN=Art Department,OU=Art,OU=Employees,DC=jdhlab,DC=local
CN=Mobile Users,OU=Groups,DC=jdhlab,DC=local
CN=Omega Mail,OU=Groups,DC=jdhlab,DC=local
CN=Sales Users,OU=Groups,DC=jdhlab,DC=local
```

Because the property is a collection, I'm using the the **-ExpandProperty** parameter to create an easier-to-read list. The groups listed here are what you would see when looking at the MemberOf tab for Roy G. Biv in Active Directory Users and Computers; with the exception of Domain Users, which is a special group that is never returned. However, you can just as easily use the **Get-ADPrincipalGroupMembership** cmdlet to return all the groups that the user belongs to directly:

```
PS C:\> Get-ADPrincipalGroupMembership "rbiv" | Select name

name
----
Domain Users
Sales Users
Omega Mail
Mobile Users
Art Department
```

But what about nested group membership? If the Art Department group belongs to another group, that membership will affect Roy, but it won't be reflected here. What you need is a tool to get all the immediate groups that Roy belongs to, and then check each one to see if it belongs to any groups. That's what my **Get-ADMemberOf** script accomplishes:

Get-ADMemberOf.ps1

```
Function Get-ADMemberOf {

[cmdletBinding()]

Param(
    [Parameter(Position=0,Mandatory=$True,
    HelpMessage="Enter a user's SAMAccountname or distinguishedname",
    ValueFromPipeline=$True,ValueFromPipelineByPropertyName=$True)]
    [ValidateNotNullorEmpty()]
    [string]$identity
)

Begin {
    Write-Verbose "Starting"
    Import-Module ActiveDirectory
    #define a function used for getting all the nested group information
    Function Get-GroupMemberOf {
        Param([string]$identity)
        #get each group and see what it belongs to
        $group=Get-ADGroup -Identity $Identity -Properties *
        #write the group to the pipeline
        $group

        #if there is MemberOf property, recursively call this function
        if ($group.MemberOf) {
            $group | Select -expandProperty MemberOf | Foreach {
              Get-GroupMemberOf -identity $_
              }
        }
    } #end function
} #close Begin

Process {
    Write-Verbose "Getting all groups for $identity"
    Get-ADUser -identity $identity -Properties memberof | Select -ExpandProperty MemberOf |
Foreach {
        Get-GroupMemberOf -identity $_
    } #foreach
} #close process

End {
    Write-Verbose "Finished"
 }
} #end function
```

The main part of this script is actually a nested function that is called recursively:

```
Function Get-GroupMemberOf {
    Param([string]$identity)
    #get each group and see what it belongs to
    $group=Get-ADGroup -Identity $Identity -Properties *
    #write the group to the pipeline
    $group

    #if there is MemberOf property, recursively call this function
    if ($group.MemberOf) {
        $group | Select -expandProperty MemberOf | Foreach {
          Get-GroupMemberOf -identity $_
          }
    }
} #end function
```

This script uses the **Get-ADGroup** cmdlet to retrieve a group and its **MemberOf** property. If this property has a value, then it is passed back to the function, thus recursively going through every group. Running the main function takes the user name, retrieves the **MemberOf** property, and then passes each value to the nested function. The function writes the complete group object to the pipeline so that I can run a cmdlet like this:

```
PS C:\> Get-ADMemberof -identity "rbiv" | Select Name,Description,Groupscope,GroupCategory

Name                    Description                        Groupscope      GroupCategory
----                    -----------                        ----------      -------------
Art Department                                             Global               Security
Promotions              Sales and Advertising prom...      Global               Security
Mobile Users            users with mobile and exte...      Universal            Security
Omega Mail                                                 Universal        Distribution
Sales Users                                                Global               Security
AlphaGroup                                                 Universal            Security
Test Rollup             testing group rollup               Universal            Security
```

Now I can see Roy's effective group membership. My **Get-ADMemberOf** script returns all group properties so you can display anything you want without having to get the group again.

Remove a Member

Removing a group member follows the same format as adding a group member, using the **Remove-ADGroupMember** cmdlet. Suppose I want to remove Rick Vincent from the AD Admins group:

```
PS C:\> Remove-ADGroupMember -Identity "AD Admins"  -Members "r.vincent"

Confirm
Are you sure you want to perform this action?
Performing operation "Set" on Target "CN=AD Admins,OU=Groups,DC=jdhlab,DC=local".
[Y] Yes  [A] Yes to All  [N] No  [L] No to All  [S] Suspend  [?] Help (default is "Y"):
```

You can also specify more than one member as a comma-separated list. This approach assumes you know the SAMAccountname. But perhaps you don't, or you want to remove members based on some other logic. Given that the AD Admins group is sensitive, perhaps I want to remove all members that have di

First, let me see w

```
PS C:\> Get-ADGroupMember -Identity "AD Admins" | Get-ADUser | where {-not $_.Enabled} |
>> Select name
>>

name
----
Bettina Tamburri
Cedric Wolke
Loyd Sawaya
Claudio Kleinschmidt
```

I passed every member to the **Get-ADUser** cmdlet so I could use the Enabled property. User accounts that are enabled are filtered out. Knowing that this works, I can pipe this to the **ForEach-Object** construct and remove each member:

```
PS C:\> Get-ADGroupMember -Identity "AD Admins" | Get-ADUser | where {-not $_.Enabled} |
>> Foreach {
>>  Remove-ADGroupMember -identity "AD Admins" -members $_.distinguishedname -Confirm:$False
>>  }
```

I set the **-Confirm** parameter on the **Remove-ADGroupMember** cmdlet to suppress the confirmation message for each user.

The Active Directory module also offers a cmdlet so you can do this from the user side, with the **Remove-ADPrincipalGroupMembership** cmdlet:

```
PS C:\> Remove-ADPrincipalGroupMembership -Identity "fdrake" -MemberOf "Group-3"

Remove members from group
Do you want to remove all the specified member(s) from the specified group(s)?
[Y] Yes  [A] Yes to All  [N] No  [L] No to All  [S] Suspend  [?] Help (default is "Y"):
```

Here, the identity is the user account and MemberOf is the group name. This only removes the user from an immediate group.

Where this might come in handy is when you have a disabled user and want to remove all their group memberships. To keep things clear, I'll first save all the user's current groups to a variable:

```
PS C:\> $groups= Get-ADPrincipalGroupMembership -Identity "c.barry"
```

Now I can call the **Remove-ADPrincipalGroupMembership** cmdlet and use my variable as the value for the **-MemberOf** parameter:

```
PS C:\> Remove-ADPrincipalGroupMembership -Identity "c.barry" -MemberOf $groups -PassThru

Remove members from group
Do you want to remove all the specified member(s) from the specified group(s)?
[Y] Yes  [A] Yes to All  [N] No  [L] No to All  [S] Suspend  [?] Help (default is "Y"): a
WARNING: Could not remove member(s) from ADGroup: 'CN=Domain Users,CN=Users,DC=jdhlab,DC=lo
cal'. Error is: 'The
user cannot be removed from a group because the group is currently the user's primary group'.
Remove-ADPrincipalGroupMembership : Could not remove member(s) to one or more ADGroup.
At line:1 char:34
+ Remove-ADPrincipalGroupMembership <<<<  -Identity "c.barry" -MemberOf $groups -PassThru
    + CategoryInfo          : OperationStopped: (Microsoft.Activ...ement.ADGroup[]:ADGroup[])
[Remove-ADPrincipalGroup
   Membership], ADException
```

```
    + FullyQualifiedErrorId : 1,Microsoft.ActiveDirectory.Management.Commands.
RemoveADPrincipalGroupMembership
```

Well, it mostly worked. The user was removed from all groups except Domain Users, which can't be touched. You can avoid this error by setting the common parameter -**ErrorActionPreference** to SilentlyContinue on the **Remove-ADPrincipalGroupMembership** cmdlet or make sure Domain Users isn't in the collection of group memberships. In fact, here's a script you can run to do this for all disabled accounts in your domain, or at least within a specified path:

Remove-DisabledGroupMembership.ps1

```
#requires -version 2.0

[cmdletbinding(SupportsShouldProcess=$True)]

Param([string]$searchBase="OU=Employees,DC=jdhlab,DC=local")


Write-Verbose "Starting script"
#load the ActiveDirectory module if not already running
If (-not (get-module "ActiveDirectory")) {
    Try {
        Import-Module "ActiveDirectory" -errorAction "Stop"
        }
    Catch {
        Write-Warning "Can't find or load the Active Directory Module"
        Break
    }
}

Write-Host "Finding disabled users in $searchBase" -ForegroundColor Yellow

Get-ADUser -filter "enabled -eq '$false'" -SearchBase $searchBase | Foreach {
    Write-Verbose "Getting group memberships for $($_.name)"
    $groups=Get-ADPrincipalGroupMembership -Identity $_ | where {$_.name -notmatch "domain
users"}
    $count=($groups | Measure-Object).count
    #only remove if user belongs to any groups
    if ($count -gt 0) {
        Write-Host "Removing $($_.name) from $count groups" -ForegroundColor Green
        #use the default confirmation for each user
        Remove-ADPrincipalGroupMembership -Identity $_ -MemberOf $groups
      }
}
Write-Verbose "Ending script"
```

The main part of the **Remove-DisabledGroupMembership** script uses the **Get-ADUser** cmdlet to find all disabled accounts within a given search base. For each user, the function gets their group memberships other than Domain Users:

```
    $groups=Get-ADPrincipalGroupMembership -Identity $_ | where {$_.name -notmatch "domain
users"}
```

The $groups variable is then used with the **Remove-ADPrincipalGroupMembership** cmdlet to delete memberships:

```
        Remove-ADPrincipalGroupMembership -Identity $_ -MemberOf $groups
```

Because the script uses cmdlet binding, you can pass parameters like **-WhatIf** and **-Verbose**:

```
PS C:\> R:\Remove-DisabledGroupMembership.ps1  -whatif
Finding disabled users in OU=Employees,DC=jdhlab,DC=local
Removing Chas Lango from 3 groups
What if: Removes all the specified member(s) from the specified group(s).
Removing Darin Policz from 3 groups
What if: Removes all the specified member(s) from the specified group(s).
...
```

The default behavior is to confirm every deletion:

```
PS C:\> R:\Remove-DisabledGroupMembership.ps1
Finding disabled users in OU=Employees,DC=jdhlab,DC=local
Removing Berry Holyfield from 3 groups

Remove members from group
Do you want to remove all the specified member(s) from the specified group(s)?
[Y] Yes  [A] Yes to All  [N] No  [L] No to All  [S] Suspend  [?] Help (default is "Y"):
```

But you may elect to simply process all users without any confirmation:

```
PS C:\> R:\Remove-DisabledGroupMembership.ps1 -confirm:$false
Finding disabled users in OU=Employees,DC=jdhlab,DC=local
Removing Berry Holyfield from 3 groups
Removing Tiffani Fabello from 3 groups
Removing Mario Sutton from 3 groups
...
```

Using QADGroupMember Cmdlets

You can use a number of Quest cmdlets that work with the QADGroupMember object:

- **Add-QADGroupMember**
- **Get-QADGroupMember**
- **Remove-QADGroupMember**

I think you'll find these work in much the same way as the Active Directory cmdlets, with the added benefit that they include more information by default, which can simplify your work.

Add a Member

To add a new member, use the **Add-QADGroupMember** cmdlet. All you need to specify are the group name and the name of the member to add:

```
PS C:\> Add-QADGroupmember -identity "mobile users" -member "jfrost"

Name                          Type          DN
----                          ----          --
Jack Frost                    user          CN=Jack Frost,OU=Payroll,OU=Employees,Dc=jdhlab
```

The **-Identity** and **-Member** parameters are positional, meaning you don't have to explicitly include them, but I wanted you to understand how the cmdlet worked. Eventually you can simply specify the group name and a comma-separated list of new members. The cmdlet wrote the user object to the pipeline so let's take a look at it, specifically the **MemberOf** property:

```
PS C:\> Get-QADuser -Identity "jfrost" | Select MemberOf

MemberOf
--------
{CN=Mobile Users,OU=Groups,DC=jdhlab,DC=local}
```

Apparently, Jack only belongs to one group.

Using PowerShell to manage group membership via the pipeline accomplishes a lot of work with minimal effort. I will show you some different examples. First, here's how easy it is to find related users and add them to a group:

```
PS C:\> Get-QADuser -city "boston" | Add-QADGroupmember -identity "Northeast Region"
```

This expression finds all Boston-based users and adds them to the "Northeast Region" group. For more complex expressions, you might need to use the **Where-Object** cmdlet:

```
PS C:\> Get-QADUser -department Executive | Where {$_.title -notmatch "Executive Assistant"} |
>> Add-QADGroupmember "Executive Users" | Select name
>>

Name
----
Joseph Moore
Sheila Wells
Annette Olson
Roy Howard
Tamara Nguyen
Hannah Newton
```

In this expression, I want to find all users in the Executive department, but I don't want any users with the title "Executive Assistant", which the **Where** expression removes. Any remaining user objects are added to the "Executive Users" group. The **Select Name** expression returns the names of the users that were added to the group.

You will likely want to combine creating a new user account and group membership in a single process. Here's an example you can use as the basis for a provisioning script:

ProvisionDemo.ps1

```
#requires -version 2.0
#requires -pssnapin Quest.ActiveRoles.ADManagement

#groups for the new hire to belong to
$groups="Sales Users","Mobile Users","Las Vegas Staff"

#organizational unit for new user
$OU="OU=Sales,OU=Employees,Dc=jdhlab,DC=local"

$user=New-QADUser -name "Cass Ino" -ParentContainer $OU `
-samAccountName "cino " -UserPassword "P@ssw0rd" `
-firstname "Cass" -LastName "Ino" -Displayname "Cass Ino" `
-userprincipalname "cass@jdhlab.com" -City "Las Vegas" `
```

```
-department "Sales" -Title "Account Rep" -description "Western sales rep" `
-office "LV87" -company "JDH Labs" |
Set-QADUser -UserMustChangePassword $True

#add the user to each group
$groups | Foreach {Add-QADGroupMember -identity $_ -member $user} | Out-Null

#verify results
Get-QADUser $user | Select Name,Title,Department,City,MemberOf
```

The $groups variable contains an array of groups the new user will belong to. The $OU variable is the path to the parent container. The **New-QADuser** expression should look familiar by now. The user account is created and enabled, and then the account is set to Change Password at next logon.

The collection of groups is piped to the **ForEach-Object** construct, which uses the **Add-QADGroupMember** cmdlet to add the new user to each group:

```
$groups | Foreach {Add-QADGroupMember $_ $user} | Out-Null
```

The last line merely summarizes the new account:

```
Name       : Cass Ino
Title      : Account Rep
Department : Sales
City       : Las Vegas
MemberOf   : {CN=Las Vegas Staff,OU=Groups,DC=jdhlab,DC=local, CN=Mobile Users,OU=Groups,
             DC=jdhlab,DC=local, CN=Sales Users,OU=Groups,DC=jdhlab,DC=local}
```

Enumerating Membership

I'm sure you deduced by now to use the **Get-QADGroupMember** cmdlet to see a group's members:

```
PS C:\> Get-QADGroupmember -identity "mobile users" | Select Name

Name
----
Cass Ino
Skip Towne
Dee Bignell
Efrain Rayes
Jim Shortz
Roy G. Biv
Andrea Dunker
Don Richardson
```

This returns the immediate members of the group.

Enumerating Nested Membership

Enumerating nested group membership is accomplished using the **Get-QADObject** cmdlet and the **-Indirect** parameter; much the same as using the Microsoft cmdlet. First, let's see the immediate membership of a group that contains nested group members:

```
PS C:\> Get-QADGroupmember -identity "Promotions"

Name                      Type       DN
----                      ----       --
Art Department            group      CN=Art Department,OU=Art,OU=Employees,DC=jdhlab,...
Sales Managers            group      CN=Sales Managers,OU=Sales,OU=Employees,DC=jdhla...
Marketing Staff           group      CN=Marketing Staff,OU=Groups,DC=jdhlab,DC=local
```

Adding the **-Indirect** parameter produces this result:

```
PS C:\> Get-QADGroupmember -identity "Promotions" -Indirect

Name                      Type       DN
----                      ----       --
Art Department            group      CN=Art Department,OU=Art,OU=Employees,DC=jdhlab,...
Roy G. Biv                user       CN=Roy G. Biv,OU=Employees,DC=jdhlab,DC=local
Sales Managers            group      CN=Sales Managers,OU=Sales,OU=Employees,DC=jdhla...
Skip Towne                user       CN=Skip Towne,OU=Sales,OU=Employees,DC=jdhlab,DC...
Margo Rida                user       CN=Margo Rida,OU=Sales,OU=Employees,DC=jdhlab,DC...
Andrea Dunker             user       CN=Andrea Dunker,OU=Sales,OU=Employees,DC=jdhlab...
Don Richardson            user       CN=Don Richardson,OU=Sales,OU=Employees,DC=jdhla...
Marketing Staff           group      CN=Marketing Staff,OU=Groups,DC=jdhlab,DC=local
```

Notice that this expression writes both user and group objects to the pipeline. If you're like me, you most likely are only interested in user objects:

```
PS C:\> Get-QADGroupmember -identity "Promotions" -Indirect | where {$_.type -match "user"}

Name                      Type       DN
----                      ----       --
Roy G. Biv                user       CN=Roy G. Biv,OU=Employees,DC=jdhlab,DC=local
Skip Towne                user       CN=Skip Towne,OU=Sales,OU=Employees,DC=jdhlab,DC...
Margo Rida                user       CN=Margo Rida,OU=Sales,OU=Employees,DC=jdhlab,DC...
Andrea Dunker             user       CN=Andrea Dunker,OU=Sales,OU=Employees,DC=jdhlab...
Don Richardson            user       CN=Don Richardson,OU=Sales,OU=Employees,DC=jdhla...
```

Because you have real user objects, you can take this a step further:

```
PS C:\> Get-QADGroupmember -identity "Promotions" -Indirect | where {$_.type -match "user"} |
>> Select Name,Title,Department
>>

Name                                Title                               Department
----                                -----                               ----------
Roy G. Biv                          Manager                             Art
Skip Towne                          Regional Sales Manager              Sales
Margo Rida                          Southwest Sales Manager
Andrea Dunker                       Western Sales Manager               Sales
Don Richardson                      Eastern Sales Manager               Sales
```

MemberOf

The MemberOf property works the same way with the Quest cmdlets:

```
PS C:\> Get-QADUser "jshortz" | Select -ExpandProperty MemberOf
CN=Mobile Users,OU=Groups,DC=jdhlab,DC=local
```

```
CN=Legal,OU=Groups,DC=jdhlab,DC=local
CN=IT Admins,OU=Groups,DC=jdhlab,DC=local
CN=AlphaGroup,OU=Groups,DC=jdhlab,DC=local
```

A nice touch to the **Get-QADUser** cmdlet is the -**MemberOf** parameter. If you specify a group name, the cmdlet will see if the user belongs to that group:

```
PS C:\> Get-QADUser "jshortz" -MemberOf "Legal"

Name                           Type        DN
----                           ----        --
Jim Shortz                     user        CN=Jim Shortz,OU=Legal,OU=Employees,DC=jdhlab,DC...
```

This means you can add some logic and add a user to a group only when they don't belong:

```
PS C:\> if (Get-QADUser "jshortz" -MemberOf "Omega Mail") {
>> Write-Host "User already belongs to group"} else {
>> Add-QADGroupMember -Identity "Omega Mail" -Member "jshortz"
>> }
>>

Name                           Type        DN
----                           ----        --
Jim Shortz                     user        CN=Jim Shortz,OU=Legal,OU=Employees,DC=jdhlab,DC...
```

Because Jim did not belong to the Omega Mail group, his account was added to the group. By the way, if you don't specify a user account, you'll get all users that belong to the group:

```
PS C:\> Get-QADUser -MemberOf "Omega Mail" | Select name

Name
----
Roy G. Biv
Jim Shortz
Sanford Noh
Rick Catoire
Jamison Teets
Rick Moe
Rashad Schiel
Jarred Huseman
Rodney Koguchi
```

But it gets even better! You can use the -**IndirectMemberOf** parameter to determine if a user belongs to a group via a nested group. If true, the user account is returned. For example, you know from earlier in the chapter that Roy G. Biv has a nested membership in the Promotions group. You can verify it with the **Get-QADUser** cmdlet:

```
PS C:\> Get-QADUser "rbiv" -IndirectMemberOf "Promotion"

Name                           Type           DN
----                           ----           --
Roy G. Biv                     user           CN=Roy G. Biv,OU=Employees,DC=jdhlab,DC=local
```

Or find all users who are indirect members:

```
PS C:\> Get-QADUser -IndirectMemberOf "Promotion" | Select DN

DN
--
CN=Don Richardson,OU=Sales,OU=Employees,DC=jdhlab,DC=local
CN=Andrea Dunker,OU=Sales,OU=Employees,DC=jdhlab,DC=local
CN=Roy G. Biv,OU=Employees,DC=jdhlab,DC=local
CN=Margo Rida,OU=Sales,OU=Employees,DC=jdhlab,DC=local
CN=Skip Towne,OU=Sales,OU=Employees,DC=jdhlab,DC=local
```

Depending on the number of groups in your domain, you could test each one for indirect membership:

```
PS C:\> Get-QADGroup | Foreach { if (Get-QADUser -Identity rbiv -IndirectMemberOf $_) {write
$_}}

Name                           Type        DN
----                           ----        --
Domain Users                   group       CN=Domain Users,CN=Users,DC=jdhlab,DC=local
Sales Users                    group       CN=Sales Users,OU=Groups,DC=jdhlab,DC=local
AlphaGroup                     group       CN=AlphaGroup,OU=Groups,DC=jdhlab,DC=local
Omega Mail                     group       CN=Omega Mail,OU=Groups,DC=jdhlab,DC=local
Mobile Users                   group       CN=Mobile Users,OU=Groups,DC=jdhlab,DC=local
Art Department                 group       CN=Art Department,OU=Art,OU=Employees,DC=jdhlab,...
Promotions                     group       CN=Promotions,OU=Groups,DC=jdhlab,DC=local
Test Rollup                    group       CN=Test Rollup,OU=Groups,DC=jdhlab,DC=local
```

Every group that the **Get-QADGroup** cmdlet writes to the pipeline is used as an IndirectMemberOf value in the **Get-QADUser** expression. If the user is found, then the group is written to the pipeline. But perhaps a better way to get the user's effective group membership is from the user side, like you did earlier. Here is a Quest-based version:

Get-QADMemberOf.ps1

```
#requires -version 2.0
#requires -pssnapin Quest.ActiveRoles.ADManagement

Function Get-QADMemberOf {

[cmdletBinding()]

Param(
    [Parameter(Position=0,Mandatory=$True,
    HelpMessage="Enter a user's SAMAccountname or distinguishedname",
    ValueFromPipeline=$True,ValueFromPipelineByPropertyName=$True)]
    [ValidateNotNullorEmpty()]
    [string]$identity
)

Begin {
    Write-Verbose "Starting"

    #define a function used for getting all the nested group information
    Function Get-QADGroupMemberOf {
        Param([string]$identity)

        #get each group and see what it belongs to
        $group=Get-QADGroup -Identity $Identity
        #write the group to the pipeline
```

```
        $group

        #if there is MemberOf property, recursively call this function
        if ($group.MemberOf) {
            $group | Select -expandProperty MemberOf | Foreach {
              Get-QADGroupMemberOf -identity $_
              }
        }
    } #end function
} #close Begin

Process {
    Write-Verbose "Getting all groups for $identity"
    Get-QADUser -identity $identity | Select -ExpandProperty MemberOf | Foreach {
        Get-QADGroupMemberOf -identity $_
    } #foreach
} #close process

End {
    Write-Verbose "Finished"
 }
} #end function
```

The only things that really changed were the cmdlet names and a few parameters. The results are the same:

```
PS C:\> Get-QADMemberof "rbiv"

Name                           Type        DN
----                           ----        --
Art Department                 group       CN=Art Department,OU=Art,OU=Employees,DC=jdhlab,...
Promotions                     group       CN=Promotions,OU=Groups,DC=jdhlab,DC=local
Mobile Users                   group       CN=Mobile Users,OU=Groups,DC=jdhlab,DC=local
Omega Mail                     group       CN=Omega Mail,OU=Groups,DC=jdhlab,DC=local
Sales Users                    group       CN=Sales Users,OU=Groups,DC=jdhlab,DC=local
AlphaGroup                     group       CN=AlphaGroup,OU=Groups,DC=jdhlab,DC=local
Test Rollup                    group       CN=Test Rollup,OU=Groups,DC=jdhlab,DC=local
```

Remove a Member

To delete a group member, I use the **Remove-QADGroupMember** cmdlet to easily undo my last step:

```
PS C:\> Remove-QADGroupmember "mobile users" "jfrost"
Name                           Type        DN
----                           ----        --
Jack Frost                     user        CN=Jack Frost,OU=Payroll,OU=Employees,DC=jdhlab...
```

As you saw with the Microsoft cmdlets, you can leverage the pipeline to remove multiple users, or users where you don't even know their name. Here's the scenario. A number of users from the Phoenix office have been relocated to Las Vegas. They need to be removed from the PHXUsers group and added to the Las Vegas Staff group:

```
PS C:\> Get-QADGroupmember -Identity "PHXUsers" | where {$_.city -match "Las Vegas"} |
>> Foreach {
>>     Remove-QADGroupMember -Identity "PHXUsers" -member $_ | Out-Null
>>     Add-QADGroupMember -Identity "Las Vegas Staff" -member $_
```

```
>> } | Select Name,Title,Department,City
>>

Name                        Title                 Department           City
----                        -----                 ----------           ----
Horace Woldt                Manager               Customer Service     Las Vegas
Vicente Stoot               Telephone Staff       Customer Service     Las Vegas
Wyatt Kraebel               Manager               Customer Service     Las Vegas
Cordell Deguzman            Telephone Staff       Customer Service     Las Vegas
Jame Harle                  Manager               Customer Service     Las Vegas
Mose Hawman                 Telephone Lead        Customer Service     Las Vegas
Barney Kersten              Manager               Customer Service     Las Vegas
Otis Goltra                 Assistant Manager     Customer Service     Las Vegas
Saul Militano               Telephone Staff       Customer Service     Las Vegas
Dewey Bhat                  Assistant Manager     Customer Service     Las Vegas
Vicente Fileds              Telephone Staff       Customer Service     Las Vegas
Cleveland Balasco           Telephone Staff       Customer Service     Las Vegas
Hector Giardini             Assistant Manager     Customer Service     Las Vegas
Royce Lohnes                Assistant Manager     Customer Service     Las Vegas
Myron Ellestad              Telephone Lead        Customer Service     Las Vegas
Morgan Hibbard              Manager               Sales                Las Vegas
Noah Ravens                 Telephone Staff       Customer Service     Las Vegas
Jere Connon                 Telephone Lead        Customer Service     Las Vegas
Kenneth Replin              Assistant Manager     Customer Service     Las Vegas
Huey Challacombe            Assistant Manager     Customer Service     Las Vegas
```

Each member of PHXUsers was piped to the **ForEach-Object** construct. Within this construct the user was removed from the group and added to the Las Vegas group. Because the cmdlets write the user object to the pipeline, I didn't need to see each user object twice, so I piped the first expression to the **Out-Null** cmdlet to suppress pipeline output:

```
Remove-QADGroupMember -Identity "PHXUsers" -member $_ | Out-Null
```

The **Add-QADGroupMember** cmdlet writes the user object to the pipeline so I take advantage and display a few user properties.

Allow Manager to Update Members

When you have a manager assigned to a group, there is a check box in Active Directory Users and Computers for allowing the manager to manage group membership. Checking this box modifies the object's access control list, giving the manager an Allow privilege for the "Write Members" permission.

First, let's make sure you can get the **ManagedBy** property for a given group. Here's how using the Active Directory module and provider:

```
PS C:\> Get-ADGroup -Identity "HRUsers" -Properties "ManagedBy" | Select Name,ManagedBy

Name                                   ManagedBy
----                                   ---------
HR Users                               CN=Sandy Bottom,OU=HR,OU=Employees,DC=jdhlab,DC=local
```

Unfortunately, there is not an easy-to-use cmdlet to give Sandy permission to manage group members. Instead you need to use the **Get-ACL** cmdlet with the Active Directory PSDrive. Let me walk you through it.

First, you'll define the GUID for the **Members** property on a group object:

```
[system.guid]$GUID="bf9679c0-0de6-11d0-a285-00aa003049e2"
```

Using the **Get-ACL** cmdlet, you'll retrieve the group's access control list from the group via the PSDrive:

```
$acl=Get-Acl -path "AD:\CN=HR Users,OU=Groups,DC=jdhlab,DC=local"
```

Next, you need a user. In this case, the user account specified by the **ManagedBy** property of the group object, which is Sandy Bottom:

```
$mb=(Get-ADGroup "hrusers" -Properties ManagedBy).ManagedBy
```

To keep things clear, I'll save her SID to a variable:

```
$sid=(Get-ADUser $mb).sid
```

Now, you need to create a security principal object using Sandy's SID:

```
$principal = New-Object System.Security.Principal.SecurityIdentifier $sid
```

Finally, you're ready to create a new access control entry to give Sandy Read/Write permissions on the **Members** property:

```
$ace = New-Object System.DirectoryServices.ActiveDirectoryAccessRule $principal,
"ReadProperty,WriteProperty", "Allow", $GUID
```

You'll add this object to the existing ACL:

```
$acl.AddAccessRule($ace)
```

All that's left at this point is to add the access control entry (ACE) to the ACL using the **Set-ACL** cmdlet:

```
Set-Acl -ACLObject $acl -Path "AD:\CN=HR Users,OU=Groups,DC=jdhlab,DC=local"
```

That's all there is to it. The next time you check the group object, you'll see that Sandy now has permission to manage group membership.

This is not necessarily a complicated task, merely tedious. Therefore, I put together a simple script to grant the ManagedBy user permission to manage group members:

Grant-ManageMember.ps1

```
Function Grant-ManageMember {

[cmdletBinding(SupportsShouldProcess=$True)]

Param (
    [Parameter(Position=0,Mandatory=$True,
    HelpMessage="Enter an identity for an Active Directory group",
    ValueFromPipeline=$True,ValueFromPipelineByPropertyName=$True)]
```

```
    [ValidateNotNullorEmpty()]
    [object[]]$identity
    )

Begin {
    Write-Verbose "Beginning function"
    #the GUID for the Members property on the Group object
    [system.guid]$GUID="bf9679c0-0de6-11d0-a285-00aa003049e2"
}

Process {
    Foreach ($item in $identity) {
        #try to get the group
        Try {
            $group=Get-ADGroup -Identity $item -properties ManagedBy -ErrorAction "Stop"
        }
        Catch {
            Write-warning "Failed to find $item"
            $group=$false
        }
        if ($group) {
            Write-Verbose "Found $group.distinguishedname"
            $path=Join-Path -Path "AD:\" -ChildPath $group.distinguishedname

            #get managedBy user
            $mb=$group.ManagedBy

            #only process if something is found for ManagedBy
            if ($mb) {
                #get the group ACL
                Write-Verbose "Getting ACL for $path"
                $acl=Get-Acl -path $path


                #get the user's SID
                $sid=(Get-ADUser $mb).sid

                #create a security principal object
                Write-Verbose "Creating the security principal for $mb"
                $principal = New-Object System.Security.Principal.SecurityIdentifier $sid

                #Create and ACE to Read/Write the Members property
                Write-Verbose "Creating the ACE"
                $ace = New-Object System.DirectoryServices.ActiveDirectoryAccessRule $princi-
pal, "ReadProperty,WriteProperty", "Allow", $GUID

                #Add the ACE to ACL
                Write-Verbose "Adding the ACE to the ACL"
                $acl.AddAccessRule($ace)

                #Set the ACL
                Write-Verbose "Setting the new ACL"
                Set-Acl -ACLObject $acl -Path $path -Passthru
            } #if $mb
            else {
                Write-Warning "No ManagedBy value found for $($group.distinguishedname)"
            }
        } #if $group
    } #foreach $group
} #close Process
```

```
End {
    Write-Verbose "Finished"
    }

} #end function
```

The **Grant-ManageMember** function is essentially the same script I walked through earlier with the addition of some error handling and a few parameters. All you need to do is specify one or more groups. If a group can't be found or doesn't have a ManagedBy value, a message will be displayed. The function also supports the -WhatIf parameter, so you can test the cmdlet before making any changes:

```
PS C:\> Get-ADGroup -filter "name -like 'group*'" | Grant-Managemember -whatif
What if: Performing operation "Set-Acl" on Target "AD:\CN=Group-1,OU=Groups,DC=jdhlab,DC=lo
cal".
WARNING: No ManagedBy value found for CN=Group-10,OU=Groups,DC=jdhlab,DC=local
WARNING: No ManagedBy value found for CN=Group-2,OU=Groups,DC=jdhlab,DC=local
WARNING: No ManagedBy value found for CN=Group-3,OU=Groups,DC=jdhlab,DC=local
What if: Performing operation "Set-Acl" on Target "AD:\CN=Group-4,OU=Groups,DC=jdhlab,DC=lo
cal".
WARNING: No ManagedBy value found for CN=Group-5,OU=Groups,DC=jdhlab,DC=local
What if: Performing operation "Set-Acl" on Target "AD:\CN=Group-6,OU=Groups,DC=jdhlab,DC=lo
cal".
WARNING: No ManagedBy value found for CN=Group-7,OU=Groups,DC=jdhlab,DC=local
What if: Performing operation "Set-Acl" on Target "AD:\CN=Group-8,OU=Groups,DC=jdhlab,DC=lo
cal".
WARNING: No ManagedBy value found for CN=Group Policy Creator Owners,CN=Users,DC=jdhlab,DC=lo
cal
```

The function writes the ACL object to the pipeline:

```
PS C:\> Grant-Managemember "Art Department"

Path                                      Owner                     Access
----                                      -----                     ------
ActiveDirectory://RootDSE/CN=Art De...    JDHLAB\Domain Admins      NT AUTHORITY\SELF Allow  ...
```

If you have the latest version of the Quest Active Directory cmdlets, making this change is incredibly easy using the **Add-QADPermission** cmdlet:

```
PS C:\> Get-QADGroup "Art Department" | Add-QADPermission -account "Roy Biv" `
>>-rights "ReadProperty,WriteProperty" -property "Member"
```

The **Get-QADGroup** cmdlet is retrieving the Executive Users group and piping it to the **Add-QADPermission** cmdlet. This grants Roy Biv read and write access to the **Member** property. How easy is that?

See the chapter on managing Active Directory permissions for more in-depth coverage of this topic.

Copying Group Membership

One common request you might get as an administrator is to copy group memberships from one user to another. If you take a moment to think about this, it's not too difficult to do with PowerShell using either the Microsoft or Quest cmdlets. The process flow is the same:

1. Get source user
2. Enumerate source user group memberships
3. For each group, add the target user as a member.

Here's an example using the Microsoft Active Directory cmdlets. The scenario is that new hire, Wes Lathers, needs the same groups as Skip Towne. First you'll get Skip's groups:

```
PS C:\> $Skip=Get-ADUser -filter "name -eq 'Skip Towne'" -Properties MemberOf
```

Skip belongs to these groups:

```
PS C:\> $Skip.memberof
CN=Sales Managers,OU=Sales,OU=Employees,DC=jdhlab,DC=local
CN=Mobile Users,OU=Groups,DC=jdhlab,DC=local
CN=Sales Users,OU=Groups,DC=jdhlab,DC=local
```

You'll get an object for Wes:

```
PS C:\> $Wes=Get-ADUser -filter "name -eq 'Wes Lathers'"
```

Now you'll take each of Skip's groups and add Wes:

```
PS C:\> $Skip.memberof | Foreach { Add-ADGroupMember -Identity $_ -Members $Wes -PassThru}


DistinguishedName : CN=Sales Managers,OU=Sales,OU=Employees,DC=jdhlab,DC=local
GroupCategory     : Security
GroupScope        : Global
Name              : Sales Managers
ObjectClass       : group
ObjectGUID        : b919a7ff-2159-488d-8740-9d49eac75f4c
SamAccountName    : Sales Managers
SID               : S-1-5-21-3957442467-353870018-3926547339-5516

DistinguishedName : CN=Mobile Users,OU=Groups,DC=jdhlab,DC=local
GroupCategory     : Security
GroupScope        : Universal
Name              : Mobile Users
ObjectClass       : group
ObjectGUID        : 353a9dd3-9dbb-4e3d-b532-9babab53ea17
SamAccountName    : Mobile Users
SID               : S-1-5-21-3957442467-353870018-3926547339-5505

DistinguishedName : CN=Sales Users,OU=Groups,DC=jdhlab,DC=local
GroupCategory     : Security
GroupScope        : Global
Name              : Sales Users
ObjectClass       : group
ObjectGUID        : 1911355d-9753-401d-82e4-32fe77a1a977
SamAccountName    : SalesUsers
SID               : S-1-5-21-3957442467-353870018-3926547339-1145
```

I used the **-Passthru** parameter to verify the changes. Now when I look at Wes I see these memberships:

```
PS C:\> Get-ADUser -filter "name -eq 'Wes Lathers'" -Properties memberOf |
>> Select -ExpandProperty MemberOf
>>
CN=Sales Managers,OU=Sales,OU=Employees,DC=jdhlab,DC=local
CN=Mobile Users,OU=Groups,DC=jdhlab,DC=local
CN=Sales Users,OU=Groups,DC=jdhlab,DC=local
```

Here's the same scenario using the Quest cmdlets:

```
PS C:\> $Skip=Get-QADUser -Identity "Skip Towne"
PS C:\> $Skip.MemberOf
CN=Sales Managers,OU=Sales,OU=Employees,DC=jdhlab,DC=local
CN=Mobile Users,OU=Groups,DC=jdhlab,DC=local
CN=Sales Users,OU=Groups,DC=jdhlab,DC=local
PS C:\> $Ses=Get-QADUser -Identity "Wes Lathers"
PS C:\> $Skip.MemberOf | Foreach {Add-QADGroupMember -Identity $_ -Member $Wes}

Name                          Type        DN
----                          ----        --
Wes Lathers                   user        CN=Wes Lathers,OU=Sales,OU=Employees,DC=jdhlab,D...
Wes Lathers                   user        CN=Wes Lathers,OU=Sales,OU=Employees,DC=jdhlab,D...
Wes Lathers                   user        CN=Wes Lathers,OU=Sales,OU=Employees,DC=jdhlab,D...
```

The Quest cmdlet writes the user object to the pipeline as shown above instead of the group, but the result is the same:

```
PS C:\> Get-QADUser -Identity "Wes Lathers" | Select -ExpandProperty MemberOf
CN=Sales Managers,OU=Sales,OU=Employees,DC=jdhlab,DC=local
CN=Mobile Users,OU=Groups,DC=jdhlab,DC=local
CN=Sales Users,OU=Groups,DC=jdhlab,DC=local
```

This task would be a great project for a PowerShell function, but I'll leave that exercise for you to enjoy.

Finding Empty Groups

Using the Active Directory Module

The best way to find empty groups using the **Get-ADGroup** cmdlet is to create a filter on the **Members** property. If the property is populated it will obviously have some value. Therefore you can use a wild-card comparison operator, **-NotLike**, to find all groups that don't meet the criteria:

```
PS C:\> Get-ADGroup -filter "members -notlike '*'" | Measure-Object

Count    : 43
Average  :
Sum      :
Maximum  :
Minimum  :
Property :
```

I have 43 groups in my entire domain with no members. Some of those are built-in and legacy groups, such as Server Operators, that more than likely are empty on purpose. Let's refine the expression to only search for groups I've created and placed in my Groups organizational unit. I'll even display a few useful pieces of information:

```
PS C:\> Get-ADGroup -filter "members -notlike '*'" -properties Members,Description `
>>-searchbase "OU=Groups,DC=jdhlab,DC=local" | Select Name,Description,GroupScope,GroupCateg
ory
>>

Name                          Description                       GroupScope       GroupCategory
----                          -----------                       ----------       -------------
Group-6                                                         Universal         Distribution
Group-7                                                         Universal         Distribution
Group-8                                                         Universal         Distribution
Group-10                                                        Universal         Distribution
DL_Demo2                                                        Universal         Distribution
Marketing Staff                                                 Global                Security
Mfg Staff                     Corp. manufacturing divisio...   Universal             Security
DL_Mfg Staff                  mailing list for Corp. manu...   Universal         Distribution
UG Finance                    Universal group for all Fin...   Universal             Security
DL Human Resources            Distribution group for all ...   Global            Distribution
Test Users                                                      DomainLocal           Security
IT Developers                                                   Global                Security
Desktop Support                                                 Global                Security
```

This is something I can work with. If I wanted, I could pipe this to the **Remove-ADGroup** cmdlet, which I'll cover shortly.

Using the Quest Cmdlets

The **Get-QADGroup** cmdlet has a Boolean parameter, **-Empty**, which you can use to discover domain groups with no members defined:

```
PS C:\> Get-QADGroup -empty:$True -SearchRoot "OU=Groups,DC=jdhlab,DC=local"

Name                          Type        DN
----                          ----        --
Group-6                       group       CN=Group-6,OU=Groups,DC=jdhlab,DC=local
Group-7                       group       CN=Group-7,OU=Groups,DC=jdhlab,DC=local
Group-8                       group       CN=Group-8,OU=Groups,DC=jdhlab,DC=local
Group-10                      group       CN=Group-10,OU=Groups,DC=jdhlab,DC=local
DL_Demo2                      group       CN=DL_Demo2,OU=Groups,DC=jdhlab,DC=local
Marketing Staff               group       CN=Marketing Staff,OU=Groups,DC=jdhlab,DC=local
Mfg Staff                     group       CN=Mfg Staff,OU=Groups,DC=jdhlab,DC=local
DL_Mfg Staff                  group       CN=DL_Mfg Staff,OU=Groups,DC=jdhlab,DC=local
UG Finance                    group       CN=UG Finance,OU=Groups,DC=jdhlab,DC=local
DL Human Resources            group       CN=DL Human Resources,OU=Groups,DC=jdhlab,DC=local
Test Users                    group       CN=Test Users,OU=Groups,DC=jdhlab,DC=local
IT Developers                 group       CN=IT Developers,OU=Groups,DC=jdhlab,DC=local
Desktop Support               group       CN=Desktop Support,OU=Groups,DC=jdhlab,DC=localRAS
```

Though let me take this one step further and get some meaningful information, as I did with the **Get-ADGroup** cmdlet, so I can decide which groups might be deleted:

```
PS C:\> Get-QADGroup -empty:$True -SearchRoot "OU=Groups,DC=jdhlab,DC=local" |
>> Select DN,Name,Description,GroupType,GroupScope,WhenCreated,WhenChanged,ManagedBy
>>


DN          : CN=Group-6,OU=Groups,DC=jdhlab,DC=local
Name        : Group-6
Description :
GroupType   : Distribution
```

```
GroupScope  : Universal
whenCreated : 3/24/2010 8:33:53 AM
whenChanged : 8/26/2010 3:57:42 PM
ManagedBy   : CN=Barney Kersten,OU=Test,OU=Employees,DC=jdhlab,DC=local

DN          : CN=Group-7,OU=Groups,DC=jdhlab,DC=local
Name        : Group-7
Description :
GroupType   : Distribution
GroupScope  : Universal
whenCreated : 3/24/2010 8:33:53 AM
whenChanged : 8/26/2010 12:23:16 PM
ManagedBy   :
...
```

This expression selects some key group properties and displays them to the screen. Although if there are many groups or I'd like to do some additional analysis, creating a CSV file I can open in Microsoft Excel makes this an easier task:

```
PS C:\> Get-QADGroup -empty:$True -SearchRoot "OU=Groups,DC=jdhlab,DC=local" |
>> Select DN,Name,Description,GroupType,GroupScope,WhenCreated,WhenChanged,ManagedBy |
>> Sort WhenCreated | Export-Csv "S:\Reports\EmptyGroups.csv" -NoTypeInformation
```

This is essentially the same PowerShell expression from before except that I'm performing an initial sort on the **WhenCreated** property and the results are exported to the specified CSV file.

Assuming Microsoft Excel is installed, I can edit the file immediately using the **Invoke-Item** cmdlet:

```
PS C:\> Invoke-Item "s:\reports\emptygroups.csv"
```

Deleting Groups

When the time comes to delete a group, you can use either a Microsoft or a Quest cmdlet.

Using the Remove-ADGroup

The **Remove-ADGroup** cmdlet is pretty much no-nonsense. Specify a group and it is gone:

```
PS C:\> Remove-ADGroup -Identity "Test Users" -whatif
What if: Performing operation "Remove" on Target "CN=Test Users,OU=Groups,DC=jdhlab,DC=local".
```

Well, it is gone assuming you don't use the **-WhatIf** parameter. Otherwise, PowerShell will ask for confirmation:

```
PS C:\> Remove-ADGroup -Identity "Test Users"

Confirm
Are you sure you want to perform this action?
Performing operation "Remove" on Target "CN=Test Users,OU=Groups,DC=jdhlab,DC=local".
[Y] Yes  [A] Yes to All  [N] No  [L] No to All  [S] Suspend  [?] Help (default is "Y"):
```

Remember those empty groups? Perhaps I'd like to delete them. I can accomplish this with a one-line command:

```
PS C:\> Get-ADGroup -filter "members -notlike '*'" -searchbase "OU=Groups,DC=jdhlab,DC=local" |
>> Remove-ADGroup -whatif
>>
What if: Performing operation "Remove" on Target "CN=Group-6,OU=Groups,DC=jdhlab,DC=local".
What if: Performing operation "Remove" on Target "CN=Group-7,OU=Groups,DC=jdhlab,DC=local".
What if: Performing operation "Remove" on Target "CN=Group-8,OU=Groups,DC=jdhlab,DC=local".
What if: Performing operation "Remove" on Target "CN=Group-10,OU=Groups,DC=jdhlab,DC=local".
What if: Performing operation "Remove" on Target "CN=DL_Demo2,OU=Groups,DC=jdhlab,DC=local".
What if: Performing operation "Remove" on Target "CN=Marketing Staff,OU=Groups,DC=jdhlab,DC=lo....
What if: Performing operation "Remove" on Target "CN=Mfg Staff,OU=Groups,DC=jdhlab,DC=local".
What if: Performing operation "Remove" on Target "CN=DL_Mfg Staff,OU=Groups,DC=jdhlab,DC=local".
What if: Performing operation "Remove" on Target "CN=UG Finance,OU=Groups,DC=jdhlab,DC=local".
What if: Performing operation "Remove" on Target "CN=DL Human Resources,OU=Groups,DC=jdhlab,DC....
What if: Performing operation "Remove" on Target "CN=Test Users,OU=Groups,DC=jdhlab,DC=local".
What if: Performing operation "Remove" on Target "CN=IT Developers,OU=Groups,DC=jdhlab,DC=local".
What if: Performing operation "Remove" on Target "CN=Desktop Support,OU=Groups,DC=jdhlab,DC=lo....
```

Using Remove-QADObject

In the Quest PSSnapin, there is no group-specific cmdlet, though you can use the **Remove-QADObject** cmdlet. If you know the group's distinguished name, you can use syntax like this:

```
PS C:\> Remove-QADObject -identity "CN=My Test Group,OU=Groups,Dc=jdhlab,DC=Local"
```

You can also use the group's flat name:

```
PS C:\> Remove-QADObject -identity "jdhlab\mytestgroup"
```

Or SAMAccountname:

```
PS C:\> Remove-QADObject -identity "MyTestGroup"
```

The cmdlet prompts you to confirm the deletion. Use the **-Force** parameter to bypass the prompt:

```
PS C:\> Remove-QADObject -identity "MyTestGroup" -force
```

Chapter 6
Managing Active Directory Computer Accounts

For smaller organizations, managing Active Directory computer accounts is a minor task. Generally, a computer account is created when the computer joins the domain and is removed when the computer is decommissioned. However, in larger organizations, this is not always a smooth process. Fortunately, you can use PowerShell to get your hands around all the computer accounts in your domain.

Creating Computer Accounts

In my experience, most computer accounts are created automatically when a computer joins the domain. These accounts are created in the default container, typically Computers, unless you've modified the default location. However, you may prefer to create a computer account ahead of time. This permits you the luxury of having the account in the correct organizational unit, so that any group policy settings will apply immediately the first time the computer boots. You can also define properties such as **Description** and **ManagedBy**. Properties such as **OperatingSystem** and **ServicePack** are populated by the computer when it authenticates to the domain.

Using the New-ADComputer cmdlet

The Microsoft Active Directory module includes a dedicated cmdlet for this task, **New-ADComputer**. Table 6-1 shows the parameters you are most likely to use.

Table 6-1 Common New-ADComputer Parameters

Name	Type
AccountExpirationDate	System.Nullable`1[System.DateTime]
Description	System.String
DisplayName	System.String
DNSHostName	System.String
Enabled	System.Nullable`1[System.Boolean]
Location	System.String
ManagedBy	Microsoft.ActiveDirectory.Management.ADPrincipal
Name (Required)	System.String
OperatingSystem	System.String
OperatingSystemServicePack	System.String
OperatingSystemVersion	System.String
OtherAttributes	System.Collections.Hashtable
Path	System.String
SAMAccountName	System.String
ServicePrincipalNames	System.String[]
TrustedForDelegation	System.Nullable`1[System.Boolean]

All it takes is a very simple, one-line command to create a basic computer account. I'll create a new computer account in the Branch Office organizational unit:

```
PS C:\> New-ADComputer -Name "BranchDesk01" -Path "OU=Branch Office,DC=jdhlab,DC=local"
```

When the computer joins the domain and boots up, the rest of the computer properties will be defined. The computer account is enabled by default. But you can create it disabled. Here's another example with a few more properties defined:

```
PS C:\> New-ADComputer -Name "BranchDesk02" -Path "OU=Branch Office,DC=jdhlab,DC=local" `
>> -enabled $False -Location "Atlanta" -managedBy "S.Bishop" -description "training desktop"
```

Technically a computer account is based on the user account class so there are many similarities. However, because you can specify values like the **OperatingSystem** property, it's not too difficult to use the **New-ADComputer** cmdlet to create test computer accounts for machines that don't physically exist. I do this all the time with my test domains so I have computer accounts to work with that are pretty close to complete:

```
PS C:\> New-ADComputer -Name "Web10" -OperatingSystem "Windows Server 2003" `
>> -OperatingSystemServicePack "Service Pack 2" `
>> -Path "OU=Servers,DC=jdhlab,DC=local" -location "Corporate" `
>> -operatingSystemVersion "5.2 (3790)" -description "Test Web Server" `
>> -dnshostname "web10.jdhlab.local" -passthru
>>


DistinguishedName : CN=Web10,OU=Servers,DC=jdhlab,DC=local
DNSHostName       : web10.jdhlab.local
```

```
Enabled           : True
Name              : Web10
ObjectClass       : computer
ObjectGUID        : 5801af66-698b-4a30-bf7a-1859f9e4a8e8
SamAccountName    : Web10$
SID               : S-1-5-21-3957442467-353870018-3926547339-5424
UserPrincipalName :
```

I just created a sample computer account called Web10 in the Servers organizational unit. The server is running Windows Server 2003 Service Pack 2. You can find operating system values by looking at existing, "real" servers in your domain.

One nice fact about the **New-ADComputer** cmdlet is that it accepts pipelined input for operating system information. Here's how I leverage that. First, I have a CSV file with operating system information:

OS.csv

```
Class,OperatingSystem,OperatingSystemServicePack,OperatingSystemVersion
"server","Windows Server 2003","Service Pack 2","5.2 (3790)"
"client","Windows XP Professional","Service Pack 2","5.1 (2600)"
"client","Windows XP Professional","Service Pack 3","5.1 (2600)"
"client","Windows Vista™ Ultimate","Service Pack 2","6.0 (6002)"
"server","Windows Server® 2008 Standard","Service Pack 1","6.0 (6001)"
"client","Windows 7 Ultimate",,"6.1 (7000)"
"client","Windows 7 Professional",,"6.1 (7600)"
"server","Microsoft(R) Windows(R) Server 2003, Enterprise Edition","Service Pack
2","5.2.(3790)"
"server","Microsoft Windows Server 2008 R2 Standard",,"6.1 (7600)"
"server","Microsoft Windows Server 2008 R2 Enterprise",,"6.1 (7600)"
"server","Windows Server® 2008 Standard without Hyper-V","Service Pack 2","6.0 (6002)"
```

Next, I'll import the file and save the results to a variable:

```
PS C:\> $os=Import-Csv r:\os.csv
```

I've decided I want to create a test server using the last operating system in $os:

```
PS C:\> $os[-1] | Format-List


Class                      : server
OperatingSystem            : Windows Server® 2008 Standard without Hyper-V
OperatingSystemServicePack : Service Pack 2
OperatingSystemVersion     : 6.0 (6002)
```

All I need to do is pipe this object to the **New-ADComputer** cmdlet, specifying a few other properties:

```
PS C:\> $os[-1] | New-ADComputer -Name "DB03" -Path "OU=Servers,DC=jdhlab,DC=local" `
>> -location "Corporate"  -description "Test DB Server" -dnshostname "db03.jdhlab.local"
-passthru
>>


DistinguishedName : CN=DB03,OU=Servers,DC=jdhlab,DC=local
DNSHostName       : db03.jdhlab.local
```

```
Enabled           : True
Name              : DB03
ObjectClass       : computer
ObjectGUID        : e110e4ff-4406-4e10-bfad-4803e65fbbaf
SamAccountName    : DB03$
SID               : S-1-5-21-3957442467-353870018-3926547339-5427
UserPrincipalName :
```

Using the New-QADObject cmdlet

Quest Software doesn't have a cmdlet specific to creating new computer accounts. But you can achieve similar results with the **New-QADObject** cmdlet:

```
PS C:\> New-QADObject -ParentContainer "OU=Servers,DC=jdhlab,DC=local" -Name "Server21" `
>> -type "computer" -Description "Test Server" -ObjectAttributes @{
>> samaccountname="SERVER21$";
>> DNSHostName="server21.jdhlab.local";
>> operatingsystem="Microsoft Windows Server 2008 R2 Standard";
>> operatingSystemVersion="6.1 (7600)"}
>>

Name                          Type            DN
----                          ----            --
Server21                      computer        cn=Server21,OU=Servers,DC=jdhlab,DC=local
```

This expression created the SERVER211 computer account in the Servers organizational unit. You need to specify the type and at a minimum should use the **-ObjectAttributes** parameter to define the SAMAccountname, which in case you didn't know is always the computer name followed by a dollar sign ($). I've gone ahead and also defined a few other properties as well.

In fact, I can easily use the **New-QADObject** cmdlet to create hundreds of computer accounts in my test domain:

New-TestQADComputer.ps1

```
#Requires -version 2.0
#requires -pssnapin Quest.ActiveRoles.ADManagement

[cmdletBinding(SupportsShouldProcess=$True)]

Param (
#define default values
[Parameter(Position=0,Mandatory=$True,HelpMessage="Enter the basename for the new
computername.")]
[ValidateNotNullorEmpty()]
[string]$basename,
[string]$parent="OU=Servers,DC=JDHLab,DC=local",
[parameter(ValueFromPipelineByPropertyName=$True)]
[Alias("os")]
[string]$operatingsystem="Microsoft Windows Server 2008 R2 Standard",
[parameter(ValueFromPipelineByPropertyName=$True)]
[Alias("Version")]
[string]$operatingSystemVersion="6.1 (7600)",
[parameter(ValueFromPipelineByPropertyName=$True)]
[Alias("ServicePack")]
[string]$operatingSystemServicePack,
[int]$start=1,
[int]$end=10,
```

```
[string]$description,
[string]$location,
[string]$dnsSuffix="jdh.local",
[switch]$Disabled
)

$total=($start..$end).count

if ($disabled) {
    $UAC=4098
}
else {
    $UAC=4096
}
$i=0

$start..$end | Foreach {
    $i++
    [int]$p=($i/$total)*100
    $name="$BaseName$_"
    $sam=$name+"$"
    $dns=("{0}.{1}" -f $name.ToLower(),$dnsSuffix)
    Write-Verbose ("Creating {0} [{1}] {2}" -f $name,$sam,$dns)
    $status=("{0} [{1}] OS:{2} {3}" -f $name,$sam,$operatingsystem,$operatingSystemServicePack
)
    Write-Progress -activity "Creating Computer in $parent" -status $status `
   -CurrentOperation "$p% complete"

    New-QADObject -ParentContainer $parent -Name $name `
    -type "computer" -Description $description -ObjectAttributes @{
    samaccountname=$sam;useraccountcontrol=$UAC;location=$location; `
    operatingsystem=$operatingsystem;operatingSystemServicePack=$operatingSystemServicePack; `
    operatingSystemVersion=$operatingSystemVersion;dNSHostName=$dns }
}

Write-Progress -activity "Creating Computer" -status "Done!" -Completed
```

I wrote this script so that you could pass values as parameters. In fact, the operating system parameters are configured to accept pipelined input like the **New-ADComputer** cmdlet. I've hard-coded in some defaults you will likely want to change like the default location. The only mandatory property is the **basename**. The script creates computer accounts with a name that is a concatenation of the basename and a number. You specify the starting number and end number. The end result is a computer account like TestServer14.

The script calculates how many accounts it needs to create:

```
$total=($start..$end).count
```

Each number from the starting to the end is piped to the **ForEach-Object** cmdlet:

```
$start..$end | Foreach {
```

Within the loop a new computer account is created using the **New-QADObject** cmdlet and the parameter values you specified:

```
New-QADObject -ParentContainer $parent -Name $name `
    -type "computer" -Description $description -ObjectAttributes @{
    samaccountname=$sam;useraccountcontrol=$UAC;location=$location; `
```

```
operatingsystem=$operatingsystem;operatingSystemServicePack=$operatingSystemServicePack; `
operatingSystemVersion=$operatingSystemVersion;dNSHostName=$dns }
```

The script uses the **Write-Progress** cmdlet so you can keep track of what the script is doing. With this script I can use my operating system CSV file and create any number of test accounts. Here's one example:

New-TestClient.ps1

```
$i=0
Import-Csv r:\os.csv | where {$_.class -eq "client"}| Foreach {
$i=$i+10
$end=$i+5
write-host "$($_.OperatingSystem) $($_.OperatingSystemServicePack)" -ForegroundColor Green
#pipe the OS information to the script
$_ | R:\New-TestQADComputer.ps1 -basename "Desk-" -start $i -end $end `
-description "company desktop" -parent "OU=Staging,OU=Desktops,DC=jdhlab,DC=local"
}
```

My CSV file has several operating systems tagged as clients. This code imports the file and filters the output, keeping only the client operating systems. Each one is then piped to the **ForEach-Object** cmdlet. The operating system object is piped to my script. All I have to do is specify the other parameters. My computer accounts will all start with "Desk-" followed by a number. The first time through the loop the starting number will be 10 and the end number 15. When PowerShell processes the next operating system, $i will jump to 20 and the last number will be 25, and so on. Thus I'll end up with six computer accounts for each client operating system.

I can achieve like-wise results for servers:

New-TestServer.ps1

```
$i=0
Import-Csv r:\os.csv | where {$_.class -eq "server"}| Foreach {
$i=$i+10
$end=$i+5
write-host "$($_.OperatingSystem) $($_.OperatingSystemServicePack)" -ForegroundColor Green
#pipe the OS information to the script
$_ | R:\New-TestQADComputer.ps1 -basename "DemoSVR-" -start $i -end $end `
-description "company server" -parent "OU=Demo,OU=Servers,DC=jdhlab,DC=local"
}
```

Managing Computer Accounts

There's usually not too much you need to do with computer accounts once they are created. In the Active Directory module you can use the **Get-ADComputer** cmdlet to retrieve one or more computer objects:

```
PS C:\> Get-ADComputer -identity Client1


DistinguishedName : CN=CLIENT1,OU=Desktops,DC=jdhlab,DC=local
DNSHostName       : CLIENT1.jdhlab.local
Enabled           : True
Name              : CLIENT1
ObjectClass       : computer
```

```
ObjectGUID        : 20459a2b-a241-4962-a84b-336831c7dfbe
SamAccountName    : CLIENT1$
SID               : S-1-5-21-3957442467-353870018-3926547339-1105
UserPrincipalName :
```

Like the **Get-ADUser** cmdlet, you need to specify one or more properties if you want anything other than the default you see here. Let me select all properties for Client1:

```
PS C:\> Get-ADComputer -identity Client1 -Properties *


AccountExpirationDate              :
accountExpires                     : 9223372036854775807
AccountLockoutTime                 :
AccountNotDelegated                : False
AllowReversiblePasswordEncryption  : False
BadLogonCount                      : 0
badPasswordTime                    : 0
badPwdCount                        : 0
CannotChangePassword               : False
CanonicalName                      : jdhlab.local/Desktops/CLIENT1
Certificates                       : {}
CN                                 : CLIENT1
codePage                           : 0
countryCode                        : 0
Created                            : 3/1/2010 5:01:30 PM
createTimeStamp                    : 3/1/2010 5:01:30 PM
Deleted                            :
Description                        :
DisplayName                        :
DistinguishedName                  : CN=CLIENT1,OU=Desktops,DC=jdhlab,DC=local
DNSHostName                        : CLIENT1.jdhlab.local
DoesNotRequirePreAuth              : False
dSCorePropagationData              : {6/22/2010 2:51:59 PM, 3/3/2010 10:08:03 AM, 12/31/1600 7...
Enabled                            : True
HomedirRequired                    : False
HomePage                           :
instanceType                       : 4
IPv4Address                        : 172.16.10.192
IPv6Address                        :
isCriticalSystemObject             : False
isDeleted                          :
LastBadPasswordAttempt             :
LastKnownParent                    :
lastLogoff                         : 0
lastLogon                          : 129249850150269463
LastLogonDate                      : 7/25/2010 5:50:40 PM
lastLogonTimestamp                 : 129245682405782592
localPolicyFlags                   : 0
Location                           :
LockedOut                          : False
logonCount                         : 298
ManagedBy                          :
MemberOf                           : {CN=AlphaGroup,OU=Groups,DC=jdhlab,DC=local}
MNSLogonAccount                    : False
Modified                           : 7/25/2010 5:50:40 PM
modifyTimeStamp                    : 7/25/2010 5:50:40 PM
msDS-SupportedEncryptionTypes      : 28
msDS-User-Account-Control-Computed : 0
Name                               : CLIENT1
nTSecurityDescriptor               : System.DirectoryServices.ActiveDirectorySecurity
ObjectCategory                     : CN=Computer,CN=Schema,CN=Configuration,DC=jdhlab,DC=local
```

```
ObjectClass                       : computer
ObjectGUID                        : 20459a2b-a241-4962-a84b-336831c7dfbe
objectSid                         : S-1-5-21-3957442467-353870018-3926547339-1105
OperatingSystem                   : Windows 7 Ultimate
OperatingSystemHotfix             :
OperatingSystemServicePack        :
OperatingSystemVersion            : 6.1 (7600)
PasswordExpired                   : False
PasswordLastSet                   : 7/5/2010 10:00:02 AM
PasswordNeverExpires              : False
PasswordNotRequired               : False
PrimaryGroup                      : CN=Domain Computers,CN=Users,DC=jdhlab,DC=local
primaryGroupID                    : 515
ProtectedFromAccidentalDeletion   : False
pwdLastSet                        : 129228120024167942
SamAccountName                    : CLIENT1$
sAMAccountType                    : 805306369
sDRightsEffective                 : 15
ServiceAccount                    : {}
servicePrincipalName              : {ldap/CLIENT1.jdhlab.local, ldap/CLIENT1.jdhlab.local:389,...
ServicePrincipalNames             : {ldap/CLIENT1.jdhlab.local, ldap/CLIENT1.jdhlab.local:389,...
SID                               : S-1-5-21-3957442467-353870018-3926547339-1105
SIDHistory                        : {}
TrustedForDelegation              : False
TrustedToAuthForDelegation        : False
UseDESKeyOnly                     : False
userAccountControl                : 4096
userCertificate                   : {}
UserPrincipalName                 :
uSNChanged                        : 397467
uSNCreated                        : 53357
whenChanged                       : 7/25/2010 5:50:40 PM
whenCreated                       : 3/1/2010 5:01:30 PM
```

You can use any of these properties to build a search filter for the cmdlet:

```
PS C:\> Get-ADComputer -filter "operatingsystem -like 'Windows 7*'" `
>>-Properties Description,OperatingSystem | Select Name,Description,OperatingSystem
>>

Name                                Description                     OperatingSystem
----                                -----------                     ---------------
CLIENT1                                                             Windows 7 Ultimate
Desk-40                             company desktop                 Windows 7 Ultimate
Desk-41                             company desktop                 Windows 7 Ultimate
Desk-42                             company desktop                 Windows 7 Ultimate
Desk-43                             company desktop                 Windows 7 Ultimate
Desk-44                             company desktop                 Windows 7 Ultimate
Desk-45                             company desktop                 Windows 7 Ultimate
Desk-50                             company desktop                 Windows 7 Professional
Desk-51                             company desktop                 Windows 7 Professional
Desk-52                             company desktop                 Windows 7 Professional
Desk-53                             company desktop                 Windows 7 Professional
Desk-54                             company desktop                 Windows 7 Professional
Desk-55                             company desktop                 Windows 7 Professional
```

With this one-line command I found all the computers in my domain running some version of Windows 7. I can use the **Set-ADComputer** cmdlet to modify these accounts. Let me change the description to reflect their OS and also set the **-ManagedBy** parameter:

```
PS C:\> Get-ADComputer -filter "operatingsystem -like 'Windows 7*'" |
>> Set-ADComputer -Description "Win7 company desktop" -ManagedBy "DesktopSupport"
```

The **-ManagedBy** parameter value is the SAMAccountname of the Desktop Support group. If you want to get rid of a value, set it to $Null.

The **Set-ADComputer** cmdlet doesn't write anything to the pipeline, which means when you run the command you'll get no output. If you want to force the cmdlet to write to the pipeline you must use the **-Passthru** parameter.

You can achieve similar results using the Quest **Get-QADComputer** cmdlet:

```
PS C:\> Get-QADComputer mail | Select *


objectClass                 : {top, person, organizationalPerson, user...}
objectSid                   : 0105000000000005150000000A3C7E1EBC2A017158B5B0AEA8D130000
userAccountControl          : 4096
whenCreated                 : 6/22/2010 12:24:22 PM
objectGUID                  : 3D6CF9DA77B1AD46894447E85B2DE5BF
whenChanged                 : 7/29/2010 5:16:53 PM
operatingSystemVersion      : 6.0 (6002)
operatingSystem             : Windows Server® 2008 Standard without Hyper-V
operatingSystemServicePack : Service Pack 2
dNSHostName                 : Mail.jdhlab.local
edsvaNamingContextDN        :
mS-DS-CreatorSID            :
ComputerName                : MAIL$
ComputerRole                : Member
CreatorSid                  :
DnsName                     : Mail.jdhlab.local
Location                    :
ManagedBy                   :
SecondaryOwners             : {}
OSName                      : Windows Server® 2008 Standard without Hyper-V
OSVersion                   : 6.0 (6002)
OSServicePack               : Service Pack 2
OSHotFix                    :
TrustedForDelegation        : False
AccountIsDisabled           : False
NTAccountName               : JDHLAB\MAIL$
SamAccountName              : MAIL$
Security                    : Quest.ActiveRoles.ArsPowerShellSnapIn.UI.SecurityDescriptor
Domain                      : JDHLAB\
LastKnownParent             :
MemberOf                    : {CN=Exchange Install Domain Servers,CN=Microsoft Exchange System O...
NestedMemberOf              : {CN=Exchange Servers,OU=Microsoft Exchange Security Groups,DC=jdhl...
Notes                       :
AllMemberOf                 : {CN=Exchange Install Domain Servers,CN=Microsoft Exchange System O...
Keywords                    : {}
ProxyAddresses              : {}
PrimarySMTPAddress          :
PrimarySMTPAddressPrefix    :
PrimarySMTPAddressSuffix    :
PrimaryX400Address          :
PrimaryMSMailAddress        :
PrimaryCCMailAddress        :
PrimaryMacMailAddress       :
PrimaryLotusNotesAddress    :
PrimaryGroupWiseAddress     :
EmailAddressPolicyEnabled   : False
Path                        : LDAP://COREDC01.jdhlab.local/CN=MAIL,CN=Computers,DC=jdhlab,DC=local
```

```
DN                         : CN=MAIL,CN=Computers,DC=jdhlab,DC=local
CanonicalName              : jdhlab.local/Computers/MAIL
CreationDate               : 6/22/2010 12:24:22 PM
ModificationDate           : 7/29/2010 5:16:53 PM
ParentContainer            : jdhlab.local/Computers
ParentContainerDN          : CN=Computers,DC=jdhlab,DC=local
Name                       : MAIL
ClassName                  : computer
Type                       : computer
Guid                       : daf96c3d-b177-46ad-8944-47e85b2de5bf
Sid                        : S-1-5-21-3957442467-353870018-3926547339-5005
Description                :
DisplayName                : MAIL$
OperationID                :
OperationStatus            : Unknown
Cache                      : Quest.ActiveRoles.ArsPowerShellSnapIn.BusinessLogic.ObjectCache
Connection                 : Quest.ActiveRoles.ArsPowerShellSnapIn.Data.ArsADConnection
DirectoryEntry             : System.DirectoryServices.DirectoryEntry
```

You should see a lot of the same properties. You can use the **Set-QADComputer** cmdlet to modify the account:

```
PS C:\> Set-QADComputer -Identity Mail -Description "Exchange 2007" -Location "Corporate"

Name                           Type            DN
----                           ----            --
MAIL                           computer        CN=MAIL,CN=Computers,DC=jdhlab,DC=local
```

The cmdlet also accepts pipelined input. Let me update the **-ManagedBy** parameter for all servers in the Corporate location:

```
PS C:\> Get-QADComputer -Location corporate -SearchRoot "OU=Servers,DC=jdhlab,DC=local" |
>> Set-QADComputer -ManagedBy "ITAdmins" -ObjectAttributes @{Info="$(get-Date) Modified
ManagedBy $env:userdomain\$env:username"}
>>

Name                           Type            DN
----                           ----            --
File-1                         computer        CN=File-1,OU=Servers,DC=jdhlab,DC=local
File-2                         computer        CN=File-2,OU=Servers,DC=jdhlab,DC=local
File-3                         computer        CN=File-3,OU=Servers,DC=jdhlab,DC=local
File-4                         computer        CN=File-4,OU=Servers,DC=jdhlab,DC=local
File-5                         computer        CN=File-5,OU=Servers,DC=jdhlab,DC=local
File-6                         computer        CN=File-6,OU=Servers,DC=jdhlab,DC=local
File-7                         computer        CN=File-7,OU=Servers,DC=jdhlab,DC=local
File-8                         computer        CN=File-8,OU=Servers,DC=jdhlab,DC=local
File-9                         computer        CN=File-9,OU=Servers,DC=jdhlab,DC=local
File-10                        computer        CN=File-10,OU=Servers,DC=jdhlab,DC=local
Web10                          computer        CN=Web10,OU=Servers,DC=jdhlab,DC=local
DB03                           computer        CN=DB03,OU=Servers,DC=jdhlab,DC=local
```

The Active Directory Users and Computers management console doesn't expose the **Info** or **Note** properties. But you can use PowerShell to verify the change:

```
PS C:\> Get-QADComputer -Location corporate -SearchRoot "OU=Servers,DC=jdhlab,DC=local" `
>> -includedproperties Info | Select Name,Info | Format-Table -auto
>>
```

```
Name    info
----    ----
File-1  07/30/2010 14:10:37 Modified ManagedBy JDHLAB\Administrator
File-2  07/30/2010 14:10:37 Modified ManagedBy JDHLAB\Administrator
File-3  07/30/2010 14:10:37 Modified ManagedBy JDHLAB\Administrator
...
```

Searching Computer Accounts

You've already seen ways you can search for computers using the **Get-ADComputer** or **Get-QADComputer** cmdlets. The former requires a filter of some sort, either PowerShell or LDAP. Suppose I want to find all servers running some version of Windows 2003 in my domain with a location of "Omaha"? The **Get-ADComputer** cmdlet will require a filter:

```
PS C:\> Get-ADComputer -filter "operatingsystem -like '*2003*' -AND Location -eq 'Omaha'" |
>> Select distinguishedname,name

distinguishedname                                    name
-----------------                                    ----
CN=DemoSVR-10,OU=Demo,OU=Servers,DC=jdhlab,DC=local  DemoSVR-10
CN=DemoSVR-11,OU=Demo,OU=Servers,DC=jdhlab,DC=local  DemoSVR-11
CN=DemoSVR-12,OU=Demo,OU=Servers,DC=jdhlab,DC=local  DemoSVR-12
CN=DemoSVR-13,OU=Demo,OU=Servers,DC=jdhlab,DC=local  DemoSVR-13
CN=DemoSVR-14,OU=Demo,OU=Servers,DC=jdhlab,DC=local  DemoSVR-14
CN=DemoSVR-15,OU=Demo,OU=Servers,DC=jdhlab,DC=local  DemoSVR-15
```

I can get a similar result using the **Get-QADComputer** cmdlet:

```
PS C:\> Get-QADComputer -OSName "*2003*" -Location "Omaha" | Select DN,Name

DN                                                   Name
--                                                   ----
CN=DemoSVR-10,OU=Demo,OU=Servers,DC=jdhlab,DC=local  DemoSVR-10
CN=DemoSVR-11,OU=Demo,OU=Servers,DC=jdhlab,DC=local  DemoSVR-11
CN=DemoSVR-12,OU=Demo,OU=Servers,DC=jdhlab,DC=local  DemoSVR-12
CN=DemoSVR-13,OU=Demo,OU=Servers,DC=jdhlab,DC=local  DemoSVR-13
CN=DemoSVR-14,OU=Demo,OU=Servers,DC=jdhlab,DC=local  DemoSVR-14
CN=DemoSVR-15,OU=Demo,OU=Servers,DC=jdhlab,DC=local  DemoSVR-15
```

One big difference I'm sure you noticed between the Microsoft and Quest cmdlets is that the Quest cmdlet exposes much more via parameters, which makes it more admin friendly.

Find Servers

Active Directory can't really distinguish a server from a desktop. Your best option is to search for computer accounts based on operating system as I demonstrated earlier. Let's build a report of all servers organized by operating system. First, it might be helpful to know what operating systems are currently in use:

```
PS C:\> Get-QADComputer -OSName * | Sort OSName | Select OSName -Unique

OSName
------
Microsoft Windows Server 2008 R2 Enterprise
Microsoft Windows Server 2008 R2 Standard
Microsoft(R) Windows(R) Server 2003, Enterprise Edition
```

```
Windows 7 Professional
Windows 7 Ultimate
Windows Server 2003
Windows Server 2008 R2 Enterprise
Windows Server 2008 R2 Standard
Windows Server® 2008 Standard
Windows Server® 2008 Standard without Hyper-V
Windows Vista™ Ultimate
Windows XP Professional
```

It seems clear then that I need to search for any operating system with "server" as part of the name:

```
PS C:\> Get-QADComputer -OSName "*server*" | Sort OSName |
>> Format-table -groupBy OSName  -property DN,Name,OSServicePack,Location,Description
>>


   OSName: Microsoft Windows Server 2008 R2 Enterprise

DN                        Name            OSServicePack     Location        Description
--                        ----            -------------     --------        -----------
CN=DemoSVR-50,OU=Dem... DemoSVR-50                                          company server
CN=DemoSVR-54,OU=Dem... DemoSVR-54                                          company server
CN=DemoSVR-53,OU=Dem... DemoSVR-53                                          company server
CN=DemoSVR-51,OU=Dem... DemoSVR-51                                          company server
CN=DemoSVR-55,OU=Dem... DemoSVR-55                                          company server
CN=DemoSVR-52,OU=Dem... DemoSVR-52                                          company server


   OSName: Microsoft Windows Server 2008 R2 Standard

DN                        Name         OSServicePack       Location         Description
--                        ----         -------------       --------         -----------
CN=File-8,OU=Servers... File-8                             Corporate
CN=DemoSVR-42,OU=Dem... DemoSVR-42                                          company server
CN=File-9,OU=Servers... File-9                             Corporate
…
```

Or perhaps you'd simply like a quick head count by operating system:

```
PS C:\> Get-QADComputer -OSName "*server*" | Group-Object -Property OSName |
>> Sort Count -descending | Select Name,Count
>>

Name                                                                        Count
----                                                                        -----
Microsoft Windows Server 2008 R2 Standard                                      28
Windows Server® 2008 Standard without Hyper-V                                   8
Windows Server 2003                                                             7
Microsoft Windows Server 2008 R2 Enterprise                                     6
Windows Server® 2008 Standard                                                   6
Microsoft(R) Windows(R) Server 2003, Enterprise Edition                         6
Windows Server 2008 R2 Standard                                                 1
Windows Server 2008 R2 Enterprise                                               1
```

I took all the computers running a server operating system and grouped them using the **Group-Object** cmdlet. That cmdlet writes a new object to the pipeline with the **Name** (OSName value) and **Count** (number of items in each group) properties.

Don't Assume

Don't assume that the operating system information you find in Active Directory is what is actually on the server. The Active Directory information usually gets updated when the computer boots up. If you've installed a service pack, for example, and have yet to reboot, the information in Active Directory won't be 100% accurate.

This expression works but it also returns domain controllers, which perhaps I don't want. For a more granular approach you can search based on the **ComputerRole** property using the **Get-QADComputer** cmdlet. This won't work with the **Get-ADComputer** cmdlet. The possible values are DomainController or Member:

```
PS C:\> Get-QADComputer -OSName "*server*" -computerrole "Member"| Group-Object -Property
OSName |
>> Sort Count -descending | Select Name,Count
>>

Name                                                                                Count
----                                                                                -----
Microsoft Windows Server 2008 R2 Standard                                              28
Windows Server® 2008 Standard without Hyper-V                                           8
Windows Server 2003                                                                     7
Microsoft Windows Server 2008 R2 Enterprise                                             6
Windows Server® 2008 Standard                                                           6
Microsoft(R) Windows(R) Server 2003, Enterprise Edition                                 6
Windows Server 2008 R2 Enterprise                                                       1
```

In my domain I only have a single domain controller running Windows Server 2008 R2 Standard, which if you look closely you'll see is not in the list.

Are you beginning to see some utility here? You can easily create a list of member servers that need the latest service pack:

```
PS C:\> Get-QADComputer -osname "*2003*" -OSServicePack "Service Pack 1" -computerrole
"member"|
>> Select Name,OSName,Location | Tee-Object -file "2003sp1.txt"

Name                                    OSName                                  Location
----                                    ------                                  --------
DemoSVR-10                              Windows Server 2003                     Omaha
DemoSVR-11                              Windows Server 2003                     Omaha
DemoSVR-12                              Windows Server 2003                     Omaha
DemoSVR-13                              Windows Server 2003                     Omaha
DemoSVR-14                              Windows Server 2003                     Omaha
DemoSVR-15                              Windows Server 2003                     Omaha
```

With this expression, I've found all my Windows 2003 servers still at Service Pack 1. I've used the **Tee-Object** cmdlet to display the results to the console and save them to a text file, which I can hand off to a server operator for remediation.

You actually can achieve similar results with the **Get-ADComputer** cmdlet, but it requires a more complex filter:

```
Get-ADComputer -filter "primarygroupid -ne '516' -AND OperatingSystem -like '*2003*' -AND
OperatingSystemServicePack -eq 'Service Pack 1'" -Properties "OperatingSystem","Location" |
Select Name,OperatingSystem,Location | Tee-object -file "2003sp1.txt"
```

I'll get the same results with this expression. One thing I've done that is a little different is to find computer accounts that do not have a PrimaryGroupID of 516. All domain controllers should have a PrimaryGroupID of 516 so this should have the effect of returning all member servers.

Find Desktops

To find desktop computers, you should be able to simply filter for all non-server operating systems. Fortunately the **Get-QADComputer** cmdlet accepts an array of operating system names, including wildcards:

```
PS C:\> Get-QADComputer -OSName "*XP*",*"Windows 7*","*Vista*" | Sort OSName |
>> Select Name,OSName,OSServicePack
>>

Name                                    OSName                                  OSServicePack
----                                    ------                                  -------------
Desk-52                                 Windows 7 Professional
Desk-51                                 Windows 7 Professional
Desk-50                                 Windows 7 Professional
Desk-55                                 Windows 7 Professional
Desk-54                                 Windows 7 Professional
Desk-53                                 Windows 7 Professional
Desk-41                                 Windows 7 Ultimate
Desk-40                                 Windows 7 Ultimate
CLIENT1                                 Windows 7 Ultimate
Desk-42                                 Windows 7 Ultimate
Desk-45                                 Windows 7 Ultimate
Desk-44                                 Windows 7 Ultimate
Desk-43                                 Windows 7 Ultimate
Desk-34                                 Windows Vista™ Ultimate                 Service Pack 2
Desk-35                                 Windows Vista™ Ultimate                 Service Pack 2
Desk-32                                 Windows Vista™ Ultimate                 Service Pack 2
Desk-33                                 Windows Vista™ Ultimate                 Service Pack 2
Desk-31                                 Windows Vista™ Ultimate                 Service Pack 2
Desk-30                                 Windows Vista™ Ultimate                 Service Pack 2
Desk-14                                 Windows XP Professional                 Service Pack 2
Desk-12                                 Windows XP Professional                 Service Pack 2
Desk-13                                 Windows XP Professional                 Service Pack 2
Desk-22                                 Windows XP Professional                 Service Pack 3
Desk-10                                 Windows XP Professional                 Service Pack 2
Desk-11                                 Windows XP Professional                 Service Pack 2
Desk-23                                 Windows XP Professional                 Service Pack 3
```

Disabling and Enabling Computer Accounts

To disable or enable a computer account, it is a matter of flipping the rights bits in the object's UserAccountControl flag. Fortunately both Microsoft and Quest have cmdlets to handle this task for you. Let's disable a computer account:

```
PS C:\> Disable-ADAccount -Identity "DemoSVR-10$"
```

Remember, a computer account is like a user account so the easy way is to specify the computer's SAMAccountname. Although you can leverage the pipeline as well to find one or more computer accounts:

```
PS C:\> "App-1","File-1","DB03" | Get-ADComputer | Disable-ADAccount -whatif
What if: Performing operation "Set" on Target "CN=App-1,OU=Servers,DC=jdhlab,DC=local".
What if: Performing operation "Set" on Target "CN=File-1,OU=Servers,DC=jdhlab,DC=local".
What if: Performing operation "Set" on Target "CN=DB03,OU=Servers,DC=jdhlab,DC=local".
```

The three computer names are piped to the **Get-ADComputer** cmdlet, which retrieves the account, and then pipes the objects to the **Disable-ADAccount** cmdlet.

The Quest version is a little easier since all you have to do is specify the Active Directory name:

```
PS C:\> Disable-QADComputer -Identity "DemoSVR-20"

Name                              Type        DN
----                              ----        --
DemoSVR-20                        computer    CN=DemoSVR-20,OU=Demo,OU=Servers,DC=jdhlab,DC=local
```

Use the **Enable-ADAccount or Enable-QADComputer** cmdlets to go the other way:

```
PS C:\> Enable-QADComputer -Identity "DemoSVR-20"

Name                              Type        DN
----                              ----        --
DemoSVR-20                        computer    CN=DemoSVR-20,OU=Demo,OU=Servers,DC=jdhlab,DC=local
PS C:\> Enable-ADAccount -Identity "Desk-25$" -PassThru


DistinguishedName : CN=Desk-25,OU=XP,OU=Desktops,DC=jdhlab,DC=local
Enabled           : True
Name              : Desk-25
ObjectClass       : computer
ObjectGUID        : 90fd523a-17f8-4769-a018-28256c8977bf
SamAccountName    : Desk-25$
SID               : S-1-5-21-3957442467-353870018-3926547339-5380
UserPrincipalName :
```

Naturally, you might also want a way to find all disabled computer accounts. With the **Get-ADComputer** cmdlet, it's just a matter of the right filter:

```
PS C:\> Get-ADComputer -filter "enabled -eq '$false'" | Select distinguishedname

distinguishedname
-----------------
CN=test1,OU=Servers,DC=jdhlab,DC=local
CN=Desk-15,OU=XP,OU=Desktops,DC=jdhlab,DC=local
CN=App-7,OU=Servers,DC=jdhlab,DC=local
CN=File-9,OU=Servers,DC=jdhlab,DC=local
CN=BranchDesk02,OU=Branch Office,DC=jdhlab,DC=local
CN=DemoSVR-10,OU=Demo,OU=Servers,DC=jdhlab,DC=local
```

When using the **Get-QADComputer** cmdlet, I'm going to search the UserAccountControl flag. A disabled computer account typically has a value of 4098:

```
PS C:\> Get-QADComputer -searchattributes @{"UserAccountControl"=4098}

Name                              Type        DN
----                              ----        --
test1                             computer    CN=test1,OU=Servers,DC=jdhlab,DC=local
Desk-15                           computer    CN=Desk-15,OU=XP,OU=Desktops,DC=jdhlab,DC=local
```

```
App-7                       computer    CN=App-7,OU=Servers,DC=jdhlab,DC=local
File-9                      computer    CN=File-9,OU=Servers,DC=jdhlab,DC=local
BranchDesk02                computer    CN=BranchDesk02,OU=Branch Office,DC=jdhlab,DC=local
DemoSVR-10                  computer    CN=DemoSVR-10,OU=Demo,OU=Servers,DC=jdhlab,DC=local
```

Or you can use the LDAP filter which is probably a little more accurate:

```
PS C:\> Get-QADComputer -LdapFilter "(userAccountControl:1.2.840.113556.1.4.803:=2)"
```

The results will be the same.

Finding Obsolete Accounts

Computer accounts are very similar to user accounts. You may not know it, but behind the scenes a computer updates its password with the domain on a periodic basis, usually no more than every 21-30 days. The easiest way to find obsolete computer accounts is to check when the password was last set. If the password age is greater than 90 days, that computer is probably no longer around, although you should verify that before doing anything drastic like deleting accounts.

The **Get-ADComputer** cmdlet exposes a **PasswordLastSet** property in a friendly format:

```
PS C:\> Get-ADComputer -filter "*" -properties PasswordLastSet |
>> Sort PasswordLastSet -Descending | Select name,PasswordLastSet
>>

name                                    PasswordLastSet
----                                    ---------------
DB03                                    7/30/2010 9:04:48 AM
Web10                                   7/29/2010 8:28:00 PM
BranchDesk02                            7/29/2010 8:19:33 PM
BranchDesk01                            7/29/2010 8:09:51 PM
MAIL                                    7/27/2010 2:27:56 PM
CLIENT1                                 7/5/2010 10:00:02 AM
COREDC01                                7/5/2010 9:58:39 AM
SERVER01                                6/14/2010 4:00:27 PM
...
```

Using the **Get-QADComputer** cmdlet isn't that much more difficult. Here's a version that also includes some calculated information:

Get-ComputerAge.ps1

```
#get GMT offset
$wmi=Get-WmiObject -Class Win32_OperatingSystem

Get-QADComputer -sizelimit 0 -includedProperties pwdLastSet |
Select Name,@{Name="PasswordLastSet";
Expression={($_.pwdLastSet).AddMinutes($wmi.CurrentTimeZone)}}, `
@{Name="PasswordAge";
Expression={(get-date)-($_.pwdLastSet).AddMinutes($wmi.CurrentTimeZone)}} |
Sort PasswordAge
```

This short block of code returns computer objects, including the **pwdLastSet** property. I use the current time zone from WMI to convert it to a local date time format. I also calculate a time span object indicating the password age. Running the code should produce results like this:

```
Name                    PasswordLastSet                 PasswordAge
----                    ---------------                 -----------
SERVER01                8/2/2010 12:24:17 PM            00:15:40.5882436
DB03                    7/30/2010 9:04:48 AM            3.03:35:10.6477398
Web10                   7/29/2010 8:28:00 PM            3.16:11:58.4737063
BranchDesk02            7/29/2010 8:19:33 PM            3.16:20:24.6714103
BranchDesk01            7/29/2010 8:09:51 PM            3.16:30:07.3141853
MAIL                    7/27/2010 2:27:56 PM            5.22:12:01.6555122
CLIENT1                 7/5/2010 10:00:02 AM            28.02:39:55.7155364
COREDC01                7/5/2010 9:58:39 AM             28.02:41:19.0699207
test1                   12/31/1600 8:00:00 PM           149597.16:39:58.1479556
Desk-11                 12/31/1600 8:00:00 PM           149597.16:39:58.1635806
...
```

The last two computer accounts have never set a password, which means they are accounts for computers that have yet to contact the domain.

The **Get-QADComputer** cmdlet (assuming you are running at least version 1.4) also offers a few other parameters you might use to determine whether an account is active:

- NotLoggedOnFor
- PasswordNotChangedFor
- InactiveFor
- Inactive

The first parameter checks the **LastLogon** property:

```
PS C:\> Get-QADComputer client1 -includedproperties lastlogon | Select name,lastlogon

Name                                          lastLogon
----                                          ---------
CLIENT1                                       8/2/2010 3:46:59 PM
```

The **-NotLoggedOnFor** parameter takes an integer value that represents the number of days since the last logon. Here's an example showing computers that have not logged on in at least 120 days. The **-Service** parameter indicates the name of a domain controller in another domain since my test domain doesn't have enough computer accounts for an effective demonstration:

```
PS C:\> Get-QADComputer -NotLoggedOnFor 120 -Service "jdhit-dc01" `
>> -IncludedProperties LastLogon | Sort LastLogon | Select Name,LastLogon

Name                                          lastLogon
----                                          ---------
GODOT                                         10/24/2004 8:43:38 PM
SWITCH                                        10/14/2005 11:41:25 PM
PORTAL                                        10/15/2005 1:23:27 AM
PROSPERO                                      11/7/2008 1:46:35 PM
DOGTOY                                        3/20/2010 1:53:56 PM
```

Or I can use the **-PasswordNotChangedFor** parameter and get similar results:

```
PS C:\> Get-QADComputer -PasswordNotChangedFor 120 -Service "jdhit-dc01" `
>>-IncludedProperties pwdLastSet | Sort PwdLastSet | Select Name,pwdLastSet
>>
```

```
Name                                          pwdLastSet
----                                          ----------
GODOT                                         10/24/2004 5:43:09 PM
SWITCH                                        9/14/2005 9:07:27 PM
PORTAL                                        10/14/2005 11:41:32 PM
PROSPERO                                      11/7/2008 1:45:01 PM
DOGTOY                                        3/20/2010 1:53:56 PM
```

The **-InactiveFor** parameter is quite useful as it checks multiple conditions. It will return any computer objects that meet this condition where X is the value specified by the parameter:

- The account has an Expired status for at least X number of days.
- The account has not had a password change for at least X number of days.
- The account has not logged on for at least X number of days:

```
PS C:\> Get-QADComputer -InactiveFor 1000 -Service "jdhit-dc01" `
>> -IncludedProperties LastLogon,pwdLastSet | Select  Name,pwdLastSet,lastlogon
>>

Name                        pwdLastSet                  lastLogon
----                        ----------                  ---------
SWITCH                      9/14/2005 9:07:27 PM        10/14/2005 11:41:25 PM
PORTAL                      10/14/2005 11:41:32 PM      10/15/2005 1:23:27 AM
GODOT                       10/24/2004 5:43:09 PM       10/24/2004 8:43:38 PM
```

In this domain I found three computers that have been inactive for at least 1000 days. Lastly, the Quest cmdlets have a policy that wraps this all up into a neat package. The policy applies to both user and computer accounts. Use the **Get-QADInactiveAccountsPolicy** cmdlet to view the current settings:

```
PS C:\> Get-QADInactiveAccountsPolicy

     AccountExpiratonPeriod     PasswordNotChangedPeriod     NotLoggedOnPeriod
     ----------------------     ------------------------     -----------------

                          0                          120                    30
```

When you use the **-Inactive** parameter, any computer account that meets the policy setting is returned:

```
PS C:\> Get-QADComputer -Inactive
```

If you would like to define a new policy, then use the **Set-QADInactiveAccountPolicy** cmdlet:

```
PS C:\>Set-QADInactiveAccountsPolicy -AccountNotLoggedOnPeriod 60 -PasswordNotChangedPeriod
120
```

This policy is intended to work with Quest's commercial Active Directory product. You can modify the policy without the product, but it is stored locally. Thus if you run the command on two different computers you may get two different results.

Let me wrap up this section with a short script example that will create a report of all computer accounts. This is information I think you would find of most use when conducting an inventory or attempting to identify obsolete accounts:

Get-ComputerReport.ps1

```
#requires -pssnapin Quest.ActiveRoles.ADManagement

$wmi=Get-WmiObject -Class Win32_OperatingSystem

Get-QADComputer -sizelimit 0 -includedproperties LastLogon,pwdlastset  |
select Name,Description,ComputerRole,Location,OSName,OSServicePack, AccountIsDisabled, `
@{Name="Created";Expression={$_.CreationDate}}, `
@{Name="LastModified";Expression={$_.ModificationDate}}, `
@{Name="LastLogon";Expression={$_.LastLogon.AddMinutes($wmi.CurrentTimeZone)}},`
@{Name="LogonAge";Expression={((get-date)-$_.lastLogon).TotalDays -as [int]}}, `
@{Name="PasswordLastSet";Expression={($_.pwdLastSet).AddMinutes($wmi.CurrentTimeZone)}}, `
@{Name="PasswordAge";Expression={(get-date)-($_.pwdLastSet).AddMinutes($wmi.CurrentTimeZone)}}
```

This script re-uses code from earlier in the chapter to calculate some new properties or provide a short, more admin-friendly name. You should get output like this for each computer in the domain:

```
Name              : MAIL
Description       : Exchange 2007
ComputerRole      : Member
Location          : Corporate
OSName            : Windows Server® 2008 Standard without Hyper-V
OSServicePack     : Service Pack 2
AccountIsDisabled : False
Created           : 6/22/2010 12:24:22 PM
LastModified      : 7/30/2010 2:06:07 PM
LastLogon         : 7/27/2010 5:52:57 PM
LogonAge          : 6
PasswordLastSet   : 7/27/2010 2:27:56 PM
PasswordAge       : 6.00:45:33.6698432
```

You could take the results of this script and sort, filter, export, convert, print, or do just about anything else can think of.

Moving and Deleting Computer Accounts

Moving a computer account from one organizational unit to another, or deleting a computer account, uses the same expressions and techniques as you use for a user account. Please refer back to the chapter on Active Directory user accounts. Replace the user accounts with the computer accounts you want to manage and it should all work well.

Managing Computers Client-Side

While most of this chapter has focused on managing computer accounts in Active Directory, there are a few related actions you can perform in PowerShell from the client.

Add-Computer

It is possible to add a computer to a domain, or workgroup, using PowerShell and the **Add-Computer** cmdlet:

```
PS C:\> Add-Computer -domainname "JDHLAB.Local" -credential "jdhlab\administrator"
```

You will most likely need to specify a domain credential. This will add the computer to the default computer container. If you know the organizational unit, you can specify it:

```
PS C:\> Add-Computer -domainname "JDHLAB.Local" -credential "jdhlab\administrator" `
>> OUPath="OU=Desktops,DC=jdhlab,DC=local"
```

If you would like to take the computer out of the domain and put it back in a workgroup, you'll still need to specify a domain credential with proper permissions:

```
PS C:\> Add-Computer -workgroup "Workgroup" -credential "jdhlab\administrator"
```

In any event, you'll need to restart the computer for the change to take effect:

```
PS C:\> Restart-Computer
```

Test-ComputerSecureChannel

When troubleshooting, you might need to verify that the secure channel between the member computer and the domain is working properly. Use the **Test-ComputerSecureChannel** cmdlet. This is run from the domain member:

```
PS C:\> Test-ComputerSecureChannel
True
```

Right now, I have no problems. If there were, I could try the command with the **-Repair** parameter.

Reset-ComputerMachinePassword

One final remedy would be to reset the computer password using the **Reset-ComputerMachinePassword** cmdlet:

```
PS C:\> Reset-ComputerMachinePassword
```

That's all there is to it. The cmdlet will use any available domain controller. If you want to specify one, then use the **-Server** parameter:

```
PS C:\> Reset-ComputerMachinePassword -server "coredc01"
```

Chapter 7
Managing Organizational Units and Containers

A well designed Active Directory has an organizational structure that reflects your management requirements, not necessarily your organizational chart. While you may not spend a lot of time repeating the process of creating organizational units, you may want to incorporate it with other PowerShell provisioning and management scripts.

Creating Containers and Organizational Units

You can create both containers and organizational units (OUs). The primary difference between the two is that you cannot apply group policy or delegate permissions to a container. Examples of containers are the built-in Users or Computers folder you see in Active Directory Users and Computers. For the most part, you will want to create OUs, though I will show you how to create both.

Using the Active Directory Module

The Microsoft Active Directory module offers a few cmdlets for working with OUs. You can very easily create an OU like this with the **New-ADOrganizationalUnit** cmdlet:

```
PS C:\> New-ADOrganizationalUnit -Name "Offices"
```

This will create an OU called "Offices" in the domain root. As you might have guessed, the **Get-ADOrganizationalUnit** cmdlet can retrieve it:

```
PS C:\> Get-ADOrganizationalUnit -filter "name -eq 'Offices'"


City                     :
Country                  :
DistinguishedName        : OU=Offices,DC=jdhlab,DC=local
LinkedGroupPolicyObjects : {}
ManagedBy                :
Name                     : Offices
ObjectClass              : organizationalUnit
ObjectGUID               : 31ecd010-1fba-42c4-8c5b-5b7c5c8dbc39
PostalCode               :
State                    :
StreetAddress            :
```

You'll notice that the distinguished name indicates the OU was created in the domain root. If you want the OU somewhere else, you need to specify the parent path:

```
PS C:\> New-ADOrganizationalUnit -name "Atlanta" -Path "OU=Offices,DC=JDHLab,DC=Local"
-passthru


City                     :
Country                  :
DistinguishedName        : OU=Atlanta,OU=Offices,DC=JDHLab,DC=Local
LinkedGroupPolicyObjects : {}
ManagedBy                :
Name                     : Atlanta
ObjectClass              : organizationalUnit
ObjectGUID               : e833b7be-951e-4c88-85c9-952bce406d05
PostalCode               :
State                    :
StreetAddress            :
```

The parent container must already exist or you'll get an error. If your organizational units are related to physical locations, the **New-ADOrganizationalUnit** cmdlet offers a number of parameters you might want to use:

```
PS C:\> New-ADOrganizationalUnit -name "Chicago" -Path "OU=Offices,DC=JDHLab,DC=Local"  `
>>-city "Chicago" -streetaddress "1060 West Addison Street" -postalcode 60613 -state "IL" `
>> -country "US" -description "Chicago Marketing" -managedBy "a.aske"  `
>> -protectedFromAccidentalDeletion $True -passthru
>>


City                     : Chicago
Country                  : US
DistinguishedName        : OU=Chicago,OU=Offices,DC=JDHLab,DC=Local
LinkedGroupPolicyObjects : {}
ManagedBy                : CN=Alonzo Aske,OU=Executive,OU=Employees,DC=jdhlab,DC=local
Name                     : Chicago
ObjectClass              : organizationalUnit
ObjectGUID               : 0f56e845-542b-4d1c-8a14-9df65074caa9
PostalCode               : 60613
State                    : IL
StreetAddress            : 1060 West Addison Street
```

This cmdlet created an OU with just about everything filled out that you could want. I also used the

-ProtectedFromAccidentialDeletion parameter to explicitly set security so the OU can't accidentally be deleted. This is usually the default but I wanted to demonstrate the parameter in action. Set the value to $False if you don't want to protect it.

Pass It On

By default the **New-ADOrganizationalUnit** cmdlet doesn't write anything to the pipeline. That's why I used the **-Passthru** parameter. Otherwise I would have not seen any result.

If for some reason you wish to create a container, then you'll need to use the **New-ADObject** cmdlet:

```
PS C:\> New-ADObject -Type container -Name "MyContainer" -PassThru

DistinguishedName             Name             ObjectClass        ObjectGUID
-----------------             ----             -----------        ----------
cn=MyContainer,DC=jdhlab,D... MyContainer      container          aff6a4cd-4113-4952-82...
```

You can also create OUs using Active Directory PSDrive. First, you need to change to the domain root:

```
PS C:\> cd AD:
AD:\
PS AD:\> cd "DC=jdhlab,DC=local"
AD:\DC=jdhlab,DC=local
```

Let's create another office location under the Offices organizational unit:

```
PS AD:\DC=jdhlab,DC=local> cd OU=Offices
AD:\OU=Offices,DC=jdhlab,DC=local
```

You'll use the **New-Item** cmdlet to create an OU in the current "directory":

```
PS AD:\OU=Offices,DC=jdhlab,DC=local> new-item -Name "OU=Las Vegas" -ItemType "organizationalunit"

Name                 ObjectClass          DistinguishedName
----                 -----------          -----------------
Las Vegas            organizationalUnit   OU=Las Vegas,OU=Offices,DC=jdhlab,DC=local
```

The **New-Item** cmdlet doesn't allow you to specify other object properties, although you can pipe the new item to the **Set-ItemProperty** cmdlet to define a single value:

```
PS AD:\OU=Offices,DC=jdhlab,DC=local> New-Item -Name "OU=Miami" `
>> -ItemType "organizationalunit" |
>> Foreach {
>> Set-ItemProperty -path $_.PSPath -name "Description" -value "Customer Service" -passthru
>> }
>>


PSPath       : ActiveDirectory::/RootDSE/OU=Miami,OU=Offices,DC=jdhlab,DC=local
PSParentPath : ActiveDirectory::/RootDSE/OU=Offices,DC=jdhlab,DC=local
PSChildName  : OU=Miami
```

```
PSProvider    : ActiveDirectory
Description   : Customer Service
```

I can't pipe directly to the **Set-ItemProperty** cmdlet because it can't identify a path property on the incoming object. Thus, I have to use a **ForEach-Object** expression so that I can specify the value.

If you prefer, you can use the helper function **mkdir** or its alias **md**. This is a wrapper for the **New-Item** cmdlet:

```
PS AD:\OU=Offices,DC=jdhlab,DC=local> md "OU=Staging"
```

This is a fast and easy way to create additional OUs if you don't need to define any additional values.

Creating a container isn't that much different:

```
PS AD:\OU=Offices,DC=jdhlab,DC=local> New-Item -path "AD:\DC=jdhlab,DC=Local" `
>> -name "CN=Omega" -itemType "Container"
>>

Name                ObjectClass         DistinguishedName
----                -----------         -----------------
Omega               container           CN=Omega,DC=jdhlab,DC=Local
```

Because I'm still in the Offices "directory", I use the **-Path** parameter to specify the parent path for the new container, Omega.

If you simply need to create a lot of containers or organizational units, the PSDrive provider is fine; but not if you also want to define additional properties.

Using Quest Cmdlets

There is no specific cmdlet for creating containers or OUs by using Quest Cmdlets, though you can use the **New-QADObject** cmdlet. Using the parameters to define properties makes this pretty simple:

```
PS C:\> New-QADObject -parentcontainer "dc=jdhlab,dc=local" -name "Temporary" `
>>-type container -description "Temporary storage container"

Name                          Type          DN
----                          ----          --
Temporary                     container     cn=Temporary,dc=jdhlab,dc=local
```

The **New-QADObject** cmdlet creates a new container called Temporary under the domain root and sets a description property. Do you want to create an OU? I bet you can figure it out by now:

```
PS C:\> New-QADObject -parentcontainer "ou=employees,dc=mycompany,dc=local" -name "Legal" `
>> -type organizationalunit -description "Legal and Paralegal users" `
>> -objectattributes @{"street"="10 Wall Street";"l"="New York";"st"="NY";"postalcode"=10005}
>>

Name                       Type                DN
----                       ----                --
Legal                      organization...     ou=Legal,ou=employees,dc=jdhlab,dc=local
```

This should look very similar to the previous example. Notice, however, that the type is organizationalunit. Since it is an organizational unit, I can set additional properties such as address information. In this example, the Legal OU may contain contacts or user accounts from a New York City law firm. I use the **-ObjectAttributes** parameter to specify the additional properties.

This approach does not create a protected object by default like the Microsoft cmdlets. However, you can pipe the new object to the **Add-QADPermission** cmdlet to configure it accordingly:

```
PS C:\> New-QADObject -parentcontainer "ou=Employees,DC=jdhlab,DC=local" -name "Hourly" `
>> -type organizationalunit -description "Hourly and non salaried" |
>> Add-QADPermission  -Deny -Account Everyone -ApplyTo ThisObjectOnly -Rights
DeleteTree,Delete
>>

Ctrl    Account                         Rights                  Source          AppliesTo
----    -------                         ------                  ------          ---------
Deny    Everyone                        Special                 Not inherited   This object only
```

Permissions and security are covered in more detail in Chapter 13.

Modifying Containers and Organizational Units

The organizational unit and standard container don't have many properties you can, or need, to set. Though, it is pretty easy to do using the Microsoft or Quest cmdlets.

Microsoft has a dedicated cmdlet, **Set-ADOrganizationalUnit**, with parameters for most properties you would typically define:

```
PS C:\> Set-ADOrganizationalUnit  "OU=Atlanta,OU=Offices,DC=jdhlab,DC=local" `
>> -description "SouthEast Regional Office" -street "1 Philips Drive NW" -city "Atlanta" `
>> -state "GA" -postalcode "30303" -managedBy "D.Otta" -passthru
>>


City                     : Atlanta
Country                  :
DistinguishedName        : OU=Atlanta,OU=Offices,DC=jdhlab,DC=local
LinkedGroupPolicyObjects : {}
ManagedBy                : CN=Daniel Otta,OU=Executive,OU=Employees,DC=jdhlab,DC=local
Name                     : Atlanta
ObjectClass              : organizationalUnit
ObjectGUID               : e833b7be-951e-4c88-85c9-952bce406d05
PostalCode               : 30303
State                    : GA
StreetAddress            : 1 Philips Drive NW
```

The **Set-ADOrganizationalUnit** cmdlet gets the Atlanta organizational unit by its distinguished name and defines a number of properties. For the -**ManagedBy** parameter, all I specified was the SAMAccountname and the cmdlet took care of the rest.

Remember, there are no OU-specific cmdlets from Quest, though you can use the **Set-QADObject** cmdlet:

```
PS C:\> Set-QADObject "Miami" -Description "Regional Customer Service Center" `
>> -objectattributes @{l="Boca Raton";st="FL"}
>>
```

```
Name                          Type            DN
----                          ----            --
Miami                         organization... OU=Miami,OU=Offices,DC=jdhlab,DC=local
```

The **Set-QADObject** cmdlet requires an input object, which in my example is the Miami OU. Because I only have one object with a name of "Miami" this works just fine. Otherwise specify the distinguished name. The **Set-QADObject** cmdlet updates the description; I need to use the **-ObjectAttributes** parameter to define additional properties. In this example, I'm setting the locality or city (l) property and the state. You'll need to use the LDAP property names.

Renaming

Occasionally you may have the need to rename a container or OU. You'll need to use a more generic rename cmdlet. In the Active Directory module that would be the **Rename-ADObject** cmdlet:

```
PS C:\> Rename-ADObject -Identity "OU=JDHTest,DC=jdhlab,DC=local" -NewName "Private Test" `
>> -passthru
>>

DistinguishedName             Name              ObjectClass           ObjectGUID
-----------------             ----              -----------           ----------
OU=Private Test,DC=jdhlab,... Private Test      organizationalUnit    8fad8162-c195-459f-...
```

You need to specify the object's distinguished name and specify a new name. The **Rename-ADObject** cmdlet doesn't write anything to the pipeline unless you use the **-Passthru** parameter.

An alternative is to use the **Get-ADOrganizationalUnit** cmdlet and pipe the result to the **Rename-ADObject** cmdlet:

```
PS C:\> Get-ADOrganizationalUnit -Filter "name -eq 'Foobar'" |
>> Rename-ADObject -NewName "Babylon" -passthru
>>

DistinguishedName             Name              ObjectClass           ObjectGUID
-----------------             ----              -----------           ----------
OU=Bablyon,DC=jdhlab,DC=local Babylon           organizationalUnit    cefec88c-6f9a-402c-...
```

If I don't know the full path to the Foobar OU, I can use the **Get-ADOrganizationalUnit** cmdlet to retrieve the path, and then rename it.

You do almost the same thing when using the Quest cmdlets with the **Rename-QADObject** cmdlet:

```
PS C:\> Rename-QADObject "OU=Servers,DC=jdhlab,DC=local" -newName "Enterprise Servers"

Name                          Type            DN
----                          ----            --
OU=Enterprise Servers         organization... OU=Enterprise Servers,DC=jdhlab,DC=local
```

This example uses the **-NewName** parameter to rename the Servers organizational unit to "Enterprise Servers". Likewise you can retrieve the OU first, and then rename it:

```
PS C:\> Get-QADObject "Desktops" -Type organizationalunit |
>> Rename-QADObject -NewName "Company Desktops"
>>
```

```
Name                            Type            DN
----                            ----            --
Company Desktops                organization... ou=Company Desktops,DC=jdhlab,DC=local
```

Because there is no specific cmdlet for getting organizational units, you need to use the **Get-QADObject** cmdlet. I'm also specifying the object type so there is no confusion about what I wish to rename.

Permissions and Delegation

You may be wondering if you can script or automate delegation or permissions changes with Active Directory containers. While it is possible, I recommend you continue to use the delegation of control wizard, unless you are doing very simple and broad permission assignments. First, this is likely not an administrative task you will be repeating. Second, the delegation of control wizard makes very granular permission changes that are simply too time-consuming to do manually in PowerShell. Plus, if you make a mistake, there are security implications. Later in this book I will cover how to manage broad permission assignments of Active Directory objects.

Deleting

When using the Active Directory module, you can use the **Remove-ADOrganizationalUnit** cmdlet:

```
PS C:\> Remove-ADOrganizationalUnit -Identity "OU=Private Test,DC=jdhlab,DC=local" -whatif
What if: Performing operation "Remove" on Target "OU=Private Test,DC=jdhlab,DC=local".
```

Let's try it for real:

```
PS C:\> Remove-ADOrganizationalUnit -Identity "OU=Private Test,DC=jdhlab,DC=local"

Confirm
Are you sure you want to perform this action?
Performing operation "Remove" on Target "OU=Private Test,DC=jdhlab,DC=local".
[Y] Yes  [A] Yes to All  [N] No  [L] No to All  [S] Suspend  [?] Help (default is "Y"): y
Remove-ADOrganizationalUnit : Access is denied
At line:1 char:28
+ Remove-ADOrganizationalUnit <<<<  -Identity "OU=Private Test,DC=jdhlab,DC=local"
    + CategoryInfo          : PermissionDenied: (OU=Private Test,DC=jdhlab,DC=local:ADOrganiza
tionalUnit) [Remove-ADOrganizationalUnit], UnauthorizedAccessException  + FullyQualifiedErrorId
: Access is
denied,Microsoft.ActiveDirectory.Management.Commands.RemoveADOrganizationalUniT
```

Well that didn't work.

Are You Using Windows Server 2008?

If you create an organizational unit with a Windows Server 2008 domain controller, it is protected from automatic deletion by default. You'll notice a new check box when you create a new OU. This check box sets a deny access rule for the Everyone group, which prevents deletion. If you want to delete an OU, you first need to remove the access rule. This also means that you will get an Access Denied error message if you try to delete the OU from PowerShell.

The OU is protected so I need to change that first. I can accomplish this with a one-line expression:

```
PS C:\> Set-ADOrganizationalUnit -Identity "OU=Private Test,DC=jdhlab,DC=local" `
>> -protectedfromaccidentaldeletion $false -passthru |
>> Remove-ADOrganizationalUnit -recursive
>>

Are you sure you want to remove the item and all its children?
Performing recursive remove on Target: 'OU=Private Test,DC=jdhlab,DC=local'.
[Y] Yes  [A] Yes to All  [N] No  [L] No to All  [S] Suspend  [?] Help (default is "Y"):
```

First I use the **Set-ADOrganizationalUnit** cmdlet to change the protection level. I have to use the **-Passthru** parameter so that it writes an object to the pipeline. This is picked up by the **Remove-ADOrganizationalUnit** cmdlet. Because I knew there were child objects, I used the **-Recursive** parameter. If there are child objects and you don't specify **-Recursive**, PowerShell will throw an exception.

Caution!
Be careful here. Whenever you delete an OU and its objects, everything is deleted, even if you have protected child organizational units. Take the example above: The Private Test organizational unit contained user accounts and a child OU. The child OU was marked as protected. Yet when I was able to delete the Private Test OU, even the protected child OU was deleted.

The Quest cmdlets follow the same rules when you use the **Remove-QADObject** cmdlet, especially for containers that aren't empty:

```
PS C:\> Remove-QADObject -Identity "OU=Temporary Testing,DC=jdhlab,DC=local"

Warning!
Are you sure you want to delete this object: OU=Temporary Testing,DC=jdhlab,DC=local?
[Y] Yes  [A] Yes to All  [N] No  [L] No to All  [S] Suspend  [?] Help (default is "Y"): y
Remove-QADObject : The directory service can perform the requested operation only on a leaf
object.
At line:1 char:17
+ Remove-QADObject <<<<  -Identity "OU=Temporary Testing,DC=jdhlab,DC=local"
    + CategoryInfo          : NotSpecified: (:) [Remove-QADObject],
DirectoryServicesCOMException
    + FullyQualifiedErrorId : System.DirectoryServices.DirectoryServicesCOMException,Quest.
ActiveRoles.ArsPowerShellSn
   apIn.Cmdlets.RemoveObjectCmdlet
```

If the OU had been empty, this would have worked without any errors. If you intentionally want to remove the OU and its children, then use the **-DeleteTree** parameter:

```
PS C:\> Remove-QADObject -Identity "OU=Temporary Testing,DC=jdhlab,DC=local" -deleteTree

Warning!
Are you sure you want to delete this object and its children: OU=Temporary
Testing,DC=jdhlab,DC=local?
[Y] Yes  [A] Yes to All  [N] No  [L] No to All  [S] Suspend  [?] Help (default is "Y"):
```

In this particular situation, the organizational unit was not marked as protected. You get the same Access Denied message when you try:

```
PS C:\> Remove-QADObject -Identity "OU=Protected Test,DC=jdhlab,DC=local" -deleteTree

Warning!
Are you sure you want to delete this object and its children: OU=Protected
Test,DC=jdhlab,DC=local?
[Y] Yes  [A] Yes to All  [N] No  [L] No to All  [S] Suspend  [?] Help (default is "Y"):
Remove-QADObject : Access is denied. (Exception from HRESULT: 0x80070005 (E_ACCESSDENIED))
At line:1 char:17
+ Remove-QADObject <<<<  -Identity "OU=Protected Test,DC=jdhlab,DC=local" -deleteTree
    + CategoryInfo          : NotSpecified: (:) [Remove-QADObject], UnauthorizedAccessException
    + FullyQualifiedErrorId : System.UnauthorizedAccessException,
Quest.ActiveRoles.ArsPowerShellSnapIn.Cmdlets.RemoveObjectCmdlet
```

As before, you need to remove the protection. You must do it as a separate step using the **Get-QADPermission** and **Remove-QADPermission** cmdlets:

```
PS C:\> Get-QADPermission -Identity "OU=Protected Test,DC=jdhlab,DC=local" -deny |
>> remove-qadpermission
```

This example removes the explicitly Deny permission on the OU (presumably the only one) and pipes the permission object to the **Remove-QADPermission** cmdlet, which does the deed. Then you can run the **Remove-QADObject** expression.

Finally, what about using the Active Directory PSDrive provider? Here, you can see there are child organizational units under the domain root:

```
PS AD:\DC=jdhlab,DC=local> dir | where {$_.objectclass -eq "organizationalunit"}

Name                   ObjectClass          DistinguishedName
----                   -----------          -----------------
Branch Office          organizationalUnit   OU=Branch Office,DC=jdhlab,DC=local
Company Desktops       organizationalUnit   OU=Company Desktops,DC=jdhlab,DC=local
Contacts               organizationalUnit   OU=Contacts,DC=jdhlab,DC=local
Disabled Users         organizationalUnit   OU=Disabled Users,DC=jdhlab,DC=local
Domain Controllers     organizationalUnit   OU=Domain Controllers,DC=jdhlab,DC=local
Employees              organizationalUnit   OU=Employees,DC=jdhlab,DC=local
Enterprise Servers     organizationalUnit   OU=Enterprise Servers,DC=jdhlab,DC=local
Groups                 organizationalUnit   OU=Groups,DC=jdhlab,DC=local
Microsoft Exchang...   organizationalUnit   OU=Microsoft Exchange Security Groups,DC=jdhlab,DC=local
Obsolete               organizationalUnit   OU=Obsolete,DC=jdhlab,DC=local
Offices                organizationalUnit   OU=Offices,DC=jdhlab,DC=local
Orlando Temporary      organizationalUnit   OU=Orlando Temporary,DC=jdhlab,DC=local
Templates              organizationalUnit   OU=Templates,DC=jdhlab,DC=local
```

Let's delete the Orlando Temporary OU:

```
PS AD:\DC=jdhlab,DC=local> del "OU=Orlando Temporary"

Are you sure you want to remove?
OU=Orlando Temporary,DC=jdhlab,DC=local
[Y] Yes  [N] No  [S] Suspend  [?] Help (default is "Y"):
Remove-Item : Access is denied
At line:1 char:4
+ del <<<<  "OU=Orlando Temporary"
    + CategoryInfo          : PermissionDenied: (OU=Orlando Temporary,DC=jdhlab,DC=local:Str
ing) [Remove-Item], Unaut
   horizedAccessException
    + FullyQualifiedErrorId :
ADProvider:RemoveItem:AccessDenied,Microsoft.PowerShell.Commands.RemoveItemCommand
```

Hopefully you weren't too surprised by the access denied message. If it wasn't protected, PowerShell would have deleted it. If the OU has child objects you need to use the **-Recurse** parameter. In my example I'm using the common alias, del, in place of the **Remove-Item** cmdlet. But back to the protection issue.

Removing the permission will require editing the access control rule using the **Get-ACL** and **Set-ACL** cmdlets. The protected permission is a single deny entry for the Everyone group, which you can see in the access control list:

```
PS AD:\DC=jdhlab,DC=local> $acl=Get-Acl "ou=Orlando Temporary"
PS AD:\DC=jdhlab,DC=local> $acl.access |
>> where {$_.IdentityReference -eq "Everyone" -AND $_.AccessControlType -eq "Deny"}
>>


ActiveDirectoryRights : DeleteChild, DeleteTree, Delete
InheritanceType       : None
ObjectType            : 00000000-0000-0000-0000-000000000000
InheritedObjectType   : 00000000-0000-0000-0000-000000000000
ObjectFlags           : None
AccessControlType     : Deny
IdentityReference     : Everyone
IsInherited           : False
InheritanceFlags      : None
PropagationFlags      : None
```

What you have to do is remove this rule from the ACL. To make it easier to follow the process, I'll first save the rule to a variable:

```
PS AD:\DC=jdhlab,DC=local> $rule=$acl.access |
>> where {$_.IdentityReference -eq "Everyone" -AND $_.AccessControlType -eq"Deny"}
```

Next, you'll remove this rule from the ACL:

```
PS AD:\DC=jdhlab,DC=local> $acl.RemoveAccessRule($rule)
True
```

All that's left now is to apply the revised ACL to the object:

```
PS AD:\DC=jdhlab,DC=local> Set-Acl -Path "OU=Orlando Temporary" -AClObject $acl
```

Now you can delete the item without error:

```
PS AD:\DC=jdhlab,DC=local> del "OU=Orlando Temporary" -recurse

Are you sure you want to remove the item and all its children?
OU=Orlando Temporary,DC=jdhlab,DC=local
[Y] Yes  [N] No  [S] Suspend  [?] Help (default is "Y"):
```

Importing and Exporting

From time to time, you may need to export your organizational hierarchy for reporting purposes or perhaps to recreate it in a test environment. You can use either the Microsoft or Quest cmdlets.

You can export to CSV or XML format. Using the **Export-Clixml** cmdlet produces the most complete results, especially if you will be re-importing into PowerShell:

```
PS C:\> Get-ADOrganizationalUnit -filter "*" -properties * | Export-Clixml c:\work\OU.xml
```

Or using the Quest **Get-QADObject** cmdlet, which will create slightly different objects:

```
PS C:\> Get-QADObject -Type organizationalunit -includeAllProperties | Export-Clixml QOU.xml
```

In either case you could also specify a smaller subset of properties to export.

I want to wrap up this section with an exercise. I want to recreate the OU structure under my Employees OU to a new OU called Backup, which already has been created. It is important to remember that I am only exporting and importing the structure, not any users or groups contained within the organizational units. The Microsoft cmdlets offer a pretty easy solution which I've wrapped up in this short script:

Recreate-OUs.ps1

```
#requires -version 2.0

Import-Module "ActiveDirectory"

$base="OU=Employees,DC=jdhlab,DC=local"
Get-ADOrganizationalUnit -filter "name -ne 'Employees'" -searchbase $base -properties * |
Sort canonicalname | Foreach {
    #replace OU=Employees with OU=Backup
    $dn=$_.Distinguishedname.Replace("OU=Employees","OU=Backup")
    #define the parent path by parsing the distinguishedname
    $path=$dn.substring($dn.indexof(",")+1)
    $_ | Add-Member -MemberType "NoteProperty" -Name "Path" -value $path -force
    $_ | Add-Member -MemberType "NoteProperty" -Name "DistinguishedName" -value $dn -force
-passthru
 } |  New-ADOrganizationalUnit -passthru | Select Distinguishedname
```

The **Recreate-OUs** script uses the **Get-ADOrganizationalUnit** cmdlet to retrieve all OUs in the specified base, filtering out the base itself. I also grab all the properties:

```
Get-ADOrganizationalUnit -filter "name -ne 'Employees'" -searchbase $base -properties * |
```

I decided to sort the results by their canonical name. This way I get a hierarchy of sorts since I have to make sure any parent OU exists before creating any child OUs. Here's the tricky part: Because the **New-ADOrganizationalUnit** cmdlet works so well in the pipeline, all I have to do is make sure the incoming objects have the correct values. This means I need to specify the path for each OU. I accomplish that by grabbing the current distinguished name and replacing Employees with Backup to reflect the new location:

```
$dn=$_.Distinguishedname.Replace("OU=Employees","OU=Backup")
```

Then I can parse out the parent path by selecting the last part of the distinguished name:

```
$path=$dn.substring($dn.indexof(",")+1)
```

These values are added to the OU object with the **Add-Member** cmdlet, forcing a rewrite of existing values:

```
$_ | Add-Member -MemberType "NoteProperty" -Name "Path" -value $path -force
$_ | Add-Member -MemberType "NoteProperty" -Name "DistinguishedName" -value $dn -force -
passthru
```

Each modified object is piped to the **New-ADOrganizationalUnit** cmdlet, which creates the OU under the Backup OU. The end result is a duplicated hierarchy complete with all properties like **Description**, **City**, and **ManagedBy**. This script doesn't go as far to duplicate any custom permissions, although that is possible.

You can achieve similar results using the Quest cmdlets. This is my solution:

Recreate-OU-2.ps1

```
#requires -version 2.0

Add-pssnapin Quest.ActiveRoles.ADManagement

#define some variables

#the starting OU
$base="OU=Employees,DC=jdhlab,DC=local"

#the name of the XML file to create
$file="c:\work\qou.xml"

#the new OU
$target="OU=Quest"

#additional properties to export
$properties="DisplayName","Description","Street","l","State","PostalCode","c","ManagedBy"

#export to an XML file.
Write-Host "Exporting OUs from $base to $file" -ForegroundColor Green
Get-QADObject -Type organizationalunit -IncludedProperties $properties -searchroot $base `
-LdapFilter "(!(name=Employees))" | Export-Clixml -Path $file

$imported= Import-Clixml -Path $File
Write-host "Imported $($imported.count) organizational units from $base" -ForegroundColor
Green

$imported | Sort Canonicalname | Foreach {
  #replace OU=Employees with OU=Backup
  $dn=$_.dn.Replace("OU=Employees",$target)
  #define the parent path by parsing the distinguishedname
  $path=$dn.substring($dn.indexof(",")+1)
  $_ | Add-Member -MemberType "NoteProperty" -Name "ParentContainer" -value $path -force
  $_ | Add-Member -MemberType "NoteProperty" -Name "DistinguishedName" -value $dn -force
-passthru
 } |
foreach {
    #create a variable for the imported object to avoid pipeline confusion
    $ou=$_
    Write-Host "Creating $($_.name) in $($_.parentcontainer)" -foregroundcolor Yellow

    #define a hash of new properties
    $hash=@{}
    Foreach ($property in $properties) { $hash.Add($property,$ou.$property) }
```

```
#recreate the OU
New-QADObject  -type "OrganizationalUnit" -Name $ou.Name `
-ParentContainer $ou.ParentContainer  -ObjectAttributes $hash
}
```

Unfortunately the Quest version is a little more complicated and not nearly as complete. The first part of the script is similar to the Microsoft version. One main difference is that I need to define the properties on the recreated organizational units:

```
$properties="DisplayName","Description","Street","l","State","PostalCode","c","ManagedBy"
```

This variable holds the most commonly used properties. I also specify these same properties when I export all Employee OUs to an XML file:

```
Get-QADObject -Type organizationalunit -IncludedProperties $properties -searchroot $base `
-LdapFilter "(!(name=Employees))" | Export-Clixml -Path $file
```

When I re-import the XML, I go through the same sleight of hand to adjust paths:

```
$imported | Sort Canonicalname | Foreach {
  #replace OU=Employees with OU=Backup
  $dn=$_.dn.Replace("OU=Employees",$target)
  #define the parent path by parsing the distinguishedname
  $path=$dn.substring($dn.indexof(",")+1)
  $_ | Add-Member -MemberType "NoteProperty" -Name "ParentContainer" -value $path -force
  $_ | Add-Member -MemberType "NoteProperty" -Name "DistinguishedName" -value $dn -force
-passthru
 } |
```

To create the OUs under OU=Quest,DC=Jdhlab,DC=Local, each imported and tweaked OU object is piped to the **ForEach-Object** cmdlet, which passes it to the **New-QADObject** cmdlet. In the looping construct I define a hash table with all the properties I need to set:

```
#create a variable for the imported object to avoid pipeline confusion
$ou=$_
Write-Host "Creating $($_.name) in $($_.parentcontainer)" -foregroundcolor Yellow

#define a hash of new properties
$hash=@{}
foreach ($property in $properties) { $hash.Add($property,$ou.$property) }
```

This hash table is then used when I create the "new" organizational unit:

```
new-QADObject  -type "OrganizationalUnit" -Name $ou.Name `
-ParentContainer $ou.ParentContainer  -ObjectAttributes $hash
```

Of course, if you simply want to serialize information to either a CSV or XML file, you don't need to go through all of this nonsense.

Using the PowerShell Community Extensions

Before I end this chapter let me at least briefly introduce you to another tool that you might want to use. The free PowerShell Community Extensions is a community-driven effort to extend

PowerShell. Think of it as a free resource kit full of extra functions, cmdlets, and providers. You can download the latest version from http://pscx.codeplex.com. Allow me to offer a little taste of the AD-related features.

The extensions are delivered as a module so the first step is to import the module:

```
PS C:\> Import-Module PSCX
```

Of interest is the DirectoryServices provider. This allows you to "map" a PSDrive to Active Directory. This is very similar to the Microsoft provider with some subtle differences. The PSCX provider works with any Active Directory from Windows 2003 and up. You don't need the Active Directory web service at all. You can use both providers in the same PowerShell session.

To create a drive using the PSCX provider, the root is specified as an ADSI path:

```
PS C:\> New-PSDrive JDHLAB -PSProvider DirectoryServices -root "LDAP://DC=jdhlab,DC=local"
PS C:\> cd jdhlab:
JDHLAB:\
```

I've just created a drive mapped to my domain root. See?

```
PS JDHLAB:\> dir

      LastWriteTime Type                  Name
      ------------- ----                  ----
   8/3/2010  5:31 PM organizationalUnit    Backup
  7/16/2010  1:14 PM organizationalUnit    Branch Office
  1/24/2010  3:02 PM builtinDomain         Builtin
   8/3/2010  2:38 PM organizationalUnit    Company Desktops
  1/24/2010  3:02 PM container             Computers
   7/6/2010  7:43 PM organizationalUnit    Contacts
  7/27/2010  7:09 PM organizationalUnit    Disabled Users
  1/24/2010  3:02 PM organizationalUnit    Domain Controllers
   7/5/2010 10:49 AM organizationalUnit    Employees
   8/3/2010  2:36 PM organizationalUnit    Enterprise Servers
  1/24/2010  3:02 PM container             ForeignSecurityPrincipals
   3/3/2010 10:14 AM organizationalUnit    Groups
  1/24/2010  3:02 PM infrastructureUpdate  Infrastructure
  1/24/2010  3:02 PM lostAndFound          LostAndFound
  1/24/2010  3:02 PM container             Managed Service Accounts
  6/22/2010  2:51 PM organizationalUnit    Microsoft Exchange Security Groups
  6/22/2010  2:51 PM msExchSystemObjec...  Microsoft Exchange System Objects
   8/2/2010  4:39 PM container             MyContainer
  1/24/2010  3:02 PM msDS-QuotaContainer   NTDS Quotas
  7/26/2010  4:48 PM organizationalUnit    Obsolete
   8/2/2010  4:20 PM organizationalUnit    Offices
   8/3/2010 10:33 AM container             Omega
  1/24/2010  3:02 PM container             Program Data
   8/4/2010  3:00 PM organizationalUnit    Quest
  1/24/2010  3:02 PM container             System
  7/20/2010  1:09 PM organizationalUnit    Templates
   8/3/2010 10:47 AM container             Temporary
  1/24/2010  3:02 PM container             Users
```

Changing "directories" is pretty easy. Let me change to the Employees organizational unit and get a "directory" listing:

```
PS JDHLAB:\> cd employees
JDHLAB:\employees
PS JDHLAB:\employees> dir

        LastWriteTime Type                 Name
        ------------- ----                 ----
     8/3/2010  4:28 PM organizationalUnit  Accounting
     8/3/2010  4:31 PM organizationalUnit  Art
    7/28/2010  3:57 PM user                Cassie O'Pia
    7/28/2010  3:57 PM user                Chris Barry
     3/4/2010 12:50 PM organizationalUnit  Customer Service
    7/28/2010  4:41 PM user                DA_Hicks
     6/1/2010  2:20 PM organizationalUnit  Engineering
     6/1/2010  4:45 PM organizationalUnit  Executive
    7/26/2010  1:23 PM organizationalUnit  Finance
    7/28/2010  3:57 PM user                Francis Drake
     8/3/2010 10:58 AM organizationalUnit  Hourly
     3/4/2010 12:50 PM organizationalUnit  HR
     6/1/2010  2:20 PM organizationalUnit  IT
     8/4/2010 10:44 AM user                Jim Shortz
    7/28/2010  3:57 PM user                John Plumber
    7/28/2010  3:57 PM user                Johnson Apacible
     8/3/2010 10:49 AM organizationalUnit  Legal
     6/1/2010  2:19 PM organizationalUnit  Marketing
    7/26/2010  1:23 PM organizationalUnit  Payroll
    7/28/2010  4:40 PM user                Prithvi Raj
    7/28/2010  3:50 PM user                Roy G. Biv
    7/12/2010  3:35 PM organizationalUnit  Sales
     6/1/2010  2:19 PM organizationalUnit  Shipping
     8/3/2010  4:22 PM organizationalUnit  Temp
    7/15/2010  3:43 PM organizationalUnit  Test
    7/28/2010  3:57 PM user                Toby Nixon
    7/28/2010  3:57 PM user                William Flash
```

A new cmdlet in PSCX that I like is the **Show-Tree** cmdlet. This is a PowerShell version of a venerable DOS tool. Used within this context provides a very nice tree view of your OU hierarchy:

```
PS JDHLAB:\employees> show-tree
JDHLAB:\employees
├──Accounting
│  └──Consultants
├──Art
├──Customer Service
├──Engineering
├──Executive
├──Finance
├──Hourly
├──HR
│  └──Benefits
├──IT
├──Legal
├──Marketing
├──Payroll
│  └──Operations
├──Sales
│  ├──Agents
│  │  └──Mobile
│  └──Sales Managers
├──Shipping
├──Temp
│  └──Omicron
└──Test
```

If you use the **-ShowLeaf** parameter, then the command will display all the users, groups, and computers as well. Take it a step further with the **-ShowProperty** parameter and you'll get an additional listing of the object's properties. You can use the **Show-Tree** cmdlet with the Microsoft Active Directory provider, but because of the way the provider is implemented you get slightly different results. Personally, I prefer to use the **Show-Tree** cmdlet with the PSCX provider.

You probably won't have occasion to frequently automate organizational unit and container management, but as you've seen there a number of approaches that all will get the job done very quickly and all without a GUI.

Chapter 8
Managing Group Policy

If you are using Group Policy in your Active Directory environment, a practice I whole-heartedly endorse, you may be eager to manage it with PowerShell. Ideally, you are managing it now with the Group Policy Management Console (GPMC). This COM-based solution has been Microsoft's answer for the last several years. Many people, myself included, had in the past created VBScript and PowerShell scripts based on this object model. Fortunately, with the release of Windows Server 2008 R2 there is now a Group Policy module. This is separate from the Active Directory module, so you'll need to import it before using it:

```
PS C:\> Import-Module GroupPolicy
```

This module contains these cmdlets, many of which I'll discuss in this chapter.

Table 8-1 Group Policy Module Cmdlets

Name	Synopsis
Backup-GPO	Backs up one GPO or all the GPOs in a domain.
Copy-GPO	Copies a GPO.
Get-GPInheritance	Retrieves Group Policy inheritance information for a specified domain or OU.
Get-GPO	Gets one GPO or all the GPOs in a domain.

Get-GPOReport	Generates a report either in XML or HTML format for a specified GPO or for all GPOs in a domain.
Get-GPPermissions	Gets the permission level for one or more security principals on a specified GPO.
Get-GPPrefRegistryValue	Retrieves one or more Registry preference items under either Computer Configuration or User Configuration in a GPO.
Get-GPRegistryValue	Retrieves one or more Registry-based policy settings under either Computer Configuration or User Configuration in a GPO.
Get-GPResultantSetOfPolicy	Outputs the Resultant Set of Policy (RSoP) information for a user a computer or both to a file.
Get-GPStarterGPO	Gets one Starter GPO or all Starter GPOs in a domain.
Import-GPO	Imports the Group Policy settings from a backed-up GPO into a specified GPO.
New-GPLink	Links a GPO to a site domain or organizational unit (OU).
New-GPO	Creates a new GPO.
New-GPStarterGPO	Creates a new Starter GPO.
Remove-GPLink	Removes a GPO link from a site domain or OU.
Remove-GPO	Deletes a GPO.
Remove-GPPrefRegistryValue	Removes one or more Registry preference items from either Computer Configuration or User Configuration in a GPO.
Remove-GPRegistryValue	Removes one or more Registry-based policy settings from either Computer Configuration or User Configuration in a GPO.
Rename-GPO	Assigns a new display name to a GPO.
Restore-GPO	Restores one GPO or all GPOs in a domain from one or more GPO backup files.
Set-GPInheritance	Blocks or unblocks inheritance for a specified domain or organizational unit (OU).
Set-GPLink	Sets the properties of the specified GPO link.
Set-GPPermissions	Grants a level of permissions to a security principal for one GPO or all the GPOs in a domain.
Set-GPPrefRegistryValue	Configures a Registry preference item under either Computer Configuration or User Configuration in a GPO.

Set-GPRegistryValue	Configures one or more Registry-based policy settings under either Computer Configuration or User Configuration in a GPO.

Unlike the Active Directory module, nothing special needs to be running on a domain controller. When you install the Remote Server Administration Tools on your Windows 7 desktop, check the boxes to manage Group Policy and you'll get the module. You should be able to manage Group Policy on any domain controller running Windows Server 2003 and later.

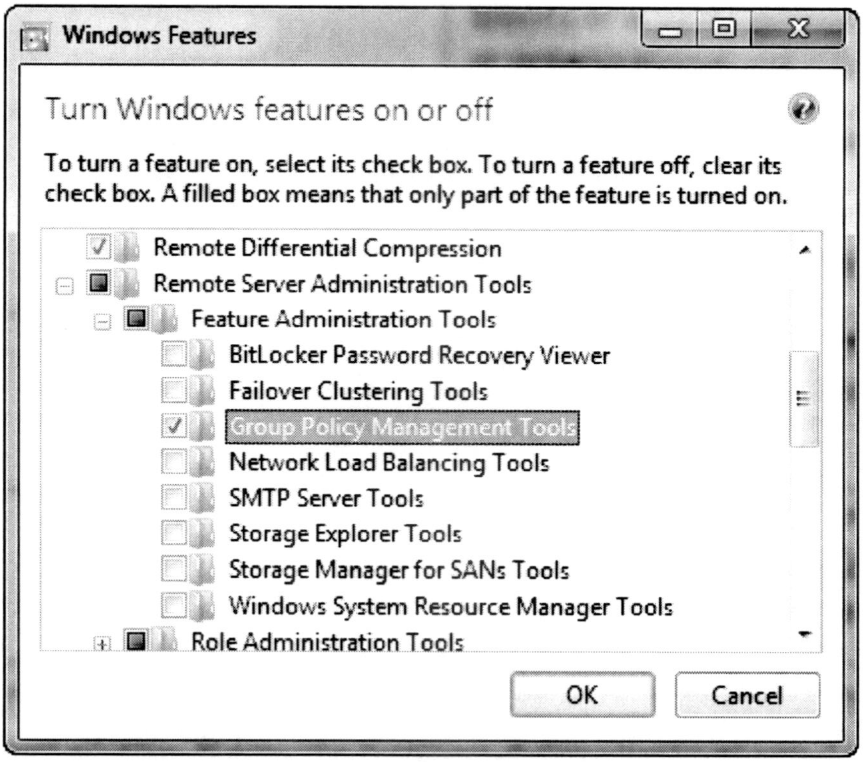

Figure 8-1 Configuring Group Policy Management Tools

But I Can't Use This Module!
If you are stuck with a down-level client like Windows XP and still have to run PowerShell 1.0, an alternative for managing Group Policy is to use a free solution from Group Policy MVP, Darren Mar-Elia, also known as The GPO Guy. Darren has developed a collection of free PowerShell cmdlets that wrap around the GPMGMT.GPM COM objects so you don't have to deal with the complexities of this object model. You can download these cmdlets, currently at version 1.3, from his blog, www.gpoguy.com, at http://tinyurl.com/37g9577. The free cmdlets can also be installed on PowerShell 2.0, but require manual intervention since they were never designed for PowerShell 2.0. I'd only recommend them if you can't use the Microsoft module.

After you download and install, you will need to add the SDMSoftware.PowerShell.GPMC PSSnapin to your session. You'll find that many of the cmdlets function like the Microsoft cmdlets I'll review in this chapter.

Darren also offers a number of other GPO tools at http://tinyurl.com/24kfpbj.

In this chapter I'll focus on the Microsoft cmdlets and give you a taste of some other third-party, PowerShell-based solutions for managing Group Policy.

Where's Quest?
The Quest PSSnapin does not have any cmdlets designed to work specifically with Group Policy. Some Group Policy information is stored in Active Directory, so you could use the **Get-QADObject** cmdlet, but I think you'll find it much easier to use the cmdlets I'm going to discuss in this chapter.

GPO Reporting

Finding GPOs

To retrieve information about a GPO, use the **Get-GPO** cmdlet. You can specify a GPO by name:

```
PS C:\> Get-GPO -Name "Default Domain Policy"


DisplayName      : Default Domain Policy
DomainName       : jdhlab.local
Owner            : JDHLAB\Domain Admins
Id               : 31b2f340-016d-11d2-945f-00c04fb984f9
GpoStatus        : AllSettingsEnabled
Description      :
CreationTime     : 1/24/2010 3:02:46 PM
ModificationTime : 8/16/2010 10:04:44 AM
UserVersion      : AD Version: 0, SysVol Version: 0
ComputerVersion  : AD Version: 10, SysVol Version: 10
WmiFilter        :
```

You can also refer to a GPO by its GUID or ID using the **-GUID** parameter. But since I rarely have any of those memorized, I don't use this approach often. One exception might be in a large, multi-domain forest where I might have duplicate GPO names. In this situation, programmatically referencing by GUID makes more sense.

You can also use the **-All** parameter to return all GPOs in your domain:

```
PS C:\> Get-GPO -all | Measure-Object


Count    : 13
Average  :
Sum      :
Maximum  :
Minimum  :
Property :
```

The **Get-GPO** cmdlet defaults to the domain of the current user. You can use the **-Domain** parameter to query GPOs in a different domain. You can also use the **-Server** parameter to query a specific server. Unfortunately, there is no provision for alternate credentials, so whatever account you are logged on with must have appropriate permission in any other domain you might query:

```
PS C:\> Get-GPO -all -Domain "jdhitsolutions.local" | Measure-Object


Count    : 9
Average  :
Sum      :
Maximum  :
Minimum  :
Property :
```

Unlike some of the Active Directory cmdlets, the **Get-GPO** cmdlet doesn't offer any filtering. This means you'll need to pipe GPO objects to the **Where-Object** cmdlet. For example, let's say I want to find all GPOs where the user configuration setting is disabled:

```
PS C:\> Get-GPO -all | where {$_.gpostatus -eq "UserSettingsDisabled"}


DisplayName      : Lab Computers
DomainName       : jdhlab.local
Owner            : JDHLAB\Domain Admins
Id               : 78d0bec3-82c2-45e2-a22f-0391654e5281
GpoStatus        : UserSettingsDisabled
Description      :
CreationTime     : 7/12/2010 4:05:45 PM
ModificationTime : 8/31/2010 12:21:30 PM
UserVersion      : AD Version: 0, SysVol Version: 0
ComputerVersion  : AD Version: 0, SysVol Version: 0
WmiFilter        :

DisplayName      : Firefox Config
DomainName       : jdhlab.local
Owner            : JDHLAB\Domain Admins
Id               : a1ecc28f-4854-4afb-b31f-b4d61d038a1b
GpoStatus        : UserSettingsDisabled
Description      :
CreationTime     : 3/22/2010 1:17:31 PM
ModificationTime : 7/13/2010 9:01:12 AM
UserVersion      : AD Version: 8, SysVol Version: 8
ComputerVersion  : AD Version: 0, SysVol Version: 0
WmiFilter        :
```

WMI Filters and Other Details

You're probably feeling this is pretty easy so you decide to find GPOs that have a WMI filter:

```
PS C:\> Get-GPO -all | where {$_.wmifilter} | Select Displayname,ComputerVersion,WMIFilter

DisplayName                                      ComputerVersion     WmiFilter
-----------                                      ---------------     --------
Win7 Special                                                         Microsoft.GroupPolicy.WmiFilter
XP Special                                                           Microsoft.GroupPolicy.WmiFilter
```

That doesn't look right. Turns out the cmdlet designers added a bit of behind-the-scenes tweaking when you run the **Get-GPO** cmdlet. The default view contains a few properties constructed on the fly. You can still capture the information you want, but it requires a bit more work. Pipe one of the GPOs to the **Select-Object** cmdlet displaying all properties:

```
PS C:\> Get-GPO -Name "Win7 Special" | Select *


Id               : 16b56faf-0746-4197-8860-c223b593e5af
DisplayName      : Win7 Special
Path             : cn={16B56FAF-0746-4197-8860-C223B593E5AF},cn=policies,cn=system,DC=jdhlab,DC...
Owner            : JDHLAB\Domain Admins
DomainName       : jdhlab.local
CreationTime     : 7/12/2010 4:05:38 PM
ModificationTime : 8/31/2010 12:37:16 PM
User             : Microsoft.GroupPolicy.UserConfiguration
Computer         : Microsoft.GroupPolicy.ComputerConfiguration
GpoStatus        : AllSettingsEnabled
WmiFilter        : Microsoft.GroupPolicy.WmiFilter
Description      :
```

Properties like **User**, **Computer**, and **WmiFilter** are nested objects. Let's save a GPO to a variable to make life simple:

```
PS C:\> $gpo=Get-GPO -Name "Win7 Special"
```

Now you can look at these properties and see that they are in fact additional objects:

```
PS C:\> $gpo.computer


Policy         : Microsoft.GroupPolicy.PolicySettings
Preference     : Microsoft.GroupPolicy.PreferenceSettings
DSVersion      : 4
SysvolVersion  : 4
Enabled        : True


PS C:\> $gpo.wmifilter

Description                             Name                        Path
-----------                             ----                        ----
Any Win7 flavor                         Windows 7                   MSFT_SomFilter.ID=...
```

Naturally, you might be interested to know the WMI filter definition. That information isn't displayed as a property, but there is a WMI filter method called **GetQueryList()** that will help:

```
PS C:\> ($gpo.wmifilter).GetQueryList()
root\CIMv2;Select * from win32_operatingsystem where caption like '%Windows 7%'
```

Once you know what you're looking for, you can construct a slightly more advanced PowerShell expression with the **Select-Object** cmdlet and a few hash tables:

```
PS C:\> Get-GPO -all | where {$_.wmifilter} |
>> Select Displayname,@{Name="ADVersion";Expression={$_.Computer.DSVersion}},
>> @{Name="SysVersion";Expression={$_.computer.Sysvolversion }},
>> @{Name="WMIFilter";Expression={$_.WMIFilter.Name}},
>> @{Name="WMIQuery";Expression={($_.WMIFilter).GetQueryList()}}
>>


DisplayName : Win7 Special
ADVersion   : 5
SysVersion  : 5
WMIFilter   : Windows 7
WMIQuery    : root\CIMv2;Select * from win32_operatingsystem where caption like '%Windows 7%'

DisplayName : Engineering Desktop
ADVersion   : 1
SysVersion  : 1
WMIFilter   : Windows 7
WMIQuery    : root\CIMv2;Select * from win32_operatingsystem where caption like '%Windows 7%'

DisplayName : XP Special
ADVersion   : 4
SysVersion  : 4
WMIFilter   : XP Systems
WMIQuery    : root\CIMv2;Select * from win32_operatingsystem where caption like '%XP%'
```

Creating HTML and XML Reports

Another typical Group Policy administrative task is preparing reports that document a GPO's settings. Most administrators prefer to prepare HTML reports because they are the easiest to view. The **Get-GPOReport** cmdlet will create such a report from one or more GPOs:

```
PS C:\> Get-GPOReport -Name "Default Domain Policy" -ReportType HTML `
>> -Path c:\work\DefaultDomain.html
```

The **-ReportType** parameter expects a value of HTML or XML. The **-Path** parameter reflects the name of the file to create. You can view this file using the **Invoke-Item** cmdlet:

```
PS C:\> Invoke-Item "c:\work\defauldomain.html"
```

Assuming your default browser is Internet Explorer, you might need to allow the ActiveX control. But then you should see a report like Figure 8-2.

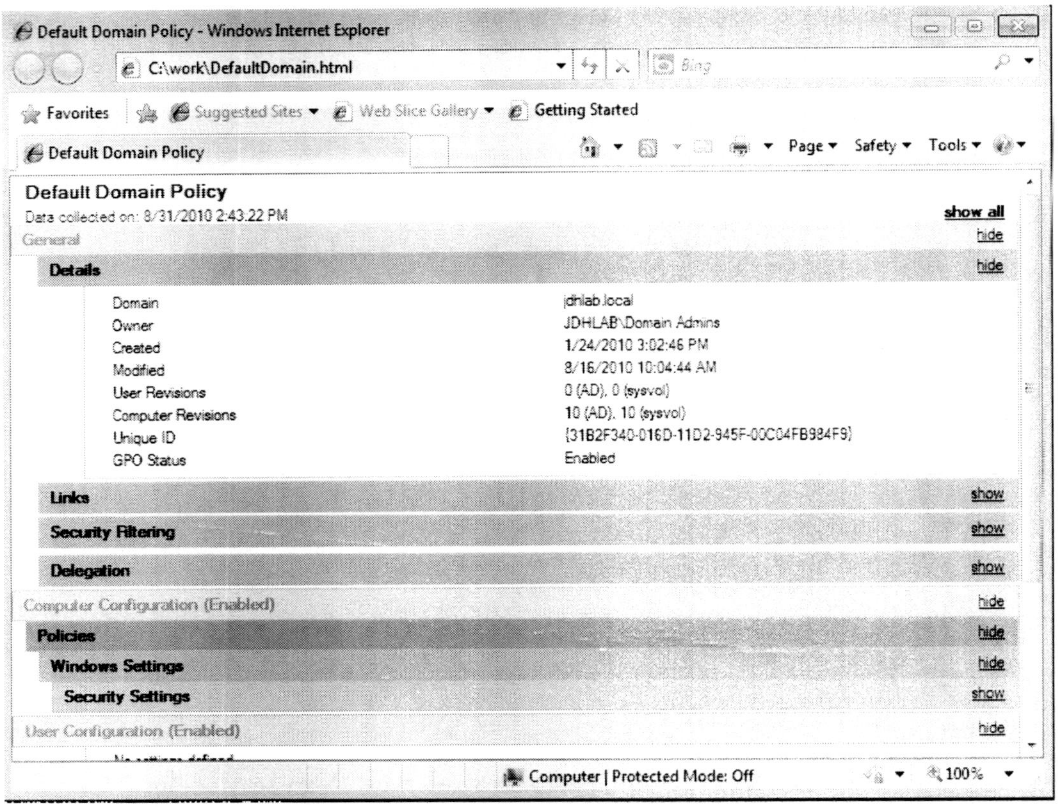

Figure 8-2 GPO HTML-based Report

If you prefer you can create a single HTML report for all GPOs using the **-All** parameter:

```
PS C:\> Get-GPOReport -All -ReportType HTML -Path "c:\work\AllGPOs.html"
```

Personally, I prefer to have a separate HTML report for each GPO, typically using the GPO name for the file name:

Create-AllGPOReports.ps1

```
Get-GPO -All | Foreach {
    #replace spaces in GPO names with dashes
    $file="C:\work\reports\{0}.html" -f ($_.displayname).Replace(" ","-")
    Write-Host "Creating $file" -ForegroundColor Green
    Get-GPOReport -Name $_.Displayname -ReportType HTML -Path $file
    #show the new file in the directory
    Get-Item $file
}
```

With the **ForEach-Object** cmdlet, I take the incoming GPO and define a report file name using the GPO's displayname. Personally, I don't like spaces in file names so I'm using the **Replace()** method to change all spaces to dashes:

```
$file="C:\work\reports\{0}.html" -f ($_.displayname).Replace(" ","-")
```

I use this file reference with the **Get-GPOReport** cmdlet:

```
Get-GPOReport -Name $_.Displayname -ReportType HTML -Path $file
```

Because the cmdlet doesn't write anything to the pipeline, I decided to use the **Get-Item** cmdlet to write each file object to the pipeline:

```
Get-Item $file
```

If you prefer to create XML-based reports, you can use everything I've just presented, substituting XML for HTML:

```
PS C:\> Get-GPOReport -All -ReportType XML -Path "c:\work\AllGPOs.xml"
```

If you are an XML aficionado, here's a technique you might find interesting. If you run the **Get-GPOReport** cmdlet and do not use the **-Path** parameter, the cmdlet writes either HTML or XML to the pipeline. This means you can create an XML object you can work with interactively in the shell:

```
PS C:\> [xml]$xml=Get-GPOReport -Name "WinRM Configuration" -ReportType XML
```

I cast $xml as an [xml] object, otherwise, $xml would be a very long string. But as an [xml] type, I can navigate it:

```
PS C:\> $xml

xml                                                                         GPO
---                                                                         ---
version="1.0" encoding="utf-16"                                             GPO

PS C:\> $xml.gpo


xsi                 : http://www.w3.org/2001/XMLSchema-instance
xsd                 : http://www.w3.org/2001/XMLSchema
xmlns               : http://www.microsoft.com/GroupPolicy/Settings
Identifier          : Identifier
Name                : WinRM Configuration
IncludeComments     : true
CreatedTime         : 2010-03-26T12:15:42
ModifiedTime        : 2010-08-24T15:49:56
ReadTime            : 2010-08-31T19:36:58.5063411Z
SecurityDescriptor  : SecurityDescriptor
FilterDataAvailable : true
Computer            : Computer
User                : User
LinksTo             : LinksTo


PS C:\> $xml.gpo.computer

VersionDirectory                VersionSysvol             Enabled             ExtensionData
----------------                -------------             -------             -------------
13                              13                        true                ExtensionData
```

```
PS C:\> $xml.gpo.computer.ExtensionData.Extension

q1                                          type                  Policy
--                                          ----                  ------
http://www.microsoft.com/GroupPolicy/S... q1:RegistrySettings  {Windows Firewall: Allow inb...
```

See how I navigated the XML document? The ExtensionData node contains information about what is actually in the GPO. Let's take a look at the Policy setting in a bit more detail:

```
PS C:\> $xml.gpo.computer.ExtensionData.Extension.policy | Select Name,State

Name                                                             State
----                                                             -----
Windows Firewall: Allow inbound remote administration excep... Enabled
Windows Firewall: Allow local port exceptions                   Enabled
Windows Firewall: Define inbound port exceptions                Enabled
Trusted Hosts                                                    Enabled
Allow automatic configuration of listeners                      Enabled
Allow Remote Shell Access                                        Enabled
Specify maximum number of processes per Shell                   Enabled
Specify maximum number of remote shells per user                Enabled
```

There are other policy properties, but many of them are simple explanatory. I'm more interested in the actual settings.

Finding Links

Unfortunately, there is no cmdlet for easily displaying what links are defined for each GPO. The best approach I've come up with is to generate an XML report for the GPO and pull link information from the report. To do this manually, you'll create an XML report like you did earlier, and save the results to a variable:

```
PS C:\> [xml]$gpo=Get-GPOReport -name "WinRM Configuration" -ReportType XML
```

Link information is part of the LinksTo node, which you can access directly:

```
PS C:\> $gpo.gpo.linksto

SOMName                       SOMPath                     Enabled        NoOverride
-------                       -------                     -------        ----------
jdhlab                        jdhlab.local                true           false
```

Based on this information I can see that the GPO is linked to the domain root. Since the module lacks a tool, I wrote my own:

Get-GPOLink.ps1

```
#requires -version 2.0

Function Get-GPOLink {

    [cmdletbinding()]

    Param(
```

```
        [Parameter(Position=0,Mandatory=$True,HelpMessage="Enter a GPO name",
        ValueFromPipeline=$True,ValueFromPipelineByPropertyName=$True)]
        [ValidateNotNullorEmpty()]
        [Alias("Displayname")]
        [string[]]$Name
    )
    Begin {
        Write-Verbose "Starting function"
        Write-Verbose "Checking for Group Policy Module and loading it if necessary."
        $mod="GroupPolicy"
        If (-not (get-module $mod)) {
        Try {
            Import-Module $mod -errorAction "Stop"
            }
        Catch {
            Write-Warning "Can't find or load the $mod Module"
            Break
        }
    }

    }
    Process {
        Foreach ($item in $name) {
            Write-Verbose "Getting links for $item"
            Try {
                [xml]$gpo=Get-GPOReport -name $item -ReportType XML -ErrorAction "Stop"
                $Links=$gpo.GPO.LinksTo
                #only proceed if links were found
                if ($links) {
                    #add GPO Name to the object
                    $Links | Add-Member -MemberType NoteProperty -Name "GPO" -Value $gpo.GPO.
Name -PassThru
                }
                Else {
                    Write-Verbose "No links found"
                }

            }
            Catch {
                Write-Warning "Failed to get XML data for $item"
            }
        } #foreach $item

    } #Process
    End {
        Write-Verbose "Finished function"
    }

} #end function
```

The **Get-GPOLink** script takes a GPO name and returns a custom object that shows the link information and the GPO:

```
PS C:\> Get-GPOLink "WinRM Configuration"


GPO        : WinRM Configuration
SOMName    : jdhlab
SOMPath    : jdhlab.local
Enabled    : true
NoOverride : false
```

The script is designed to accept pipeline input and can work with the **Get-GPO** cmdlet. I can find all GPOs linked to a scope of management:

```
PS C:\> Get-GPO -all | Get-GPOlink | where {$_.SOMPath -eq "jdhlab.local/Employees/Test"}


GPO        : FoxitReader
SOMName    : Test
SOMPath    : jdhlab.local/Employees/Test
Enabled    : false
NoOverride : false

GPO        : Firefox Config
SOMName    : Test
SOMPath    : jdhlab.local/Employees/Test
Enabled    : true
NoOverride : false

GPO        : Define Local Admins
SOMName    : Test
SOMPath    : jdhlab.local/Employees/Test
Enabled    : true
NoOverride : false
```

Note, that I can't determine the link order. Or I can prepare a report showing all links:

```
PS C:\> Get-GPO -all | Get-GPOlink | Sort GPO |
>> Format-Table -GroupBy GPO -Property SOMPath,Enabled,NoOverride
>>


   GPO: Default Domain Controllers Policy

SOMPath                                  Enabled                                  NoOverride
-------                                  -------                                  ----------
jdhlab.local/Domain Controllers          true                                     false


   GPO: Default Domain Policy

SOMPath                                  Enabled                                  NoOverride
-------                                  -------                                  ----------
jdhlab.local                             true                                     false


   GPO: Define Local Admins

SOMPath                                  Enabled                                  NoOverride
-------                                  -------                                  ----------
jdhlab.local/Company Desktops            true                                     false
jdhlab.local/Branch Office               false                                    false
jdhlab.local/Employees/Test              true                                     false


   GPO: Firefox Config

SOMPath                                  Enabled                                  NoOverride
-------                                  -------                                  ----------
jdhlab.local/Employees                   true                                     false
jdhlab.local/Employees/Test              true                                     false
jdhlab.local/Branch Office               true                                     false
```

```
   GPO: FoxitReader

SOMPath                                 Enabled                                 NoOverride
-------                                 -------                                 ----------
jdhlab.local/Employees/Test             false                                   false
jdhlab.local/Employees                  true                                    false


   GPO: WinRM Configuration

SOMPath                                 Enabled                                 NoOverride
-------                                 -------                                 ----------
jdhlab.local                            true                                    false
```

GPO Security Settings

Another piece of GPO information you might like to track are permissions. What permissions apply to which users or groups for a given GPO? The Group Policy module includes a cmdlet, **Get-GPPermissions**. It will display a version of what you see on the Delegation tab in the Group Policy Management Console. Figure 8-3 shows the security settings on the Default Domain Policy GPO.

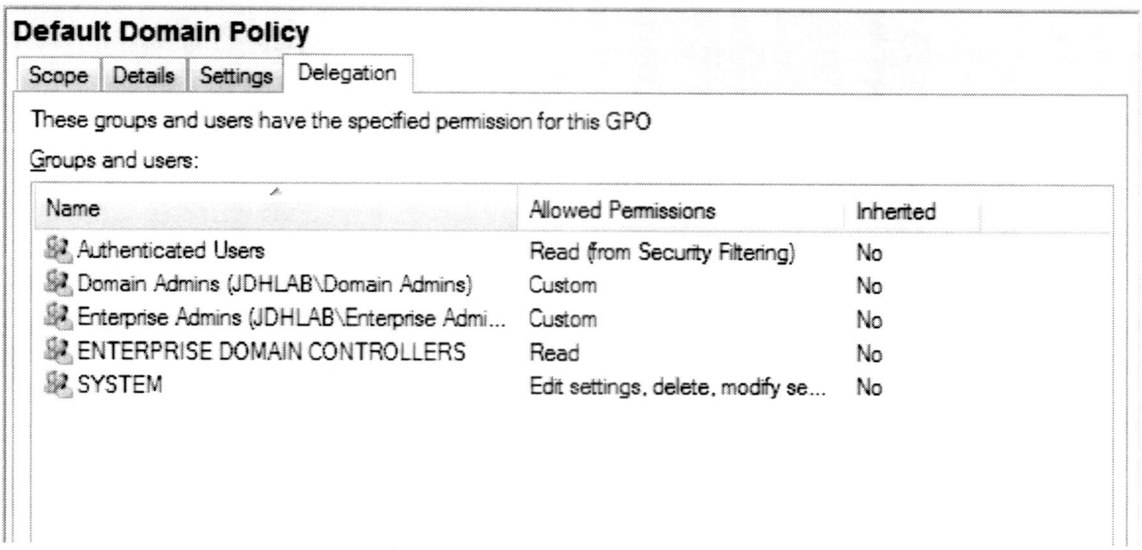

Figure 8-3 Default Domain Policy Security

In PowerShell, I can get the same information like this, referencing the GPO by name or GUID:

```
PS C:\> Get-GPPermissions -Name "default domain policy" -all


Trustee     : Domain Admins
TrusteeType : Group
Permission  : GpoCustom
Inherited   : False

Trustee     : Enterprise Admins
TrusteeType : Group
Permission  : GpoCustom
Inherited   : False
```

```
Trustee     : SYSTEM
TrusteeType : WellKnownGroup
Permission  : GpoEditDeleteModifySecurity
Inherited   : False

Trustee     : Authenticated Users
TrusteeType : WellKnownGroup
Permission  : GpoApply
Inherited   : False

Trustee     : ENTERPRISE DOMAIN CONTROLLERS
TrusteeType : WellKnownGroup
Permission  : GpoRead
Inherited   : False
```

If you know the security principal name and type, you can restrict the display using the **-TargetName** and **-TargetType** parameters:

```
PS C:\> Get-GPPermissions -Name "default domain policy" -TargetName "Domain Admins" `
>> -TargetType Group
>>


Trustee     : Domain Admins
TrusteeType : Group
Permission  : GpoCustom
Inherited   : False
```

This GPO has the default permissions. Let's look at another GPO that has been customized. I want to see what permissions have been applied for all by well known groups like SYSTEM:

```
PS C:\> Get-GPPermissions -Name "finance desktop" -all |
>> where {$_.Trustee -ne "WellKnownGroup"} | Select Trustee,Permision,Inherited
>>

Trustee                                        Permission          Inherited
-------                                        ----------          ---------
Microsoft.GroupPolicy.GPTrustee                  GpoApply          False
Microsoft.GroupPolicy.GPTrustee                  GpoApply          False
Microsoft.GroupPolicy.GPTrustee       GpoEditDeleteModifySecurity  False
Microsoft.GroupPolicy.GPTrustee                   GpoEdit          False
Microsoft.GroupPolicy.GPTrustee       GpoEditDeleteModifySecurity  False
Microsoft.GroupPolicy.GPTrustee                   GpoRead          False
Microsoft.GroupPolicy.GPTrustee       GpoEditDeleteModifySecurity  False
```

Once again, you are thwarted. Based on the output you saw earlier, you would think this expression would work. However, once again you're looking at nested objects that are parsed for the default display. You'll need to do some parsing of your own to get the results you want. Looking at the output object in the **Get-Member** cmdlet, you can see the trustee is something other than a simple string object:

```
PS C:\> Get-GPPermissions -Name "finance desktop" -all | Get-Member


   TypeName: Microsoft.GroupPolicy.GPPermission
```

```
Name        MemberType Definition
----        ---------- ----------
Equals      Method     bool Equals(System.Object obj)
GetHashCode Method     int GetHashCode()
GetType     Method     type GetType()
ToString    Method     string ToString()
Denied      Property   System.Boolean Denied {get;}
Inheritable Property   System.Boolean Inheritable {get;}
Inherited   Property   System.Boolean Inherited {get;}
Permission  Property   Microsoft.GroupPolicy.GPPermissionType Permission {get;}
Trustee     Property   Microsoft.GroupPolicy.GPTrustee Trustee {get;}
```

Since I know the Everyone group is included, let's look at it more closely to discover more about this Microsoft.GroupPolicy.GPTrustee object:

```
PS C:\> Get-GPPermissions -Name "finance desktop" -TargetName System -TargetType Group |
>> Select -ExpandProperty Trustee
>>


Domain  : NT AUTHORITY
DSPath  :
Name    : SYSTEM
Sid     : S-1-5-18
SidType : WellKnownGroup
```

With this information you can construct a better PowerShell expression:

```
PS C:\> Get-GPPermissions -Name "finance desktop" -all |
>> where {$_.Trustee.SidType -ne "WellKnownGroup"} |
>> Select @{Name="Group";Expression={"{0}\{1}" -f $_.Trustee.domain,$_.Trustee.Name}},
>> Permission,Inherited
>>

Group                                                   Permission     Inherited
-----                                                   ----------     ---------
JDHLAB\FinanceUsers                                       GpoApply     False
JDHLAB\Finance Managers                                   GpoApply     False
JDHLAB\Domain Admins                   GpoEditDeleteModifySecurity     False
JDHLAB\HelpDesk                                            GpoEdit     False
JDHLAB\Enterprise Admins               GpoEditDeleteModifySecurity     False
```

I used hash tables to define new properties with the **Select-Object** cmdlet. These permissions, by the way, also include those from security filtering.

Most of the permissions are pretty clear I think, except GpoCustom, which you saw as the Domain Admins permission on the Default Domain Policy. Unfortunately, there's no way with Get-GPPermissions to determine what that exactly means. What you can do, however, is get the GPO from the Active Directory PSDrive and look at its access control list.

Using the **Get-GPO** cmdlet, you can identify the object's Active Directory path:

```
PS C:\> Get-GPO -Name "Default domain policy" | Select path

Path
----
cn={31B2F340-016D-11D2-945F-00C04FB984F9},cn=policies,cn=system,DC=jdhlab,DC=local
```

For the sake of simplicity, let's build a variable for the PSDrive path:

```
PS C:\> $path=Join-path "AD:\" (Get-GPO -Name "Default domain policy").Path
```

Now you can get the object's access control list using the **Get-ACL** cmdlet:

```
PS C:\> $acl=Get-Acl $path
```

It's not very pretty, but by parsing out the Access property, you can divine the actual GPO permissions for the Domain Admins group:

```
PS C:\> $acl.access | where {$_.identityreference -match "domain admins"} |
>> Select AccessControlType,ActiveDirectoryRIghts,InheritanceFlags,PropagationFlags |
Format-List


AccessControlType     : Allow
ActiveDirectoryRights : CreateChild, Self, WriteProperty, GenericRead, WriteDacl, WriteOwner
InheritanceFlags      : None
PropagationFlags      : None

AccessControlType     : Allow
ActiveDirectoryRights : CreateChild, DeleteChild, Self, WriteProperty, DeleteTree, Delete,
                        GenericRead, WriteDacl, WriteOwner
InheritanceFlags      : ContainerInherit
PropagationFlags      : InheritOnly

AccessControlType     : Allow
ActiveDirectoryRights : CreateChild, Self, WriteProperty, GenericRead, WriteDacl, WriteOwner
InheritanceFlags      : None
PropagationFlags      : None
```

However, I believe most of your GPO security needs will be a bit more basic. You can use the **Set-GPPermissions** cmdlet to make simple or sweeping changes to one or all of your GPOs:

```
PS C:\> Set-GPPermissions -Name "Finance Desktop" -TargetName "Payroll Users" `
>>-TargetType "Group" -PermissionLevel GPOApply
>>


DisplayName      : Finance Desktop
DomainName       : jdhlab.local
Owner            : JDHLAB\Domain Admins
Id               : b3772e21-ff64-40c5-8777-c54e6b0516ab
GpoStatus        : AllSettingsEnabled
Description      :
CreationTime     : 9/2/2010 7:25:12 AM
ModificationTime : 9/2/2010 7:26:08 AM
UserVersion      : AD Version: 0, SysVol Version: 0
ComputerVersion  : AD Version: 0, SysVol Version: 0
WmiFilter        :
```

With this expression, I've modified security on the Finance Desktop GPO so that it now also applies to the Payroll Users group. The TargetType must be either User, Group, or Computer. The PermissionLevel must be one of these pre-defined settings:

- GpoRead
- GpoApply
- GpoEdit
- GpoEditDeleteModifySecurity
- None

You can use the **-Replace** parameter to edit current permissions. Let's take Payroll Users out of the Finance Desktop access control list:

```
PS C:\> Set-GPPermissions -Name "Finance Desktop" -TargetName "Payroll Users" `
>> -TargetType Group -PermissionLevel None -replace
>>


DisplayName      : Finance Desktop
DomainName       : jdhlab.local
Owner            : JDHLAB\Domain Admins
Id               : b3772e21-ff64-40c5-8777-c54e6b0516ab
GpoStatus        : AllSettingsEnabled
Description      :
CreationTime     : 9/2/2010 7:25:12 AM
ModificationTime : 9/2/2010 3:32:28 PM
UserVersion      : AD Version: 0, SysVol Version: 0
ComputerVersion  : AD Version: 0, SysVol Version: 0
WmiFilter        :
```

I replaced their existing permission with "None".

The **Set-GPPermissions** cmdlet has one other powerful option and that is the ability to set an access control entry on all GPOs in the domain by using the **-All** parameter. Cmdlet syntax is the same except that instead of specifying a GPO name, use **-All**.

For example, the Help Desk group often needs to look at Group Policy settings when troubleshooting a problem. I want to give them the GpoRead permission on all GPOs in my domain:

```
PS C:\> Set-GPPermissions -All -TargetName "Help Desk" -TargetType Group `
>> -PermissionLevel GPORead -Replace | Select Displayname
>>

DisplayName
-----------
HR Desktop
Win7 Special
Sales Desktop
Default Domain Policy
WinRM Configuration
ADMDemo
FoxitReader
Default Domain Controllers Policy
Corp Desktop
Lab Computers
XP Special
Firefox Config
Define Local Admins
Restricted Admins
Finance Desktop
```

With this one-line command, I updated security on all GPOs in my domain to give the Help Desk group Read permissions.

Scope of Management Security Settings

The last piece of GPO-related reporting is security settings at the Scope of Management (SOM) level. For example, who can create a GPO at the domain level? What group has permissions to link a GPO to an OU or run an Resultant Set of Policy (RSoP) logging report? The bad news is that the Group Policy module doesn't offer any cmdlets for these settings. The good news is that I've written an advanced functionGet-SOMPermission, for you to fill in the gap.

Another Option
If you are able to get the free SDM Software Group Policy cmdlets loaded, there is a cmdlet called **Get-SDMSOMSecurity** that you can use.

The Get-SOMPermission function relies on the underlying Group Policy management console COM object. This object can retrieve security settings for a given SOM. However, the permission value is an integer. You can decode the value from the GPMC constants object. To make life more PowerShell-friendly, I use this simple script to define a hash table of all the relevant permission values:

GPMC-Permissions.ps1

```
#a hash table of GPMC permission constants

$GPPerms=@{
"permGPOApply"                  = 65536;
"permGPORead"                   = 65792;
"permGPOEdit"                   = 65793;
"permGPOEditSecurityAndDelete"  = 65794;
"permGPOCustom"                 = 65795;
"permWMIFilterEdit"             = 131072;
"permWMIFilterFullControl"      = 131073;
"permWMIFilterCustom"           = 131074;
"permSOMLink"                   = 1835008;
"permSOMLogging"                = 1573120;
"permSOMPlanning"               = 1573376;
"permSOMGPOCreate"              = 1049600;
"permSOMWMICreate"              = 1049344;
"permSOMWMIFullControl"         = 1049345;
"permStarterGPORead"            = 197888;
"permStarterGPOEdit"            = 197889;
"permStarterGPOFullControl"     = 197890;
"permStarterGPOCustom"          = 197891;
}
```

I'll use the **GPMC-Permissions** hash table in this **Get-SOMPermission** function I wrote for you:

Get-SOMPermission.ps1

```
Function Get-SOMPermission {

Param (
    [Parameter(Position=0,Mandatory=$True,
    HelpMessage="Enter a scope of management's distinguishedname",
```

```
        ValueFromPipeline=$True,
        ValueFromPipelineByPropertyName=$True)]
        [ValidateNotNullorEmpty()]
        [Alias("Path ","Name")]
        [string[]]$DistinguishedName,
        [string]$Domain="jdhlab.local"
    )

    Begin {
        Write-Verbose "Starting Function"
        #define the permission constants hash table
        $GPPerms=@{
            "permGPOApply"                  = 65536;
            "permGPORead"                   = 65792;
            "permGPOEdit"                   = 65793;
            "permGPOEditSecurityAndDelete" = 65794;
            "permGPOCustom"                 = 65795;
            "permWMIFilterEdit"             = 131072;
            "permWMIFilterFullControl"      = 131073;
            "permWMIFilterCustom"           = 131074;
            "permSOMLink"                   = 1835008;
            "permSOMLogging"                = 1573120;
            "permSOMPlanning"               = 1573376;
            "permSOMGPOCreate"              = 1049600;
            "permSOMWMICreate"              = 1049344;
            "permSOMWMIFullControl"         = 1049345;
            "permStarterGPORead"            = 197888;
            "permStarterGPOEdit"            = 197889;
            "permStarterGPOFullControl"     = 197890;
            "permStarterGPOCustom"          = 197891;
            }

        #define the GPMC COM Objects
        $gpm=New-Object -ComObject "GPMGMT.GPM"
        $gpmConstants=$gpm.GetConstants()
        $gpmDomain=$gpm.GetDomain($domain,"",$gpmConstants.UseAnyDC)
    } #Begin

    Process {
        Foreach ($item in $DistinguishedName) {
            Write-Verbose "Getting SOM $item"
            $som=$gpmDomain.GetSOM($item)
            if ($som) {
            $security=$som.GetSecurityInfo()
            Write-Verbose "Found $($security.count) security entries"
            $security | Select @{Name="SOM";Expression={$item}},
            @{Name="Identity";Expression={
            "{0}\{1}" -f $_.Trustee.TrusteeDomain,$_.Trustee.TrusteeName}},
            Inherited,Denied,@{Name="Permission";Expression={
                $p=$_.Permission
                #verify permission is in the hash table
                if ($gpperms.ContainsValue($p)) {
                    #define an enumerator
                    $e=$gpperms.GetEnumerator()
                    #get the key name
                    $match=$e | where {$_.value -match $p}
                    $match.name
                }
                else {
                    #permission is not in hash so write the raw permission value
                    $p
                }
              }}
```

```
        } #if $som
        else {
            Write-Warning "Failed to retrieve SOM $item"
        }
    } #foreach

} #process

End {
    Write-Verbose "Finished"
 } #end
} #end function
```

Once you load the function into your shell, you specify the distinguished name of an OU and your domain. I've set the default domain value to my domain; you might want to change it for yours. I won't take time to explain the inner workings since most of it you'll never have to worry about. Instead, dot source the script and use it like a cmdlet:

```
PS R:\> Get-SOMPermission -Path "OU=Employees,DC=jdhlab,DC=local" |
>> where {-not $_.Inherited -and $_.identity -match "jdhlab"} | Select Identity,Permission
>>

Identity                                                        Permission
--------                                                        ----------
JDHLAB\Help Desk                                                permSOMLogging
JDHLAB\Help Desk                                                permSOMPlanning
JDHLAB\AD Admins                                                permSOMLink
JDHLAB\Domain Admins                                            permSOMLogging
JDHLAB\Domain Admins                                            permSOMPlanning
JDHLAB\Domain Admins                                            permSOMLink
```

I used my **Get-SOMPermission** function to find all non-inherited permissions for domain members (which skips items like System) on the Employees organizational unit. The permissions, I hope, are self-explanatory. Because the function takes pipelined input, you might want to document all SOM security settings with a CSV file, assuming you've loaded the Active Directory module:

```
PS C:\> dir "AD:\DC=jdhlab,DC=local" -recurse |
>> where {$_.objectclass -match "organizationalunit"} |
>> Get-SOMPermission | Export-csv -Path "C:\work\AllSOMPerms.csv" -NoTypeInformation
```

Naturally if you get SOM permissions you might want to set them as well. For that you'll need to use this custom function:

Set-SOMPermission.ps1

```
Function Set-SOMPermission {

[cmdletBinding(SupportsShouldProcess=$True)]

Param (
    [Parameter(Position=0,Mandatory=$True,
    HelpMessage="Enter a scope of management's distinguishedname",
    ValueFromPipeline=$True,
    ValueFromPipelineByPropertyName=$True)]
    [ValidateNotNullorEmpty()]
    [Alias("Path","Name")]
    [string[]]$DistinguishedName,
```

```
    [Parameter(Position=1,Mandatory=$True,
    HelpMessage="Enter the name of a group or user in domain\name format")]
    [ValidatePattern("\w+\\\w+")]
    [string]$Identity,

    [Parameter(Position=2,Mandatory=$True,
    HelpMessage="Enter the name of one or more SOM permissions. Valid choices are permSOMLink,
permSOMLogging,permSOMPlanning, and permSOMGPOCreate")]
    [ValidateSet("permSOMLink","permSOMLogging","permSOMPlanning","permSOMGPOCreate")]
    [string[]]$Permission,
    [string]$Domain="jdhlab.local",
    [Switch]$Remove

)

Begin {
    Write-Verbose "Starting Function"
    #define the permission constants hash table
    $GPPerms=@{
        "permGPOApply"                  = 65536;
        "permGPORead"                   = 65792;
        "permGPOEdit"                   = 65793;
        "permGPOEditSecurityAndDelete" = 65794;
        "permGPOCustom"                 = 65795;
        "permWMIFilterEdit"             = 131072;
        "permWMIFilterFullControl"      = 131073;
        "permWMIFilterCustom"           = 131074;
        "permSOMLink"                   = 1835008;
        "permSOMLogging"                = 1573120;
        "permSOMPlanning"               = 1573376;
        "permSOMGPOCreate"              = 1049600;
        "permSOMWMICreate"              = 1049344;
        "permSOMWMIFullControl"         = 1049345;
        "permStarterGPORead"            = 197888;
        "permStarterGPOEdit"            = 197889;
        "permStarterGPOFullControl"     = 197890;
        "permStarterGPOCustom"          = 197891;
        }

    #define the GPMC COM Objects
    $gpm=New-Object -ComObject "GPMGMT.GPM"
    $gpmConstants=$gpm.GetConstants()
    $gpmDomain=$gpm.GetDomain($domain,"",$gpmConstants.UseAnyDC)
    #parse out identity
    $IDDomain=$identity.Split("\")[0]
    $IDPrincipal=$identity.Split("\")[1]
} #Begin

Process {
    Foreach ($item in $DistinguishedName) {
        Write-Verbose "Getting SOM $item"
        $som=$gpmDomain.GetSOM($item)
        if ($som) {
            $security=$som.GetSecurityInfo()
            Write-Verbose "Found $($security.count) security entries for $($som.path)"
                 foreach ($perm in $permission) {
                   #get the permission value
                    $value=$gpperms.$($Perm)
                 if ($remove) {

                    $perm=$security |
                    where {$_.trustee.trusteename -eq $idprincipal -AND $_.trustee.trusteedo-
main -eq $IDDomain -AND $_.permission -eq $value}
                    if ($perm) {
```

```
                    Write-Verbose "Removing $value entry for $identity"
                    $security.Remove($Perm)
                }
                else {
                    Write-Verbose "No matching rule found"
                }
            }
            else {
                #create new permission
                Write-Verbose "Creating $perm permission ($value) for $identity"
                $newPerm=$gpm.CreatePermission($identity,$value,$True)
                Write $newperm

                #add the permission
                Write-Verbose "Adding the permission entry"
                $security.Add($newPerm)
            } #else

        } #foreach $perm in $permission
        #set security unless -Whatif
        #define a target message
        $target="{0} for {1}" -f $($som.path),$identity
        if ($pscmdlet.ShouldProcess($target)) {
            Write-Verbose "Setting security information"
            $som.SetSecurityInfo($security)
        } #whatif
    } #if $som
    else {
        Write-Warning "Failed to retrieve SOM $item"
    }
  } #foreach
} #process

End {
    Write-Verbose "Finished"
 } #end
} #end function
```

Most of this code is the same as the **Get-SOMPermission** function. The **Set-SOMPermission** function also requires the name of a user or group, in the format domain\username, and a comma-separated list of permissions. The function uses the GPMC COM object to create a new permission object:

```
$newPerm=$gpm.CreatePermission($identity,$value,$True)
```

$Value is the numeric value of the specified permission. Each permission is then added to the security object:

```
$security.Add($newPerm)
```

After all the permissions have been set, the SOM's security descriptor is updated:

```
$som.SetSecurityInfo($security)
```

The function also supports removing one or more permissions for a user or group. The function searches the existing security information for a match and, if found, removes it:

```
if ($remove) {

$perm=$security |
where {$_.trustee.trusteename -eq $idprincipal -AND $_.trustee.trusteedomain -eq $IDDomain
-AND $_.permission -eq $value}
if ($perm) {
Write-Verbose "Removing $value entry for $identity"
$security.Remove($Perm)
}
```

Because the **Set-SOMPermission** function is making a change to security, I included support for the **-WhatIf** parameter:

```
PS C:\> set-sompermission "OU=Test,OU=Employees,DC=jdhlab,dc=local" `
>> -identity "jdhlab\alphagroup permSOMLogging,permSOMPlanning -whatif
>>


Inherited   : False
Inheritable : True
Denied      : False
Permission  : 1573120
Trustee     : System.__ComObject

Inherited   : False
Inheritable : True
Denied      : False
Permission  : 1573376
Trustee     : System.__ComObject

What if: Performing operation "Set-SOMPermission" on Target "OU=Test,OU=Employees,DC=jdhlab,DC=...
```

If I had omitted **-WhatIf**, I would have granted members of the AlphaGroup permission on the Test organizational unit to perform RSoP logging and planning sessions.

Creating a GPO Framework

Create an Empty GPO

You can create empty GPOs using the **New-GPO** cmdlet:

```
PS C:\> New-GPO -Name "Executive Laptop" -Comment "configure C-level laptops"


DisplayName      : Executive Laptop
DomainName       : jdhlab.local
Owner            : JDHLAB\Domain Admins
Id               : af6f4a88-5e8a-49ce-84f7-f04677a7d80d
GpoStatus        : AllSettingsEnabled
Description      : configure C-level laptops
CreationTime     : 9/8/2010 8:36:10 AM
ModificationTime : 9/8/2010 8:36:11 AM
UserVersion      : AD Version: 0, SysVol Version: 0
ComputerVersion  : AD Version: 0, SysVol Version: 0
WmiFilter        :
```

This cmdlet created a GPO, called "Executive Laptop", which I can use to configure computer settings. Nothing is defined in the policy and it isn't linked anywhere, but I'll get to that in a bit. Or I could open the Group Policy editor and begin modifying the policy.

Using Starter GPOs

Microsoft also offers a collection of starter GPOs. These are pre-configured GPOs with common or recommended settings for a variety of operating systems. You can use them as is, or as a starting point for your own customization. Use the **Get-GPStarterGPO** cmdlet to see them:

```
PS C:\> Get-GPStartergpo -All
```

You should see a collection of starter GPOs like Table 8-2.

Table 8-2 Starter Group Policy Objects

DisplayName	Description
Windows XP SP2 SSLF User	Contains the user Group Policy settings recommended for the Specialized Security Limited Functionality (SSLF) client environment described in the Windows XP security guide.
Windows XP SP2 EC Computer	Contains the computer Group Policy settings recommended for the Enterprise Client (EC) environment described in the Windows XP security guide.
Windows Vista SSLF User	Contains the user Group Policy settings recommended for the Specialized Security Limited Functionality (SSLF) client environment described in the Windows Vista security guide.
Windows Vista EC Computer	Contains the computer Group Policy settings recommended for the Enterprise Client (EC) environment described in the Windows Vista security guide.
Windows Vista SSLF Computer	Contains the computer Group Policy settings recommended for the Specialized Security Limited Functionality (SSLF) client environment described in the Windows Vista security guide.
Windows Vista EC User	Contains the user Group Policy settings recommended for the Enterprise Client (EC) environment described in the Windows Vista security guide.
Windows XP SP2 EC User	Contains the user Group Policy settings recommended for the Enterprise Client (EC) environment described in the Windows XP security guide.

Windows XP SP2 SSLF Computer	Contains the computer Group Policy settings recommended for the Specialized Security Limited Functionality (SSLF) client environment described in the Windows XP security guide.

To create a new GPO based on one of these starter GPOs, you'll use the **New-GPO** cmdlet and reference the starter by name or GUID:

```
PS C:\> New-GPO -StarterGPOName "Windows Vista EC User" -name "Branch Office User"


DisplayName      : Branch Office User
DomainName       : jdhlab.local
Owner            : JDHLAB\Domain Admins
Id               : 74edb1e6-4073-4c37-977c-0bbf7384f3f4
GpoStatus        : AllSettingsEnabled
Description      :
CreationTime     : 9/8/2010 8:53:16 AM
ModificationTime : 9/8/2010 8:53:16 AM
UserVersion      : AD Version: 1, SysVol Version: 1
ComputerVersion  : AD Version: 1, SysVol Version: 1
WmiFilter        :
```

The new GPO, "Branch Office User" is already configured with settings from the starter GPO. I could use it as is or modify.

One great feature about starter GPOs is that you can create your own using the **New-GPStarterGPO** cmdlet:

```
PS C:\> New-GPStarterGPO -Name "Corp Desktop Starter" -comment "standard desktop settings"


DisplayName       : Corp Desktop Starter
Id                : a02f2559-3c2d-45e9-9047-977b7978412e
Owner             : BUILTIN\Administrators
CreationTime      : 9/8/2010 9:16:14 AM
ModificationTime  : 9/8/2010 9:16:14 AM
UserVersion       : 0
ComputerVersion   : 0
StarterGpoVersion :
StarterGpoType    : Custom
Author            :
Description       : standard desktop settings
```

The **New-GPStarterGPO** cmdlet will create an empty starter GPO. After you configure it, you can use it to create new GPOs like any other starter. Another approach to jump start GPO deployment is to copy an existing GPO. I'll cover that later in the chapter.

GPO Provisioning

The Group Policy module offers some functionality for provisioning or configuring GPOs.

Managing User Settings

If you have a GPO that has no user configuration settings, you may wish to disable the user configuration node:

```
PS C:\> $gpo=Get-GPO -Name "HR Desktop"
PS C:\> $gpo.user


Policy        : Microsoft.GroupPolicy.PolicySettings
Preference    : Microsoft.GroupPolicy.PreferenceSettings
DSVersion     : 0
SysvolVersion : 0
Enabled       : True
```

As you can see, the user configuration node of the HR Desktop GPO is enabled. You can disable it by setting the **Enabled** property to $False:

```
PS C:\> $gpo.User.enabled=$false
```

That's it. The change is immediate.

Managing Computer Settings

Likewise, you can also modify computer settings:

```
PS C:\> $gpo=Get-gpo "Branch Office User"
PS C:\> $gpo.Computer


Policy        : Microsoft.GroupPolicy.PolicySettings
Preference    : Microsoft.GroupPolicy.PreferenceSettings
DSVersion     : 1
SysvolVersion : 1
Enabled       : True

PS C:\> $gpo.Computer.Enabled=$false
```

Again, the change is immediate.

Managing Links

Earlier in the chapter I showed how to discover where a GPO is linked. To create a new link you'll use the **New-GPLink** cmdlet:

```
PS C:\> New-GPLink -Name "Executive Laptop" `
>> -Target "OU=Laptops,OU=Company Desktops,DC=jdhlab,DC=local" -LinkEnabled "Yes"
>>


GpoId       : af6f4a88-5e8a-49ce-84f7-f04677a7d80d
DisplayName : Executive Laptop
Enabled     : True
Enforced    : False
Target      : OU=Laptops,OU=Company Desktops,DC=jdhlab,DC=local
Order       : 1
```

If I had wanted to also enforce the GPO I would have included the **-Enforced** parameter:

```
New-GPLink -Name "Executive Laptop" -Target "OU=Laptops,OU=Company
Desktops,DC=jdhlab,DC=local"
-LinkEnabled "Yes" -Enforced "Yes"
```

But since I didn't, I can use the **Set-GPLink** cmdlet to modify it:

```
PS C:\> Set-GPLink -Name "Executive Laptop"
>> -Target "OU=Laptops,OU=Company Desktops,DC=jdhlab,DC=local" -Enforced "Yes"


GpoId       : af6f4a88-5e8a-49ce-84f7-f04677a7d80d
DisplayName : Executive Laptop
Enabled     : True
Enforced    : True
Target      : OU=Laptops,OU=Company Desktops,DC=jdhlab,DC=local
Order       : 1
```

You can also use the **Set-GPLink** cmdlet to modify the **Enabled** and **Order** properties:

```
PS C:\> Set-GPLink -Name "Corp Desktop" -Target "OU=Company Desktops,DC=jdhlab,DC=local" `
>> -Enforce "Yes" -Order -1


GpoId       : cb903cce-8e60-4e83-bbcd-944cc4ccc0eb
DisplayName : Corp Desktop
Enabled     : True
Enforced    : True
Target      : OU=Company Desktops,DC=jdhlab,DC=local
Order       : 3
```

With this command I enforced the Corp Desktop GPO that is linked to the Company Desktops organizational unit and moved it to the last order position using -1.

When it comes time to remove a link, the **Remove-GPLink** cmdlet is the answer:

```
PS C:\>  Remove-GPLink -Name "Firefox Config" -Target "OU=Employees,DC=jdhlab,DC=local"


DisplayName      : Firefox Config
DomainName       : jdhlab.local
Owner            : JDHLAB\Domain Admins
Id               : a1ecc28f-4854-4afb-b31f-b4d61d038a1b
GpoStatus        : UserSettingsDisabled
Description      :
CreationTime     : 3/22/2010 1:17:31 PM
ModificationTime : 9/2/2010 5:00:16 PM
UserVersion      : AD Version: 8, SysVol Version: 8
ComputerVersion  : AD Version: 0, SysVol Version: 0
WmiFilter        :
```

The **Remove-GPLink** cmdlet writes the GPO to the pipeline.

Another way to look at links is from the scope of management. That is, what GPOs are linked to an OU or site? Again, there are no cmdlets you can use, but there is the Group Policy Management COM object that you've used before. Once you have a reference to a SOM you can retrieve the linked GPOs:

```
    $som=$gpmDomain.GetSOM($item)
    if ($som) {
        $links=$Som.GetGPOLinks()
```

I wrote a function, **Get-SOMLink**, that simplifies the entire process:

Get-SOMLink.ps1

```
Function Get-SOMLink {

Param (
    [Parameter(Position=0,Mandatory=$True,
    HelpMessage="Enter a scope of management's distinguishedname",
    ValueFromPipeline=$True,
    ValueFromPipelineByPropertyName=$True)]
    [ValidateNotNullorEmpty()]
    [Alias("Path","Name")]
    [string[]]$DistinguishedName,
    [string]$Domain="jdhlab.local"
)

Begin {
    Write-Verbose "Starting Function"
    #define the permission constants hash table
    $GPPerms=@{
        "permGPOApply"                  = 65536;
        "permGPORead"                   = 65792;
        "permGPOEdit"                   = 65793;
        "permGPOEditSecurityAndDelete" = 65794;
        "permGPOCustom"                 = 65795;
        "permWMIFilterEdit"             = 131072;
        "permWMIFilterFullControl"      = 131073;
        "permWMIFilterCustom"           = 131074;
        "permSOMLink"                   = 1835008;
        "permSOMLogging"                = 1573120;
        "permSOMPlanning"               = 1573376;
        "permSOMGPOCreate"              = 1049600;
        "permSOMWMICreate"              = 1049344;
        "permSOMWMIFullControl"         = 1049345;
        "permStarterGPORead"            = 197888;
        "permStarterGPOEdit"            = 197889;
        "permStarterGPOFullControl"     = 197890;
        "permStarterGPOCustom"          = 197891;
        }

    #define the GPMC COM Objects
    $gpm=New-Object -ComObject "GPMGMT.GPM"
    $gpmConstants=$gpm.GetConstants()
    $gpmDomain=$gpm.GetDomain($domain,"",$gpmConstants.UseAnyDC)
} #Begin

Process {
    Foreach ($item in $DistinguishedName) {
        Write-Verbose "Getting SOM $item"
        $som=$gpmDomain.GetSOM($item)
        if ($som) {
            $links=$Som.GetGPOLinks()
            if ($links) {
                #add the GPO name
```

```
                Write-Verbose ("Found {0} GPO links" -f ($links | Measure-Object).count)
                $links | Select @{Name="Name";Expression={($gpmDomain.GetGPO($_.GPOID)).
DisplayName}},
                @{Name="Description";Expression={($gpmDomain.GetGPO($_.GPOID)).Description}},
                GPOID,Enabled,Enforced,GPODomain,SOMLinkOrder,
                @{Name="SOM";Expression={$_.SOM.Path}}
            } #if $links

        } #if $som
        else {
            Write-Warning "Failed to retrieve SOM $item"
        }
    } #foreach

} #process

End {
    Write-Verbose "Finished"
 } #end
} #end function
```

The **Get-SOMLink** function takes the distinguished name of an organizational unit and your domain as parameters. I've set the domain default, which you'll want to modify. Here's an example of the function in action:

```
PS C:\> Get-SOMLink "OU=Test,OU=Employees,DC=Jdhlab,DC=local"


Name         : Define Local Admins
Description  : Control membership in local admins group
GPOID        : {A263EFB9-1BFE-4918-ADA1-A075325513F7}
Enabled      : True
Enforced     : False
GPODomain    : jdhlab.local
SOMLinkOrder : 1
SOM          : OU=Test,OU=Employees,DC=Jdhlab,DC=local

Name         : Firefox Config
Description  :
GPOID        : {A1ECC28F-4854-4AFB-B31F-B4D61D038A1B}
Enabled      : True
Enforced     : False
GPODomain    : jdhlab.local
SOMLinkOrder : 2
SOM          : OU=Test,OU=Employees,DC=Jdhlab,DC=local
```

What this won't do is get site-linked GPOs. For that, you'll need to use another function I wrote, **Get-GPSiteLink**:

Get-GPSiteLink.ps1

```
Function Get-GPSiteLink {

Param (
    [Parameter(Position=0,ValueFromPipeline=$True)]
    [string]$SiteName="Default-First-Site-Name",
    [Parameter(Position=1)]
    [string]$Domain="jdhlab.local",
    [Parameter(Position=2)]
    [string]$Forest="jdhlab.local"
```

```
)

Begin {
    Write-Verbose "Starting Function"
    #define the permission constants hash table
    $GPPerms=@{
        "permGPOApply"                  = 65536;
        "permGPORead"                   = 65792;
        "permGPOEdit"                   = 65793;
        "permGPOEditSecurityAndDelete" = 65794;
        "permGPOCustom"                 = 65795;
        "permWMIFilterEdit"             = 131072;
        "permWMIFilterFullControl"      = 131073;
        "permWMIFilterCustom"           = 131074;
        "permSOMLink"                   = 1835008;
        "permSOMLogging"                = 1573120;
        "permSOMPlanning"               = 1573376;
        "permSOMGPOCreate"              = 1049600;
        "permSOMWMICreate"              = 1049344;
        "permSOMWMIFullControl"         = 1049345;
        "permStarterGPORead"            = 197888;
        "permStarterGPOEdit"            = 197889;
        "permStarterGPOFullControl"     = 197890;
        "permStarterGPOCustom"          = 197891;
        }

    #define the GPMC COM Objects
    $gpm=New-Object -ComObject "GPMGMT.GPM"
    $gpmConstants=$gpm.GetConstants()
    $gpmDomain=$gpm.GetDomain($domain,"",$gpmConstants.UseAnyDC)
} #Begin

Process {
 foreach ($item in $siteName) {
   #connect to site container
   $SiteContainer=$gpm.GetSitesContainer($forest,$domain,$null,$gpmConstants.UseAnyDC)
   Write-Verbose "Connected to site container on $($SiteContainer.domainController)"
   #get sites
   Write-Verbose "Getting $item"
   $site=$SiteContainer.GetSite($item)
   Write-Verbose ("Found {0} sites" -f ($sites | Measure-Object).count )
   if ($site) {
       Write-Verbose "Getting site GPO links"
       $links=$Site.GetGPOLinks()
       if ($links) {
          #add the GPO name
          Write-Verbose ("Found {0} GPO links" -f ($links | Measure-Object).count)
          $links | Select @{Name="Name";Expression={($gpmDomain.GetGPO($_.GPOID)).
DisplayName}},
          @{Name="Description";Expression={($gpmDomain.GetGPO($_.GPOID)).Description}},
          GPOID,Enabled,Enforced,GPODomain,SOMLinkOrder,
          @{Name="SOM";Expression={$_.SOM.Path}}
        } #if $links
   } #if $site
 } #foreach site

} #process

End {
    Write-Verbose "Finished"
 } #end
} #end function
```

This too uses the GPMGMT COM object. The function takes a site name, using the default site name as the function default and values for the forest and domain. Again, I've hard-coded defaults you will want to modify. You don't need to worry too much about the technical details here, simply use the function like a cmdlet:

```
PS C:\> Get-GPSiteLink


Name         : Network Config
Description  : IP and network related settings for all users
GPOID        : {019E061A-B032-48E7-A6AE-F0A0F37F809A}
Enabled      : True
Enforced     : False
GPODomain    : jdhlab.local
SOMLinkOrder : 1
SOM          : CN=Default-First-Site-Name,cn=Sites,CN=Configuration,DC=jdhlab,DC=local
```

Copying a GPO

You can use the **Copy-GPO** cmdlet to copy GPOs within the same domain or across domains in the forest. This is a great way of accelerating GPO deployment:

```
PS C:\> Copy-GPO -SourceName "Corp Desktop" -TargetName "Engineering Desktop"


DisplayName      : Engineering Desktop
DomainName       : jdhlab.local
Owner            : JDHLAB\Domain Admins
Id               : 6ee6fd40-03db-4dd7-91e3-8329df33cae9
GpoStatus        : UserSettingsDisabled
Description      :
CreationTime     : 9/13/2010 3:28:27 PM
ModificationTime : 9/13/2010 3:28:28 PM
UserVersion      : AD Version: 1, SysVol Version: 1
ComputerVersion  : AD Version: 1, SysVol Version: 1
WmiFilter        :
```

I just created a new GPO, Engineering Desktop, from a copy of the Corp Desktop GPO. If it was necessary, I could also have copied the access control list with the **-CopyACL** parameter.

When copying GPOs between domains you'll need to specify a migration table to handle security principal re-assignments. Creating migration tables goes beyond the scope of this book; there are no PowerShell solutions. But assuming you have a migration table, here's how you might use it:

```
PS C:\> Copy-GPO -SourceName "Corp Desktop" -TargetName "Corp Desktop" `
>> -TargetDomain "jdhitsolutions.local" -CopyAcl -MigrationTable "c:\work\migration.migtable"
```

Renaming a GPO

Should the need arise to rename a GPO, the **Rename-GPO** cmdlet does exactly what it says:

```
PS C:\> Rename-GPO -Name TestGPO -TargetName "Mobile Users"
```

```
DisplayName      : Mobile Users
DomainName       : jdhlab.local
Owner            : JDHLAB\Domain Admins
Id               : 4b669b15-5f0e-4943-88ff-96edade4155f
GpoStatus        : AllSettingsEnabled
Description      :
CreationTime     : 9/8/2010 3:35:05 PM
ModificationTime : 9/8/2010 4:00:24 PM
UserVersion      : AD Version: 5, SysVol Version: 5
ComputerVersion  : AD Version: 6, SysVol Version: 6
WmiFilter        :
```

Because the GPO ID or GUID is what really identifies a GPO, renaming is for your convenience. All you need to do is specify the GPO and its new name.

GPO Backup and Restore

It is a best practice to periodically back up your Group Policy Objects, especially before making any major modifications.

Backing Up a GPO

Backing up a GPO is a simple process of copying configuration information to a network share. The backup process allows you to use the same location repeatedly, seamlessly creating a version history for each GPO. You'll use the **Backup-GPO** cmdlet to create a backup for a single GPO or all of them:

```
PS C:\> Backup-GPO -Name "Corp Desktop" -Path \\coredc01\backup\gpo -comment "baseline backup"


DisplayName     : Corp Desktop
GpoId           : cb903cce-8e60-4e83-bbcd-944cc4ccc0eb
Id              : d7a8e6a9-dbbb-4c78-975e-69a242c1c685
BackupDirectory : \\coredc01\backup\gpo
CreationTime    : 9/13/2010 4:34:35 PM
DomainName      : jdhlab.local
Comment         : baseline backup
```

Using the **Backup-GPO** cmdlet, I created a backup copy of the Corp Desktop GPO in \\coredc01\backup\gpo:

```
PS C:\> dir \\coredc01\backup\gpo


    Directory: \\coredc01\backup\gpo


Mode                LastWriteTime     Length Name
----                -------------     ------ ----
d----         9/13/2010   4:34 PM            {D7A8E6A9-DBBB-4C78-975E-69A242C1C685}
```

You can use a local folder, a mapped drive, or a UNC. In any event, the target path must exist; the cmdlet will not create it.

You can also back up GPOs by GUID, which I typically don't use, at least interactively, since I'm not about to type one out. What I am more likely to do is back up all GPOs at once:

```
PS C:\> Backup-GPO -All -Path \\coredc01\backup\gpo -Comment "September backup"


DisplayName     : Network Config
GpoId           : 019e061a-b032-48e7-a6ae-f0a0f37f809a
Id              : 22a1a467-3edc-41d7-8633-0f8f71fcc4d1
BackupDirectory : \\coredc01\backup\gpo
CreationTime    : 9/13/2010 4:36:51 PM
DomainName      : jdhlab.local
Comment         : September backup

DisplayName     : HR Desktop
GpoId           : 07126f7c-fcc5-48ec-90dd-50ef5725708f
Id              : e1053f2b-e3fd-4309-9766-c54399d1c735
BackupDirectory : \\coredc01\backup\gpo
CreationTime    : 9/13/2010 4:36:51 PM
DomainName      : jdhlab.local
Comment         : September backup
...
```

I like using comments because it makes it easier to identify backups.

Enumerating Backups

Another shortcoming in the Group Policy module is that there is no cmdlet for finding or enumerating your backups. Instead, you have to rely once again on the GPMGMT COM object and take matters into your own hands. Actually, I took care of it with my own function, **Get-GPOBackup**:

Get-GPOBackup.ps1

```
Function Get-GPOBackup {

[CmdletBinding(DefaultParameterSetName="Single")]

Param(
    [Parameter(Position=0,Mandatory=$True,HelpMessage="Enter the GPO backup directory path.")]
    [ValidateNotNullorEmpty()]
    [string]$path,
    [Parameter(Position=1,Mandatory=$False,ParameterSetName="Single")]
    [string]$GPOName,
    [Switch]$MostRecent,
    [Parameter(ParameterSetName="All")]
    [Switch]$All
)
    Write-Verbose "Testing $path"
    if (Test-Path -Path $path) {
        #define the GPMC COM Objects
        Write-Verbose "Creating GPMGMT.GPM objects"
        $gpm=New-Object -ComObject "GPMGMT.GPM"
        $gpmConstants=$gpm.GetConstants()

        #get backup folder
        Write-Verbose "Getting backup folder $path"
        $backupDir=$gpm.getbackupdir($path)

         Write-Verbose "Creating search criteria"
         $search=$gpm.CreateSearchCriteria()

         if ($MostRecent) {
            #get most recent GPO backups
```

```
            Write-Verbose "Adding most recent search criteria"
      $search.add($gpmConstants.SearchPropertyBackupMostRecent,$gpmConstants.
SearchOpEquals,$True)
          }

          if ($gpoName) {
            Write-Verbose "Adding search for $GPOName"
     $search.add($gpmConstants.SearchPropertyGPODisplayName,$gpmConstants.
SearchOpEquals,$GPOName)
            }

            Write-Verbose "Executing search"
            $backupDir.SearchBackups($search)

    } #if Test-Path
    Else {
        Write-Warning "Failed to find $path"
    }

    Write-Verbose "Finished."
} #end function
```

The **Get-GPOBackup** function requires the path to your GPO backup folder. You can retrieve all backups for a single GPO:

```
PS C:\> Get-GPObackup -path "\\coredc01\backup\gpo" -GPOName "engineering desktop" -verbose
VERBOSE: Testing \\coredc01\backup\gpo
VERBOSE: Creating GPMGMT.GPM objects
VERBOSE: Getting backup folder \\coredc01\backup\gpo
VERBOSE: Creating search criteria
VERBOSE: Adding search for engineering desktop
VERBOSE: Executing search


ID             : {04077176-A027-4C06-9D7A-772C2D2105CF}
GPOID          : {6EE6FD40-03DB-4DD7-91E3-8329DF33CAE9}
GPODomain      : jdhlab.local
GPODisplayName : Engineering Desktop
Timestamp      : 9/14/2010 8:31:10 AM
Comment        : Pre revision
BackupDir      : \\coredc01\backup\gpo

ID             : {C885274E-49A6-4E6A-9345-F01FAC04E7D8}
GPOID          : {6EE6FD40-03DB-4DD7-91E3-8329DF33CAE9}
GPODomain      : jdhlab.local
GPODisplayName : Engineering Desktop
Timestamp      : 9/13/2010 4:36:58 PM
Comment        : September backup
BackupDir      : \\coredc01\backup\gpo

VERBOSE: Finished.
```

Or, you can get the most recent backup:

```
PS C:\> Get-GPObackup -path "\\coredc01\backup\gpo" -GPOName "engineering desktop" -MostRecent


ID             : {04077176-A027-4C06-9D7A-772C2D2105CF}
GPOID          : {6EE6FD40-03DB-4DD7-91E3-8329DF33CAE9}
GPODomain      : jdhlab.local
GPODisplayName : Engineering Desktop
```

```
Timestamp      : 9/14/2010 8:31:10 AM
Comment        : Pre revision
BackupDir      : \\coredc01\backup\gpo
```

Use the **-All** parameter to display all backups:

```
PS C:\> Get-GPOBackup -path "\\coredc01\backup\gpo" -All | Measure-Object


Count    : 25
Average  :
Sum      :
Maximum  :
Minimum  :
Property :
```

I have 25 total backups:

```
PS C:\> Get-GPObackup -path "\\coredc01\backup\gpo" -All -MostRecent | Measure-Object


Count    : 22
Average  :
Sum      :
Maximum  :
Minimum  :
Property :
```

Or, only 22 if I get just the most recent. This backup information is important, because you may need it to restore or import a GPO from backup.

Restoring a GPO

Use the **Restore-GPO** cmdlet to recover a GPO from a backup with one major caveat: The GPO you are restoring must still exist in your domain. That is, if you have deleted a GPO and attempt to restore it, the operation will fail. I'll cover your alternative in just a moment. But assuming this isn't the case, you can restore a GPO by name:

```
PS C:\> Restore-GPO -Name "sales desktop" -Path "\\coredc01\backup\gpo"


DisplayName      : Sales Desktop
DomainName       : jdhlab.local
Owner            : JDHLAB\Domain Admins
Id               : 2c92da74-d0de-4870-92ff-a1dd7a70fc95
GpoStatus        : AllSettingsEnabled
Description      :
CreationTime     : 9/2/2010 4:54:59 PM
ModificationTime : 9/14/2010 10:13:16 AM
UserVersion      : AD Version: 1, SysVol Version: 1
ComputerVersion  : AD Version: 1, SysVol Version: 1
WmiFilter        :
```

If there are multiple backups for the GPO, the cmdlet will restore the most recent one. You could also use the GPO's GUID in place of the name. But what if you want to roll back to a different backup? For those situations, you'll need the GUID of the backup GPO.

Let's say I need the September backup version of my Sales Desktop GPO. Using my **Get-GPOBackup** function, this is what I'm looking for:

```
PS C:\> Get-GPOBackup -path "\\coredc01\backup\gpo" -GPOName "Sales Desktop" |
>> where {$_.Comment -eq "September Backup"}
>>


ID             : {FBA2FB2B-90D8-4F1D-96E8-54391C1154C4}
GPOID          : {2C92DA74-D0DE-4870-92FF-A1DD7A70FC95}
GPODomain      : jdhlab.local
GPODisplayName : Sales Desktop
Timestamp      : 9/13/2010 4:36:54 PM
Comment        : September backup
BackupDir      : \\coredc01\backup\gpo
```

I can combine this with the **Restore-GPO** cmdlet:

```
PS C:\> Get-GPOBackup -path "\\coredc01\backup\gpo" -GPOName "Sales Desktop" |
>> where {$_.Comment -eq "September Backup"} | Restore-GPO -path "\\coredc01\backup\gpo
-confirm"
>>

Confirm
Are you sure you want to perform this action?
Restore a GPO to the jdhlab.local domain from the GPO backup with backup ID
{fba2fb2b-90d8-4f1d-96e8-54391c1154c4} at the following location: \\coredc01\backup\gpo.
(Restore-GPO)
[Y] Yes  [A] Yes to All  [N] No  [L] No to All  [S] Suspend  [?] Help (default is "Y"):
```

As you can see from the confirmation message, this will in fact restore the correct backup.

In extreme situations, you can also restore **all** GPOs from backup:

```
PS C:\> Restore-GPO -All -Path "\\coredc01\backup\gpo" -whatif
What if: Restore all the GPOs in the jdhlab.local domain from their most recent backups found
at
the following location: \\coredc01\backup\gpo. (Restore-GPO)
```

I didn't really want to do it so I used the **-WhatIf** parameter.

Importing a GPO

Importing a GPO using the **Import-GPO** cmdlet is similar to using the **Restore-GPO** cmdlet. One way you might use the **Import-GPO** cmdlet is to restore a GPO where the original GPO has been deleted. In this example, I no longer have the Mobile User GPO but I can recover it by importing from a backup:

```
PS C:\> Import-GPO -Path \\coredc01\backup\gpo -BackupGpoName "Mobile Users" `
>> -TargetName "Mobile Users" -CreateIfNeeded
>>


DisplayName      : Mobile Users
DomainName       : jdhlab.local
Owner            : JDHLAB\Domain Admins
```

```
Id               : 8334c110-1beb-4045-829e-94708f4de60d
GpoStatus        : AllSettingsEnabled
Description      :
CreationTime     : 9/14/2010 10:31:35 AM
ModificationTime : 9/14/2010 10:31:36 AM
UserVersion      : AD Version: 1, SysVol Version: 1
ComputerVersion  : AD Version: 1, SysVol Version: 1
WmiFilter        :
```

You must use the **-CreateIfNeeded** parameter in this scenario. Otherwise, if the GPO already exists it will be overwritten.

If there are multiple backup versions, the cmdlet will import the most recent. If you want a different version, then you'll need to specify a backup GUID like you did earlier when restoring.

The primary reason you would use the **Import-GPO** cmdlet is to add GPOs from other domains or forests. In these situations, you will likely also need a migration table:

```
PS C:\> Import-GPO -BackupGpoName SecureUsers -Path "Z:\ImportBackups" `
>> -TargetName SecureMobileUsers -MigrationTable "Z:\Tables\Migtable1.mitable" -CreateIfNeeded
```

Resultant Set of Policy

The last area of Group Policy management is Resultant Set of Policy (RSoP) planning and troubleshooting. The **Get-GPResultantSetofPolicy** cmdlet will play a key role. This cmdlet makes it easier to create a logging report for some combination of user and computer. You can create either an XML or HTTP report:

```
PS C:\> Get-GPResultantSetOfPolicy -ReportType html -Computer client1 `
>> -Path "c:\work\reports\client1-rsop.html"
>>


RsopMode        : Logging
Namespace       : \\client1\Root\Rsop\NS2D6BAB2F_6AA3_406F_A6BA_ACA6093A5E96
LoggingComputer : client1
LoggingUser     : JDHLAB\Administrator
LoggingMode     : Computer
```

The **Get-GPResultantSetofPolicy** cmdlet will connect to Client1 and build a RSoP report for policy settings that affect all users. Or if I'm troubleshooting, I can generate a report for a specific user who has logged on to a specific computer by adding the **-User** parameter:

```
PS C:\> Get-GPResultantSetOfPolicy -ReportType html -Computer client1 -user "jshortz" `
>> -Path "c:\work\reports\client1-jshortz-rsop.html"
>>


RsopMode        : Logging
Namespace       : \\client1\Root\Rsop\NS74C171BC_36AC_41C9_87E4_DB57A4F84386
LoggingComputer : client1
LoggingUser     : jshortz
LoggingMode     : UserAndComputer
```

If you've worked with RSoP in the past, you may have noticed that the Microsoft cmdlet used

Logging mode only. There is no provision for generating RSoP planning information. However you are not without options.

Using GPMGMT.GPM

Using the GPMGMT COM object, you can generate RSoP planning reports. This object has a **GetRSOP()** method. This method in turn returns an RSoP object with these properties:

- Mode
- Namespace
- LoggingComputer
- LoggingUser
- LoggingFlags
- PlanningFlags
- PlanningDomainController
- PlanningSiteName
- PlanningUser
- PlanningUserSOM
- PlanningUserWMIFilters
- PlanningUserSecurityGroups
- PlanningComputer
- PlanningComputerSOM
- PlanningComputerWMIFilters
- PlanningComputerSecurityGroups

Can you begin to see how this might be useful? Instead of forcing you to work interactively, let me cut to the chase and give you a **Get-RSOPPlanning** function that creates RSoP planning reports. The GPMGMT COM object could also create logging reports, but since there is a cmdlet you can use I didn't bother re-inventing the wheel:

Get-RSOPPlanning.ps1

```
#requires -version 2.0

#this function needs the Active Directory Module
$mod="ActiveDirectory"
If (-not (get-module $mod)) {
        Try {
            Import-Module $mod -errorAction "Stop"
            }
        Catch {
            Write-Warning "Can't find or load the $mod Module"
            Break
        }
 }

Function Get-RSOPPlanning {
```

```
[CmdletBinding(DefaultParameterSetName="File")]

Param(
    [Parameter(Position=0,Mandatory=$False,
    HelpMessage="Enter the report's file name and path",ParameterSetName="File")]
    [string]$Path,
    [string]$User,
    [string]$UserSOM=(Get-ADDomain).DistinguishedName,
    [string]$Computer,
    [string]$ComputerSOM=(Get-ADDomain).DistinguishedName,
    [string]$Domain=$env:UserDNSDomain,
    [string]$Site,
    [switch]$XML,
    [Parameter(ParameterSetName="Raw")]
    [switch]$Raw
    )

   Write-Verbose "Starting function"
   $gpm=New-Object -COM "GPMGMT.GPM"
   $gpmconstants=$gpm.getconstants()
   $gpmDomain=$gpm.GetDomain($domain,"",$gpmConstants.UseAnyDC)

   #Default report type is HTML but if you specify -xml you will
   #get an XML report
   if ($XML) {
       Write-Verbose "Creating an XML report"
       $Report=$gpmconstants.ReportXML
   }
   else {
       Write-Verbose "Creating an HTML report"
       $Report=$gpmconstants.ReportHTML
   }

   $rsop=$gpm.GetRSOP($gpmconstants.RSOPModePlanning,$null,0)

   #use the current domain controller. This is a required value
   $rsop.PlanningDomainController=$gpmDomain.DomainController

   #$User takes precedence over $UserSOM
   if ($user) {
       $rsop.PlanningUser=$User
   }
   else {
       $rsop.PlanningUserSOM=$UserSOM
   }
    #$Computer takes precedence over $ComputerSOM
   if ($Computer) {
       $rsop.PlanningComputer=$Computer
   }
   else {
       $rsop.PlanningComputerSOM=$ComputerSOM
   }

   if ($site) {
       Write-Verbose "Adding site $site"
       $rsop.PlanningSiteName=$site
   }

   Write-Verbose ($RSOP | Out-String)

   $rsop.CreateQueryResults()

   if ($Path) {
      Write-Verbose "Generating report $path"
```

```
      $rsop.GenerateReportToFile($Report,$Path)
     #display the report
     Invoke-Item $path
    }
    else {
      Write-Verbose "Writing Raw data"
      $rpt=$rsop.GenerateReport($Report)
      #write the result property to the pipeline
      write $rpt.Result
    }

    Write-Verbose "Finished."
} #end function
```

My **Get-RSOPPlanning** function will create either an XML or HTML resultant set of policy planning report for any combination of a specific user or computer and/or a user or computer scope of management. The user or computer name should either be specified by their distinguished name or down-level name, e.g. jdhlab\jeff. The scope of management must be a distinguished name. The default is the domain root, which is retrieved by using the **Get-ADDomain** cmdlet from the Active Directory module.

For example, suppose I want to know the RSoP for user Roy G. Biv when he logs on to any computer with an account in the Company Desktops organizational unit; here's how I can create an HTML report:

```
PS C:\> Get-RSOPPlanning -Path "c:\work\reports\biv-rsop.html" -User "jdhlab\rbiv" `
>> -ComputerSOM "OU=Company Desktops,DC=jdhlab,DC=local"
>>

Status                                                      Result
------                                                      ------
System.__ComObject                                          c:\work\reports\biv-rsop.html
```

The function creates the report using the GPMGMT COM object and displays it. Or perhaps I want to know what will happen for any user account that logs on to Client1. But I want this information in an XML file:

```
PS C:\> Get-RSOPPlanning -Path "c:\work\reports\client1-rsop.xml" `
>> -UserSOM "OU=Employees,DC=jdhlab,DC=local" -Computer "jdhlab\client1" -XML
>>

Status                                                      Result
------                                                      ------
System.__ComObject                                          c:\work\reports\biv-rsop.xml
```

I expect that most of the time you'll simply want these types of reports. But I also added a feature to allow access to the raw RSoP data. This works best when using the XML format type. The best approach is to save the raw results from the **Get-RSOPPlanning** cmdlet as an XML object:

```
PS C:\> [xml]$raw=Get-RSOPPlanning -User "jdhlab\rbiv" `
>> -ComputerSOM "OU=Company Desktops,DC=jdhlab,DC=local" -XML -Raw
>>

PS C:\> $raw
```

```
xml                                                         Rsop
---                                                         ----
version="1.0" encoding="utf-16"                             Rsop
```

I now have an XML object I can navigate in the shell:

```
PS C:\> $raw.rsop


xsi             : http://www.w3.org/2001/XMLSchema-instance
xsd             : http://www.w3.org/2001/XMLSchema
xmlns           : http://www.microsoft.com/GroupPolicy/Rsop
ReadTime        : 2010-09-14T19:38:49.9193696Z
DataType        : PlanningData
UserResults     : UserResults
ComputerResults : ComputerResults



PS C:\> $raw.rsop.userresults


Version         : 2228228
Name            : jdhlab\rbiv
Domain          : jdhlab.local
SOM             : jdhlab.local/Employees/Temp
SearchedSOM     : {SearchedSOM, SearchedSOM, SearchedSOM}
SecurityGroup   : {Name, Name, Name, Name...}
SlowLink        : false
Loopback        : None
ExtensionStatus : {Group Policy Infrastructure, Registry}
GPO             : {Default Domain Policy, FoxitReader, WinRM Configuration}
ExtensionData   : ExtensionData



PS C:\> $raw.rsop.userresults.gpo


Name             : Default Domain Policy
Path             : Path
VersionDirectory : 0
VersionSysvol    : 0
Enabled          : true
IsValid          : true
FilterAllowed    : true
AccessDenied     : false
Link             : Link

Name             : FoxitReader
Path             : Path
VersionDirectory : 12
VersionSysvol    : 12
Enabled          : true
IsValid          : true
FilterAllowed    : true
AccessDenied     : false
Link             : Link

Name             : WinRM Configuration
Path             : Path
VersionDirectory : 0
```

```
VersionSysvol     : 0
Enabled           : true
IsValid           : true
FilterAllowed     : true
AccessDenied      : false
Link              : Link
```

Since everyone will have slightly different needs and different reports, I won't spend any more time on this topic. The more XML experience you have, the more you'll be able to get out of it.

Get-GPOPlanning Limitations

Even though my **Get-GPOPlanning** function accomplishes most tasks I think you'll need, it is not a 100% PowerShell version of what you can accomplish using the Group Policy Management Console. There are a few limitations. While I include an option to include a site name, like Default-First-Site-Name, the function doesn't offer a way for RSOP planning that takes WMI filters, loopback processing, or group memberships into account. You'll need to rely on the management console, 3rd party products or revise the function.

Third-party Products

If you have significant Group Policy management responsibilities, you might want to consider some third-party tools, especially if they support Windows PowerShell. SDMSoftware, which is run by Group Policy MVP Darren Mar-Elia, offers a few such tools. Some are free and others are licensed products. Let me give you a quick peek at some of them.

Group Policy Health

The free, GPExpert Group Policy Health cmdlet can give you a quick "stop light" view of how your GPOs are applied to computers in your domain, making it easy to identify problems. I won't go into the details of what the cmdlet does, but it writes an object to the pipeline for each computer with an overall status property. A value of green is good. Red is bad.

The cmdlet installs as a 32-bit PSSnapin. On x64 systems you'll need to make sure you launch the x86 PowerShell session, and then add the snapin:

```
PS C:\> Add-PSSnapin SDMSoftware.PowerShell.GroupPolicyHealth
```

The snapin includes a single cmdlet, **Get-SDMGPHealth**. The cmdlet takes a computer name as a parameter and returns a health object:

```
PS C:\> Get-SDMGPHealth -ComputerName Client1


OverallStatus              : green
TimeLogged                 : 9/14/2010 8:48:57 PM
HostName                   : Client1
Domain                     : jdhlab.local
OSVersion                  : Microsoft Windows 7 Ultimate ,
ComputerCoreStatus         : The operation completed successfully
UserCoreStatus             : The operation completed successfully
FastLogonEnabled           : True
ComputerSlowLinkDetected   : False
```

```
Loopback                  : None
DCUsed                    : \\COREDC01.jdhlab.local
ComputerElapsedTime       : 00:00:02
CurrentLoggedOnUser       : JDHLAB\Administrator
UserSlowLinkDetected      : False
UserElapsedTime           : 00:00:02
ComputerGPOsProcessed     : {Local Group Policy, Network Config, WinRM Configuration, Default D...}
UserGPOsProcessed         : {Local Group Policy, Network Config, WinRM Configuration, Default D...}
ComputerCSEsProcessed     : {Group Policy Environment, Registry, Security, Group Policy Service...}
UserCSEsProcessed         : {}
```

You can use this cmdlet as another means of getting RSoP logging results. Here I can see what computer GPOs were applied to Client1:

```
PS C:\> Get-SDMGPHealth -ComputerName Client1 | Select -ExpandProperty ComputerGPOsProcessed


DisplayName          GPLink                                 Version
-----------          ------                                 -------
Local Group Policy   Local                                  GPT Version: 0000, GPC Version: 0000
Network Config       CN=Default-First-Site-Name,CN=Sites,... GPT Version: 0000, GPC Version: 0000
WinRM Configuration  DC=jdhlab,DC=local                     GPT Version: 000D, GPC Version: 000D
Default Domain Policy DC=jdhlab,DC=local                    GPT Version: 000A, GPC Version: 000A
Corp Desktop         OU=Company Desktops,DC=jdhlab,DC=local GPT Version: 0007, GPC Version: 0007
Win7 Special         OU=Company Desktops,DC=jdhlab,DC=local GPT Version: 0005, GPC Version: 0005
```

I also like that you can use the **-Domain** parameter to search every computer in Active Directory:

```
PS C:\> Get-SDMGPHealth  -DomainName jdhlab -ErrorAction "SilentlyContinue"  |
>> Select Hostname,OverallStatus,TimeLogged
>>

HostName                           OverallStatus          TimeLogged
--------                           -------------          ----------
COREDC01                           green                  9/14/2010 9:06:34 PM
CLIENT1                            green                  9/14/2010 9:06:37 PM
...
```

By selecting only a few properties, I can tell at a glance where I have problems. Visit http://www.sdmsoftware.com/freeware.php to learn more.

GPO Compare

Very often you will create new GPOs from copies of existing GPOs. Or you may have two very similar GPOs and would like to know where they match up and where they differ. SDMSoftware offers a graphical tool called GPO Compare, but it also ships a cmdlet equivalent.

The product installs as a 32-bit module:

```
PS C:\> Import-Module SDM-GPOCompare
```

The module consists of a single cmdlet, **Compare-SDMGPO**. I have two GPOs that are very similar, and I would like to create a comparison report. The cmdlet will show where settings are missing and where they are different. Here's a quick look at just the differences between two GPOs:

```
PS C:\> Compare-SDMGPO -GpoNameA "Executive Laptop" -GpoNameB "Sales Laptop" |
>> where {$_.DiffType -eq "Different"} | Format-List
>>


Path      : Computer Configuration|Preferences|Control Panel Settings|Power Options
SettingA : Power Plan (Windows Vista)|High performance
SettingB : Power Plan (Windows Vista)|Balanced
DiffType : Different

Path      : Computer Configuration|Policies|Administrative Templates|Control Panel/User
            Accounts|Apply the default user logon picture to all users|State
SettingA : Enabled
SettingB : Disabled
DiffType : Different
```

You can also compare using GPO backups as well as across domains. Learn more at http://www.sdmsoftware.com/group_policy_compare.php.

GPO Export

It turns out there are other ways to report on or audit your GPOs. Using SDMSoftware's GPO Exporter you can get a very granular report on only the critical GPO settings that matter to you.

Like the GPO Compare cmdlet, this tool ships as a 32-bit module:

```
PS C:\> Import-Module SDM-GPOExporter
```

The cmdlet is **Export-SDMGPSettings**. With this cmdlet you can export one or more GPOs to a custom object with as much detail as you need:

```
PS C:\> Export-SDMGPSettings -GpoNames "Default Domain Policy"  -metadata

GPOName                         SettingPath                              SettingValue
-------                         -----------                              ------------
Default Domain Policy           METADATA|GUID                            {31B2F340-016D-...
Default Domain Policy           METADATA|Status
Default Domain Policy           METADATA|Created Time                    1/24/2010 8:02:...
Default Domain Policy           METADATA|Modified Time                   9/2/2010 9:00:...
Default Domain Policy           METADATA|Version|Computer|AD             10
Default Domain Policy           METADATA|Version|Computer|SYSVOL         10
Default Domain Policy           METADATA|Version|User|AD                 0
Default Domain Policy           METADATA|Version|User|SYSVOL             0
Default Domain Policy           METADATA|Links                           jdhlab.local
Default Domain Policy           METADATA|Links|jdhlab.local|Link Ena...  True
Default Domain Policy           METADATA|Links|jdhlab.local|Link Enf...  False
Default Domain Policy           METADATA|Delegation                      NT AUTHORITY\Au...
Default Domain Policy           METADATA|Delegation|NT AUTHORITY\Aut...  Allow
Default Domain Policy           METADATA|Delegation|NT AUTHORITY\Aut...  ApplyGroupPolicy
Default Domain Policy           METADATA|Delegation                      NT AUTHORITY\E...
Default Domain Policy           METADATA|Delegation|NT AUTHORITY\ENT...  Allow
Default Domain Policy           METADATA|Delegation|NT AUTHORITY\ENT...  Read
Default Domain Policy           METADATA|Delegation                      NT AUTHORITY\S...
Default Domain Policy           METADATA|Delegation|NT AUTHORITY\SYS...  Allow
Default Domain Policy           METADATA|Delegation|NT AUTHORITY\SYS...  Editdeletemodi...
Default Domain Policy           METADATA|Delegation                      JDHLAB\Help Desk
Default Domain Policy           METADATA|Delegation|JDHLAB\Help Desk...  Allow
Default Domain Policy           METADATA|Delegation|JDHLAB\Help Desk...  Read
Default Domain Policy           Windows Settings|Security Settings|A...  False
```

```
Default Domain Policy           Windows Settings|Security Settings|A...  7
Default Domain Policy           Windows Settings|Security Settings|A...  30
...
```

Combine this with a few other PowerShell cmdlets and you have a pretty potent reporting tool:

```
PS C:\> Get-GPO -all | where {$_.displayname -match "laptop"} | Foreach {
>> Export-SDMGPSettings -GpoNames $_.Displayname
>> } | Export-Csv -Path R:\LaptopGPOs.csv -NoTypeInformation
```

With the Get-GPO cmdlet I found all GPOs with "laptop" in the name and exported the GPO settings from each. All results were then saved to a CSV file, which I can open in Microsoft Excel for further review.

The GPO Compare and GPO Exporter tools are primarily graphical, but these PowerShell cmdlets offer some tantalizing possibilities. Details on the GPO Exporter can be found at http://www.sdm-software.com/group_policy_export.php.

Group Policy Automation Engine

What if you didn't have to use the Group Policy editor to define individual settings? How handy would be it to do everything from PowerShell? SDM Software has a commercial product, the GPExpert™ Group Policy Automation Engine (GPAE) that allows you to use PowerShell to automate Group Policy settings in areas such as Folder Redirection and Administrative Templates. You can use the GPAE to read and write information for GPO settings. The GPAE offers more functionality than I cover here, though I'll show you a few ways to use it. I also encourage you to look through the product's help file, which is full of additional examples and documentation.

The Group Policy Automation Engine installs as a PSSnapin with a single cmdlet, **Get-SDMgpobject**:

```
PS C:\> Add-PSSnapin GetGPObjectPSSnapin
```

Not only can the GPAE read group policy settings, it can write them as well. Let me give you a quick peek. I will first use the **Get-SDMgpobject** cmdlet to retrieve a GPO:

```
PS C:\> $gpo=Get-SDMgpobject "gpo://jdhlab.local/Finance Desktop" -openbyname $true
PS C:\> $gpo


GPName                         : gpo://jdhlab.local/Finance Desktop
UserName                       :
Password                       :
AuthEnum                       : None
OpenByName                     : True
CentralStore                   :
Containers                     : {Computer Configuration, User Configuration}
GPCComputerVersion             : 0
GPCUserVersion                 : 1
GPTComputerVersion             : 0
GPTUserVersion                 : 1
Name                           : Finance Desktop
Guid                           : CE106638-C25F-47F5-A511-3BF2DADFA659
DisableComputerConfiguration   : False
DisableUserConfiguration       : False
Type                           : AD
```

```
ADRoot                    : System.DirectoryServices.DirectoryEntry
FSPath                    : \\COREAD.jdhlab.local\SYSVOL\jdhlab.local\Policies\{CE10663
PolFileManager            : GPOSDK.Providers._Common.PolFileManager
AdmManager                : GPOSDK.Providers._Common.AdmManager
```

The syntax is a little different. I specify the domain name, the name of the GPO, and a Boolean parameter indicating I want to open it by its name, as opposed to the GUID:

```
PS C:\> $gpo=Get-SDMgpobject "gpo://jdhlab.local/Finance Desktop" -openbyname $true
```

Within this policy I want to configure folder redirection, but I don't want to be bothered using the Group Policy editor. Instead I'll use the GPAE. There are a number of settings for this policy, although I will be accepting most of the defaults. First, I'll create an object for the GPO's folder redirection setting:

```
PS C:\> $container=$gpo.GetObject("User Configuration/Windows Settings/Folder Redirection")
```

Next, I'll create an object for the "Documents" redirection setting:

```
PS C:\> $documents=$container.Settings.ItemByName("Documents")
```

I'm going to set the same path for all users:

```
PS C:\> $documents.put("Behavior",[GPOSDK.FolderRedirectionBehavior]"Simple")
PS C:\> $documents.put("Basic_FolderPath", "\\FILE01\Redirected\%USERNAME%")
PS C:\> $documents.save()
```

The **Put()** method writes the policy and the **Save()** method commits the change. The cmdlet help has some additional examples, which I encourage you to look at.

One extra special feature of the GPAE is its ability to manage group policy settings on the local machine. This is very handy when you need to configure systems that may not be able to always retrieve domain policies. With the GPAE, in combination with the Microsoft Group Policy module, you could create an entire GPO provisioning process using Windows PowerShell and never have to touch a graphical interface. Visit http://www.sdmsoftware.com/group_policy_scripting.php to learn more.

Chapter 9
Active Directory Security and Permissions

If you work in a small Windows environment, the default Active Directory security settings and permissions are usually sufficient. In larger organizations, however, customizations are often required to meet corporate or regulatory guidelines. As with most Windows products and services, managing security and permissions is not an easy task. Active Directory is no different.

Using the Active Directory Module

It is possible to manage Active Directory permissions using the Active Directory Module and the Active Directory PSDrive. There are no cmdlets specifically designed for managing permissions so you have to rely on the PowerShell cmdlets **Get-ACL** and **Set-ACL**.

Get Permission

Let's jump right in and look at getting permissions for an Active Directory user object using the Microsoft module. First, I'm going to create a new PSDrive, rooted to the Employees organizational unit:

```
PS C:\> New-PSDrive -Name "Employees" -psprovider ActiveDirectory `
>> -Root "OU=Employees,DC=jdhlab,dc=local"
>>

Name           Used (GB)     Free (GB) Provider      Root                          CurrentLocation
----           ---------     --------- --------      ----                          ---------------
Employees                              ActiveDire... //RootDSE/OU=Employees,D...
PS C:\> cd employees:
```

```
PS Employees:\> cd ou=sales
PS Employees:\OU=sales>
```

I've changed to the Sales organizational unit. To keep things a little clearer, I'll get a user and save it to a variable:

```
PS Employees:\ou=sales> $user=get-item "CN=Skip Towne"
```

In order to use the **Get-ACL** cmdlet, I need to specify a path to the object that the cmdlet will recognize:

```
PS Employees:\OU=sales> Get-Acl -Path $user.pspath

Path                                      Owner                   Access
----                                      -----                   ------
ActiveDirectory://RootDSE/CN=Skip Tow... JDHLAB\Domain Admins    NT AUTHORITY\SELF Allow  ...
```

The ACL object has a property called **Access**, which will return a collection of access rule objects. Here's a sample:

```
PS Employees:\ou=sales> $acl=Get-Acl -Path $user.pspath
PS Employees:\ou=sales> $acl.access

ActiveDirectoryRights : GenericRead
InheritanceType       : None
ObjectType            : 00000000-0000-0000-0000-000000000000
InheritedObjectType   : 00000000-0000-0000-0000-000000000000
ObjectFlags           : None
AccessControlType     : Allow
IdentityReference     : NT AUTHORITY\SELF
IsInherited           : False
InheritanceFlags      : None
PropagationFlags      : None

ActiveDirectoryRights : ReadControl
InheritanceType       : None
ObjectType            : 00000000-0000-0000-0000-000000000000
InheritedObjectType   : 00000000-0000-0000-0000-000000000000
ObjectFlags           : None
AccessControlType     : Allow
IdentityReference     : NT AUTHORITY\Authenticated Users
IsInherited           : False
InheritanceFlags      : None
PropagationFlags      : None

ActiveDirectoryRights : GenericAll
InheritanceType       : None
ObjectType            : 00000000-0000-0000-0000-000000000000
InheritedObjectType   : 00000000-0000-0000-0000-000000000000
ObjectFlags           : None
AccessControlType     : Allow
IdentityReference     : NT AUTHORITY\SYSTEM
IsInherited           : False
InheritanceFlags      : None
PropagationFlags      : None
...
```

You are most likely to be interested in the access right, and who possesses it. Here's a more specific approach:

```
PS Employees:\ou=sales> $acl.access |
>> Select ActiveDirectoryRights,ObjectType,IdentityReference,AccessControlType | Format-List
>>

ActiveDirectoryRights : ReadProperty
ObjectType            : 1f298a89-de98-47b8-b5cd-572ad53d267e
AccessControlType     : Allow
IdentityReference     : NT AUTHORITY\Authenticated Users

ActiveDirectoryRights : ReadProperty, WriteProperty, ExtendedRight
ObjectType            : 91e647de-d96f-4b70-9557-d63ff4f3ccd8
AccessControlType     : Allow
IdentityReference     : NT AUTHORITY\SELF

ActiveDirectoryRights : GenericRead
ObjectType            : 00000000-0000-0000-0000-000000000000
AccessControlType     : Allow
IdentityReference     : JDHLAB\Exchange Recipient Administrators

ActiveDirectoryRights : GenericAll
ObjectType            : 00000000-0000-0000-0000-000000000000
AccessControlType     : Allow
IdentityReference     : JDHLAB\Enterprise Admins
...
```

Each access rule is associated with a specific object property. But what property? The property is identified or associated with a GUID, which you can see in the ObjectType property. The GUID can refer to a *Standard Property Set* such as Personal Information, an *Extended Right* such as "Change Password", or a *Control Access Right* defined in the schema such as "Generate-RSoP-Planning" for an organizational unit object. These last rights are sometimes referred to as *Specific Rights*. Let's look at all of these in a bit more detail.

Standard Property Sets

Standard Property Sets are stored in the Extended-Rights container in the configuration naming context of Active Directory. Each property set is defined by a GUID. A set of common GUIDs are shown in Table 9-1.

Table 9-1 Active Directory Standard Property Sets

Property Set	GUID	Comments
DNS Host Name Attributes	72e39547-7b18-11d1-adef-00c04fd8d5cd	DNS-Host-Name and ms-DS- objects.
Other Domain Parameters	b8119fd0-04f6-4762-ab7a-4986c76b3f9a	Applies to the DomainDNS object.
Domain Password and Lockout Policies	c7407360-20bf-11d0-a768-00aa006e0529	Account and password age attributes. Applies to Domain and DomainDNS objects.

Phone and Mail Options	e45795b2-9455-11d1-aebd-0000f80367c1	Properties for user email-related information. Applies to User, Group, and inetOrgPerson objects.
General Information	59ba2f42-79a2-11d0-9020-00c04fc2d3cf	General user information properties.
Group Membership	bc0ac240-79a9-11d0-9020-00c04fc2d4cf	Properties for group objects.
Personal Information	77b5b886-944a-11d1-aebd-0000f80367c1	Personal user information. Applies to User, Contact, Computer, and inetOrgPerson objects.
Public Information	e48d0154-bcf8-11d1-8702-00c04fb96050	Public information. Applies to User, Computer, and inetOrgPerson objects.
Account Restrictions	4c164200-20c0-11d0-a768-00aa006e0529	Property set related to account restrictions. Applies to User, Computer, and inetOrgPerson objects.
Logon Information	5f202010-79a5-11d0-9020-00c04fc2d4cf	Property set related to user logon information. Applies to User and inetOrgPerson objects.
Web Information	{e45795b3-9455-11d1-aebd-0000f80367c1	Property set related to user web-related information. Applies to User, Contact, and inetOrgPerson objects.

These property sets act as collections for a group of related properties. So instead of having to set multiple individual properties, you can select a set of related properties.

Active Directory Extended Rights

Extended rights are also stored in the Extended-Rights container within the configuration naming context. Here's a short PowerShell script that demonstrates how to list all extended rights. This also includes Standard Property Sets:

Get-ExtendedRights.ps1

```
Import-Module ActiveDirectory

$rootDSE=Get-ADRootDSE
$context=$rootDSE.ConfigurationNamingContext
$container="CN=Extended-Rights,$context"
$path=Join-Path -Path "AD:" -ChildPath $container
Get-ChildItem -Path $path -Properties Displayname,RightsGUID,AppliesTo |
Select Name,Displayname,RightsGUID,AppliesTo
```

To avoid hard-coding domain names, and to make the code more transportable, I'm using the RootDSE object so that I can programmatically identify the configuration naming context. The script then constructs a path that will work with the Active Directory PSDrive provider:

```
$path=Join-Path -Path "AD:" -ChildPath $container
```

Each child item in this container is an extended right. For our purposes all you need are the name and RightsGUID. This last property is not included by default so I'm using the **-Properties** parameter to include it. I'm also going to display a few other properties, which you'll need momentarily:

```
Get-ChildItem -Path $path -Properties Displayname,RightsGUID,AppliesTo |
Select Name,Displayname,RightsGUID,AppliesTo
```

Running the script should give you a result like this:

```
PS R:\> .\get-extendedrights.ps1 | Format-List

Name        : Add-GUID
Displayname : Add GUID
RightsGUID  : 440820ad-65b4-11d1-a3da-0000f875ae0d
AppliesTo   : {19195a5b-6da0-11d0-afd3-00c04fd930c9}

Name        : Allocate-Rids
Displayname : Allocate Rids
RightsGUID  : 1abd7cf8-0a99-11d1-adbb-00c04fd8d5cd
AppliesTo   : {f0f8ffab-1191-11d0-a060-00aa006c33ed}

Name        : Allowed-To-Authenticate
Displayname : Allowed to Authenticate
RightsGUID  : 68B1D179-0D15-4d4f-AB71-46152E79A7BC
AppliesTo   : {4828cc14-1437-45bc-9b07-ad6f015e5f28, bf967aba-0de6-11d0-a285-00aa003049e2,
              ce206244-5827-4a86-ba1c-1c0c386c1b64, bf967a86-0de6-11d0-a285-00aa003049e2}

Name        : Apply-Group-Policy
Displayname : Apply Group Policy
RightsGUID  : edacfd8f-ffb3-11d1-b41d-00a0c968f939
AppliesTo   : {f30e3bc2-9ff0-11d1-b603-0000f80367c1}

Name        : Certificate-Enrollment
Displayname : Enroll
RightsGUID  : 0e10c968-78fb-11d2-90d4-00c04f79dc55
AppliesTo   : {e5209ca2-3bba-11d2-90cc-00c04fd91ab1}

Name        : Change-Domain-Master
Displayname : Change Domain Master
RightsGUID  : 014bf69c-7b3b-11d1-85f6-08002be74fab
AppliesTo   : {ef9e60e0-56f7-11d1-a9c6-0000f80367c1}
...
```

I've truncated the output and formatted the output as list so it's easier to read here. Depending on your Active Directory version or modifications, you may see different extended rights.

Control Access Rights

The other location for possible rights is the schema. Each object class, such as user or computer, has its own set of control access rights. In the output above, this is where the **AppliesTo** property comes into play. That value is associated with an object class in the Active Directory schema. Here is a script that connects everything together. This script uses the **Get-ExtendedRights** script and assumes your current location is the scripts folder:

Get-ControlAccessRights.ps1

```
Param ([string]$class="user")

Import-Module ActiveDirectory

#call Get-ExtendedRights.ps1 script
$erights=.\Get-ExtendedRights.ps1

$rootDSE=Get-ADRootDSE
$context=$rootDSE.SchemaNamingContext
$container="CN=$Class,$context"
$path=Join-Path -Path "AD:" -ChildPath $container
#get the schema class GUID
[system.guid]$item=(Get-Item -Path $path -Properties SchemaIDGUID).SchemaIDGUID
#find the associated right
$eRights | where {$_.AppliesTo -contains $item.guid} |
Select Name,Displayname,RightsGUID
```

The **Get-ControlAccessRights** script takes a parameter for a schema class like user, computer, group, or organizational unit. It runs the **Get-ExtendedRights** script and saves the result to a variable:

```
$erights=.\Get-ExtendedRights.ps1
```

Like the **Get-ExtendedRights** script, this too connects a naming context, in this case the schema naming context, and gets the GUID for the specified class. I cast the property as a System.GUID so that PowerShell will properly format the value:

```
[system.guid]$item=(Get-Item -Path $path -Properties SchemaIDGUID).SchemaIDGUID
```

Here's an excerpt of what you can expect to see when you run this script:

```
PS R:\> .\get-controlaccessrights -class user | Format-List

Name        : Allowed-To-Authenticate
Displayname : Allowed to Authenticate
RightsGUID  : 68B1D179-0D15-4d4f-AB71-46152E79A7BC

Name        : Email-Information
Displayname : Phone and Mail Options
RightsGUID  : E45795B2-9455-11d1-AEBD-0000F80367C1

Name        : Exchange-Information
Displayname : Exchange Information
RightsGUID  : 1F298A89-DE98-47b8-B5CD-572AD53D267E

Name        : Exchange-Personal-Information
Displayname : Exchange Personal Information
RightsGUID  : B1B3A417-EC55-4191-B327-B72E33E38AF2

Name        : General-Information
Displayname : General Information
RightsGUID  : 59ba2f42-79a2-11d0-9020-00c04fc2d3cf

Name        : Membership
Displayname : Group Membership
RightsGUID  : bc0ac240-79a9-11d0-9020-00c04fc2d4cf
```

```
Name        : Personal-Information
Displayname : Personal Information
RightsGUID  : 77B5B886-944A-11d1-AEBD-0000F80367C1

Name        : Private-Information
Displayname : Private Information
RightsGUID  : 91e647de-d96f-4b70-9557-d63ff4f3ccd8

Name        : Public-Information
Displayname : Public Information
RightsGUID  : e48d0154-bcf8-11d1-8702-00c04fb96050

Name        : RAS-Information
Displayname : Remote Access Information
RightsGUID  : 037088f8-0ae1-11d2-b422-00a0c968f939
...
```

Now, let's put this all together to report on access rights and permissions for a given Active Directory object:

Get-ADUserPermission.ps1

```
Function Get-ADUserPermission {

[cmdletBinding()]

Param(
    [Parameter(Position=0,Mandatory=$True,HelpMessage="Enter a user's identity",
    ValueFromPipeline=$True,ValueFromPipelineByPropertyName=$True)]
    [ValidateNotNullOrEmpty()]
    [Alias("name")]
    [string[]]$identity
    )

Begin {
    Import-Module ActiveDirectory
    #get the Extended rights
    Write-Verbose "Getting extended rights"
    $eRights=.\Get-ExtendedRights.ps1
}
Process {

    Foreach ($user in $identity) {
        Write-Verbose "Getting $user"
        $aduser=Get-ADUser -Identity $user -Properties NTSecurityDescriptor
        $access=$adUser.NTSecurityDescriptor.Access
        $access | Select IdentityReference,AccessControlType,ActiveDirectoryRights,
        @{Name="Right";Expression={
         $g=$_.ObjectType
         $right= $erights | where {$_.RightsGUID -match "^$g"}
         if ($right)
         {
            $right.Name
         }
         else
         {
            $g
         }
         }}
    } #foreach

}
```

```
End {
    Write-Verbose "Finished"
}

} #end function
```

This function uses the **Get-ADUser** cmdlet to retrieve the user object. The user object has a property called **NTSecurityDescriptor**. The information in this property is the same as what you would get using the PSDrive. The cmdlet makes it easier to retrieve a user object and get at the access control list:

```
$aduser=Get-ADUser -Identity $user -Properties NTSecurityDescriptor
$access=$adUser.NTSecurityDescriptor.Access
```

The primary feature of the function is that it "decodes" the RightsGUID value. In the function, I create a variable to hold the results of my **Get-ExtendedRights** script:

```
$eRights=.\Get-ExtendedRights.ps1
```

The function selects a few access properties and uses the $eRights variable as part of hash table to define a new property. The expression finds the extended right that has a RightsGUID value that matches the ObjectType property:

```
@{Name="Right";Expression={
 $g=$_.ObjectType
 $right= $erights | where {$_.RightsGUID -match "^$g"}
 if ($right)
 {
    $right.Name
 }
 else
 {
    $g
 }
```

If there is no match, then the ObjectType GUID is displayed. Once the function is loaded into your session, here's how you might use it:

```
PS R:\> Get-ADUserpermission jfrost | Format-List


IdentityReference      : NT AUTHORITY\SELF
AccessControlType      : Allow
ActiveDirectoryRights : GenericRead
Right                  : 00000000-0000-0000-0000-000000000000

IdentityReference      : NT AUTHORITY\Authenticated Users
AccessControlType      : Allow
ActiveDirectoryRights : ReadControl
Right                  : 00000000-0000-0000-0000-000000000000

IdentityReference      : NT AUTHORITY\SYSTEM
AccessControlType      : Allow
ActiveDirectoryRights : GenericAll
Right                  : 00000000-0000-0000-0000-000000000000
```

```
IdentityReference     : S-1-5-32-548
AccessControlType     : Allow
ActiveDirectoryRights : GenericAll
Right                 : 00000000-0000-0000-0000-000000000000

IdentityReference     : JDHLAB\Domain Admins
AccessControlType     : Allow
ActiveDirectoryRights : GenericAll
Right                 : 00000000-0000-0000-0000-000000000000

IdentityReference     : Everyone
AccessControlType     : Allow
ActiveDirectoryRights : ExtendedRight
Right                 : User-Change-Password

IdentityReference     : NT AUTHORITY\SELF
AccessControlType     : Allow
ActiveDirectoryRights : ReadProperty, WriteProperty
Right                 : Email-Information

IdentityReference     : NT AUTHORITY\SELF
AccessControlType     : Allow
ActiveDirectoryRights : ReadProperty, WriteProperty
Right                 : Personal-Information

IdentityReference     : NT AUTHORITY\SELF
AccessControlType     : Allow
ActiveDirectoryRights : ReadProperty, WriteProperty
Right                 : Web-Information

IdentityReference     : NT AUTHORITY\SELF
AccessControlType     : Allow
ActiveDirectoryRights : ExtendedRight
Right                 : User-Change-Password
...
```

There are many ways you might want to use this information. Here are the permissions that Jack Frost has on his own account:

```
PS R:\> Get-ADUserpermission jfrost | where {$_.IdentityReference -match "Self"} |
>> Select AccessControlType,ActiveDirectoryRights,Right
>>

AccessControlType                          ActiveDirectoryRights Right
-----------------                          --------------------- -----
            Allow                                    GenericRead
00000000-0000-0000-0000-000000000000
            Allow                    ReadProperty, WriteProperty Email-Information
            Allow                    ReadProperty, WriteProperty Personal-Information
            Allow                    ReadProperty, WriteProperty Web-Information
            Allow                                  ExtendedRight User-Change-Password
            Allow                                  ExtendedRight Send-As
            Allow                                  ExtendedRight Receive-As
            Allow ReadProperty, WriteProperty, ExtendedRight Private-Information
```

Here's one more example: I want to find all the domain members that have some sort of permission on Penny Lane's account. I filter for the domain and filter out the Exchange related principals:

```
PS R:\> Get-ADUserpermission plane | where {($_.IdentityReference -match $env:userdomain) -AND
>> ($_.IdentityReference -notmatch "Exchange")} |
```

```
>> Select IdentityReference,AccessControlType,ActiveDirectoryRights,Right
>>

IdentityReference          AccessControlType       ActiveDirectoryRights Right
-----------------          -----------------       --------------------- -----
JDHLAB\Domain Admins                   Allow                  GenericAll 00000000-0000-0000-00...
JDHLAB\sbottom                         Allow ReadProperty, GenericExecute 00000000-0000-0000-00...
JDHLAB\Cert Publishers                 Allow  ReadProperty, WriteProperty bf967a7f-0de6-11d0-a2...
JDHLAB\RAS and IAS Servers             Allow                ReadProperty RAS-Information
JDHLAB\RAS and IAS Servers             Allow                ReadProperty Membership
JDHLAB\RAS and IAS Servers             Allow                ReadProperty User-Logon
JDHLAB\RAS and IAS Servers             Allow                ReadProperty User-Account-Restrict...
JDHLAB\sbottom                         Allow               ExtendedRight User-Force-Change-Pas...
JDHLAB\sbottom                         Allow               ExtendedRight User-Change-Password
JDHLAB\Help Desk                       Allow               ExtendedRight Generate-RSoP-Planning
JDHLAB\Help Desk                       Allow               ExtendedRight Generate-RSoP-Logging
JDHLAB\AD Admins                       Allow                ReadProperty f30e3bbe-9ff0-11d1-b6...
JDHLAB\AD Admins                       Allow                ReadProperty f30e3bbf-9ff0-11d1-b6...
JDHLAB\AD Admins                       Allow               WriteProperty f30e3bbe-9ff0-11d1-b6...
JDHLAB\AD Admins                       Allow               WriteProperty f30e3bbf-9ff0-11d1-b6...
JDHLAB\Enterprise Admins               Allow       GenericAll 00000000-0000-0000-0000-0000000...
```

Set Permission

Unfortunately there aren't any dedicated cmdlets for modifying permissions on an Active Directory object. However, you can accomplish modest changes using the PSDrive and a few .NET classes. Let me walk you through the process. The first step is to create a new access control list entry. To create this type of object you will need a security principal object for the user or group that is being granted the permission, you need to know what type of extended right you're granting, whether this is an Allow or Deny permission, and the extended right GUID.

In my example I want to grant Jack B. Nimble the Send-As permission for Jack B. Quick. I'll start by defining a few variables:

```
$Identity="JDHLAB\jnimble"
$ExtendedRight="Send-As"
$permission="Allow"
```

I'll also use my **Get-ExtendedRights** script so that I can find the Send-As GUID:

```
$erights=.\get-extendedRights.ps1
```

I need to create a special .NET object that represents Jack B. Nimble as a security principal. I know it seems like programming but it's pretty simple:

```
$account  = New-Object System.Security.Principal.NTAccount($identity)
```

The identity value could just as easily have been a group like JDHLAB\Admins.

Next, I'm going to define another .NET object that represents object inheritance. You shouldn't need to modify this at all:

```
[System.DirectoryServices.ActiveDirectorySecurityInheritance]$inherit = "All"
```

The last piece of information I need before I can create the new rule is the GUID associated with the Send-As extended right. I can pipe $eRights to the **Where-Object** cmdlet looking for extended rights and returning the RightsGUID property:

```
[system.guid]$ERGuid=($erights | where {$_.name -eq $ExtendedRight}).RightsGUID
```

I'm specifically casting the variable $ERGuid as a System.GUID, otherwise the variable would be a string and creating the access rule would fail. Now it's time to create the access rule object, specifying the appropriate values as part of the constructor:

```
$ace = New-Object System.DirectoryServices.ActiveDirectoryAccessRule($account,
"ExtendedRight",
$permission, $ERGuiD, $Inherit)
```

All that's left now is to add it to Jack B. Quick's user object. I can use the **Get-ADUser** cmdlet to retrieve the object and its security descriptor:

```
$user=Get-ADUser -identity "jquick" -properties nTSecurityDescriptor
```

Case Doesn't Matter

I realize the property name looks a little odd, but that's the way it is stored in Active Directory. However, you should be able to use any capitalization, or none, that you prefer.

To keep things simple (honestly), I'll save the security descriptor to a variable and add the access rule to it:

```
$acl=$user.nTSecurityDescriptor
$acl.AddAccessRule($ace)
```

Finally, all that is left is to commit the change to Active Directory. To accomplish that, I'll use the standard **Set-ACL** cmdlet. This will require a path to the user object; for that you can take advantage of the Active Directory PSDrive. I can construct a path using the user object's distinguished name:

```
$path=join-path -Path "AD:\" -ChildPath $user.distinguishedname
```

With this final piece of information, the **Set-ACL** cmdlet finishes the task:

```
Set-Acl -AclObject $acl -Path $path
```

You can see the result in Figure 9-1.

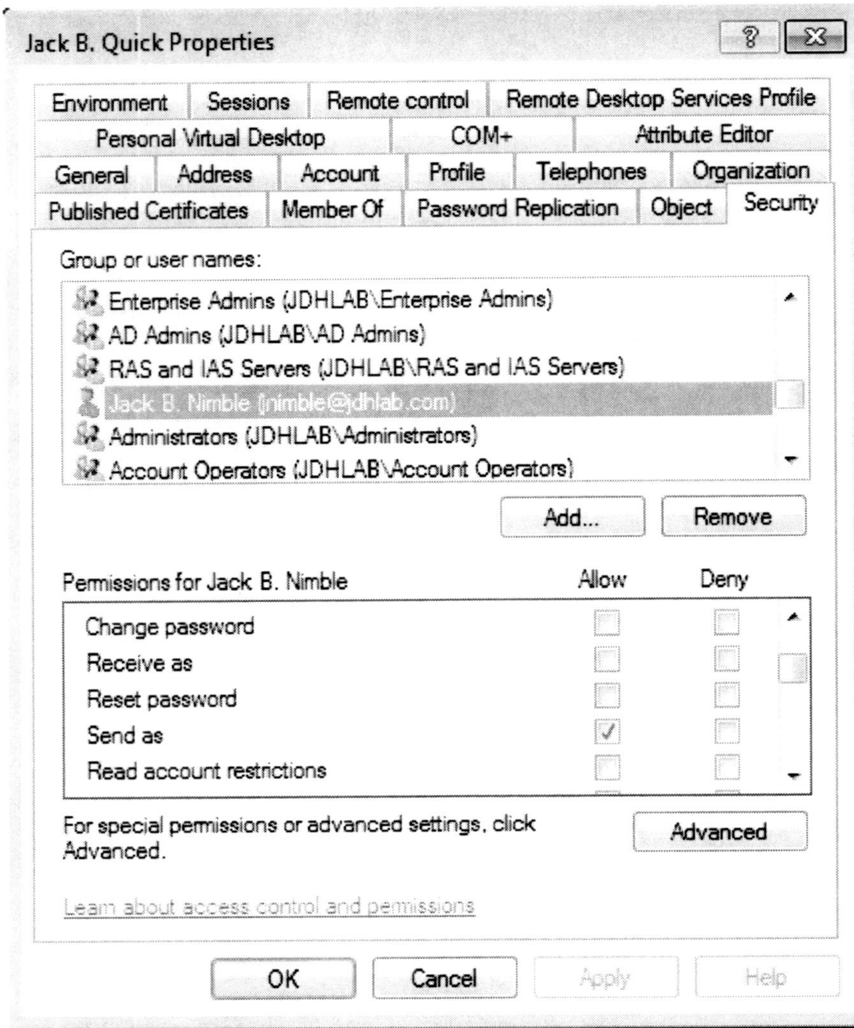

Figure 9-1 New Access Control Rule

I'll be the first to admit this is a lot of work and you'll most likely want to develop a set of functions or scripts to meet your business needs. An alternative is to skip PowerShell and use a command line tool like DSACLS.EXE, which is designed for this task. Or keep reading and you'll see how to manage this using the Quest cmdlets.

Remove Permission

Removing permission is a little bit easier. Let's undo the change you just made and remove Jack B. Nimble's Send-As permission. First, connect to the Active Directory object:

```
$user=Get-ADUser -identity "jquick" -properties nTSecurityDescriptor
```

Next get the security object's rules:

```
$acl=$user.nTSecurityDescriptor
```

Now to find the access rule or rules to be removed:

```
$remove = $acl | where {$_.IdentityReference -match "jnimble"}
```

In this example, I'm searching for any rule with jnimble as the part of the identity name. Just as I can add an access rule, I can also remove it:

```
$acl.RemoveAccessRule($remove)
```

As before, the **Set-ACL** cmdlet commits the change:

```
Set-Acl -AclObject $acl -Path $path
```

Obviously, there's some risk involved when modifying permissions, especially when creating your own scripts and functions so please be very, very careful.

Using Quest Active Directory Cmdlets

You're probably thinking by now that there has to be a better way to manage Active Directory permissions. With the Quest permission cmdlets, there is.

Get-QADPermission

The **Get-QADPermission** cmdlet returns a collection of access control entries (ACE) from the specified Active Directory object's discretionary access control list (DACL). At its simplest, the cmdlet returns any permissions applied directly to the object:

```
PS C:\> Get-QADPermission "Roy Biv"
Permissions for: jdhlab.local/Employees/Executive/Roy Biv

Ctrl Account                        Rights         Source        AppliesTo
---- -------                        ------         ------        ---------
     jdhlab.local\mwashington       Special        Not inherited This object only
     jdhlab.local\mwashington       Reset Password Not inherited This object only
     jdhlab.local\mwashington       Receive As     Not inherited This object only
     jdhlab.local\mwashington       Send As        Not inherited This object only
```

This example shows that mwashington has rights for the Reset Password, Receive As, and Send As permissions. You can also use the **-Inherited** and **-SchemaDefault** parameters to display additional permissions.

Suppose you want to find what permissions a particular security principal has. You can use an expression like this:

```
PS C:\> Get-QADPermission "OU=Employees,DC=jdhlab,DC=local" -inherited -schemadefault `
>> -account "jdhlab\help desk" | Select RightsDisplay,Source,Rights,AccessControlType
>>
Permissions for: jdhlab.local/Employees
```

```
RightsDisplay             Source                         Rights           AccessControlType
-------------             ------                         ------           -----------------
Read/Write pwdLastSet         NotInherited    ReadProperty, WriteProperty               Allow
Reset Password                NotInherited                  ExtendedRight               Allow
Read/Write member                Inherited    ReadProperty, WriteProperty               Allow
Create computer                  Inherited                    CreateChild               Allow
```

The result shows all direct or inherited permissions applied to the Employees organizational unit, which apply to the Help Desk group. Another way you might use this is to export any permission setting that specifically applies to the special SELF account:

```
PS C:\> Get-QADUser -sizelimit 0 | Get-QADPermission -account "SELF" | Export-Csv "selfperms.
csv"
```

You can then re-import the CSV and get any information you want:

```
PS C:\> Import-Csv selfperms.csv | Sort AccessControlType |
>> Select TargetObject,AccessControlType,RightsDisplay
>>

TargetObject                              AccessControlType          RightsDisplay
------------                              -----------------          -------------
CN=krbtgt,CN=Users,DC=jdhlab,DC=...       Allow                      Special
CN=Jeffery Hicks,OU=Information Tech... Allow                        Special
CN=svcDirectoryUpdate,OU=Service Acc... Allow                        Special
CN=Administrator,CN=Users,DC=mycomp...   Allow                       Special
CN=jeff,CN=Users,DC=jdhlab,DC=local      Allow                       Special
CN=Jane Smith,OU=Disabled Accounts,O... Deny                         Change Password
CN=Guest,CN=Users,DC=jdhlab,DC=l...      Deny                        Change Password
CN=Tom Sawyer,OU=Sales,OU=Employees,... Deny                         Change Password
CN=Jack Frost,OU=Payroll,OU=Employee... Deny                         Change Password
```

The end result is a report of all user accounts where a specific permission for the SELF account has been directly applied. The **Get-QADPermission** cmdlet has a few more parameters for retrieving some very granular permission information, so be sure to look at the help documentation.

Add-QADPermission

Adding an access control rule or permission is straightforward—just specify the security principal and what rights or permissions to apply:

```
PS C:\> Get-QADObject "Boston" -type organizationalunit |
>> Add-QADPermission -account "Jdhlab\Boston Admins" -rights "GenericAll" | Select *display


RightsDisplay                                    ApplyToDisplay
-------------                                    --------------
Create/Delete Child objects                      This object and all child objects
Read/Write all properties                        This object and all child objects
All extended rights                              This object and all child objects
All validated writes                             This object and all child objects
Special                                          This object and all child objects
```

In this example, I use the **Get-QADObject** cmdlet to retrieve the Boston organizational unit object. The output is piped to the **Add-QADPermission** cmdlet, which grants the GenericAll permission to the Boston Admins group.

Or consider this example:

```
PS C:\> Get-QADGroup "Las Vegas" |
>> Add-QADPermission -account "jdhlab\las vegas admins" -property "Member" `
>> -ApplyToType "Group" -rights "ReadProperty,WriteProperty" | Select TargetObject
>>

TargetObject
------------
CN=Las Vegas Admins,OU=Groups,DC=jdhlab,DC=local
CN=Las Vegas Engineering,OU=Groups,DC=jdhlab,DC=local
CN=Las Vegas Staff,OU=Groups,DC=jdhlab,DC=local
```

The **Get-QADGroup** cmdlet pipes all groups with Las Vegas in the name to the **Add-QADPermission** cmdlet. cmdlet will grant Read and Write access to the **Member** property, to the "Las Vegas Admins" group. This allows members of this group permission to modify group membership of any Las Vegas group.

You can also use the **Add-QADPermission** cmdlet to copy permissions from one object to another:

```
PS C:\> Get-QADUuser -department "Sales" |
>> Add-QADPermission -inputpermission (Get-QADPermission "sales user")
```

With this expression, I'm getting all users in the Sales department and adding the permission object from the Sales User account. This will not copy any schema-defined or inherited permissions. This expression assumes the Sales User account has one or more special permissions already defined.

Remove-QADPermission

You can remove any Access Control Entry (ACE) with the **Remove-QADPermission** cmdlet. The easiest approach is to use the **Get-QADPermission** cmdlet to return one or more ACEs and pipe them to the **Remove-QADPermission** cmdlet:

```
PS C:\> Get-QADUser -department "Sales" | Get-QADPermission -account "Sales IT" |
>> Remove-QADPermission
```

Or, you might like to use an expression like this:

```
PS C:\> Get-QADuser -sizelimit 0 -enabled | Get-QADPermission -deny |
>> Remove-QADPermission -confirm
```

Every enabled user account is piped to the **Get-QADPermission** cmdlet, which returns all Deny permissions. Each permission object is piped to the **Remove-QADPermission** cmdlet, with the **-Confirm** parameter, so you can remove permissions selectively.

There is always a high degree of risk when working with permissions, so please read the cmdlet documentation and test thoroughly in a non-production environment. With some practice, I think you'll find managing permissions with the Quest cmdlets to be an enjoyable experience.

Chapter 10
The Active Directory Recycle Bin and Recovered Objects

In the past, recovering deleted objects from Active Directory was a time-consuming and tedious task. But with the arrival of Windows Server 2008 R2, Active Directory administrators now have a critical new feature, the Active Directory Recycle Bin. Without going into technical details, when this feature is enabled, if you delete an object from Active Directory, it is moved to a special container instead of being simply tombstoned. Because the object retains all of its original properties, restoring an object from the Recycle Bin is a quick, easy, and painless process. Objects remain in the recycle bin for the duration of the tombstone period. You can recover them at any time. After the tombstone period expires the objects are permanently deleted.

Enabling Optional Features

The Recycle Bin is one of the first "optional features" that you can enable for Active Directory. As of this writing, it is pretty much the only feature. The Microsoft Active-Directory module includes a cmdlet that will display information about all optional features:

```
PS C:\> Get-ADOptionalFeature -Filter *


DistinguishedName  : CN=Recycle Bin Feature,CN=Optional Features,CN=Directory Service,CN=Windows
                     NT,CN=Services,CN=Configuration,DC=jdhlab,DC=local
EnabledScopes      : {}
FeatureGUID        : 766ddcd8-acd0-445e-f3b9-a7f9b6744f2a
FeatureScope       : {ForestOrConfigurationSet}
IsDisableable      : False
Name               : Recycle Bin Feature
ObjectClass        : msDS-OptionalFeature
```

```
ObjectGUID          : f04ae2c2-8bb4-43a6-983f-a71ec99648e1
RequiredDomainMode :
RequiredForestMode : Windows2008R2Forest
```

As you can see, the Recycle Bin is it. You can also get the feature by name:

```
PS C:\> Get-ADOptionalFeature -identity "Recycle Bin Feature"
```

Before you can enable the Recycle Bin feature, make sure you have met all the requirements. I suggest checking the latest information from Microsoft TechNet (http://tinyurl.com/2e2oped). When you are ready, use the **Enable-ADOptionalFeature** cmdlet:

```
PS C:\> Enable-ADOptionalFeature -Identity "Recycle Bin Feature" `
>> -Scope ForestOrConfigurationSet -Target "jdhlab.local"  `
>> -Server coredc01 -whatif
>>

WARNING: Enabling 'Recycle Bin Feature' on 'CN=Partitions,CN=Configuration,DC=jdhlab,DC=local'
is an irreversible action!
You will not be able to disable 'Recycle Bin Feature' on 'CN=Partitions,CN=Configuration,DC=jdh
lab,DC=local' if you proceed.
What if: Performing operation "Enable" on Target "Recycle Bin Feature".
```

The scope can be either the Forest, as I show in this example, or the Domain. Actually, as of this writing, the Domain value does not work. You will get an exception. The only parameter value that works is ForestOrConfigurationSet. Perhaps at some point in time, Domain will work as expected.

The **-Target** parameter is the scope for the new feature. In this example I'm configuring the Recycle Bin for the jdhlab.local forest. You don't have to specify a domain controller, if you only have one and it has all of the FSMO roles. Otherwise, the domain controller you specify must hold the domain-naming FSMO role. I'll go ahead and enable the feature in my domain:

```
PS C:\> Enable-ADOptionalFeature -Identity "Recycle Bin Feature" `
>> -Scope ForestOrConfigurationSet -Target "jdhlab.local" -Server coredc01
>>
WARNING: Enabling 'Recycle Bin Feature' on 'DC=jdhlab,DC=local' is an irreversible action! You
will not be able to disable
'Recycle Bin Feature' on 'DC=jdhlab,DC=local' if you proceed.

Confirm
Are you sure you want to perform this action?
Performing operation "Enable" on Target "Recycle Bin Feature".
[Y] Yes  [A] Yes to All  [N] No  [L] No to All  [S] Suspend  [?] Help (default is "Y"):
```

The Recycle Bin feature can't be disabled or uninstalled so there is no need to worry about learning how to use the **Disable-ADOptionalFeature** cmdlet right now.

One major caveat is that you can't begin to recover items until after you enable the feature. Any objects deleted prior to enabling the Recycle Bin remain unaffected. If you need to restore them, you'll need to use traditional methods. Only objects deleted *after* the Recycle Bin has been enabled can be recovered using the cmdlets in this chapter.

Enumerating Deleted Objects

When you delete an object and the Recycled Bin feature is enabled, the object is moved to a special, super-secret, protected container and, aside from a few minor modifications, remains essentially intact. This is critical because when you restore the object, it is fully restored to its previous state.

What this also means is that a deleted user or group is still a user or group object, which means you use the same tools, most of the time. The only thing new is a parameter to include deleted objects.

Using the Active Directory Module

To get user objects in the Active Directory module, you know to use the **Get-ADUser** cmdlet. However, when it comes to finding deleted user objects, or any other type for that matter, you need to turn to the **Get-ADObject** cmdlet.

To find only deleted objects, you'll need to work out a specific query. In know I have a deleted user account for Francis Drake. Using the **Get-ADObject** cmdlet, I'll get that object. Notice I'm including a new parameter you haven't seen before called the **-IncludeDeletedObjects** parameter:

```
PS C:\> Get-ADObject -Filter 'Samaccountname -eq "fdrake"' -IncludeDeletedObjects


Deleted           : True
DistinguishedName : CN=Francis Drake\0ADEL:058c0fc3-0dc6-425c-a291-b793e35c38ad,CN=Deleted
                    Objects,DC=jdhlab,DC=local
Name              : Francis Drake
                    DEL:058c0fc3-0dc6-425c-a291-b793e35c38ad
ObjectClass       : user
ObjectGUID        : 058c0fc3-0dc6-425c-a291-b793e35c38ad
```

There are actually more properties for this object that I can display:

```
PS C:\> Get-ADObject -Filter 'Samaccountname -eq "fdrake"' -IncludeDeletedObjects -Properties *


accountExpires                  : 9223372036854775807
badPasswordTime                 : 129246310266007794
badPwdCount                     : 5
CanonicalName                   : jdhlab.local/Deleted Objects/Francis Drake
                                  DEL:058c0fc3-0dc6-425c-a291-b793e35c38ad
CN                              : Francis Drake
                                  DEL:058c0fc3-0dc6-425c-a291-b793e35c38ad
codePage                        : 0
company                         : JDH Lab
countryCode                     : 0
Created                         : 7/19/2010 2:50:51 PM
createTimeStamp                 : 7/19/2010 2:50:51 PM
Deleted                         : True
department                      : IT
Description                     : Created 07/19/2010 14:50:26
DisplayName                     : Francis Drake
DistinguishedName               : CN=Francis Drake\0ADEL:058c0fc3-0dc6-425c-a291-b793e35c38ad,
                                  CN=Deleted Objects,DC=jdhlab,DC=local
division                        : Operations
dSCorePropagationData           : {9/9/2010 12:20:33 PM, 9/3/2010 11:05:03 AM, 9/3/2010 11:04:53
                                  AM, 9/3/2010 11:04:31 AM...}
givenName                       : Francis
instanceType                    : 4
isDeleted                       : True
```

```
LastKnownParent                 : OU=Temp,OU=Employees,DC=jdhlab,DC=local
lastLogoff                      : 0
lastLogon                       : 0
lockoutTime                     : 129246310266007794
logonCount                      : 0
memberOf                        : {CN=Group-6,OU=Groups,DC=jdhlab,DC=local}
Modified                        : 9/16/2010 6:35:19 PM
modifyTimeStamp                 : 9/16/2010 6:35:19 PM
msDS-LastKnownRDN               : Francis Drake
msDS-SupportedEncryptionTypes   : 0
Name                            : Francis Drake
                                  DEL:058c0fc3-0dc6-425c-a291-b793e35c38ad
nTSecurityDescriptor            : System.DirectoryServices.ActiveDirectorySecurity
ObjectCategory                  :
ObjectClass                     : user
ObjectGUID                      : 058c0fc3-0dc6-425c-a291-b793e35c38ad
objectSid                       : S-1-5-21-3957442467-353870018-3926547339-5047
physicalDeliveryOfficeName      : 5-South-233
primaryGroupID                  : 513
ProtectedFromAccidentalDeletion : False
pwdLastSet                      : 129264575046643798
sAMAccountName                  : FDrake
sDRightsEffective               : 15
sn                              : Drake
title                           : Sr. Engineer
userAccountControl              : 512
userPrincipalName               : FDrake@jdhlab.com
uSNChanged                      : 468889
uSNCreated                      : 385338
whenChanged                     : 9/16/2010 6:35:19 PM
whenCreated                     : 7/19/2010 2:50:51 PM
```

There are a few key properties I want to draw your attention to:

```
PS C:\> Get-ADObject -Filter 'Samaccountname -eq "fdrake"' `
>> -IncludeDeletedObjects -Properties * |
>> Select Displayname,Name,samaccountname,IsDeleted,LastKnownParent
>>


Displayname     : Francis Drake
Name            : Francis Drake
                  DEL:058c0fc3-0dc6-425c-a291-b793e35c38ad
samaccountname  : FDrake
IsDeleted       : True
LastKnownParent : OU=Temp,OU=Employees,DC=jdhlab,DC=local
```

The **IsDeleted** property is a Boolean value that indicates exactly what the name says. The **LastKnownParent** property is populated when the object is deleted. The value reflects where the object resided in Active Directory prior to its deletion. When an object is restored, it is restored to this location. You can also use this property in a filtering query:

```
PS C:\> Get-ADObject -Filter 'objectclass -eq "user" -and IsDeleted -eq $True' `
>> -IncludeDeletedObjects -Properties SAMAccountname,LastKnownParent |
>> Select Name,SamAccountname,LastKnownParent
>>
```

```
Name                                SamAccountname        LastKnownParent
----                                --------------        ---------------
William Flash...                    W.Flash               OU=Temp,OU=Employees,DC=j...
Monroe Demonbreun...                M.Demonbreun          OU=Obsolete,DC=jdhlab,DC=...
Marc Bordes...                      M.Bordes              OU=Alpha\0ADEL:2ce9b887-e...
Otto Nejaime...                     O.Nejaime             OU=Obsolete,DC=jdhlab,DC...
Jack Stanier...                     J.Stanier             OU=Alpha\0ADEL:2ce9b887-e...
Ivan Alberda...                     I.Alberda             OU=Finance,OU=Employees,D...
Man Beauchamp...                    M.Beauchamp           OU=Finance,OU=Employees,D...
...
```

Or perhaps you'd like to know how many accounts were deleted from the Temp organizational unit under Employees? All I need is to modify my filtering query:

```
PS C:\> Get-ADObject -Filter 'objectclass -eq "user" -and IsDeleted -eq $True
>> -and LastKnownParent -eq "OU=Temp,OU=Employees,DC=jdhlab,dc=local"' `
>> -IncludeDeletedObjects -Properties SAMAccountname,LastKnownParent |
>> Select Name,SamAccountname,LastKnownParent

Name                                          SamAccountname LastKnownParent
----                                          -------------- ---------------
William Flash...                              W.Flash        OU=Temp,OU=Employees,DC=j...
Francis Drake...                              FDrake         OU=Temp,OU=Employees,DC=j...
```

Given this, you would think you should be able to use the **-Like** parameter in the filter and find all user objects from anywhere in the Employees organizational unit hierarchy with an expression like this:

```
Get-ADObject -Filter 'objectclass -eq "user" -and IsDeleted -eq $True -and LastKnownParent
-like "*OU=Employees*"' -IncludeDeletedObjects -Properties *
```

But for some reason that I haven't learned yet, this fails to return any results. Instead I've had to resort to late filtering with the **Where-Object** cmdlet:

```
PS C:\> Get-ADObject -Filter 'objectclass -eq "user" -and IsDeleted -eq $True' `
>> -IncludeDeletedObjects  -Properties SAMAccountname,LastKnownParent |
>> Where {$_.LastKnownParent -like "*OU=Employees*"} |
>> select Samaccountname,LastKnownParent
>>

Samaccountname                       LastKnownParent
--------------                       ---------------
W.Flash                              OU=Temp,OU=Employees,DC=jdhlab,DC=local
I.Alberda                            OU=Finance,OU=Employees,DC=jdhlab,DC=local
M.Beauchamp                          OU=Finance,OU=Employees,DC=jdhlab,DC=local
L.Ngov                               OU=Finance,OU=Employees,DC=jdhlab,DC=local
FDrake                               OU=Temp,OU=Employees,DC=jdhlab,DC=local
```

But this isn't too bad. The more specific you can make the filter for the **Get-ADObject** cmdlet, the better this will perform.

Using Quest Cmdlets

Using the Quest cmdlets takes a slightly different approach. The cmdlets you use to get computers, users, and groups all have a **-Tombstone** parameter to return only the deleted object type:

```
PS C:\> Get-QADGroup -Tombstone

Name                            Type        DN
----                            ----        --
Group-100ADEL:99f2d2fa-fde5... group       CN=Group-10\0ADEL:99f2d2fa-fde5-446f-a764-90d0af...
Art Department0ADEL:1c16f96... group       CN=Art Department\0ADEL:1c16f960-cf48-4f2b-a683-...
PS C:\> Get-QADUser -Tombstone | Measure-Object


Count    : 18
Average  :
Sum      :
Maximum  :
Minimum  :
Property :
```

As you can see, I have two deleted groups I can recover and 18 users. Let's look at one of these user objects in more detail:

```
PS C:\> Get-QADUuser -Identity "fdrake" -Tombstone |
>> Select Name,DisplayName,SamAccountname,LastKnownParent,WhenChanged
>>


Name            : Francis Drake0ADEL:058c0fc3-0dc6-425c-a291-b793e35c38ad
DisplayName     : Francis Drake
SamAccountName  : FDrake
LastKnownParent : OU=Temp,OU=Employees,DC=jdhlab,DC=local
whenChanged     : 9/16/2010 6:35:19 PM
```

The properties are essentially the same as what you get with the Microsoft cmdlet. Even better, the **LastKnownParent** property is a parameter for the **Get-QADUser** cmdlet:

```
PS C:\> Get-QADuser -LastKnownParent "OU=Finance,OU=Employees,DC=jdhlab,DC=local" -tombstone |
>> Select Samaccountname
>>

SamAccountName
--------------
I.Alberda
M.Beauchamp
L.Ngov
```

The value for the **LastKnownParent** property must be an exact match. Here, I've found all deleted users from the Finance organizational unit and displayed their SAMAccountnames. If I want to find any user from Employees, I'll again need to use the **Where-Object** cmdlet:

```
PS C:\> Get-QADUuser -tombstone | where {$_.LastKnownParent -like "*OU=Employees*"} |
>> Select SAMAccountname,LastKnownParent

SamAccountName                                   LastKnownParent
--------------                                   ---------------
W.Flash                                          OU=Temp,OU=Employees,DC=jdhlab,DC=local
I.Alberda                                        OU=Finance,OU=Employees,DC=jdhlab,DC=local
M.Beauchamp                                      OU=Finance,OU=Employees,DC=jdhlab,DC=local
L.Ngov                                           OU=Finance,OU=Employees,DC=jdhlab,DC=local
FDrake                                           OU=Temp,OU=Employees,DC=jdhlab,DC=local
```

Since deleted objects aren't modified, the **WhenChanged** property actually reflects when they were deleted. This might come in handy. Suppose I want to find all the user accounts deleted in the last seven days:

```
PS C:\> Get-QADUser -LastChangedAfter (Get-Date).AddDays(-7) -Tombstone |
>> Where {$_.Classname -eq "user"} | Select SAMAccountname,WhenChanged,LastKnownParent,Classn
ame |
>> Sort WhenChanged
>>

SamAccountName                        whenChanged                   LastKnownParent
--------------                        -----------                   ---------------
hdemo14                               9/16/2010 4:47:55 PM          CN=Users,DC=jdhlab,DC=l...
M.Demonbreun                          9/16/2010 4:48:44 PM          OU=Obsolete,DC=jdhlab,D...
O.Nejaime                             9/16/2010 4:48:44 PM          OU=Obsolete,DC=jdhlab,D...
J.Stanier                             9/16/2010 4:49:26 PM          OU=Alpha\0ADEL:2ce9b887...
F.Botten                              9/16/2010 4:49:26 PM          OU=Alpha\0ADEL:2ce9b887...
L.Cofrancesco                         9/16/2010 4:49:26 PM          OU=Alpha\0ADEL:2ce9b887...
M.Claessens                           9/16/2010 4:49:26 PM          OU=Alpha\0ADEL:2ce9b887...
M.Bordes                              9/16/2010 4:49:26 PM          OU=Alpha\0ADEL:2ce9b887...
N.Deschepper                          9/16/2010 4:49:26 PM          OU=Alpha\0ADEL:2ce9b887...
M.Beauchamp                           9/16/2010 5:23:08 PM          OU=Finance,OU=Employees...
I.Alberda                             9/16/2010 5:23:09 PM          OU=Finance,OU=Employees...
L.Ngov                                9/16/2010 5:23:09 PM          OU=Finance,OU=Employees...
W.Flash                               9/16/2010 5:35:08 PM          OU=Temp,OU=Employees,DC...
FDrake                                9/16/2010 6:35:19 PM          OU=Temp,OU=Employees,DC...
A.Andersen                            9/17/2010 12:58:00 PM         OU=Test,OU=Employees,DC...
```

When using the **Get-QADUser** cmdlet to retrieve deleted objects, the cmdlet also returns deleted computer accounts, since they are derived from the user class. To filter them out, I use the **Where-Object** cmdlet:

```
Where {$_.Classname -eq "user"}
```

My output is also sorted by the **WhenChanged** property. The reason I'm spending all this time on finding deleted accounts is because it is easier to recover objects if you know what you are looking for.

What About -Recycled?

If you look at cmdlet help for **Get-QADUser**, you'll come across the **-Recycled** parameter. In order to use this parameter you must specify a domain root for the search root and the Recycle Bin must be enabled. The **Get-QADUser** cmdlet will then display all deleted user accounts. However, what you will see will be all the accounts that were deleted before you enabled the Recycle Bin. You cannot restore any of these objects with the techniques in this chapter. I realize it is a little confusing, but stick to using the **-Tombstone** parameter to identify deleted objects that can be restored.

Recovering Deleted Objects

Finally, we get to the main event. Now that you know how to identify deleted objects, let's restore them.

Using the Active Directory Module

I know that I have accidentally deleted the Francis Drake account:

```
PS C:\> Get-ADObject -filter 'samaccountname -eq "fdrake"' -includeDeletedObjects


Deleted           : True
DistinguishedName : CN=Francis Drake\0ADEL:058c0fc3-0dc6-425c-a291-b793e35c38ad,CN=Deleted
                    Objects,DC=jdhlab,DC=local
Name              : Francis Drake
                    DEL:058c0fc3-0dc6-425c-a291-b793e35c38ad
ObjectClass       : user
ObjectGUID        : 058c0fc3-0dc6-425c-a291-b793e35c38ad
```

The easiest way to restore this object is to pipe this object to the **Restore-ADObject** cmdlet:

```
PS C:\> Get-ADObject -filter 'samaccountname -eq "fdrake"' -includeDeletedObjects |
>> Restore-ADObject -whatif
>>
What if: Performing operation "Restore" on Target "CN=Francis Drake\0ADEL:058c0fc3-0dc6-425c-
a291-b793e35c38ad,CN=Deleted Objects,DC=jdhlab,DC=local".
```

Looks OK, so let's do it for real:

```
PS C:\> Get-ADObject -filter 'samaccountname -eq "fdrake"' -includeDeletedObjects |
>> Restore-ADObject -passthru
>>


DistinguishedName                 Name              ObjectClass   ObjectGUID
-----------------                 ----              -----------   ----------
cn=Francis Drake,OU=Temp,OU=...  Francis Drake     user          058c0fc3-0dc6-425c-a291-b79...


PS C:\> Get-ADUser -Identity "fdrake"


DistinguishedName : CN=Francis Drake,OU=Temp,OU=Employees,DC=jdhlab,DC=local
Enabled           : True
GivenName         : Francis
Name              : Francis Drake
ObjectClass       : user
ObjectGUID        : 058c0fc3-0dc6-425c-a291-b793e35c38ad
SamAccountName    : FDrake
SID               : S-1-5-21-3957442467-353870018-3926547339-5047
Surname           : Drake
UserPrincipalName : FDrake@jdhlab.com
```

By default, the **Restore-ADObject** cmdlet doesn't write anything to the pipeline, which is why I included the **-Passthru** parameter. I then retrieved the object with the **Get-ADUser** cmdlet to prove it was restored. By the way, the value for the **LastKnownParent** property remains. This is useful when you want to identify restored accounts:

```
PS C:\> Get-ADUser -filter "LastknownParent -like '*'" `
>> -SearchBase "OU=Employees,DC=jdhlab,DC=local"
>>
```

```
DistinguishedName : CN=Adam Patsy,OU=Test,OU=Employees,DC=jdhlab,DC=local
Enabled           : True
GivenName         : Adam
Name              : Adam Patsy
ObjectClass       : user
ObjectGUID        : 905d96b4-9ab5-4057-bb80-f8bd1efd0341
SamAccountName    : A.Patsy
SID               : S-1-5-21-3957442467-353870018-3926547339-4330
Surname           : Patsy
UserPrincipalName : A.Patsy@jdhlab.com

DistinguishedName : CN=Francis Drake,OU=Temp,OU=Employees,DC=jdhlab,DC=local
Enabled           : True
GivenName         : Francis
Name              : Francis Drake
ObjectClass       : user
ObjectGUID        : 058c0fc3-0dc6-425c-a291-b793e35c38ad
SamAccountName    : FDrake
SID               : S-1-5-21-3957442467-353870018-3926547339-5047
Surname           : Drake
UserPrincipalName : FDrake@jdhlab.com
```

Right now, I've only restored two accounts under the Employee's organizational unit.

The **Restore-ADObject** cmdlet also permits you to rename an object upon restoration. I'm going to restore the deleted Lisa Andrews account and rename it to Lisa Jones:

```
PS C:\> Get-ADObject -filter 'samaccountname -eq "l.andrews"' -includeDeletedObjects |
>> Restore-ADObject -NewName "Lisa Jones" -passthru
>>

DistinguishedName                Name              ObjectClass        ObjectGUID
-----------------                ----              -----------        ----------
cn=Lisa Jones,OU=Sales,OU=Em... Lisa Jones        user               1019ec03-09be-4f08-...
```

Before you get too excited though, check out the restored object:

```
PS C:\> Get-ADUser -Identity "l.andrews" -Properties *name


DistinguishedName : CN=Lisa Jones,OU=Sales,OU=Employees,DC=jdhlab,DC=local
Enabled           : True
GivenName         : Lisa
Name              : Lisa Jones
ObjectClass       : user
ObjectGUID        : 1019ec03-09be-4f08-96e0-10716a2e291f
SamAccountName    : L.Andrews
SID               : S-1-5-21-3957442467-353870018-3926547339-1115
Surname           : Andrews
UserPrincipalName : L.Andrews@jdhlab.com
```

All you did was change the display name. Other critical properties like SAMAccountname and UserPrincipalName are unchanged; although you can now modify them with PowerShell if you wish. By the way, there is no provision for restoring an object to a different location.

Here's another situation you might run into. You've deleted an organizational unit with user accounts. What should you do? First, I'll make sure I can find the deleted OU:

```
PS C:\> Get-ADObject -filter 'Objectclass -eq "organizationalunit" -and IsDeleted -eq $True
>> -and Name -like "Alpha*"' -IncludeDeletedObjects
>>


Deleted           : True
DistinguishedName : OU=Alpha\0ADEL:2ce9b887-e0d4-4242-b798-8fef36e341a0,CN=Deleted Objects,...
Name              : Alpha
                    DEL:2ce9b887-e0d4-4242-b798-8fef36e341a0
ObjectClass       : organizationalUnit
ObjectGUID        : 2ce9b887-e0d4-4242-b798-8fef36e341a0
```

Restoring this object is no different than what I did earlier:

```
PS C:\> Get-ADObject -filter 'Objectclass -eq "organizationalunit" -and IsDeleted -eq $True
>> -and Name -like "Alpha*"' -IncludeDeletedObjects  | Restore-ADObject
```

The organizational unit is restored. But when I look, there are no user accounts. They are still deleted:

```
PS C:\> Get-ADObject -filter 'IsDeleted -eq $True -AND
>> LastKnownParent -eq "OU=Alpha,OU=Omega,DC=jdhlab,DC=local"' -includeDeletedObjects |
>> Select Name
>>

Name
----
Marc Bordes...
Jack Stanier...
Lawrence Cofrancesco...
Numbers Deschepper...
Franklyn Botten...
Marilee Claessens...
```

Restoring these objects is just as easy:

```
PS C:\> Get-ADObject -filter 'IsDeleted -eq $True -AND
>> LastKnownParent -eq "OU=Alpha,OU=Omega,DC=jdhlab,DC=local"' -includeDeletedObjects |
>> Restore-ADObject -PassThru
>>

DistinguishedName                Name                    ObjectClass     ObjectGUID
-----------------                ----                    -----------     ----------
cn=Marc Bordes,OU=Alpha,OU=O... Marc Bordes             user            53a98f20-fb22-4...
cn=Jack Stanier,OU=Alpha,OU=... Jack Stanier            user            62a0bf85-0129-4...
cn=Lawrence Cofrancesco,OU=A... Lawrence Cofrancesco    user            84cc48d5-0ef1-4...
cn=Numbers Deschepper,OU=Alp... Numbers Deschepper      user            a2e698a3-ff69-4...
cn=Franklyn Botten,OU=Alpha,... Franklyn Botten         user            d8ef9f2a-0228-4...
cn=Marilee Claessens,OU=Alph... Marilee Claessens       user            81c3f850-a45a-4...
```

Just like that all the users have been restored. If you attempt to restore an object before you restore the parent, you'll get an error:

```
PS C:\> Get-ADObject -filter 'samaccountname -eq "g.brentano"' -IncludeDeletedObjects |
>> Restore-ADObject -PassThru
>>

Restore-ADObject : The operation could not be performed because the object's parent is either
```

```
uninstantiated or deleted
At line:1 char:97
+ Get-ADObject -filter 'samaccountname -eq "g.brentano"' -IncludeDeletedObjects | Restore-
ADObject <<<<  -PassThru
    + CategoryInfo          : InvalidOperation: (CN=Garrett Bren...jdhlab,DC=local:ADObject)
[Restore-ADObject], ADExceptio
   n
    + FullyQualifiedErrorId : 0,Microsoft.ActiveDirectory.Management.Commands.RestoreADObject

Restore-ADObject : Directory object not found
At line:1 char:97
+ Get-ADObject -filter 'samaccountname -eq "g.brentano"' -IncludeDeletedObjects | Restore-
ADObject <<<<  -PassThru
    + CategoryInfo          : ObjectNotFound: (CN=Garrett Bren...jdhlab,DC=local:ADObject)
[Restore-ADObject], ADIdentityNo
   tFoundException
    + FullyQualifiedErrorId : Directory object not
found,Microsoft.ActiveDirectory.Management.Commands.RestoreADObject
```

Remember to restore the container first, and then restore the child objects.

Using Restore-QADDeletedObject

Using the Quest cmdlets is not that much different. I accidentally deleted the Art Department group and need to recover it. You can see the deleted object with the **Get-QADGroup** cmdlet:

```
PS C:\> Get-QADGgroup "Art Department" -Tombstone

Name                            Type            DN
----                            ----            --
Art Department0ADEL:1c16f96... group           CN=Art
Department\0ADEL:1c16f960-cf48-4f2b-a683-...
```

You might be curious about how this affects group membership. The deleted object has no members, which seems only right since the object is deleted after all:

```
PS C:\> Get-QADGroup "Art Department" -Tombstone | Select Members

Members
-------
{}
```

I'll restore the group using the **Restore-QADDeletedObject** cmdlet:

```
PS C:\> Get-QADGroup "Art Department" -Tombstone | Restore-QADDeletedObject

Name                            Type        DN
----                            ----        --
Art Department                  group       CN=Art Department,OU=Art,OU=Employees,DC=jdhlab,...
```

Now when I look at the restored group, the membership has been restored:

```
PS C:\> Get-QADGroup "Art Department"| Select Members

Members
-------
{CN=Roy G. Biv,OU=Executive,OU=Employees,DC=jdhlab,DC=local}
```

Recovering a user account is the same. I'll recover Leo Ngov who belongs in the Finance OU:

```
PS C:\> Get-QADObject -identity "l.ngov" -Tombstone

Name                          Type        DN
----                          ----        --
Leo Ngov0ADEL:bfe38077-7877... user       CN=Leo Ngov\0ADEL:bfe38077-7877-4c49-a32b-d90c8e...


PS C:\> Get-QADObject -identity "l.ngov" -Tombstone | Restore-QADDeletedObject

Name                          Type        DN
----                          ----        --
Leo Ngov                      user        CN=Leo Ngov,OU=Finance,OU=Employees,DC=jdhlab,DC...
```

But there is a major difference when it comes to recovering organizational units or containers. I've also accidentally deleted the Customer Service organizational unit:

```
PS C:\> Get-QADObject -Identity "Customer Service" -Tombstone

Name                          Type            DN
----                          ----            --
Customer Service0ADEL:133a5... organization... OU=Customer Service\0ADEL:133a50a9-02af-4498-bd3...
```

I could restore this object then search for all child objects and restore them. But the Quest cmdlet makes this much easier:

```
PS C:\> Get-QADObject -Identity "Customer Service" -Tombstone |
>> Restore-QADDeletedObject -RestoreChildren
>>

Name                     Type             DN
----                     ----             --
Customer Service         organization...  OU=Customer Service,OU=Quest,DC=jdhlab,DC=local
Gaylord Nachor           user             CN=Gaylord Nachor,OU=Customer Service,OU=Quest,D...
Gaston Halcott           user             CN=Gaston Halcott,OU=Customer Service,OU=Quest,D...
Fidel Szysh              user             CN=Fidel Szysh,OU=Customer Service,OU=Quest,DC=j...
Filiberto Randrup        user             CN=Filiberto Randrup,OU=Customer Service,OU=Ques...
Garrett Brentano         user             CN=Garrett Brentano,OU=Customer Service,OU=Quest...
Francisco Teder          user             CN=Francisco Teder,OU=Customer Service,OU=Quest,...
Gene Everman             user             CN=Gene Everman,OU=Customer Service,OU=Quest,DC=...
```

The **-RestoreChildren** parameter does it all! If you need to be more selective about what child objects you restore, then you'll need to manage that on your own. But when you need to recover a deleted container, it doesn't get any easier than this.

Before You Begin

The Recycle Bin feature is truly a life (and job) saver. But before you jump into restoring objects in your production environment, please, please, test everything from this chapter in a lab setting. Deleting and restoring objects has a number of ramifications.

Chapter 11

Using the Active Directory PSDrive Provider

When you install the Microsoft Active Directory module on a domain member, you will also get a PSDrive "mapped" to Active Directory, called AD:

```
PS C:\> Get-PSDrive AD

Name           Used (GB)     Free (GB) Provider      Root                CurrentLocation
----           ---------     --------- --------      ----                ---------------
AD                                     ActiveDire... //RootDSE/
```

If your computer does not belong to a domain, you won't see the drive and will get a warning message, which you can ignore.

To use the drive, simply change your location to it:

```
PS C:\> cd AD:
PS AD:\>
PS AD:\> dir

Name                ObjectClass         DistinguishedName
----                -----------         -----------------
jdhlab              domainDNS           DC=jdhlab,DC=local
Configuration       configuration       CN=Configuration,DC=jdhlab,DC=local
Schema              dMD                 CN=Schema,CN=Configuration,DC=jdhlab,DC=local
DomainDnsZones      domainDNS           DC=DomainDnsZones,DC=jdhlab,DC=local
ForestDnsZones      domainDNS           DC=ForestDnsZones,DC=jdhlab,DC=local
```

Navigating

Now you can navigate your Active Directory domain as if it were a file system, although changing "directories" requires you to use a distinguished name:

```
PS AD:\> cd "DC=jdhlab,DC=local"
PS AD:\DC=jdhlab,DC=local> dir

Name                 ObjectClass          DistinguishedName
----                 -----------          -----------------
Backup               organizationalUnit   OU=Backup,DC=jdhlab,DC=local
Branch Office        organizationalUnit   OU=Branch Office,DC=jdhlab,DC=local
Builtin              builtinDomain        CN=Builtin,DC=jdhlab,DC=local
Company Desktops     organizationalUnit   OU=Company Desktops,DC=jdhlab,DC=local
Computers            container            CN=Computers,DC=jdhlab,DC=local
Contacts             organizationalUnit   OU=Contacts,DC=jdhlab,DC=local
Disabled Users       organizationalUnit   OU=Disabled Users,DC=jdhlab,DC=local
Domain Controllers   organizationalUnit   OU=Domain Controllers,DC=jdhlab,DC=local
Employees            organizationalUnit   OU=Employees,DC=jdhlab,DC=local
Enterprise Servers   organizationalUnit   OU=Enterprise Servers,DC=jdhlab,DC=local
ForeignSecurityPr... container            CN=ForeignSecurityPrincipals,DC=jdhlab,DC=local
Groups               organizationalUnit   OU=Groups,DC=jdhlab,DC=local
Infrastructure       infrastructureUpdate CN=Infrastructure,DC=jdhlab,DC=local
LostAndFound         lostAndFound         CN=LostAndFound,DC=jdhlab,DC=local
Managed Service A... container            CN=Managed Service Accounts,DC=jdhlab,DC=local
Microsoft Exchang... organizationalUnit   OU=Microsoft Exchange Security Groups,DC=jdhlab,DC=local
Microsoft Exchang... msExchSystemObjec... CN=Microsoft Exchange System Objects,DC=jdhlab,DC=local
MyContainer          container            CN=MyContainer,DC=jdhlab,DC=local
NTDS Quotas          msDS-QuotaContainer  CN=NTDS Quotas,DC=jdhlab,DC=local
Obsolete             organizationalUnit   OU=Obsolete,DC=jdhlab,DC=local
Offices              organizationalUnit   OU=Offices,DC=jdhlab,DC=local
Program Data         container            CN=Program Data,DC=jdhlab,DC=local
Project Omega        organizationalUnit   OU=Project Omega,DC=jdhlab,DC=local
Quest                organizationalUnit   OU=Quest,DC=jdhlab,DC=local
System               container            CN=System,DC=jdhlab,DC=local
Templates            organizationalUnit   OU=Templates,DC=jdhlab,DC=local
Temporary            container            CN=Temporary,DC=jdhlab,DC=local
Test Desktops        organizationalUnit   OU=Test Desktops,DC=jdhlab,DC=local
Users                container            CN=Users,DC=jdhlab,DC=local
```

Organizational units are the equivalent of directories so you can navigate simply by changing "directories". You don't need the complete distinguished name at this point, only the first part:

```
PS AD:\DC=jdhlab,DC=local> cd "OU=Enterprise Servers"
PS AD:\OU=Enterprise Servers,DC=jdhlab,DC=local> dir

Name                 ObjectClass          DistinguishedName
----                 -----------          -----------------
App-1                computer             CN=App-1,OU=Enterprise Servers,DC=jdhlab,DC=local
App-10               computer             CN=App-10,OU=Enterprise Servers,DC=jdhlab,DC=local
App-2                computer             CN=App-2,OU=Enterprise Servers,DC=jdhlab,DC=local
App-3                computer             CN=App-3,OU=Enterprise Servers,DC=jdhlab,DC=local
App-4                computer             CN=App-4,OU=Enterprise Servers,DC=jdhlab,DC=local
App-5                computer             CN=App-5,OU=Enterprise Servers,DC=jdhlab,DC=local
App-6                computer             CN=App-6,OU=Enterprise Servers,DC=jdhlab,DC=local
App-7                computer             CN=App-7,OU=Enterprise Servers,DC=jdhlab,DC=local
App-8                computer             CN=App-8,OU=Enterprise Servers,DC=jdhlab,DC=local
App-9                computer             CN=App-9,OU=Enterprise Servers,DC=jdhlab,DC=local
DB03                 computer             CN=DB03,OU=Enterprise Servers,DC=jdhlab,DC=local
```

```
Demo                  organizationalUnit  OU=Demo,OU=Enterprise Servers,DC=jdhlab,DC=local
File-1                computer            CN=File-1,OU=Enterprise Servers,DC=jdhlab,DC=local
File-10               computer            CN=File-10,OU=Enterprise Servers,DC=jdhlab,DC=local
File-2                computer            CN=File-2,OU=Enterprise Servers,DC=jdhlab,DC=local
File-3                computer            CN=File-3,OU=Enterprise Servers,DC=jdhlab,DC=local
File-4                computer            CN=File-4,OU=Enterprise Servers,DC=jdhlab,DC=local
File-5                computer            CN=File-5,OU=Enterprise Servers,DC=jdhlab,DC=local
File-6                computer            CN=File-6,OU=Enterprise Servers,DC=jdhlab,DC=local
File-7                computer            CN=File-7,OU=Enterprise Servers,DC=jdhlab,DC=local
File-8                computer            CN=File-8,OU=Enterprise Servers,DC=jdhlab,DC=local
File-9                computer            CN=File-9,OU=Enterprise Servers,DC=jdhlab,DC=local
Server21              computer            CN=Server21,OU=Enterprise Servers,DC=jdhlab,DC=local
test1                 computer            CN=test1,OU=Enterprise Servers,DC=jdhlab,DC=local
Web10                 computer            CN=Web10,OU=Enterprise Servers,DC=jdhlab,DC=local
```

I've now changed to the "Enterprise Servers" directory, which is really an organizational unit. An object within one of these "directories" is equivalent to a file. You can't access any content, but each object has plenty of properties you can work with. I'm going to change to the HR organizational unit:

```
PS AD:\OU=Enterprise Servers,DC=jdhlab,DC=local> cd "..\OU=HR,OU=Employees"
```

You can use the DIR alias for the **Get-ChildItem** cmdlet to display all objects within the container. But for anything more selective you need to use an LDAP filter. For example, here's how I can show only the user, Sandy Bottom:

```
PS AD:\OU=HR,OU=Employees,DC=jdhlab,DC=local> dir -Filter "name=Sandy Bottom"

Name                 ObjectClass     DistinguishedName
----                 -----------     -----------------
Sandy Bottom         user            CN=Sandy Bottom,OU=HR,OU=Employees,DC=jdhlab,DC=local
```

Of course, I could simply use the **Get-Item** cmdlet to retrieve the user object:

```
PS AD:\OU=HR,OU=Employees,DC=jdhlab,DC=local> Get-Item "CN=Sandy Bottom" | Select *


PSPath            : ActiveDirectory:://RootDSE/CN=Sandy Bottom,OU=HR,OU=Employees,
                    DC=jdhlab,DC=local
PSParentPath      : ActiveDirectory:://RootDSE/OU=HR,OU=Employees,DC=jdhlab,DC=local
PSChildName       : CN=Sandy Bottom
PSDrive           : AD
PSProvider        : ActiveDirectory
PSIsContainer     : True
distinguishedName : CN=Sandy Bottom,OU=HR,OU=Employees,DC=jdhlab,DC=local
name              : Sandy Bottom
objectClass       : user
objectGUID        : 78176ca7-b117-40a9-88a8-af9285cdd1b1
PropertyNames     : {distinguishedName, name, objectClass, objectGUID}
PropertyCount     : 4
```

In this example, the Sandy Bottom user object is listed using the **Get-Item** cmdlet, which is then piped to the **Select-Object** cmdlet to display all properties. Like the **Get-ADUser** cmdlet, the provider doesn't return any more properties than it has to. But you can use the **Get-ItemProperty** cmdlet to display more information:

```
PS AD:\OU=HR,OU=Employees,DC=jdhlab,DC=local> Get-ItemProperty -Path ".\CN=Sandy Bottom" `
>> -Name name,samaccountname,description,title,telephonenumber
>>


PSPath          : ActiveDirectory:://RootDSE/CN=Sandy Bottom,OU=HR,OU=Employees,DC=jdhlab,DC=
local
PSParentPath    : ActiveDirectory:://RootDSE/OU=HR,OU=Employees,DC=jdhlab,DC=local
PSChildName     : CN=Sandy Bottom
PSDrive         : AD
PSProvider      : ActiveDirectory
Name            : Sandy Bottom
samaccountname  : sbottom
description     : Project Omega
title           : Benefits Administrator
telephonenumber : x567
```

Personally, I find the extra properties annoying so I would use an expression like this:

```
PS AD:\OU=HR,OU=Employees,DC=jdhlab,DC=local> Get-ItemProperty -Path ".\CN=Sandy Bottom" `
>> -name name,samaccountname,description,title | Select Name,Samaccountname,Description,Title
>>

name                      samaccountname      description              title
----                      --------------      -----------              -----
Sandy Bottom              sbottom             Project Omega            Benefits Administrator
```

Once you have a feel for the objects, you can incorporate other PowerShell cmdlets:

```
PS AD:\OU=Employees,DC=jdhlab,DC=local> dir -recurse `
>>-filter "(&(objectcategory=person)(objectclass=user))" | Foreach {
>> get-itemproperty $_.pspath -name Name,DistinguishedName,WhenChanged } |
>> where {$_.WhenChanged -gt (Get-Date).AddDays(-7)} |
>> Select DistinguishedName,Name,WhenChanged
>>

DistinguishedName              Name                          WhenChanged
-----------------              ----                          -----------
CN=Jim Shortz,OU=Legal,OU=...  Jim Shortz                    9/14/2010 11:54:41 AM
CN=Francis Drake,OU=Temp,O...  Francis Drake                 9/9/2010 12:20:33 PM
CN=Cassie O'Pia,OU=Temp,OU...  Cassie O'Pia                  9/9/2010 12:20:33 PM
CN=Chris Barry,OU=Temp,OU=...  Chris Barry                   9/9/2010 12:20:33 PM
CN=Johnson Apacible,OU=Tem...  Johnson Apacible              9/9/2010 12:20:33 PM
CN=Prithvi Raj,OU=Temp,OU=...  Prithvi Raj                   9/9/2010 12:20:33 PM
CN=William Flash,OU=Temp,O...  William Flash                 9/9/2010 12:20:33 PM
CN=Toby Nixon,OU=Temp,OU=E...  Toby Nixon                    9/9/2010 12:20:33 PM
CN=John Plumber,OU=Temp,OU...  John Plumber                  9/9/2010 12:20:33 PM
CN=Roy G. Biv,OU=Temp,OU=E...  Roy G. Biv                    9/14/2010 11:46:49 AM
CN=Leif Matsko,OU=Temp,OU=...  Leif Matsko                   9/9/2010 12:23:50 PM
```

This expression recursively found all user objects under the Employees organizational unit, and filtered out all but accounts changed in the last 7 days.

Creating New Drives

You are not limited to having a single Active Directory PSDrive. You can create additional PSDrives and root them to specific containers or organizational units:

```
PS C:\> New-PSDrive -Name Miami -PSProvider ActiveDirectory `
>> -Root "OU=Miami,OU=Offices,DC=jdhlab,DC=local"
>>

Name       Used (GB)     Free (GB) Provider      Root                                CurrentLocation
----       ---------     --------- --------      ----                                ---------------
Miami                              ActiveDire... //RootDSE/OU=Miami,OU=Offices,DC...


PS C:\> cd miami:
PS Miami:\> dir

Name                 ObjectClass     DistinguishedName
----                 -----------     -----------------
Andra Papallo        user            CN=Andra Papallo,OU=Miami,OU=Offices,DC=jdhlab,DC=local
Caren Heimsoth       user            CN=Caren Heimsoth,OU=Miami,OU=Offices,DC=jdhlab,DC=local
Chassidy Gribben     user            CN=Chassidy Gribben,OU=Miami,OU=Offices,DC=jdhlab,DC=...
Donella Males        user            CN=Donella Males,OU=Miami,OU=Offices,DC=jdhlab,DC=local
Indira Trudics       user            CN=Indira Trudics,OU=Miami,OU=Offices,DC=jdhlab,DC=local
Mariam Granberry     user            CN=Mariam Granberry,OU=Miami,OU=Offices,DC=jdhlab,DC=...
```

I've now created a new drive called "Miami" rooted to OU=Miami,OU=Offices,DC=jdhlab,DC=lo cal. Since this is the drive root, I can't navigate to other parts of Active Directory, but if all I want to administer is this organizational unit, this PSDrive makes life easier.

Creating New Objects

The ability to create new objects within the PSDrive is slightly limited. Though creating a new OU isn't too difficult. Use the **New-Item** cmdlet and specify "organizationalUnit" as the type. Here's how I created a new OU in the Miami PS Drive called Temporary Hires:

```
PS Miami:\> New-Item -Path . -Name "OU=Temporary Hires" -ItemType "organizationalUnit"

Name              ObjectClass          DistinguishedName
----              -----------          -----------------
Temporary Hires   organizationalUnit   OU=Temporary Hires,OU=Miami,OU=Offices,DC=jdhlab,DC=local
```

Read the Examples

Many PowerShell cmdlets work in the Active Directory PSDrive. Even better, cmdlet help is provider aware. By that I mean, if your location is in the Active Directory PSDrive and you look at either full cmdlet help, or help examples, you'll see examples that use the PSDrive. Check it out.

Of course, if you can create one, you can create many. This expression pipes a list of locations to the **ForEach-Object** construct, which uses the **New-Item** cmdlet to create new organizational units underneath the current PSDrive location. As you can see from the prompt, I've changed locations:

```
PS AD:\OU=Offices,dc=jdhlab,dc=local> "Detroit","New York","Denver","London" | Foreach {
>> New-Item -Path . -Name "OU=$_" -ItemType "organizationalUnit"
>> }
>>
```

```
Name                 ObjectClass          DistinguishedName
----                 -----------          -----------------
Detroit              organizationalUnit   OU=Detroit,OU=Offices,dc=jdhlab,dc=local
New York             organizationalUnit   OU=New York,OU=Offices,dc=jdhlab,dc=local
Denver               organizationalUnit   OU=Denver,OU=Offices,dc=jdhlab,dc=local
London               organizationalUnit   OU=London,OU=Offices,dc=jdhlab,dc=local
```

I piped the collection of names to the **ForEach-Object** construct, passing each name as part of the new organizational unit.

Use an Old Friend

PowerShell includes an alias md, which is an alias of mkdir that, in turn, is a wrapper function for the **New-Item** cmdlet. You can also use md or mkdir to create new organizational units.

You can create a group just as easily. I'm going to create a group called Telecommuters in the Groups OU:

```
PS AD:\OU=Groups,dc=jdhlab,dc=local> $newgroup=New-Item -Path . -Name "CN=Telecommuters" `
>> -ItemType "Group"
>>

PS AD:\OU=Groups,dc=jdhlab,dc=local> $newgroup

Name                 ObjectClass          DistinguishedName
----                 -----------          -----------------
Telecommuters        group                CN=Telecommuters,OU=Groups,dc=jdhlab,dc=local
```

I've just created a group called Telecommuters, which has a distinguished name of CN=Telecommuters,OU=Groups,DC=jdhlab,DC=local. The **New-Item** cmdlet creates generic objects from the specified type. In this case, the Telecommuters group is a global security group, which is the default group type. However there is a problem with this approach. Look at the group's SAMAccountname:

```
PS AD:\OU=Groups,dc=jdhlab,dc=local> Get-ADGroup -Filter "name -eq 'Telecommuters'"


DistinguishedName : CN=Telecommuters,OU=Groups,DC=jdhlab,DC=local
GroupCategory     : Security
GroupScope        : Global
Name              : Telecommuters
ObjectClass       : group
ObjectGUID        : d9cc23fc-70f7-4c60-b8e6-fa22088e78d0
SamAccountName    : $LC5000-PL5FF4GJ2S0H
SID               : S-1-5-21-3957442467-353870018-3926547339-5525
```

Because I didn't specify a SAMAccountname, Active Directory created one for me. Let me delete this group and I'll show you how to fix this problem:

```
PS AD:\OU=Groups,dc=jdhlab,dc=local> Get-ADGroup -Filter "name -eq 'Telecommuters'" |
>> Remove-ADGroup
>>

Confirm
Are you sure you want to perform this action?
```

```
Performing operation "Remove" on Target "CN=Telecommuters,OU=Groups,DC=jdhlab,DC=local".
[Y] Yes  [A] Yes to All  [N] No  [L] No to All  [S] Suspend  [?] Help (default is "Y"):
PS AD:\OU=Groups,dc=jdhlab,dc=local> $newgroup=New-Item -Path . -Name "CN=Telecommuters" `
>> -ItemType "Group" `
>> -Value @{Samaccountname="Telecommuters";Description="telecommuting and remote employees"}
>>
PS AD:\OU=Groups,dc=jdhlab,dc=local> Get-ADGroup Telecommuters -Properties Description


Description       : telecommuting and remote employees
DistinguishedName : CN=Telecommuters,OU=Groups,DC=jdhlab,DC=local
GroupCategory     : Security
GroupScope        : Global
Name              : Telecommuters
ObjectClass       : group
ObjectGUID        : ffcd9457-9d08-43ae-a630-466a3feb6723
SamAccountName    : Telecommuters
SID               : S-1-5-21-3957442467-353870018-3926547339-5526
```

Now I have a properly created group. The trick is to use the **-Value** parameter with the **New-Item** cmdlet and specify a hash table of properties and values. I set values for the SAMAccountname and description.

Creating a user object isn't that much more difficult, at least initially:

```
PS AD:\OU=Temp,OU=Employees,DC=Jdhlab,DC=local> $user=New-Item -Name "CN=Walt Whitman" `
>> -Itemtype User -Value @{samaccountname="wwhitman";givenname="Walt";
>> sn="Whitman";userprincipalname="wwhitman@jdhlab.com";
>> description="Contract author";department="Marketing"}
>>

PS AD:\OU=Temp,OU=Employees,DC=Jdhlab,DC=local> $user | Select *


PSPath            : ActiveDirectory::/RootDSE/CN=Walt Whitman,OU=Temp,OU=Employees,DC=Jdhlab,...
PSParentPath      : ActiveDirectory::/RootDSE/OU=Temp,OU=Employees,DC=Jdhlab,DC=local
PSChildName       : CN=Walt Whitman
PSDrive           : AD
PSProvider        : ActiveDirectory
PSIsContainer     : True
department        : Marketing
description       : Contract author
distinguishedName : CN=Walt Whitman,OU=Temp,OU=Employees,DC=Jdhlab,DC=local
givenName         : Walt
name              : Walt Whitman
objectClass       : user
objectGUID        : 938c67d0-6a39-4c84-9443-8729c16e5fab
sAMAccountName    : wwhitman
sn                : Whitman
userPrincipalName : wwhitman@jdhlab.com
PropertyNames     : {department, description, distinguishedName, givenName...}
PropertyCount     : 10
```

The biggest challenge is discovering the correct LDAP property names such as "sn" for surname. But it wasn't that difficult to create the Walt Whitman user account. Unfortunately there's no provision with this object for setting or changing the user password. As you'll see in a moment you can change other properties, but for the password, you are out of luck. You'll have to stick to the password cmdlets I covered earlier in the book.

Modifying Objects

First off, be very careful when using the PSDrive provider. The DEL alias for the **Remove-Item** cmdlet works faster than you can say: "Uh-oh." It's also a good practice to keep the "protect from accidental deletion" setting on new organizational units. Fortunately, if you haven't modified the shell, you should get prompted when you attempt to delete an object:

```
PS AD:\OU=Temp,OU=Employees,DC=Jdhlab,DC=local> del "CN=toby nixon"

Are you sure you want to remove?
CN=toby nixon,OU=Temp,OU=Employees,DC=Jdhlab,DC=local
[Y] Yes  [N] No  [S] Suspend  [?] Help (default is "Y"):
```

But if you use an expression like this:

```
PS AD:\OU=Temp,OU=Employees,DC=Jdhlab,DC=local> del "CN=toby nixon"  -force
```

Toby Nixon will be gone, no questions asked. Although there is one caveat: the **-Force** parameter will not work if the object is protected from accidental deletion.

Let's return to the Telecommuters group object I created earlier and see about modifying it. To make it easy to follow, I'll get the group and save it to a variable:

```
PS AD:\ou=groups,dc=jdhlab,dc=local> $group=Get-Item "CN=Telecommuters" -properties *
```

Using the **Get-Item** cmdlet, I included all properties. Here's what you have to start with:

```
PS AD:\ou=groups,dc=jdhlab,dc=local> $group | Select *


PSPath                 : ActiveDirectory:://RootDSE/CN=Telecommuters,ou=groups,dc=jdhlab,dc=local
PSParentPath           : ActiveDirectory:://RootDSE/ou=groups,dc=jdhlab,dc=local
PSChildName            : CN=Telecommuters
PSDrive                : AD
PSProvider             : ActiveDirectory
PSIsContainer          : True
cn                     : Telecommuters
description            : telecommuting and remote employees
distinguishedName      : CN=Telecommuters,ou=groups,dc=jdhlab,dc=local
dSCorePropagationData  : {12/31/1600 7:00:00 PM}
groupType              : -2147483646
instanceType           : 4
name                   : Telecommuters
nTSecurityDescriptor   : System.DirectoryServices.ActiveDirectorySecurity
objectCategory         : CN=Group,CN=Schema,CN=Configuration,DC=jdhlab,DC=local
objectClass            : group
objectGUID             : ffcd9457-9d08-43ae-a630-466a3feb6723
objectSid              : S-1-5-21-3957442467-353870018-3926547339-5526
sAMAccountName         : Telecommuters
sAMAccountType         : 268435456
uSNChanged             : 468735
uSNCreated             : 468735
whenChanged            : 9/15/2010 7:09:10 PM
whenCreated            : 9/15/2010 7:09:10 PM
PropertyNames          : {cn, description, distinguishedName, dSCorePropagationData...}
PropertyCount          : 18
```

I want to change the group description. This is the current setting:

```
PS AD:\ou=groups,dc=jdhlab,dc=local> $group.description
telecommuting and remote employees
```

Now to change it using the **Set-ItemProperty** cmdlet:

```
PS AD:\ou=groups,dc=jdhlab,dc=local> Set-ItemProperty -path $group.pspath -Name "Description" `
>> -Value "Corporate Telecommuters"
```

The change is immediate:

```
PS AD:\ou=groups,dc=jdhlab,dc=local> Get-ADGroup "Telecommuters" -Properties Description |
>> Select Name,Description
>>

Name                                                        Description
----                                                        -----------
Telecommuters                                               Corporate Telecommuters
```

While I'm on the topic of groups, let's look at group membership. If a group has members, then the object's **Member** property will have a value:

```
PS AD:\ou=groups,dc=jdhlab,dc=local> Get-Item "CN=AlphaGroup" -property Member |
>> Select -ExpandProperty Member
>>
CN=Sam Apple,OU=HR,OU=Employees,DC=jdhlab,DC=local
CN=Jim Shortz,OU=Legal,OU=Employees,DC=jdhlab,DC=local
CN=Sales Users,OU=Groups,DC=jdhlab,DC=local
```

All I did was take the **Member** property and pipe it to the **Select-Object** cmdlet, where I expanded it because the value is stored as an array. Adding a group member is not much different than what I've already showed you. Let's turn back to the Telecommuters group, which is still saved as a $group variable. Once more I'll use the **Set-ItemProperty** cmdlet to set a value for the **Member** property. The value will be an array of user (or group) distinguished names:

```
PS AD:\ou=groups,dc=jdhlab,dc=local> Set-ItemProperty -path $group.pspath -Name "Member" `
>>-value ("CN=Sam Apple,OU=HR,OU=Employees,Dc=jdhlab,DC=local",
>> "CN=Alonzo Aske,OU=Executive,OU=Employees,DC=jdhlab,DC=local")
```

The change is immediate:

```
PS AD:\ou=groups,dc=jdhlab,dc=local> Get-ADGroupMember "Telecommuters"


distinguishedName : CN=Alonzo Aske,OU=Executive,OU=Employees,DC=jdhlab,DC=local
name              : Alonzo Aske
objectClass       : user
objectGUID        : 8b8eb2ce-48df-4c52-aee7-5c46d4f7f11b
SamAccountName    : A.Aske
SID               : S-1-5-21-3957442467-353870018-3926547339-4544

distinguishedName : CN=Sam Apple,OU=HR,OU=Employees,DC=jdhlab,DC=local
name              : Sam Apple
```

```
objectClass        : user
objectGUID         : 06e051f1-edd5-4324-8271-ad56a01421ab
SamAccountName     : sapple
SID                : S-1-5-21-3957442467-353870018-3926547339-5064
```

Without a doubt it is easier to use the cmdlets designed for working with groups, but I wanted to share with you other possibilities.

Moving Objects

The PSDrive provider does not support copying objects, which makes sense since this would likely violate uniqueness requirements. However, you can easily move objects from one location to another. In my Temp organizational unit is the Roy G. Biv user account, which needs to be moved to the Executive organizational unit. I can accomplish this using the standard **Move-Item** cmdlet. All I need to do is specify a source and target name:

```
PS AD:\OU=Temp,OU=Employees,DC=jdhlab,dc=local> move-Item -path ".\CN=Roy G. Biv" `
>> -destination "\OU=Executive,OU=Employees,DC=jdhlab,DC=local"
```

Using the **Move-Item** cmdlet, you can move an entire OU from one location to another:

```
PS AD:\> move-item -path "OU=Alpha,dc=jdhlab,dc=local" `
>> -destination "OU=Omega,DC=jdhlab,DC=local"  -passthru
>>

Name                 ObjectClass          DistinguishedName
----                 -----------          -----------------
Alpha                organizationalUnit   OU=Alpha,OU=Omega,DC=jdhlab,DC=local
```

This moved the Alpha OU and all of its child objects to the Omega OU:

```
PS AD:\> dir "OU=Omega,DC=jdhlab,DC=local" -recurse

Name                 ObjectClass          DistinguishedName
----                 -----------          -----------------
Omega                organizationalUnit   OU=Omega,DC=jdhlab,DC=local
Alpha                organizationalUnit   OU=Alpha,OU=Omega,DC=jdhlab,DC=local
Lawrence Cofrancesco user                 CN=Lawrence Cofrancesco,OU=Alpha,OU=Omega,DC=jdhlab,D...
Marilee Claessens    user                 CN=Marilee Claessens,OU=Alpha,OU=Omega,DC=jdhlab,DC=l...
Marc Bordes          user                 CN=Marc Bordes,OU=Alpha,OU=Omega,DC=jdhlab,DC=local
Jack Stanier         user                 CN=Jack Stanier,OU=Alpha,OU=Omega,DC=jdhlab,DC=local
Numbers Deschepper   user                 CN=Numbers Deschepper,OU=Alpha,OU=Omega,DC=jdhlab,DC...
Franklyn Botten      user                 CN=Franklyn Botten,OU=Alpha,OU=Omega,DC=jdhlab,DC=local
```

You can even use the **Move-Item** cmdlet and the PSDrive to move objects between domains in your forest:

```
PS AD:\>  Move-Item -path "OU=Transfer Accounts,DC=jdhlab,DC=local" `
>> -destination "AD:\OU=Employees,DC=Europe,DC=jdhlab,DC=local" `
>> -CrossDomain dc01.europe.jdhlab.local
```

The **-CrossDomain** parameter is the name of a domain controller in the target domain.

Cmdlet Integration

There's no reason you can't combine objects from the Active Directory PSDrive with any of the cmdlets I've discussed in the book, either from Microsoft or even Quest Software. Let me wrap up this chapter with a quick demonstration.

My Temp OU has several objects including users and child organizational units. But all I want are the users:

```
PS AD:\ou=temp,ou=employees,dc=jdhlab,dc=local> dir `
>> -filter "(&(objectcategory=user)(objectclass=person))">>

Name                ObjectClass   DistinguishedName
----                -----------   -----------------
Cassie O'Pia        user          CN=Cassie O'Pia,OU=Temp,OU=Employees,DC=jdhlab,DC=local
Chris Barry         user          CN=Chris Barry,OU=Temp,OU=Employees,DC=jdhlab,DC=local
Francis Drake       user          CN=Francis Drake,OU=Temp,OU=Employees,DC=jdhlab,DC=local
John Plumber        user          CN=John Plumber,OU=Temp,OU=Employees,DC=jdhlab,DC=local
Johnson Apacible    user          CN=Johnson Apacible,OU=Temp,OU=Employees,DC=jdhlab,DC=local
Leif Matsko         user          CN=Leif Matsko,OU=Temp,OU=Employees,DC=jdhlab,DC=local
Prithvi Raj         user          CN=Prithvi Raj,OU=Temp,OU=Employees,DC=jdhlab,DC=local
Sally Sweet         user          CN=Sally Sweet,OU=Temp,OU=Employees,DC=jdhlab,DC=local
Walt Whitman        user          CN=Walt Whitman,OU=Temp,OU=Employees,DC=jdhlab,DC=local
William Flash       user          CN=William Flash,OU=Temp,OU=Employees,DC=jdhlab,DC=local
```

My task is to add these users to the Group-6 distribution list. I'll save these users to a variable:

```
PS AD:\ou=temp,ou=employees,dc=jdhlab,dc=local> $users=dir
>> -filter "(&(objectcategory=user)(objectclass=person))"
```

Now I can call the **Add-GroupMember** cmdlet and use the $users variable as the value for the **-Members** parameter:

```
PS AD:\ou=temp,ou=employees,dc=jdhlab,dc=local> Add-ADGroupMember -Identity "Group-6"
>> -Members $users
```

Finally, I'll verify the change:

```
PS AD:\ou=temp,ou=employees,dc=jdhlab,dc=local> Get-ADGroup -Identity "Group-6" `
>> -Properties Members | Select -ExpandProperty Members
>>

CN=Walt Whitman,OU=Temp,OU=Employees,DC=jdhlab,DC=local
CN=John Plumber,OU=Temp,OU=Employees,DC=jdhlab,DC=local
CN=Sally Sweet,OU=Temp,OU=Employees,DC=jdhlab,DC=local
CN=Francis Drake,OU=Temp,OU=Employees,DC=jdhlab,DC=local
CN=Leif Matsko,OU=Temp,OU=Employees,DC=jdhlab,DC=local
CN=William Flash,OU=Temp,OU=Employees,DC=jdhlab,DC=local
CN=Prithvi Raj,OU=Temp,OU=Employees,DC=jdhlab,DC=local
CN=Johnson Apacible,OU=Temp,OU=Employees,DC=jdhlab,DC=local
CN=Chris Barry,OU=Temp,OU=Employees,DC=jdhlab,DC=local
CN=Cassie O'Pia,OU=Temp,OU=Employees,DC=jdhlab,DC=local
```

Depending on the cmdlet you might be able to leverage a simple pipeline as I've done here. Or you might need a **ForEach-Object** construct, using the distinguished name property from the PSDrive item.

Chapter 12

Managed Service Accounts

Historically, administrators have often run special services on member servers or desktops using domain accounts. The challenge has always been managing these accounts, especially account passwords. But now there are managed service accounts. These are special Active Directory account objects that you install on a member server or desktop. The server or desktop must be running Windows 7 or Windows Server 2008 R2 or later. I encourage you to take a look at http://tinyurl.com/28cmb7r and http://tinyurl.com/35rtcsh or search Microsoft for more information, especially if your domain mode is not Windows Server 2008 R2.

Because there are no graphical tools for managing these new types of accounts, you have no choice but to use PowerShell.

Creating New Managed Service Accounts

New-ADServiceAccount

Let's create a new managed service account using the **New-ADServiceAccount** cmdlet. The only parameter is the service name. The cmdlet doesn't write to the pipeline unless you use the **-Passthru** parameter:

```
PS C:\> New-ADServiceAccount -name MSA-Web -passthru


DistinguishedName : CN=MSA-Web,CN=Managed Service Accounts,DC=jdhlab,DC=local
Enabled           : True
HostComputers     :
```

```
Name              : MSA-Web
ObjectClass       : msDS-ManagedServiceAccount
ObjectGUID        : 8662bfa6-ff88-47c1-b737-301e752a056d
SamAccountName    : MSA-Web$
SID               : S-1-5-21-3957442467-353870018-3926547339-5539
UserPrincipalName :
```

By default the account is created in the special Managed Service Accounts container that you'll find in Windows Server 2008 R2. You could use the **-Path** parameter to specify an alternate location but that really shouldn't be necessary in my opinion.

If your service requires a service principal name (SPN), you can define it at the same time you create the service account:

```
PS C:\ >New-ADServiceAccount MSA-Foo -ServicePrincipalNames "MyService/Server02.jdhlab.local"
```

Separate multiple SPNs by commas.

There are a number of optional values you might want to set. Here's a test service account that will expire at the end of 2011. Use a date format appropriate to your culture or regional settings:

```
PS C:\> New-ADServiceAccount -Name MSA-Test -DisplayName "MSCV Test"  -enabled:$false `
>>-AccountExpirationDate "12/31/2011" -Description "Test managed service account" -passthru
>>


DistinguishedName : CN=MSA-Test,CN=Managed Service Accounts,DC=jdhlab,DC=local
Enabled           : False
HostComputers     :
Name              : MSA-Test
ObjectClass       : msDS-ManagedServiceAccount
ObjectGUID        : d8470429-e2fe-404e-8f08-178fb0621f51
SamAccountName    : MSA-Test$
SID               : S-1-5-21-3957442467-353870018-3926547339-5540
UserPrincipalName :
```

The account is Enabled by default, but if you wanted to create it Disabled use the **-Enabled** parameter and set it to $False. The cmdlet will allow you to specify a password as a secure string. However, you're better off letting Windows automatically handle passwords when you begin using the account. This is a much securer approach.

Maintaining Managed Service Accounts

Get-ADServiceAccount

Use the **Get-ADServiceAccount** cmdlet to retrieve one or more objects. The cmdlet's syntax is very similar to the **Get-ADUser** or **Get-ADGroup** cmdlets:

```
PS C:\> Get-ADServiceAccount -filter * | Measure-Object


Count    : 3
Average  :
Sum      :
```

```
Maximum  :
Minimum  :
Property :
```

I have three managed service objects in my domain. Here's one of them:

```
PS C:\> Get-ADServiceAccount -Identity "MSA-Test"


DistinguishedName : CN=MSA-Test,CN=Managed Service Accounts,DC=jdhlab,DC=local
Enabled           : False
HostComputers     :
Name              : MSA-Test
ObjectClass       : msDS-ManagedServiceAccount
ObjectGUID        : d8470429-e2fe-404e-8f08-178fb0621f51
SamAccountName    : MSA-Test$
SID               : S-1-5-21-3957442467-353870018-3926547339-5540
UserPrincipalName :
```

Like the other Active Directory cmdlets, you only get a subset of properties. Use the **-Properties** parameter to retrieve the rest:

```
PS C:\> Get-ADServiceAccount -filter * -Properties * |
>> Select Name,DisplayName,Enabled,Description,AccountExpirationDate
>>


Name                  : MSA-1
DisplayName           : Managed Service 1
Enabled               : True
Description           :
AccountExpirationDate :

Name                  : MSA-Web
DisplayName           :
Enabled               : True
Description           :
AccountExpirationDate :

Name                  : MSA-Test
DisplayName           : MSCV Test
Enabled               : False
Description           : Test managed service account
AccountExpirationDate : 12/31/2011 12:00:00 AM
```

Set-ADServiceAccount

To modify a managed service account you'll rely on the **Set-ADServiceAccount** cmdlet. In fact, let's use it to enable the test account:

```
PS C:\> Set-ADServiceAccount -Identity "MSA-Test" `
>> -Description "Test Managed Service Account for ITDEV" -Enabled:$True
```

Nothing was written to the pipeline because I didn't specify the **-Passthru** parameter, but the object was, in fact, updated:

```
PS C:\> Get-ADServiceAccount -Identity "MSA-Test" -Properties Description |
>> Select Name,Enabled,Description
>>

Name                                       Enabled   Description
----                                       ----------
MSA-Test                                   True Test Managed Service Account for ITDEV
```

You might also need to modify an account to add one or more SPNs:

```
PS C:\> Set-ADServiceAccount "MSA-Test" -ServicePrincipalNames @{add="Foo/jdhlab.local"}
```

Implementing Managed Service Accounts

Add-ADComputerServiceAccount

Before you can configure any services on a Windows 7 or Windows 2008 R2 system to use the managed service account, it must be associated with a host computer and "installed". The **Add-ADComputerServiceAccount** cmdlet associates one or more service accounts with a computer:

```
PS C:\> Add-ADComputerServiceAccount -Identity "CLIENT1"-ServiceAccount "MSA-Test"
```

With this command I've added the "MSA Test" service account to computer CLIENT1. I can verify this by using the **Get-ADComputerServiceAccount** cmdlet:

```
PS C:\> Get-ADComputerServiceAccount -Identity "client1"


DistinguishedName : CN=MSA-Test,CN=Managed Service Accounts,DC=jdhlab,DC=local
Enabled           : True
HostComputers     : {CN=CLIENT1,OU=Company Desktops,DC=jdhlab,DC=local}
Name              : MSA-Test
ObjectClass       : msDS-ManagedServiceAccount
ObjectGUID        : d8470429-e2fe-404e-8f08-178fb0621f51
SamAccountName    : MSA-Test$
SID               : S-1-5-21-3957442467-353870018-3926547339-5540
UserPrincipalName :
```

If the computer had more than one managed service account, this expression would have returned all of them.

I can also check the **HostComputers** property of the service account object, which is a collection of computer distinguished names:

```
PS C:\> Get-ADServiceAccount -Identity "MSA-Test" | Select -ExpandProperty HostComputers
CN=CLIENT1,OU=Company Desktops,DC=jdhlab,DC=local
```

Install-ADServiceAccount

Now for the tricky part. Before you can configure a service to use the account it must be installed on the domain member. You must run the following command ON the member server or desktop.

This will require that the Active Directory module be installed, which you can get from the Remote Server Administration Tools. You'll also need .NET Framework version 3.5.1 or later. Don't forget any service packs as well. Then with an administrative account in an elevated session run the **Install-ADServiceAccount** cmdlet specifying the service account name.

Here's what I would run when in a PowerShell session on CLIENT1:

```
PS C:\> Install-ADServiceAccount -Identity "MSA-Test"
```

If the service account is already associated with a different host you will get an error about a duplicate backlink. You can only install a service account on one computer, although a single computer can have multiple managed service accounts.

Assuming no errors, now you can use the Services management console to configure your service to use this service account. But where's the fun in that? Let's use PowerShell.

First, you'll use WMI to get the service:

```
PS C:\> $service=Get-WmiObject -Class Win32_Service -filter "name='MyTestSvc'"
```

To change the start name you'll invoke the **Change()** method. You must specify the account name in the domain\samaccountname format, which means make sure you use the SAMAccountname which should end in a **$**. The password should be left blank as the whole point of managed service accounts is to let the computers manage the passwords:

```
PS C:\> $service.Change($null,$null,$null,$null,$null,$null,"jdhlab\MSA-test$",$null)


__GENUS          : 2
__CLASS          : __PARAMETERS
__SUPERCLASS     :
__DYNASTY        : __PARAMETERS
__RELPATH        :
__PROPERTY_COUNT : 1
__DERIVATION     : {}
__SERVER         :
__NAMESPACE      :
__PATH           :
ReturnValue      : 0
```

A value of 0 indicates success.

Removing Managed Service Accounts

If you decide to retire a managed service account, you need to undo the steps you took to install it.

Uninstall-ADServiceAccount

If you no longer need the service account on a given computer, but think you might need to reuse it elsewhere or later, you can uninstall it. Run this command on the host computer:

```
PS C:\> Uninstall-ADServiceAccount -Identity "MSA-Test"
```

This will leave the service account in Active Directory. Don't forget to change the service as well using either the GUI or the **Get-WMIObject** cmdlet.

Remove-ADComputerServiceAccount

If for some reason the host is no longer available, you can remove the association using the **Remove-ADComputerServiceAccount** cmdlet:

```
PS C:\> Remove-ADComputerServiceAccount -Identity "Client1" -ServiceAccount "MSA-Test" `
>> -PassThru -confirm

Confirm
Are you sure you want to perform this action?
Performing operation "Set" on Target "CN=CLIENT1,OU=Company Desktops,DC=jdhlab,DC=local".
[Y] Yes  [A] Yes to All  [N] No  [L] No to All  [S] Suspend  [?] Help (default is "Y"): y


DistinguishedName : CN=CLIENT1,OU=Company Desktops,DC=jdhlab,DC=local
DNSHostName       : CLIENT1.jdhlab.local
Enabled           : True
Name              : CLIENT1
ObjectClass       : computer
ObjectGUID        : 20459a2b-a241-4962-a84b-336831c7dfbe
SamAccountName    : CLIENT1$
SID               : S-1-5-21-3957442467-353870018-3926547339-1105
UserPrincipalName :
```

This will remove the host but leave the service account in Active Directory.

Remove-ADServiceAccount

After you've uninstalled or removed the service account from the computer, if you want to permanently delete the service account from Active Directory, use the **Remove-ADServiceAccount** cmdlet:

```
PS C:\> Remove-ADServiceAccount -Identity "MSA-Test"

Confirm
Are you sure you want to perform this action?
Performing operation "Remove" on Target "CN=MSA-Test,CN=Managed Service
Accounts,DC=jdhlab,DC=local".
[Y] Yes  [A] Yes to All  [N] No  [L] No to All  [S] Suspend  [?] Help (default is "Y"):
```

If you don't remove the service account from the computer first, I expect eventually your service will fail, so follow the steps I've outlined.

Read More About It

Managed Service Accounts are simple to implement as you've seen but will require a fair bit of planning and testing. To learn much more about this new Active Directory feature, take some time to read the article Managed Service Accounts: Understanding, Implementing, Best Practices, and Troubleshooting on the Ask the Directory Services team blog at http://tinyurl.com/28cpzne.

Chapter 13
Managing Active Directory Infrastructure

I'm assuming the majority of your Active Directory management centers on users, groups, and computers. I trust that if you've read this book from the beginning, you now have plenty of new PowerShell tools in your toolbox. Before I wrap up, let's look at one more management topic that is probably not a daily task: Active Directory infrastructure.

Active Directory also requires you to give attention to things likes domains, sites, subnets, global catalog servers, domain controller, replication, trusts, and DNS. You can manage quite a bit using the Active Directory model.

Domains and Forests

The Microsoft Active Directory module has a few cmdlets designed to work with domains and forests.

Getting the RootDSE

When writing Active Directory related PowerShell scripts, you goal should be to avoid hard coding domain or forest names. You should be able to use PowerShell cmdlets to "discover" your domain name. In ADSI scripting, including what I've been covering in this book, there is a concept called the RootDSE, or "Root Directory Service Entry". Think of it as a default starting point. Active Directory and other LDAP compliant services support this feature. Connecting to the RootDSE will let you automatically discover your domain name and more.

Using the Active Directory Module

In the Active Directory module, use the **Get-ADRootDSE** cmdlet:

```
PS C:\> Get-ADRootDSE


configurationNamingContext    : CN=Configuration,DC=jdhlab,DC=local
currentTime                   : 9/29/2010 10:10:34 PM
defaultNamingContext          : DC=jdhlab,DC=local
dnsHostName                   : COREDC01.jdhlab.local
domainControllerFunctionality : Windows2008R2
domainFunctionality           : Windows2008R2Domain
dsServiceName                 : CN=NTDS Settings,CN=COREDC01,CN=Servers,CN=Default-First-Site-
                                Name,CN=Sites,CN=Configuration,DC=jdhlab,DC=local
forestFunctionality           : Windows2008R2Forest
highestCommittedUSN           : 471143
isGlobalCatalogReady          : {TRUE}
isSynchronized                : {TRUE}
ldapServiceName               : jdhlab.local:coredc01$@JDHLAB.LOCAL
namingContexts                : {DC=jdhlab,DC=local, CN=Configuration,DC=jdhlab,DC=local,
                                CN=Schema,CN=Configuration,DC=jdhlab,DC=local, DC=DomainDnsZones,
                                DC=jdhlab,DC=local...}
rootDomainNamingContext       : DC=jdhlab,DC=local
schemaNamingContext           : CN=Schema,CN=Configuration,DC=jdhlab,DC=local
serverName                    : CN=COREDC01,CN=Servers,CN=Default-First-Site-Name,
                                CN=Sites,CN=Configuration,DC=jdhlab,DC=local
subschemaSubentry             : CN=Aggregate,CN=Schema,CN=Configuration,DC=jdhlab,DC=local
supportedCapabilities         : {1.2.840.113556.1.4.800 (LDAP_CAP_ACTIVE_DIRECTORY_OID),
                                1.2.840.113556.1.4.1670 (LDAP_CAP_ACTIVE_DIRECTORY_V51_OID),
                                1.2.840.113556.1.4.1791 (LDAP_CAP_ACTIVE_DIRECTORY_LDAP_INTEG_OID),
                                1.2.840.113556.1.4.1935 (LDAP_CAP_ACTIVE_DIRECTORY_V61_OID)...}
supportedControl              : {1.2.840.113556.1.4.319 (LDAP_PAGED_RESULT_OID_STRING),
                                1.2.840.113556.1.4.801 (LDAP_SERVER_
                                SD_FLAGS_OID), 1.2.840.113556.1.4.473 (LDAP_SERVER_SORT_OID),
                                1.2.840.113556.1.4.528 (LDAP_SERVER_NOTIFICATION_OID)...}
supportedLDAPPolicies         : {MaxPoolThreads, MaxDatagramRecv, MaxReceiveBuffer,
                                InitRecvTimeout...}
supportedLDAPVersion          : {3, 2}
supportedSASLMechanisms       : {GSSAPI, GSS-SPNEGO, EXTERNAL, DIGEST-MD5}
```

You can use the RootDSE to quickly discover information without having to specify domains or servers:

```
PS C:\> Get-ADRootDSE | Select DefaultNamingContext,DomainFunctionality,ForestFunctionality

DefaultNamingContext                    DomainFunctionality           ForestFunctionality
--------------------                    -------------------           -------------------
DC=jdhlab,DC=local                      Windows2008R2Domain           Windows2008R2Forest
```

With the RootDSE you can write PowerShell code that is domain agnostic:

```
PS C:\> $rootDSE=Get-ADRootDSE
PS C:\> $nc=$rootDSE.defaultNamingContext
PS C:\> Get-ADUser -filter * -SearchBase "CN=Users,$nc" | Measure-Object


Count    : 1498
Average  :
Sum      :
```

```
Maximum  :
Minimum  :
Property :
```

First, I created the RootDSE object. Then I created a variable for the default naming context. This is almost always the domain root. I wanted to count the number of users in the Users container. I accomplished this by using the **Get-ADUser** cmdlet and constructing a dynamic search base. You could run these exact lines of code without any modification.

Using the Quest Cmdlets

The Quest snapin has a similar cmdlet called **Get-QADRootDSE** that produces similar results:

```
PS C:\> Get-QADRootDSE


DomainControllerFunctionality : Windows2008R2
DomainFunctionality           : Windows2008R2
ForestFunctionality           : Windows2008R2
IsGlobalCatalogReady          : True
LdapServiceName               : jdhlab.local:coredc01$@JDHLAB.LOCAL
DefaultNamingContext          : DC=jdhlab,DC=local
DefaultNamingContextDN        : DC=jdhlab,DC=local
Domain                        : JDHLAB\
RootDomainNamingContext       : DC=jdhlab,DC=local
DsServiceName                 : CN=NTDS Settings,CN=COREDC01,CN=Servers,CN=Default-First-Site-
                                Name,CN=Sites,CN=Configuration,DC=jdhlab,DC=local
IsSynchronized                : True
ServerName                    : CN=COREDC01,CN=Servers,CN=Default-First-Site-
                                Name,CN=Sites,CN=Configuration,DC=jdhlab,DC=local
SupportedCapabilities         : {1.2.840.113556.1.4.800, 1.2.840.113556.1.4.1670,
                                1.2.840.113556.1.4.1791, 1.2.840.113556.1.4.1935...}
SupportedControl              : {1.2.840.113556.1.4.319, 1.2.840.113556.1.4.801,
                                1.2.840.113556.1.4.473, 1.2.840.113556.1.4.528...}
SupportedLDAPPolicies         : {MaxPoolThreads, MaxDatagramRecv, MaxReceiveBuffer,
                                InitRecvTimeout...}
SupportedLDAPVersion          : {3, 2}
SupportedSASLMechanisms       : {GSSAPI, GSS-SPNEGO, EXTERNAL, DIGEST-MD5}
ConfigurationNamingContext    : CN=Configuration,DC=jdhlab,DC=local
CurrentTime                   : 9/29/2010 10:32:56 PM
DnsHostName                   : COREDC01.jdhlab.local
HighestCommitedUSN            : 471150
NamingContexts                : {DC=jdhlab,DC=local, CN=Configuration,DC=jdhlab,DC=local,
                                CN=Schema,CN=Configuration,DC=jdhlab,DC=local,DC=DomainDnsZones,
                                DC=jdhlab,DC=local...}
SchemaNamingContext           : CN=Schema,CN=Configuration,DC=jdhlab,DC=local
SubschemaSubentry             : CN=Aggregate,CN=Schema,CN=Configuration,DC=jdhlab,DC=local
Cache                         : Quest.ActiveRoles.ArsPowerShellSnapIn.BusinessLogic.ObjectCache
Connection                    : Quest.ActiveRoles.ArsPowerShellSnapIn.Data.ArsADConnection
DirectoryEntry                : System.DirectoryServices.DirectoryEntry
```

There are a few Quest specific properties here, but otherwise you can use the object just as I did with the Microsoft cmdlet.

Getting the Current Domain

You can identify or retrieve a domain using the **Get-ADDomain** cmdlet. By default, the cmdlet will return the domain for the currently logged on user:

```
PS C:\> Get-ADDomain


AllowedDNSSuffixes                 : {}
ChildDomains                       : {}
ComputersContainer                 : CN=Computers,DC=jdhlab,DC=local
DeletedObjectsContainer            : CN=Deleted Objects,DC=jdhlab,DC=local
DistinguishedName                  : DC=jdhlab,DC=local
DNSRoot                            : jdhlab.local
DomainControllersContainer         : OU=Domain Controllers,DC=jdhlab,DC=local
DomainMode                         : Windows2008R2Domain
DomainSID                          : S-1-5-21-3957442467-353870018-3926547339
ForeignSecurityPrincipalsContainer : CN=ForeignSecurityPrincipals,DC=jdhlab,DC=local
Forest                             : jdhlab.local
InfrastructureMaster               : COREDC01.jdhlab.local
LastLogonReplicationInterval       :
LinkedGroupPolicyObjects           : {cn={38228A9F-F2EC-4B48-8829-4F3131E4F77C},
                                     cn=policies,cn=system,DC=jdhlab,DC=local, CN
                                     ={31B2F340-016D-11D2-945F-00C04FB984F9},CN=Policies,
                                     CN=System,DC=jdhlab,DC=local}
LostAndFoundContainer              : CN=LostAndFound,DC=jdhlab,DC=local
ManagedBy                          :
Name                               : jdhlab
NetBIOSName                        : JDHLAB
ObjectClass                        : domainDNS
ObjectGUID                         : 9db48ea5-9dea-43c9-9301-f2262b244ce2
ParentDomain                       :
PDCEmulator                        : COREDC01.jdhlab.local
QuotasContainer                    : CN=NTDS Quotas,DC=jdhlab,DC=local
ReadOnlyReplicaDirectoryServers    : {}
ReplicaDirectoryServers            : {COREDC01.jdhlab.local}
RIDMaster                          : COREDC01.jdhlab.local
SubordinateReferences              : {DC=ForestDnsZones,DC=jdhlab,DC=local, DC=DomainDnsZones,
                                     DC=jdhlab,DC=local, CN=Configuration,DC=jdhlab,DC=local}
SystemsContainer                   : CN=System,DC=jdhlab,DC=local
UsersContainer                     : CN=Users,DC=jdhlab,DC=local
```

If your computer accounts are in a separate domain from the user, you can retrieve the computer domain for the local computer:

```
PS C:\> Get-ADDomain -Current Localcomputer
```

I omitted the output since I don't have separate domains. You can also use the cmdlet to retrieve an object for some other domain. Here is a Windows 2003 domain also on my network. The domain controller is running the Active Directory Gateway Management service:

```
PS C:\> Get-ADDomain -Identity "jdhitsolutions.local"


AllowedDNSSuffixes                 : {}
ChildDomains                       : {}
ComputersContainer                 : CN=Computers,DC=jdhitsolutions,DC=local
DeletedObjectsContainer            : CN=Deleted Objects,DC=jdhitsolutions,DC=local
DistinguishedName                  : DC=jdhitsolutions,DC=local
DNSRoot                            : jdhitsolutions.local
DomainControllersContainer         : OU=Domain Controllers,DC=jdhitsolutions,DC=local
DomainMode                         : Windows2003Domain
DomainSID                          : S-1-5-21-805063240-3875113082-2769008284
ForeignSecurityPrincipalsContainer : CN=ForeignSecurityPrincipals,DC=jdhitsolutions,DC=local
Forest                             : jdhitsolutions.local
```

```
InfrastructureMaster               : jdhit-dc01.jdhitsolutions.local
LastLogonReplicationInterval       :
LinkedGroupPolicyObjects           : {cn={49B05A51-AB3C-4847-86D1-96A38257E4E6},cn=policies,
                                     cn=system,DC=jdhitsolutions,DC=local, cn={16DEE15A-AF63-49F9-
                                     B166-42F2604A5E00},cn=policies,cn=system,DC=jdhitsolutions,
                                     DC=local, cn={940E6E3C-67A5-471C-845D-66B71D6AEF6C},
                                     cn=policies,cn=system,DC=jdhitsolutions,DC=local, cn={84F8DE
                                     F3-9519-4251-96C6-D41A42BFF9B5},cn=policies,cn=system,
                                     DC=jdhitsolutions,DC=local...}
LostAndFoundContainer              : CN=LostAndFound,DC=jdhitsolutions,DC=local
ManagedBy                          :
Name                               : jdhitsolutions
NetBIOSName                        : JDHITSOLUTIONS
ObjectClass                        : domainDNS
ObjectGUID                         : debe5394-56d0-4fbe-9000-9bd4081b69da
ParentDomain                       :
PDCEmulator                        : jdhit-dc01.jdhitsolutions.local
QuotasContainer                    : CN=NTDS Quotas,DC=jdhitsolutions,DC=local
ReadOnlyReplicaDirectoryServers    : {}
ReplicaDirectoryServers            : {jdhit-dc01.jdhitsolutions.local}
RIDMaster                          : jdhit-dc01.jdhitsolutions.local
SubordinateReferences              : {DC=ForestDnsZones,DC=jdhitsolutions,DC=local,
                                     DC=DomainDnsZones,DC=jdhitsolutions,DC=local,
                                     CN=Configuration,DC=jdhitsolutions,DC=local}
SystemsContainer                   : CN=System,DC=jdhitsolutions,DC=local
UsersContainer                     : CN=Users,DC=jdhitsolutions,DC=local
```

For the most part, all of these properties are read-only.

Modifying Domain Properties

I don't expect you'll need to modify domain properties on a regular basis, or at least often enough to warrant some level of automation. Still, for the sake of completeness let me demonstrate how to modify different parts of your domain.

DNS Suffixes

One change you might want is to add one or more DNS suffixes, especially if you are using a private domain. Right now, my domain has none;

```
PS C:\> Get-ADDomain | Select AllowedDNSSuffixes

AllowedDNSSuffixes
------------------
{}
```

I'll add a new suffix using the **Set-ADDomain** cmdlet and using a hash table. The key is a verb like Add or Replace:

```
PS C:\> Set-ADDomain -identity jdhlab -AllowedDNSSuffixes @{Add="jdhlab.com"}
```

Checking again I can see the change has been made:

```
PS C:\> Get-ADDomain | Select AllowedDNSSuffixes

AllowedDNSSuffixes
------------------
{jdhlab.com}
```

The **Set-ADDomain** cmdlet doesn't write to the pipeline by default, but I could have used the **-Passthru** parameter.

Domain Functional Levels

If you want to discover your domain functional level, use Microsoft's **Get-ADDomain** cmdlet, which will return a Microsoft.ActiveDirectory.Management.Domain object that has a **DomainMode** property:

```
PS C:\> $domain=Get-ADDomain -Identity "jdhlab"
PS C:\> $domain.domainmode
Windows2008R2Domain
```

I can't raise my domain functional level any further, though you may be able to. If you can, here's how using the **Set-ADDomainMode** cmdlet from the Active Directory module. You need to specify a domain functional level, which can be one of these values:

- Windows2000Domain
- Windows2003InterimDomain
- Windows2003Domain
- Windows2008Domain
- Windows2008R2Domain.

Assuming you understand the consequences, raising the domain functional level is very easy:

```
PS C:\>Set-ADDomainMode -Identity "MyDomain.com" -DomainMode Windows2008R2Domain
```

This command succeeds only if the target mode is a legitimate upgrade from the current mode.

Getting the Current Forest

Likewise, you can use the Active Directory module to return the current forest with the **Get-ADForest** cmdlet. Like the **Get-ADDomain** cmdlet, the default is the forest for the current logged-on user:

```
PS C:\> Get-ADForest

ApplicationPartitions : {DC=ForestDnsZones,DC=jdhlab,DC=local, DC=DomainDnsZones,
                         DC=jdhlab,DC=local}
CrossForestReferences : {}
DomainNamingMaster    : COREDC01.jdhlab.local
Domains               : {jdhlab.local}
ForestMode            : Windows2008R2Forest
GlobalCatalogs        : {COREDC01.jdhlab.local}
Name                  : jdhlab.local
PartitionsContainer   : CN=Partitions,CN=Configuration,DC=jdhlab,DC=local
RootDomain            : jdhlab.local
```

```
SchemaMaster          : COREDC01.jdhlab.local
Sites                 : {Default-First-Site-Name}
SPNSuffixes           : {}
UPNSuffixes           : {jdhlab.com}
```

You can specify the forest for the current computer:

```
PS C:\> Get-ADForest -Current LocalComputer.
```

Or specify an entirely different forest by name. You can specify the forest by its Netbios name, DNS host name, or fully qualified domain name (FQDN):

```
PS S:\> Get-ADForest -Identity "mycompany.local" -Server "mycompany-dc01" `
>> -Credential "mycompany\administrator"
>>

ApplicationPartitions : {DC=DomainDnsZones,DC=RESEARCH,DC=MYCOMPANY,DC=LOCAL,DC=ForestDnsZones,
                        DC=MYCOMPANY,DC=LOCAL,DC=DomainDnsZones,DC=MYCOMPANY,DC=LOCAL}
CrossForestReferences : {}
DomainNamingMaster    : MYCOMPANY-DC01.MYCOMPANY.LOCAL
Domains               : {MYCOMPANY.LOCAL, RESEARCH.MYCOMPANY.LOCAL}
ForestMode            : Windows2003Forest
GlobalCatalogs        : {MYCOMPANY-DC01.MYCOMPANY.LOCAL, RESEARCHDC.RESEARCH.MYCOMPANY.LOCAL,
                        CORE-RODC01.RESEARCH.MYCOMPANY.LOCAL}
Name                  : MYCOMPANY.LOCAL
PartitionsContainer   : CN=Partitions,CN=Configuration,DC=MYCOMPANY,DC=LOCAL
RootDomain            : MYCOMPANY.LOCAL
SchemaMaster          : MYCOMPANY-DC01.MYCOMPANY.LOCAL
Sites                 : {Default-First-Site-Name, Branch-Alpha}
SPNSuffixes           : {}
UPNSuffixes           : {}
```

Modifying Forest Properties

There aren't too many things to modify in a forest, although you may want to easily add or remove user principal name (UPN) or Service Principal Name (SPN) suffixes.

UPN and SPN Suffixes

Let me add a new UPN suffix to my forest using the **Set-ADForest** cmdlet. The syntax and concepts are the same as with the **Set-ADDomain** cmdlet:

```
PS C:\> Set-ADForest -Identity "jdhlab.local" -UPNSuffixes @{add="jdhlab.net"}
```

To set a corresponding SPN suffix is just as easy:

```
PS C:\> Set-ADForest -Identity "jdhlab.local"-SPNSuffixes @{add="jdhlab.net"}
```

The cmdlet doesn't write to the pipeline unless you specify the **-Passthru** parameter.

Forest Functional Levels

Active Directory forests also have a functional level:

```
PS C:\> $forest=Get-ADForest
PS C:\> $forest.ForestMode
Windows2008R2Forest
```

My forest is already at the highest level. To raise the forest functional level, you use a similar approach as you did with the domain. These are the possible mode values you can use:

- Windows2000Forest
- Windows2003InterimForest
- Windows2003Forest
- Windows2008Forest
- Windows2008R2Forest.

```
PS C:\> Set-ADForestMode -Identity "Mydomain.com" -ForestMode Windows2008Forest
```

Again, I'm assuming you understand the consequences of this process; because this is a one-time task, I doubt you'll need PowerShell.

Domain Controllers

There are several Active Directory infrastructure-related tasks involving domain controllers. Therefore, you need to be able to create objects for these servers. Let me show you a little trick to get some additional information that isn't exposed through any of the cmdlets.

Without getting into too much detail, use this command to get the current domain using the .NET Framework. Trust me:

```
PS C:\> $currentdomain=[System.DirectoryServices.ActiveDirectory.Domain]::GetCurrentDomain()
```

Some of the information in this object you've seen already:

```
PS C:\> $currentdomain


Forest                  : jdhlab.local
DomainControllers       : {COREDC01.jdhlab.local}
Children                : {}
DomainMode              : Windows2008R2Domain
Parent                  :
PdcRoleOwner            : COREDC01.jdhlab.local
RidRoleOwner            : COREDC01.jdhlab.local
InfrastructureRoleOwner : COREDC01.jdhlab.local
Name                    : jdhlab.local
```

What I especially like is the **DomainControllers** property:

```
PS C:\> $currentdomain.DomainControllers
```

```
Forest                      : jdhlab.local
CurrentTime                 : 9/30/2010 3:11:32 AM
HighestCommittedUsn         : 471160
OSVersion                   : Windows Server 2008 R2 Standard
Roles                       : {SchemaRole, NamingRole, PdcRole, RidRole...}
Domain                      : jdhlab.local
IPAddress                   : 172.16.10.190
SiteName                    : Default-First-Site-Name
SyncFromAllServersCallback :
InboundConnections          : {}
OutboundConnections         : {}
Name                        : COREDC01.jdhlab.local
Partitions                  : {DC=jdhlab,DC=local, CN=Configuration,DC=jdhlab,DC=local, CN=Schema,
                              CN=Configuration,DC=jdhlab,DC=local, DC=DomainDnsZones,
                              DC=jdhlab,DC=local...}
```

This returns a collection of all domain controllers. In my domain, I only have one. But you could easily report on the state of all domain controllers in your domain:

```
PS C:\> $currentdomain.DomainControllers |
>> Select Name,IPAddress,SiteName,OSVersion,@{Name="GlobalCatalog";
>> Expression={$_.IsGlobalCatalog()}}
>>


Name          : COREDC01.jdhlab.local
IPAddress     : 172.16.10.190
SiteName      : Default-First-Site-Name
OSVersion     : Windows Server 2008 R2 Standard
GlobalCatalog : True
```

The domain controller object has a number of methods. One of which will return a Boolean value indicating if the domain controller is also a global catalog server. You'll come back to some of the other methods later in the chapter.

FSMO Roles

Since the first days of Active Directory, there have been Flexible Single Master Operational (FSMO) roles. These roles are carried out by individual domain controllers, although typically the domain controller holds one or more roles.

Enumerating FSMO Roles

The domain roles can be identified by using the **Get-ADDomain** and **Get-ADForest** cmdlets from Microsoft. Some FSMO roles are domain specific:

```
PS C:\ Get-ADDomain | Format-List *Master

InfrastructureMaster            : COREDC01.jdhlab.local
PDCEmulator                     : COREDC01.jdhlab.local
RIDMaster                       : COREDC01.jdhlab.local
```

Others are forest specific:

```
PS C:\ Get-ADForest | Format-List *Master
```

```
DomainNamingMaster      : COREDC01.jdhlab.local
SchemaMaster            : COREDC01.jdhlab.local
```

Transferring FSMO Roles

I doubt this is something you'll need to do often, but it is possible to transfer a FSMO role with PowerShell. Use Microsoft's **Move-ADDirectoryServerOperationMasterRole** cmdlet. This is best accomplished when both domain controllers are online:

```
PS C:\> Move-ADDirectoryServerOperationMasterRole -identity "DC02" `
>> -OperationsMasterRole PDCEmulator
```

With this command I transferred the PDC Emulator role to DC02. You can transfer multiple roles at once. Separate them with commas. Valid roles are:

- PDCEmulator
- RIDMaster
- InfrastructureMaster
- SchemaMaster
- DomainNamingMaster.

Seizing a FSMO Role

If the current FSMO role holder is permanently offline, you can force an FSMO role transfer. Use the same syntax as above with the addition of the **-Force** parameter.

Global Catalog Servers

Active Directory fails to function properly without one or more active and available global catalog servers. Global catalog servers can be discovered at the forest level using the **Get-ADForest** cmdlet:

```
PS C:\> Get-ADForest | Select -ExpandProperty GlobalCatalogs
MYCOMPANY-DC01.MYCOMPANY.LOCAL
RESEARCHDC.RESEARCH.MYCOMPANY.LOCAL
CORE-RODC01.RESEARCH.MYCOMPANY.LOCAL
```

The **GlobalCatalogs** property is a collection of all global catalog servers in the forest. Another approach and frankly one that offers a bit more flexibility is to use the .NET Active Directory class. Admittedly this feels like systems programming, but you don't need to do much. Let's get the current forest:

```
PS C:\> $forest=[System.DirectoryServices.ActiveDirectory.Forest]::GetCurrentForest()
```

Whereas the **Get-ADForest** cmdlet simply returns a collection of names, the **GlobalCatalogs** property offers much more information:

```
PS C:\> $forest.GlobalCatalogs | Sort Domain | Select Name,Domain,Sitename
```

```
Name                                  Domain                     SiteName
----                                  ------                     --------
MYCOMPANY-DC01.MYCOMPANY.LOCAL        MYCOMPANY.LOCAL            Default-First-Site-Name
RESEARCHDC.RESEARCH.MYCOMPANY.LOCAL   RESEARCH.MYCOMPANY.LOCAL Default-First-Site-Name
CORE-RODC01.RESEARCH.MYCOMPANY.LOCAL RESEARCH.MYCOMPANY.LOCAL Default-First-Site-Name
```

Enabling a Global Catalog Server

In the MyCompany domain, I have a new domain controller, Pluto, that I want to enable as a global catalog server. Unfortunately, while there is a **Get-ADDomainController** cmdlet, there is no counterpart to set a domain controller. Once again, you'll need to rely on the .NET Framework.

Before you can connect to the domain controller, you need to define a context object:

```
PS C:\> $ctx=New-Object System.DirectoryServices.ActiveDirectory.DirectoryContext(
>> "directoryserver","pluto.mycompany.local")
```

Now you can create a domain controller object. You can actually type this as a single-line command:

```
PS C:\> $pluto=[System.DirectoryServices.ActiveDirectory.DomainController]::GetDomainControl
ler(
>> $ctx)
```

Pluto is currently not a global catalog server:

```
PS C:\> $pluto.IsGlobalCatalog()
False
```

Call the **EnableGlobalCatalog()** method to make the change:

```
PS C:\> $pluto.EnableGlobalCatalog()


Forest                       : MYCOMPANY.LOCAL
CurrentTime                  : 10/20/2010 5:06:14 PM
HighestCommittedUsn          : 24607
OSVersion                    : Windows Server 2003
Roles                        : {}
Domain                       : MYCOMPANY.LOCAL
IPAddress                    : 172.16.10.71
SiteName                     : Default-First-Site-Name
SyncFromAllServersCallback :
InboundConnections           : {6a93842b-b2eb-4319-b271-2e1b8ca2c4bc, 8b848491-eb11-4e23-bc5e-
                                0ea35c0864b8}
OutboundConnections          : {9c0e71f8-bb54-4f87-a5eb-d81bc384bef1, 1990fe98-5dd0-4014-b8d6-
                               f4016e8aa185}
Name                         : Pluto.MYCOMPANY.LOCAL
Partitions                   : {DC=MYCOMPANY,DC=LOCAL, CN=Configuration,DC=MYCOMPANY,DC=LOCAL,
                                CN=Schema,CN=Configuration,DC=MYCOMPANY,DC=LOCAL}
```

The change is immediate, or as long as it takes to replicate.

Disabling a Global Catalog Server

If at some point I decide to remove Pluto, or any other domain controller, as a global catalog server,

I'll use a similar process. To demonstrate, I'll remove CORE-RODC01 as a global catalog server in the Research.Mycompany.local domain. First, define the context:

```
PS C:\> $ctx=New-Object System.DirectoryServices.ActiveDirectory.DirectoryContext(
>> "directoryserver","core-rodc01.research.mycompany.local")
```

Next you need to create a global catalog server object:

```
PS C:\> $gc=[System.DirectoryServices.ActiveDirectory.GlobalCatalog]::GetGlobalCatalog($ctx)
```

To make the change, call the **DisableGlobalCatalog()** method:

```
PS C:\> $gc.DisableGlobalCatalog()
```

It might be a little confusing, but notice that you need to use the DomainController class to enable a global catalog server and the GlobalCatalog log to disable it.

Trusts

Trust relationships can be managed with the .NET ActiveDirectory.Domain object. You can list, verify, create, and remove trusts. Sorry, but I'm not aware of any cmdlets. You'll create an object for the current domain like this:

```
PS C:\> $currentDomain = [System.DirectoryServices.ActiveDirectory.Domain]::GetCurrentDomain()
```

Enumerating Trusts

Listing all existing trusts is accomplished by invoking the **GetAllTrustRelationships()** method:

```
PS C:\> $currentdomain.GetAllTrustRelationships() | Format-Table -autosize

SourceName      TargetName                TrustType   TrustDirection
----------      ----------                ---------   --------------
MYCOMPANY.LOCAL RESEARCH.MYCOMPANY.LOCAL  ParentChild Bidirectional
```

This returns all trust relationships. Since I only have one, another option is to use the **GetTrustRelationship()** method, specifying the target domain name:

```
PS C:\> $currentdomain.GetTrustRelationship("research.mycompany.local")
```

This provides the same result.

Verifying Trusts

Verifying a trust requires a few steps. The ActiveDirectory.Domain object has a **VerifyTrustRelationship()** method. However this method requires two DirectoryServices. ActiveDirectory objects which must first be created:

```
PS C:\> $ctx=New-Object System.DirectoryServices.ActiveDirectory.DirectoryContext(
>> "domain","research.mycompany.local")
```

```
>>
PS C:\> $targetdomain=[System.DirectoryServices.ActiveDirectory.Domain]::GetDomain($ctx)
```

I used the **New-Object** cmdlet to create the DirectoryContext object. I specified the context type, "domain". Because I'm logged on with an enterprise administrator account, I didn't have to specify any credentials, although you can. You'll see this in a moment when I create a new trust. Armed with this context object, I then created the target domain object using the **GetDomain()** method.

The last piece I need is a TrustDirection object. In my case, since it is a two-way trust, I'm going to specify bidirectional:

```
PS C:\> $direction=[System.DirectoryServices.ActiveDirectory.TrustDirection]::bidirectional
```

Other possible choices are Inbound and Outbound. Now I can call the **VerifyTrustRelationship()** method with these objects as parameters:

```
PS C:\> $currentdomain.VerifyTrustRelationship($targetdomain,$direction)
```

This method won't return anything if the trust is successfully verified. It's a situation of "no news is good news." If there is a problem, you'll get an error message.

Creating Trusts

Creating a trust uses a similar syntax as verifying a trust. You need an ActiveDirectory.Domain object for the target domain, and a TrustDirection object indicating what type of trust to create. Let's create a new external trust with another domain:

```
PS C:\> $ctx=New-Object System.DirectoryServices.ActiveDirectory.DirectoryContext(
>> "domain","jdhitsolutions.local","jdhitsolutions\administrator","P@ssw0rd1B3")
>>
PS C:\> $targetdomain=[System.DirectoryServices.ActiveDirectory.Domain]::GetDomain($ctx)
PS C:\> $direction=[System.DirectoryServices.ActiveDirectory.TrustDirection]::bidirectional
```

Since the jdhitsolutions.local domain is external, I need to provide credentials. But now I can create the new trust by calling the **CreateTrustRelationship()** method:

```
PS C:\> $currentdomain.CreateTrustRelationship($targetdomain,$direction)
```

Checking trusts again, you see the new external trust:

```
PS C:\> $currentdomain.GetAllTrustRelationships()

SourceName       TargetName                  TrustType  TrustDirection
----------       ----------                  ---------  --------------
MYCOMPANY.LOCAL  RESEARCH.MYCOMPANY.LOCAL  ParentChild  Bidirectional
MYCOMPANY.LOCAL  jdhitsolutions.local         External  Bidirectional
```

There is also a **CreateLocalSideOfTrustRelationship()** method you can use to create a one-way trust. The syntax is similar to creating a full trust, with the addition of specifying an initial trust password:

```
PS C:\> $currentdomain.CreateLocalSideOfTrustRelationship($targetdomain,$direction,"P@ssw0rd")
```

In this situation, create $direction with a value of either Inbound or Outbound.

Repairing and Updating Trusts

Occasionally your trusts require a little attention. If you need to repair a trust, use the **RepairTrustRelationship()** method:

```
PS C:\> $currentdomain.RepairTrustRelationship($targetdomain)
```

The method uses the $targetdomain object I created above. If you want to update the trust, perhaps to change it from two-way to one-way, first define a TrustDirection object:

```
PS C:\> $direction=[System.DirectoryServices.ActiveDirectory.TrustDirection]::inbound
```

Now you can invoke the **UpdateTrustRelationship()** method and see the result:

```
PS C:\> $currentdomain.UpdateTrustRelationship($targetdomain,$direction)
```

Removing Trusts

You can choose to remove an entire trust, that is both sides, or just the local side of the trust using the **DeleteTrustRelationship()** and **DeleteLocalSideofTrustRelationship()** methods. To delete the entire trust, you need a System.DirectoryServices.ActiveDirectory.Domain object for the target domain like what is used for verifying the trust:

```
PS C:\>$currentdomain.DeleteTrustRelationship($targetdomain)
```

The $currentdomain object is the domain object used throughout this chapter. Unless there is an error, you'll get no results. If you want to delete just one side of the trust, all you need to do is specify the target domain name:

```
PS C:\>$currentdomain.DeleteLocalSideofTrustRelationship("jdhitsolutions.local")
```

Forest Trusts

You can also create forest-level trusts in much the same way as you do domain-level trusts. The method names are all the same. Instead of a domain object, use a forest object:

```
PS C:\> $forest=[System.DirectoryServices.ActiveDirectory.Forest]::GetCurrentForest()
PS C:\> $forest.GetAllTrustRelationships()
```

When you create a forest trust, you need to specify a target forest object similar to what is done when creating a domain trust:

```
PS C:\> $context=New-Object System.DirectoryServices.ActiveDirectory.DirectoryContext `
>> "forest", "sapienpress.local","sapienpress\administrator","P@ssw0rdAbC"
>>
```

```
PS C:\> $targetforest=[System.DirectoryServices.ActiveDirectory.Forest]::GetForest($context)
PS C:\> $direction=[System.DirectoryServices.ActiveDirectory.TrustDirection]::bidirectional
PS C:\> $forest.CreateTrustRelationship($targetforest,$direction)
```

From here, use the same trust management methods I demonstrated for domain trusts, except use the $forest object.

Sites and Subnets

Managing Active Directory sites and subnets is done at the forest level and is not especially difficult, especially because you can use cmdlets. However, there may still be situations where you need to rely on the .NET Framework classes.

Enumerating Sites

How easy is this?

```
PS C:\> Get-ADForest | Select -ExpandProperty Sites
Default-First-Site-Name
Branch-Alpha
```

Using the $forest object created earlier examine the **Sites** property to see all your Active Directory sites in a bit more detail:

```
PS C:\> $forest.Sites


Name                            : Default-First-Site-Name
Domains                         : {MYCOMPANY.LOCAL, RESEARCH.MYCOMPANY.LOCAL}
Subnets                         : {172.16.0.0/16}
Servers                         : {MYCOMPANY-DC01.MYCOMPANY.LOCAL, RESEARCHDC.RESEARCH.
                                  MYCOMPANY.LOCAL, CORE-RODC01.RESEARCH.MYCOMPANY.LOCAL,
                                  Pluto.MYCOMPANY.LOCAL}
AdjacentSites                   : {Branch-Alpha}
SiteLinks                       : {DEFAULTIPSITELINK}
InterSiteTopologyGenerator      : MYCOMPANY-DC01.MYCOMPANY.LOCAL
Options                         : None
Location                        : Syracuse
BridgeheadServers               : {}
PreferredSmtpBridgeheadServers  : {}
PreferredRpcBridgeheadServers   : {}
IntraSiteReplicationSchedule    : System.DirectoryServices.ActiveDirectory.ActiveDirectorySchedule

Name                            : Branch-Alpha
Domains                         : {}
Subnets                         : {10.100.50.0/24, 192.168.1.0/24}
Servers                         : {}
AdjacentSites                   : {Default-First-Site-Name}
SiteLinks                       : {DEFAULTIPSITELINK}
InterSiteTopologyGenerator      :
Options                         : None
Location                        : Las Vegas
BridgeheadServers               : {}
PreferredSmtpBridgeheadServers  : {}
PreferredRpcBridgeheadServers   : {}
IntraSiteReplicationSchedule    :
```

Each entry is a System.DirectoryServices.ActiveDirectory.ActiveDirectorySite object. If you want to see which servers are associated with each site, use this expression:

```
PS C:\> $forest.sites | Foreach {$_.servers | Select Sitename,Name}

SiteName                                        Name
--------                                        ----
Default-First-Site-Name                         MYCOMPANY-DC01.MYCOMPANY.LOCAL
Default-First-Site-Name                         RESEARCHDC.RESEARCH.MYCOMPANY.LOCAL
Default-First-Site-Name                         CORE-RODC01.RESEARCH.MYCOMPANY.LOCAL
Default-First-Site-Name                         Pluto.MYCOMPANY.LOCAL
```

My test domain has another site, Branch-Alpha, but no servers assigned to it, which is why it doesn't show up in the results. I'm assuming you have at least one domain controller in each site so if you run this expression you will get a more complete listing.

Enumerating Subnets

Subnet information is returned for each site when using the .NET classes:

```
PS C:\> $forest.sites | Foreach {$_.subnets}

Name                         Site                         Location
----                         ----                         --------
172.16.0.0/16                Default-First-Site-Name
10.100.50.0/24               Branch-Alpha
192.168.1.0/24               Branch-Alpha
```

However, you can also get this information using the **Get-ADObject** cmdlet, since subnets are defined in the Configuration container:

```
PS C:\> $rootDSE=Get-ADRootDSE
PS C:\> Get-ADObject -filter "objectClass -eq 'subnet'" -properties SiteObject `
>>-SearchBase $rootDSE.configurationNamingContext | Select Name
>>
Name                        SiteObject
----                        ----------
172.16.0.0/16               CN=Default-First-Site-Name,CN=Sites,CN=Configuration,DC=...
10.100.50.0/24              CN=Branch-Alpha,CN=Sites,CN=Configuration,DC=MYCOMPANY,D...
192.168.1.0/24              CN=Branch-Alpha,CN=Sites,CN=Configuration,DC=MYCOMPANY,D...
```

Creating a Subnet

One item of business you'll want to take care of with the new site is associating it with a subnet. You can create the subnet with a one-line command using the **New-ADObject** cmdlet and even link it to a site:

```
PS C:\> New-ADObject -Name "192.168.100.0/24" -Type subnet `
>> -Path "CN=Subnets,CN=Sites,$($rootdse.configurationNamingContext)" `
>> -OtherAttributes @{location="Chicago";
>> siteObject="CN=CHI-CORP,CN=Sites,$($rootDSE.ConfigurationNamingContext)"}
```

Creating Unlinked Subnets

While I prefer to create a subnet and associate it with a site, you can also create a subnet without a site association by omitting the **siteObject** property.

You don't have to specify a site name. One advantage to a function like this is that it's very easy to bulk create subnets:

New-Subnets.ps1

```
Import-Module ActiveDirectory
$rootDSE=Get-ADRootDSE

for ($i=10;$i -lt 250;$i+=10) {
 $name="10.100.$i.0/24"
 Write-Host "Creating $name" -ForegroundColor Green
 New-ADobject -Name $name -Type subnet -Path "CN=Subnets,CN=Sites,$($rootdse.
configurationNamingContext)"
}
```

This will create unlinked subnets 10.100.10.0/24 through 10.100.250/24.

Creating a Site

Even though you could manually create all the required objects in the Configuration naming context for a new site using the **New-ADObject** cmdlet, I think you're better off using the .NET Framework. I've created a function to make it easier:

New-ADSite.ps1

```
Function New-ADSite {

Param(
    [Parameter(Position=0,Mandatory=$True,HelpMessage="Enter the name for the new site")]
    [ValidateNotNullOrEmpty()]
    [string]$sitename,

    [Parameter(Position=1,Mandatory=$False)]
    [ValidateNotNullOrEmpty()]
    [string]$sitelink="DEFAULTIPSITELINK",

    [string[]]$subnetip,

    [string]$location
)

#import the Active Directory module if not already laoded
if (-not (get-Module ActiveDirectory))
{
    Import-Module ActiveDirectory
}
Write-Verbose "Creating the RootDSE"
$rootDSE=Get-ADRootDSE
$nc=$rootDSE.ConfigurationNamingContext
Write-verbose "naming contect is $nc"
```

```
#create a forest object with .NET
$forest=[System.DirectoryServices.ActiveDirectory.Forest]::GetCurrentForest()
Write-verbose "Forest is $forest.name"

#create a site with .NET
$context=New-Object System.DirectoryServices.ActiveDirectory.DirectoryContext("forest",$for
est.name)
Write-verbose "Creating new site $sitename"
$site=New-Object System.DirectoryServices.ActiveDirectory.ActiveDirectorySite($context,$siten
ame)

$sitedn="CN=$sitename,CN=Sites,$nc"
Write-Verbose "DN is $sitedn"

#define optional values
if ($location)
{
    Write-Verbose "Setting location to $location"
    $site.location=$location
}

$site.Save()

if ($subnetip)
{
 Foreach ($ip in $subnetip) {
    Write-Verbose "Checking for CN=$ip,CN=Subnets,CN=Sites,$nc "
    #see if subnet already exits and if so, connect it to the site
    #turn off error pipeline to supress errors when subnet not found
    $ErrorActionPreference="SilentlyContinue"
    $subnetObject=Get-ADObject -identity "CN=$ip,CN=Subnets,CN=Sites,$nc"
    #turn it back on
    $ErrorActionPreference="Continue"

    if ($subnetObject)
    {
        Write-Verbose "Adding $siteDN to $($subnetObject.name)"
        Set-ADObject $subnetObject -Add @{siteObject=$sitedn}
    }
    else
    {
        #if not, create subnet and add to site
        Write-Verbose "Creating new subnet object"
        $subnet=New-Object System.DirectoryServices.ActiveDirectory.ActiveDirectorySubnet($con
text,$ip,$sitename)
        $subnet.save()
        Write-Verbose ($subnet | out-string)
    }
  } #foreach
} #if $subnetip

#get sitelink object
$link="CN=$Sitelink,CN=IP, CN=Inter-Site Transports,CN=Sites,$nc"
Write-Verbose "Adding siteline $link"
#add new site to sitelink
Set-ADObject -Identity $link -Add @{SiteList=$($sitedn)}

#write the new site object to the piline
Get-ADObject -identity $sitedn -properties *

Write-verbose "Finished"

} #end function
```

The function accepts several parameters, but the site name is the only one that is required. The function uses the .NET Framework to create the site object:

```
$site=New-Object System.DirectoryServices.ActiveDirectory.ActiveDirectorySite($context,$siten
ame)
```

If you've specified one or more subnets, the function will check to see if they exist:

```
if ($subnetip)
{
 Foreach ($ip in $subnetip) {
    Write-Verbose "Checking for CN=$ip,CN=Subnets,CN=Sites,$nc "
    #see if subnet already exits and if so, connect it to the site
    #turn off error pipeline to supress errors when subnet not found
    $ErrorActionPreference="SilentlyContinue"
    $subnetObject=Get-ADObject -identity "CN=$ip,CN=Subnets,CN=Sites,$nc"
    #turn it back on
    $ErrorActionPreference="Continue"

    if ($subnetObject)
```

I'm using a **ForEach** loop because you could have multiple subnets associated with a site. If the site exists, then I use the **Set-ADObject** cmdlet to add the site to the subnet object:

```
     Set-ADObject $subnetObject -Add @{siteObject=$sitedn}
```

Otherwise, I create the subnet object and associate it with the site using the .NET Framework:

```
$subnet=New-Object System.DirectoryServices.ActiveDirectory.ActiveDirectorySubnet(
$context,$ip,$sitename)
$subnet.save()
```

Sites must be associated with a site link. My function uses the default, but you could specify any site link name. Again, I use the **Set-ADObject** cmdlet to add the link:

```
$link="CN=$Sitelink,CN=IP, CN=Inter-Site Transports,CN=Sites,$nc"
Write-Verbose "Adding siteline $link"
#add new site to sitelink
Set-ADObject -Identity $link -Add @{SiteList=$($sitedn)}
```

The last part of the function merely writes the new site object to the pipeline:

```
Get-ADObject -identity $sitedn -properties *
```

Here's how you can use this function:

```
PS C:\> new-adsite -sitename SYR-CORP -location NY `
>> subnetip "10.1.2.0/24","10.100.100.0/24","10.100.110.0/24"

CanonicalName                 : MYCOMPANY.LOCAL/Configuration/Sites/SYR-CORP
CN                            : SYR-CORP
Created                       : 10/22/2010 10:37:25 AM
createTimeStamp               : 10/22/2010 10:37:25 AM
Deleted                       :
```

```
Description                     :
DisplayName                     :
DistinguishedName               : CN=SYR-CORP,CN=Sites,CN=Configuration,DC=MYCOMPANY,DC=LOCAL
instanceType                    : 4
isDeleted                       :
LastKnownParent                 :
location                        : NY
Modified                        : 10/22/2010 10:37:25 AM
modifyTimeStamp                 : 10/22/2010 10:37:25 AM
Name                            : SYR-CORP
nTSecurityDescriptor            : System.DirectoryServices.ActiveDirectorySecurity
ObjectCategory                  : CN=Site,CN=Schema,CN=Configuration,DC=MYCOMPANY,DC=LOCAL
ObjectClass                     : site
ObjectGUID                      : 3c7a763e-a357-4187-b658-82ec32b9a348
ProtectedFromAccidentalDeletion : False
sDRightsEffective               : 15
showInAdvancedViewOnly          : True
siteObjectBL                    : {CN=10.1.2.0/24,CN=Subnets,CN=Sites,CN=Configuration,
                                  DC=MYCOMPANY,DC=LOCAL,CN=10.100.110.0/24,CN=Subnets,CN=Sites,
                                  CN=Configuration,DC=MYCOMPANY,DC=LOCAL, CN=10.100.100.0/24,
                                  CN=Subnets,CN=Sites,CN=Configuration,DC=MYCOMPANY,DC=LOCAL}
systemFlags                     : 1107296256
uSNChanged                      : 543882
uSNCreated                      : 543882
whenChanged                     : 10/22/2010 10:37:25 AM
whenCreated                     : 10/22/2010 10:37:25 AM
```

I created a new site, SYR-CORP, and linked it to three subnets. One of which was created and the other two already existed.

Start With This

This function is not perfect nor 100% ready for production use. For example, there is little to no error handing. I wish I could find a cmdlet to handle this task but I can't so a scripting solution is the only option. If you find yourself needing this type of automation, please use this script as a starting point or guideline.

Moving to a Site

If you have your sites and subnets properly configured, new domain controllers are automatically added to the correct site. If you manually want to move a server, you can easily accomplish this with a one-line **Move-ADDirectoryServer** expression:

```
PS C:\> Move-ADDirectoryServer -Identity "Pluto" -Site "Branch-Alpha"
```

I'm assuming you understand the implications of moving domain controllers between sites.

Deleting a Site

To delete a site, the **Remove-ADObject** cmdlet will get the job done. I'm going to remove a site called CHI-CORP from my forest. I'll build the identity or distinguished name using the **ConfigurationNamingContext** property of the RootDSE object:

```
PS C:\> $rootDSE=Get-ADRootDSE
PS C:\> Remove-ADObject -Identity "CN=CHI-CORP,CN=Sites,$($rootDSE.configurationNamingContext)"
```

```
Confirm
Are you sure you want to perform this action?
Performing operation "Remove" on Target "CN=CHI-CORP,CN=Sites,CN=Configuration,DC=MYCOMPANY,DC
=LOCAL".
[Y] Yes  [A] Yes to All  [N] No  [L] No to All  [S] Suspend  [?] Help (default is "Y"): y
```

Note, that this will not delete any subnets that might have been associated with this site.

Replication

Managing replication from PowerShell requires a few methods with the ActiveDirectory DomainController object. You also need to know which partitions you want to check. Here is the partition information for one of my domain controllers:

```
PS C:\> Get-ADDomainController pluto | Select -ExpandProperty Partitions
CN=Schema,CN=Configuration,DC=MYCOMPANY,DC=LOCAL
CN=Configuration,DC=MYCOMPANY,DC=LOCAL
DC=MYCOMPANY,DC=LOCAL
DC=RESEARCH,DC=MYCOMPANY,DC=LOCAL
```

Unfortunately, that is as far as you can go with the Active Directory module. To manage replication you'll need to rely on the .NET classes again. So let's get a domain controller object:

```
PS C:\> $myDomain=[System.DirectoryServices.ActiveDirectory.Domain]::GetCurrentDomain()
PS C:\> $pluto=$myDomain.DomainControllers | Where {$_.Name-match "Pluto"}
```

Next, I'll discuss how you might manage replication from this domain controller.

Replication Neighbors

First, it is recommended to identify all the servers Pluto replicates with using the **GetAllReplicationNeighbors()** method:

```
PS C:\> $pluto.GetAllReplicationNeighbors()


PartitionName              : DC=MYCOMPANY,DC=LOCAL
SourceServer               : MYCOMPANY-DC01.MYCOMPANY.LOCAL
TransportType              : Rpc
ReplicationNeighborOption : Writeable, ScheduledSync, CompressChanges, NoChangeNotifications
SourceInvocationId         : 7420c6ab-83d9-44ad-9e6e-9bf45c096662
UsnLastObjectChangeSynced : 542983
UsnAttributeFilter         : 542983
LastSuccessfulSync         : 10/22/2010 8:57:32 AM
LastAttemptedSync          : 10/22/2010 8:57:32 AM
LastSyncResult             : 0
LastSyncMessage            : The operation completed successfully.
ConsecutiveFailureCount    : 0

PartitionName              : CN=Configuration,DC=MYCOMPANY,DC=LOCAL
SourceServer               : MYCOMPANY-DC01.MYCOMPANY.LOCAL
TransportType              : Rpc
ReplicationNeighborOption : Writeable, ScheduledSync, CompressChanges, NoChangeNotifications
SourceInvocationId         : 7420c6ab-83d9-44ad-9e6e-9bf45c096662
UsnLastObjectChangeSynced : 543134
UsnAttributeFilter         : 543134
```

```
LastSuccessfulSync          : 10/22/2010 8:57:32 AM
LastAttemptedSync           : 10/22/2010 8:57:32 AM
LastSyncResult              : 0
LastSyncMessage             : The operation completed successfully.
ConsecutiveFailureCount     : 0
PartitionName               : CN=Schema,CN=Configuration,DC=MYCOMPANY,DC=LOCAL
SourceServer                : MYCOMPANY-DC01.MYCOMPANY.LOCAL
TransportType               : Rpc
ReplicationNeighborOption : Writeable, ScheduledSync, CompressChanges, NoChangeNotifications
SourceInvocationId          : 7420c6ab-83d9-44ad-9e6e-9bf45c096662
UsnLastObjectChangeSynced : 542940
UsnAttributeFilter          : 542940
LastSuccessfulSync          : 10/22/2010 8:57:32 AM
LastAttemptedSync           : 10/22/2010 8:57:32 AM
LastSyncResult              : 0
LastSyncMessage             : The operation completed successfully.
...
```

This method returns information about each partition, the replication partner, and replication information. If you prefer to focus on a specific partition, simply specify it as a parameter:

```
PS C:\> $pluto.GetReplicationNeighbors("dc=mycompany,dc=local")
PartitionName               : dc=mycompany,dc=local
SourceServer                : MYCOMPANY-DC01.MYCOMPANY.LOCAL
TransportType               : Rpc
ReplicationNeighborOption : Writeable, ScheduledSync, CompressChanges, NoChangeNotifications
SourceInvocationId          : 7420c6ab-83d9-44ad-9e6e-9bf45c096662
UsnLastObjectChangeSynced : 542983
UsnAttributeFilter          : 542983
LastSuccessfulSync          : 10/22/2010 8:57:32 AM
LastAttemptedSync           : 10/22/2010 8:57:32 AM
LastSyncResult              : 0
LastSyncMessage             : The operation completed successfully.
ConsecutiveFailureCount     : 0
```

Replication Metadata

One useful bit of information you can glean from PowerShell is replication metadata. The **GetReplicationMetadata()** method takes the distinguished name of an Active Directory object as a parameter and displays a list of properties with metadata:

```
PS C:\> $dn=(Get-ADUser adeco).distinguishedname
PS C:\> $dn
CN=Art Deco,OU=Employees,DC=MYCOMPANY,DC=LOCAL
PS C:\> $pluto.GetReplicationMetadata($dn)

Name                           Value
----                           -----
supplementalcredentials        System.DirectoryServices.ActiveDirectory.AttributeMetadata
countrycode                    System.DirectoryServices.ActiveDirectory.AttributeMetadata
samaccountname                 System.DirectoryServices.ActiveDirectory.AttributeMetadata
useraccountcontrol             System.DirectoryServices.ActiveDirectory.AttributeMetadata
primarygroupid                 System.DirectoryServices.ActiveDirectory.AttributeMetadata
userprincipalname              System.DirectoryServices.ActiveDirectory.AttributeMetadata
instancetype                   System.DirectoryServices.ActiveDirectory.AttributeMetadata
givenname                      System.DirectoryServices.ActiveDirectory.AttributeMetadata
pwdlastset                     System.DirectoryServices.ActiveDirectory.AttributeMetadata
lastlogontimestamp             System.DirectoryServices.ActiveDirectory.AttributeMetadata
samaccounttype                 System.DirectoryServices.ActiveDirectory.AttributeMetadata
```

```
objectsid                   System.DirectoryServices.ActiveDirectory.AttributeMetadata
ntpwdhistory                System.DirectoryServices.ActiveDirectory.AttributeMetadata
accountexpires              System.DirectoryServices.ActiveDirectory.AttributeMetadata
displayname                 System.DirectoryServices.ActiveDirectory.AttributeMetadata
sn                          System.DirectoryServices.ActiveDirectory.AttributeMetadata
codepage                    System.DirectoryServices.ActiveDirectory.AttributeMetadata
ntsecuritydescriptor        System.DirectoryServices.ActiveDirectory.AttributeMetadata
lmpwdhistory                System.DirectoryServices.ActiveDirectory.AttributeMetadata
unicodepwd                  System.DirectoryServices.ActiveDirectory.AttributeMetadata
description                 System.DirectoryServices.ActiveDirectory.AttributeMetadata
objectclass                 System.DirectoryServices.ActiveDirectory.AttributeMetadata
logonhours                  System.DirectoryServices.ActiveDirectory.AttributeMetadata
dbcspwd                     System.DirectoryServices.ActiveDirectory.AttributeMetadata
cn                          System.DirectoryServices.ActiveDirectory.AttributeMetadata
whencreated                 System.DirectoryServices.ActiveDirectory.AttributeMetadata
name                        System.DirectoryServices.ActiveDirectory.AttributeMetadata
objectcategory              System.DirectoryServices.ActiveDirectory.AttributeMetadata
```

This shows what properties have metadata information for the Art Deco object. But what types of information are stored? To see all values, I pipe the metadata to a **ForEach** loop and look at the **Values** property for each object:

```
PS C:\> $pluto.GetReplicationMetadata($dn) | Foreach {$_.values}


Name                          : objectClass
Version                       : 1
LastOriginatingChangeTime     : 8/30/2009 9:10:31 PM
LastOriginatingInvocationId : 7420c6ab-83d9-44ad-9e6e-9bf45c096662
OriginatingChangeUsn          : 292588
LocalChangeUsn                : 17905
OriginatingServer             : MYCOMPANY-DC01.MYCOMPANY.LOCAL

Name                          : cn
Version                       : 1
LastOriginatingChangeTime     : 10/20/2010 12:09:42 PM
LastOriginatingInvocationId : 13464126-1c18-447c-93f5-05fdf7c94a27
OriginatingChangeUsn          : 17905
LocalChangeUsn                : 17905
OriginatingServer             : Pluto.MYCOMPANY.LOCAL

Name                          : sn
Version                       : 1
LastOriginatingChangeTime     : 8/30/2009 9:10:31 PM
LastOriginatingInvocationId : 7420c6ab-83d9-44ad-9e6e-9bf45c096662
OriginatingChangeUsn          : 292588
LocalChangeUsn                : 17905
OriginatingServer             : MYCOMPANY-DC01.MYCOMPANY.LOCAL

Name                          : description
Version                       : 1
LastOriginatingChangeTime     : 8/30/2009 9:10:31 PM
LastOriginatingInvocationId : 7420c6ab-83d9-44ad-9e6e-9bf45c096662
OriginatingChangeUsn          : 292588
LocalChangeUsn                : 17905
OriginatingServer             : MYCOMPANY-DC01.MYCOMPANY.LOCA
...
```

The output above is truncated, though you can see that for any given property the date of the last change is shown, and from which server. Update Sequence Numbers can also be used for additional troubleshooting. If you are interested in a specific property, use an expression like this:

```
PS C:\> $pluto.GetReplicationMetadata($dn).item("description")


Name                         : description
Version                      : 1
LastOriginatingChangeTime    : 8/30/2009 9:10:31 PM
LastOriginatingInvocationId  : 7420c6ab-83d9-44ad-9e6e-9bf45c096662
OriginatingChangeUsn         : 292588
LocalChangeUsn               : 17905
OriginatingServer            : MYCOMPANY-DC01.MYCOMPANY.LOCAL
```

This shows that the **Description** property for this object was last changed on August 30, 2009, and that the change originated on MYCOMPANY-DC01.

Replication Cursors

The **GetReplicationCursors()** method shows the replication state for a given partition:

```
PS C:\> $pluto.GetReplicationCursors("dc=mycompany,dc=local")


PartitionName          : dc=mycompany,dc=local
SourceInvocationId     : 13464126-1c18-447c-93f5-05fdf7c94a27
UpToDatenessUsn        : 26792
SourceServer           : Pluto.MYCOMPANY.LOCAL
LastSuccessfulSyncTime : 10/22/2010 11:37:28 AM

PartitionName          : dc=mycompany,dc=local
SourceInvocationId     : 7420c6ab-83d9-44ad-9e6e-9bf45c096662
UpToDatenessUsn        : 543141
SourceServer           : MYCOMPANY-DC01.MYCOMPANY.LOCAL
LastSuccessfulSyncTime : 10/22/2010 8:57:32 AM
```

This is very helpful when troubleshooting a replication problem and you want to know when a server last synchronized. Getting this information for all partitions is as simple as piping the domain controller's **Partitions** property and passing the name to the **GetReplicationCursors()** method:

```
PS C:\> $pluto.partitions | Foreach {
>> Write-Host $_ -foregroundcolor Cyan
>> Write-Host ("*"*$_.Length) -foregroundcolor Cyan
>> $pluto.GetReplicationCursors($_)
>> }
>>

DC=MYCOMPANY,DC=LOCAL
*********************

PartitionName          : DC=MYCOMPANY,DC=LOCAL
SourceInvocationId     : 13464126-1c18-447c-93f5-05fdf7c94a27
UpToDatenessUsn        : 26792
SourceServer           : Pluto.MYCOMPANY.LOCAL
LastSuccessfulSyncTime : 10/22/2010 11:39:02 AM

PartitionName          : DC=MYCOMPANY,DC=LOCAL
SourceInvocationId     : 7420c6ab-83d9-44ad-9e6e-9bf45c096662
UpToDatenessUsn        : 543141
SourceServer           : MYCOMPANY-DC01.MYCOMPANY.LOCAL
LastSuccessfulSyncTime : 10/22/2010 8:57:32 AM
```

```
CN=Configuration,DC=MYCOMPANY,DC=LOCAL
**************************************
PartitionName          : CN=Configuration,DC=MYCOMPANY,DC=LOCAL
SourceInvocationId     : 13464126-1c18-447c-93f5-05fdf7c94a27
UpToDatenessUsn        : 26792
SourceServer           : Pluto.MYCOMPANY.LOCAL
LastSuccessfulSyncTime : 10/22/2010 11:39:02 AM

PartitionName          : CN=Configuration,DC=MYCOMPANY,DC=LOCAL
SourceInvocationId     : 61fbb4af-5f61-46e5-be01-7c5f372ae22d
UpToDatenessUsn        : 35136
SourceServer           :
LastSuccessfulSyncTime : 8/24/2009 12:11:23 PM

PartitionName          : CN=Configuration,DC=MYCOMPANY,DC=LOCAL
SourceInvocationId     : 70a4d59e-5063-46bc-91d9-447c3b94bf0a
UpToDatenessUsn        : 91861
SourceServer           :
LastSuccessfulSyncTime : 5/4/2009 10:15:12 AM

PartitionName          : CN=Configuration,DC=MYCOMPANY,DC=LOCAL
SourceInvocationId     : 7420c6ab-83d9-44ad-9e6e-9bf45c096662
UpToDatenessUsn        : 543141
SourceServer           : MYCOMPANY-DC01.MYCOMPANY.LOCAL
LastSuccessfulSyncTime : 10/22/2010 8:57:32 AM

PartitionName          : CN=Configuration,DC=MYCOMPANY,DC=LOCAL
SourceInvocationId     : c29ff78d-fbbe-4636-845e-a101617d71b1
UpToDatenessUsn        : 325034
SourceServer           : RESEARCHDC.RESEARCH.MYCOMPANY.LOCAL
LastSuccessfulSyncTime : 10/22/2010 8:56:48 AM
...
```

Replication Schedule

It is possible to retrieve a replication schedule, although decoding it is a little tricky. The domain controller object you've been using has two properties: **InboundConnections** and **OutboundConnections**:

```
PS C:\> $pluto.inboundconnections


Name                            : 3f57030d-e82f-428c-aaaa-50773048bf0d
SourceServer                    : RESEARCHDC.RESEARCH.MYCOMPANY.LOCAL
DestinationServer               : Pluto.MYCOMPANY.LOCAL
Enabled                         : True
TransportType                   : Rpc
GeneratedByKcc                  : True
ReciprocalReplicationEnabled    : False
ChangeNotificationStatus        : IntraSiteOnly
DataCompressionEnabled          : True
ReplicationScheduleOwnedByUser  : False
ReplicationSpan                 : IntraSite
ReplicationSchedule             : System.DirectoryServices.ActiveDirectory.
ActiveDirectorySchedule

Name                            : 82c213ca-ad85-4abb-96d4-f9861052b31c
SourceServer                    : MYCOMPANY-DC01.MYCOMPANY.LOCAL
DestinationServer               : Pluto.MYCOMPANY.LOCAL
Enabled                         : True
TransportType                   : Rpc
```

```
GeneratedByKcc                   : True
ReciprocalReplicationEnabled     : False
ChangeNotificationStatus         : IntraSiteOnly
DataCompressionEnabled           : True
ReplicationScheduleOwnedByUser : False
ReplicationSpan                  : IntraSite
ReplicationSchedule              : System.DirectoryServices.ActiveDirectory.ActiveDirectorySchedule
```

Each connection has a **ReplicationSchedule** property, which is an ActiveDirectorySchedule object. Let's look at the first one:

```
PS C:\> $pluto.inboundconnections[0].replicationschedule

RawSchedule
-----------
{True, False, False, False...}
```

What in the world is that? Turns out information is stored in a three-dimensional array. The first bit indicates the day of the week, the second bit is the hour (from 0 to 23), and the last bit indicates which 15 minute interval. Here's a specific value:

```
PS C:\> $pluto.inboundconnections[0].replicationschedule.rawSchedule[1,2,0]
True
```

This "decodes" as Monday during the first 15 minute interval during the 2:00 AM hour. The time value reflects coordinated Universal time. To help, I wrote a function called **ConvertFrom-ADRawSchedule**:

ConvertFrom-ADRawSchedule.ps1

```
Function ConvertFrom-ADRawSchedule {

[cmdletBinding()]

Param(
[Parameter(Position=0,Mandatory=$True,
HelpMessage="pass in a raw array of boolean values")]
[boolean[,,]]$Raw
)

Write-Verbose "Added $($raw.count) values"
    #process each day
    for ($d=0;$d -lt 7;$d++)
    {
        Write-Verbose "Evaluating day value $d"
        #process each hour
        for ($h=0;$h -lt 24;$h++)
        {
            Write-Verbose "Evaluating hour value $h"
            #process each 15 minute interval
            for ($i=0;$i -lt 4;$i++)
            {
                Write-Verbose "Evaluating interval value $i"
                Write-Verbose "`$array[$d,$h,$i]"
                if ($raw[$d,$h,$i])
                {
                    Switch ($d)
                    {
```

```
                    0    { $day="Sunday"    }
                    1    { $day="Monday"    }
                    2    { $day="Tuesday"   }
                    3    { $day="Wednesday"}
                    4    { $day="Thursday" }
                    5    { $day="Friday"    }
                    6    { $day="Saturday" }
                } #close Switch $d

                Switch ($i)
                {
                    0 { $interval= "00"}
                    1 { $interval= "15"}
                    2 { $interval= "30"}
                    3 { $interval= "45"}
                } #close Switch $i

                Write-Output ("{0} {1}:{2}" -f $day,$h,$interval)
            } #close if $array
        } #close for $i
    } #close for $h
  } #close for $d
} #close function
```

The function takes the raw schedule data and uses a series of **For** loop and **Switch** constructs to run through all possible array combinations and return a message for each True expression. Once the function is loaded into your PowerShell session, here's one way you might use it. Output has been truncated:

```
PS C:\> $pluto.inboundconnections | Foreach {
>> Write $_.SourceServer; ConvertFrom-ADRawSchedule $_.ReplicationSchedule.RawSchedule
>> }
>>
RESEARCHDC.RESEARCH.MYCOMPANY.LOCAL
Sunday 0:00
Sunday 1:00
Sunday 2:00
Sunday 3:00
...
MYCOMPANY-DC01.MYCOMPANY.LOCAL
Sunday 0:00
Sunday 1:00
Sunday 2:00
Sunday 3:00
...
```

Starting Replication

There are a few methods you can use to start the replication process.

Trigger Replication

You can use the **TriggerSyncReplicaFromNeighbors()** method to instruct a server's replication partner for a given partition to begin replicating:

```
PS C:\> $pluto.TriggerSyncReplicaFromNeighbors("dc=mycompany,dc=local")
```

Or, use an expression like this to trigger replication for all partitions:

```
PS C:\> $pluto.partitions | Foreach {$pluto.TriggerSyncReplicaFromNeighbors($_)}
```

Synch Replication

To force a complete synchronization, use the **SyncReplicaFromServer()** method. Again, you have to specify a partition, plus the name of a domain controller:

```
PS C:\> $pluto.SyncReplicaFromserver("dc=mycompany,dc=local","mycompany-dc01")
```

This method has another syntax variation that allows you to specify one or more options to control the synchronization process, such as whether to cross site boundaries or skip checking the replication partner. These options are listed in Table 13-1.

Table 13-1 SyncFromAllServers Options

Option	Description
None	No synchronization options.
AbortIfServerUnavailable	Aborts if the server is unreachable.
SyncAdjacentServerOnly	No transitive replication.
CheckServerAlivenessOnly	No synchronization. The replication topology is checked to identify what servers are available or not.
SkipInitialCheck	Assume that all servers are responding.
PushChangeOutward	Pushes changes to all replication partners using transitive replication.
CrossSite	Synchronizes across site boundaries. Make sure you understand the implications of using this option.

You need to create an ActiveDirectory.SyncFromAllServersOptions object like this:

```
PS C:\> $options=[System.DirectoryServices.ActiveDirectory.SyncFromAllServersOptions]::`
>> "SkipInitialCheck","PushChangeOutward",
```

The $options variable contains two values, which you can use like this:

```
PS C:\> $pluto.SyncReplicaFromAllServers("dc=mycompany,dc=local",$options)
```

Since I don't have to specify a domain controller, the server will handle its own connections based on the specified options.

Replication Connections

Use the **InboundConnections** and **OutboundConnections** properties to examine a domain controller's replication partners:

```
PS C:\> $pluto.InboundConnections


Name                            : 8b848491-eb11-4e23-bc5e-0ea35c0864b8
SourceServer                    : MYCOMPANY-DC01.MYCOMPANY.LOCAL
DestinationServer               : Pluto.MYCOMPANY.LOCAL
Enabled                         : True
TransportType                   : Rpc
GeneratedByKcc                  : True
ReciprocalReplicationEnabled    : False
ChangeNotificationStatus        : IntraSiteOnly
DataCompressionEnabled          : True
ReplicationScheduleOwnedByUser  : False
ReplicationSpan                 : InterSite
ReplicationSchedule             : System.DirectoryServices.ActiveDirectory.
ActiveDirectorySchedule


PS C:\> $pluto.OutboundConnections


Name                            : 3067a7b0-de54-4d91-9884-90bbecaa13fa
SourceServer                    : Pluto.mycompany.local
DestinationServer               : MYCOMPANY-DC01.MYCOMPANY.LOCAL
Enabled                         : True
TransportType                   : Rpc
GeneratedByKcc                  : True
ReciprocalReplicationEnabled    : False
ChangeNotificationStatus        : IntraSiteOnly
DataCompressionEnabled          : True
ReplicationScheduleOwnedByUser  : False
ReplicationSpan                 : IntraSite
ReplicationSchedule             : System.DirectoryServices.ActiveDirectory.
ActiveDirectorySchedule
```

As you can see from the **GeneratedByKCC** property, these connections were created by the Knowledge Consistency Checker (KCC).

Monitoring Replication

Monitoring a replication operation is not necessarily tricky, but you do need to be quick. Unless you have a lot of data to replicate, replication may finish before you can execute a monitoring command. If you know that replication is underway, you can use the **GetReplicationOperationInformation()** method:

```
PS C:\> $pluto.GetReplicationOperationInformation() | ForEach {$_.currentoperation}


TimeEnqueued    : 10/22/2010 12:08:16 PM
OperationNumber : 3610
Priority        : 330
OperationType   : Sync
PartitionName   : CN=Configuration,DC=mycompany,DC=local
SourceServer    : MYCOMPANY-DC01.MYCOMPANY.LOCAL
```

This will return a collection of ReplicationOperationInformation objects, which you can enumerate with the **ForEach-Object** construct. You can look at the **CurrentOperation** property as I do in this example, or the **PendingOperations** property.

Replication Failures

The easiest way to track replication errors is with an expression like this:

```
PS C:\> $pluto.GetAllReplicationNeighbors() |
>> Select PartitionName,Last*,SourceServer,ConsecutiveFailureCount
>>

PartitionName           : DC=MYCOMPANY,DC=LOCAL
LastSuccessfulSync      : 10/22/2010 12:12:52 PM
LastAttemptedSync       : 10/22/2010 12:12:52 PM
LastSyncResult          : 0
LastSyncMessage         : The operation completed successfully.
SourceServer            : MYCOMPANY-DC01.MYCOMPANY.LOCAL
ConsecutiveFailureCount : 0

PartitionName           : CN=Configuration,DC=MYCOMPANY,DC=LOCAL
LastSuccessfulSync      : 10/22/2010 12:01:11 PM
LastAttemptedSync       : 10/22/2010 12:01:11 PM
LastSyncResult          : 0
LastSyncMessage         : The operation completed successfully.

SourceServer            : RESEARCHDC.RESEARCH.MYCOMPANY.LOCAL
ConsecutiveFailureCount : 0

PartitionName           : CN=Configuration,DC=MYCOMPANY,DC=LOCAL
LastSuccessfulSync      : 10/22/2010 12:12:52 PM
LastAttemptedSync       : 10/22/2010 12:12:52 PM
LastSyncResult          : 0
LastSyncMessage         : The operation completed successfully.
SourceServer            : MYCOMPANY-DC01.MYCOMPANY.LOCAL
ConsecutiveFailureCount : 0
...
```

Generally, the **LastSyncMessage** property should give you enough information to troubleshoot any problems. If you are only concerned about a particular zone, then use the **GetReplicationNeighbors()** method:

```
PS C:\> $pluto.GetReplicationNeighbors("dc=mycompany,dc=local") |
>> Select PartitionName,Last*,SourceServer,ConsecutiveFailureCount
```

You'll get the same information, but only for the specified partition.

Other Tasks

There are several other replication-related tasks you might like to do in PowerShell, such as setting up new replication connections, or managing the replication schedule. However, the .NET classes responsible for these tasks don't lend themselves very well to PowerShell scripting. I suggest you wait until someone releases a set of cmdlets for these tasks.

Appendix A
Managing Local Users and Groups

As of this writing, I have yet to find a cmdlet set for managing local user and group accounts—despite the fact that this is an essential Windows administrative task. The majority of PowerShell's functionality and most cmdlets for managing directory services rely on the .NET Framework. Unfortunately, this framework has some limitations when it comes to local account management. In this appendix, I will demonstrate a variety of techniques for managing local users and groups. Most of my examples require that you are already running PowerShell with local administrator credentials.

Creating Accounts

The easiest way to create a new local user account is to use the ADSI type adapter and the WinNT ADSI provider. The ADSI type adapter creates an underlying System.DirectoryServices.DirectoryEntry object. Unfortunately, when used with local user accounts, there isn't a provision for alternate credentials. You must run the command under an account that has administrative credentials on any machine you are connecting to. This approach also requires RPC connectivity between your machine and any remote computer. However, you could run the commands "locally" via WinRM and a remote session.

The first step is to connect to the computer (either server or desktop):

```
PS C:\> [ADSI]$Server="WinNT://Server01"
```

You can pipe $Server to the **Get-Member** cmdlet and see some of the properties, but you won't see any methods.

Case Counts

The WinNT ADSI provider is case sensitive and must be specified exactly as in the examples shown.

However, you can still use the **Create()** method to create a local user object called jsmith:

```
PS C:\> $NewUser=$Server.Create("user","jsmith")
```

Once the local account is created, you can set a password for the account:

```
PS C:\> $NewUser.SetPassword("P@ssw0rd")
```

At this point, all that is left is to commit the change to the SAMAccount database on Server01 by calling the **SetInfo()** method:

```
PS C:\> $NewUser.setinfo()
```

Remember that with ADSI, the object isn't written to the directory service (in this case the SAMAccount database) until you call the **SetInfo()** method. With four lines of PowerShell code you've created a new local user account called jsmith on Server01. These commands create a very basic local user account. The .NET Framework System.DirectoryServices.DirectoryEntry offers a few more properties you can specify when creating a new account, as shown below using the **Put()** method:

```
PS C:\> [ADSI]$Server="WinNT://Server01"
PS C:\> $TempUser=$server.Create("user","tmpUser")
PS C:\> $TempUser.SetPassword("P@ssw0rd")
PS C:\> $TempUser.SetInfo()
PS C:\> $TempUser.put("Description","Temporary Local User Account")
PS C:\> $TempUser.put("FullName","Temporary User")
PS C:\> $TempUser.put("AccountExpirationDate","12/31/2011" -as [datetime])
PS C:\> $TempUser.SetInfo()
```

In some cases you can simply assign a value to a property, but not for every property. Using the **Put()** method appears to be the most consistent approach. In the above example, you can see how to create a temporary user account on SERVER01 that expires at the end of 2011. Note that depending on your PowerShell culture you may need to edit the date time string, e.g., 31/12/2011, in order to get this code to work.

Typing each command is likely to be tedious so wrapping this functionality into a function will make life easier:

New-LocalUser.ps1

```
Function New-LocalUser {

[cmdletbinding(SupportsShouldProcess=$True)]

    Param(
        [Parameter(Position=0,ValueFromPipeline=$True)]
        [ValidateScript({Test-Connection $_})]
        [string]$computername=$env:computername,
```

```
    [Parameter(Position=1,ValueFromPipeline=$False,
    Mandatory=$True)]
    [ValidateNotNullOrEmpty()]
    [string]$Username,

    [string]$Password="P@ssw0rd",
    [string]$Description,
    [string]$FullName,
    [datetime]$Expires,
    [string]$HomeDir,
    [string]$Profile,
    [string]$HomeDirDrive,
    [switch]$PasswordNeverExpires,
    [switch]$Disabled,
    [switch]$ForcePasswordChange,
    [switch]$NoPasswordChangeAllowed
)

Begin {
 Write-Verbose "Defining ADSI constants"
 New-Variable ADS_UF_ACCOUNTDISABLE 0x0002 -Option Constant
 New-Variable ADS_UF_PASSWD_CANT_CHANGE 0x0040 -Option Constant
 New-Variable ADS_UF_DONT_EXPIRE_PASSWD 0x10000 -Option Constant
}

Process {

  Try {

    if ($pscmdlet.ShouldProcess("\\$computername\$username")) {
      Write-Verbose "Connecting to $computername"
      [ADSI]$Server="WinNT://$computername"

      Write-Verbose "Creatingt $username"
      $NewUser=$server.Create("user",$Username)

      Write-Verbose "Setting password $password"
      $NewUser.SetPassword($password)
      $NewUser.SetInfo()

      Write-Verbose "Defining additional properties"
    if ($Description) {
        write-verbose "Description: $description"
        $NewUser.put("Description",$Description)
        }

    if ($FullName) {
        Write-Verbose "Fullname: $fullname"
        $NewUser.put("FullName",$FullName)
        }
    if ($Profile) {
        Write-Verbose "Profile: $Profile"
        $NewUser.put("Profile",$Profile)
        }

    if ($HomeDir) {
        Write-Verbose "HomeDir: $HomeDir"
        $NewUser.put("HomeDirectory",$HomeDir)
        }

    if ($HomeDirDrive) {
        Write-Verbose "HomeDirDrive: $HomeDirDrive"
```

```
            $NewUser.put("HomeDirDrive",$HomeDirDrive)
            }

        if ($Expires) {
            Write-Verbose "Expires: True"
            $NewUser.put("AccountExpirationDate",$Expires)
             }

        if ($Disabled) {
            write-verbose "Disabled: True"
            #property is technically collection
            $value=$NewUser.userflags.value -bor $ADS_UF_ACCOUNTDISABLE
            $NewUser.put("userflags",$value)
            }

        if ($PasswordNeverExpires) {
            Write-Verbose "Password Never Expires: True"
            $value=$NewUser.userflags.value -bor $ADS_UF_DONT_EXPIRE_PASSWD
            $NewUser.put("userflags",$value)
            }

        if ($ForcePasswordChange) {
            Write-Verbose "Force Password Change: True"
            $NewUser.put("PasswordExpired",1)
            }

        if ($NoPasswordChangeAllowed) {
            Write-Verbose "User Can't Change Password: True"
            $value=$NewUser.userflags.value -bor $ADS_UF_PASSWD_CANT_CHANGE
            $NewUser.put("userflags",$value)
            }

          #commit all changes

            write-verbose "Committing new user"
            $NewUser.SetInfo()
            #write new user account to the pipeline
            $newUser
        } #end if should process
      } #close Try
      Catch {
            write-warning "There was a problem creating the account."
            write-Warning $error[0].Exception.Message
       } #close Catch
    } #close process

    End {
        Write-Verbose "Finished!"
    }
} #end function
```

This **New-LocalUser** function can create a local user account, in addition to defining some frequently used properties.

The **New-LocalUser** function's parameters may look extensive, but you probably won't need to use all of them. In the example below, I've set a default value for the server name and a default password. The only required parameter is a user name and if you don't specify one, then the function will throw an error.

This function allows you to change the user account control flags, which configure the account for such things as non-expiring passwords or removing the ability for the user to change the password.

In order to set these flags, you need to do a binary OR operation with the user flag and the value of the appropriate setting. These commands from the script define some constants available that you'll use:

```
New-Variable ADS_UF_ACCOUNTDISABLE 0x0002 -Option Constant
New-Variable ADS_UF_PASSWD_CANT_CHANGE 0x0040 -Option Constant
New-Variable ADS_UF_DONT_EXPIRE_PASSWD 0x10000 -Option Constant
```

If you want to restrict the user from being able to change their password, then specify the $NoPasswordChangeAllowed. The **New-LocalUser** function is written that if $NoPasswordChangeAllowed is specified, then update the user flag property with a new value that is a binary OR (-bor) of the current user flag value and the corresponding constant value:

```
if ($NoPasswordChangeAllowed) {
        Write-Verbose "User Can't Change Password: True"
        $value=$NewUser.userflags.value -bor $ADS_UF_PASSWD_CANT_CHANGE
        $NewUser.put("userflags",$value)
        }
```

I use this same technique with a few other user flag options in the script. The example below shows how easy the **New-LocalUser** function is to use:

```
PS C:\> new-localuser -username rgbiv


distinguishedName :
Path              : WinNT://JDHLAB/CLIENT1/rgbiv
```

A new local account called rgbiv is created on the local computer with a default password of "P@ssw0rd". The function writes the new ADSI user object to the pipeline. The remaining parameters are completely optional and should be self-explanatory. Otherwise, because this is an advanced function, you can use help once the function is loaded into your shell:

```
PS C:\> help new-localuser

NAME
    New-LocalUser

SYNOPSIS
    Create a local user account


SYNTAX
    New-LocalUser [[-computername] <String>] [-Username] <String> [-Password <String>]
[-Description <String>] [-FullName <String>] [-Expires <DateTime>] [-HomeDir <String>]
[-Profile <String>] [-HomeDirDrive <String>] [-PasswordNeverExpires] [-Disabled]
[-ForcePasswordChange]
[-NoPasswordChangeAllowed] [-WhatIf] [-Confirm] [<CommonParameters>]


DESCRIPTION
    Create a local user account on a specified computer. The account
    is enabled by default but you create it disabled using -Disabled.
    You can configure other settings as well by specifying the corresponding
    parameters.
```

```
RELATED LINKS

REMARKS
    To see the examples, type: "get-help New-LocalUser -examples".
    For more information, type: "get-help New-LocalUser -detailed".
    For technical information, type: "get-help New-LocalUser -full".
```

If you need to create a local account on a remote computer that will expire 90 days from now, the example below shows how you might use the **New-LocalUser** function:

```
PS C:\> new-localuser -computer "SERVER01" -user "Temp23" -description "Temporary Account" `
>> -expires (get-date).AddDays(90) -NoPasswordChangeAllowed -Password "AzC123*()"
>>


distinguishedName :
Path              : WinNT://JDHLAB/SERVER01/Temp23
```

What About...

You may be wondering about using Windows Management Instrumentation (WMI). Unfortunately, even though you can manage existing local user accounts, there is no provision for using WMI to create them. If you are familiar with the .NET Framework, then you may be wondering about the System.DirectoryServices.AccountManagement class. While it is possible to create PowerShell scripts and functions to create and manage local users and groups, I find the scripting to be too much like systems programming. The .NET classes I'm demonstrating here are similar enough to the ADSI scripting you might be familiar with from VBScript, which I felt was more appropriate for a Windows administrator.

One last thing about the **New-LocalUser** function that I hope you'll find useful is that it supports the **–WhatIf** parameter:

```
PS C:\> new-localuser -username LocalTest -Description "Local Testing Account" -whatif
What if: Performing operation "New Variable" on Target "Name: ADS_UF_ACCOUNTDISABLE Value:
0x0002".
What if: Performing operation "New Variable" on Target "Name: ADS_UF_PASSWD_CANT_CHANGE Value:
0x0040".
What if: Performing operation "New Variable" on Target "Name: ADS_UF_DONT_EXPIRE_PASSWD Value:
0x10000".
What if: Performing operation "New-LocalUser" on Target "\\CLIENT1\LocalTest".
```

I'll show you how to add the user to a local group a bit later in the appendix.

Defining Account Properties

Modifying an existing local user is almost as easy as creating one. You still use the [ADSI] type adapter to connect to the user object. The following example shows how to connect to the local computer and check an account. You can either use localhost or the actual computer name in this example. I recommend using an actualcomputer name as opposed to a generic placeholder.. Using $env:computername will get the local computer name from the %computername% environment variable:

```
PS C:\> [ADSI]$me="WinNT://$env:computername/Jeff,user"
PS C:\> $me | Select *


UserFlags                  : {66081}
MaxStorage                 : {-1}
PasswordAge                : {1389389}
PasswordExpired            : {0}
LoginHours                 : {255 255 255 255 255 255 255 255 255 255 255 255 255 255 255 255 2...
FullName                   : {}
Description                : {}
BadPasswordAttempts        : {0}
LastLogin                  : {6/28/2010 7:10:22 AM}
HomeDirectory              : {}
LoginScript                : {}
Profile                    : {}
HomeDirDrive               : {}
Parameters                 : {}
PrimaryGroupID             : {513}
Name                       : {Jeff}
MinPasswordLength          : {0}
MaxPasswordAge             : {3628800}
MinPasswordAge             : {0}
PasswordHistoryLength      : {0}
AutoUnlockInterval         : {1800}
LockoutObservationInterval : {1800}
MaxBadPasswordsAllowed     : {0}
objectSid                  : {1 5 0 0 0 0 0 5 21 0 0 0 152 73 103 170 26 224 246 218 202 40 88 ...
AuthenticationType         : Secure
Children                   : {}
Guid                       : {D83F1060-1E71-11CF-B1F3-02608C9E7553}
ObjectSecurity             :
NativeGuid                 : {D83F1060-1E71-11CF-B1F3-02608C9E7553}
NativeObject               : System.__ComObject
Parent                     : WinNT://WORKGROUP/SERENITY
Password                   :
Path                       : WinNT://SERENITY/Jeff,user
Properties                 : {UserFlags, MaxStorage, PasswordAge, PasswordExpired...}
SchemaClassName            : User
SchemaEntry                : System.DirectoryServices.DirectoryEntry
UsePropertyCache           : True
Username                   :
Options                    :
Site                       :
Container                  :
```

User or Group

As you read, you'll notice that when I specify an ADSI object using the WinNT provider, I'm also adding User or Group to the end. This is not required and 9.5 times out of 10, you can use an expression like this with no error: $group.Add("WinNT://Win7-Desk09/Test"). However, what if there is a group and a user called Test? How can you be sure which one will be added? Specifying the object type, as shown in the examples, removes any doubt and eliminates errors. So while it is not required, it is considered a best practice with ADSI and you should follow it whenever possible.

Suppose you want to change the description property. Use the **Put()** method and save the change:

```
PS C:\> $me.put("Description","Local Admin User")
PS C:\> $me.SetInfo()
```

Remember, you need to call the **SetInfo()** method to commit the change to the local directory service. You can verify the change by refreshing the ADSI object and looking at the new description property:

```
PS C:\> $me.refreshcache()
PS C:\> $me.description
Local Admin User
PS C:\>
```

You should be able to change most properties this way.

The following sections show how you might accomplish a few other common tasks.

Force Password Change

Setting a local user account to force a password change is accomplished by setting the PasswordExpired property to 1:

```
PS C:\> [ADSI]$roy="WinNT://File02/rgbiv,user"
PS C:\> $roy.passwordexpired
0
PS C:\> $roy.Put("passwordexpired",1)
PS C:\> $roy.SetInfo()
PS C:\> $roy.refreshCache()
PS C:\> $roy.passwordexpired
1
PS C:\>
```

The above example connected the local user account rgbiv on File02. The current value of the PasswordExpired property is 0. If you change it to 1, commit the changes and refresh the object. Now that the value is 1, the user is forced to change their password at the next logon.

Disable or Enable an Account

To disable an account, you need to modify the user account control flag and perform a binary OR with the account disabled flag value:

```
PS C:\>  New-Variable ADS_UF_ACCOUNTDISABLE 0x0002 -Option Constant
PS C:\> $roy.userflags.value
8389121
PS C:\> If ($roy.userflags.value -band $ADS_UF_ACCOUNTDISABLE) {
>> "account is disabled"} else {
>> "account is enabled"}
>>
account is enabled
PS C:\> #now I'll disable the account
PS C:\> $roy.userflags.value=$roy.userflags.value -bor $ADS_UF_ACCOUNTDISABLE
PS C:\> $roy.SetInfo()
PS C:\> $roy.refreshcache()
PS C:\> $roy.userflags.value
8389123
PS C:\> If ($roy.userflags.value -band $ADS_UF_ACCOUNTDISABLE) {
>> "account is disabled"} else {
```

```
>> "account is enabled"}
>>
account is disabled
PS C:\>
```

If the result of the binary AND operation of the user account control flag and the account disabled flag value is TRUE, then the account is already disabled:

```
PS C:\> If ($roy.userflags.value -band $ADS_UF_ACCOUNTDISABLE) {
>> "account is disabled"} else {
>> "account is enabled"}
>>
account is enabled
```

Since the account in the example above is already enabled, you can update the userflags value with the result of a binary OR operation:

```
PS C:\> $roy.userflags.value=$roy.userflags.value -bor $ADS_UF_ACCOUNTDISABLE
```

To enable a disabled account is almost the same operation, except you need to use a binary XOR operator:

```
PS C:\> $roy.userflags.value=$roy.userflags.value -bxor $ADS_UF_ACCOUNTDISABLE
PS C:\> $roy.SetInfo()
PS C:\> $roy.refreshcache()
PS C:\> If ($roy.userflags.value -band $ADS_UF_ACCOUNTDISABLE) {
>> "account is disabled"} else {
>> "account is enabled"}
>>

account is enabled
PS C:\>
```

You can use the same technique with other user account control flag settings. Table Appendix-A lists the most common user flag constants and their values:

Appendix-A User Account Control Flags

Flag Constant	Flag Value (Hex)	Flag Value (Integer)
ADS_UF_SCRIPT	0x0001	1
ADS_UF_ACCOUNTDISABLE	0x0002	2
ADS_UF_HOMEDIR_REQUIRED	0x0008	8
ADS_UF_LOCKOUT	0x0010	16
ADS_UF_PASSWD_NOTREQD	0x0020	32
ADS_UF_PASSWD_CANT_CHANGE	0x0040	64
ADS_UF_ENCRYPTED_TEXT_PASSWORD_ALLOWED	0x0080	128
ADS_UF_DONT_EXPIRE_PASSWD	0x10000	65536
ADS_UF_SMARTCARD_REQUIRED	0x40000	262144
ADS_UF_PASSWD_EXPIRED	0x800000	8388608

Another way to disable or enable an account is to use WMI and the **Get-Wmiobject** cmdlet. This approach allows you specify alternate credentials:

```
PS C:\> $wmibiv=get-wmiobject win32_useraccount -filter "name='rgbiv'" -computer "FILE07" `
>> -credential mydomain\administrator
>>

PS C:\> $wmibiv.disabled
False
PS C:\> $wmibiv.disabled=$True
PS C:\> $wmibiv.put() | Out-Null
```

You can connect to server FILE07 and retrieve an instance of the Win32_UserAccount class where the name is rgbiv using the alternate credentials mydomain\administrator. You can see the account is currently not disabled. Go ahead and set this Boolean property to $True:

```
PS C:\> $wmibiv.disabled=$True
```

At this point, all you've done is update the $wmibiv object. To make the change on FILE07, call the **Put()** method, which will update the remote object. Now the account is disabled.

Modifying Account Expiration

You can configure a local user account to expire on a certain date by setting the AccountExpirationDate property. The only detail is that you need to specify a [DateTime] object:

```
PS C:\> $roy.AccountExpirationDate
MemberType          : Method
OverloadDefinitions :
TypeNameOfValue     : System.Management.Automation.PSMethod
Value               :
Name                : accountexpirationdate
IsInstance          : True
```

Currently this account never expires, which is why there is no value for "AccountExpirationDate", other than the funky method definition, which you can ignore. However, this is easily changed:

```
PS C:\> [datetime]$expires="12/31/2012"
PS C:\> $roy.put("AccountExpirationDate",$expires)
PS C:\> $roy.setinfo()
PS C:\> $roy.refreshcache()
PS C:\> $roy.AccountExpirationDate

Monday, December 31, 2012 12:00:00 AM
```

Get the User's SID

The easiest approach to retrieving a local user account SID is to use WMI:

```
PS C:\> (get-wmiobject win32_useraccount -filter "name='jeff'").SID
S-1-5-21-1877886752-145991758-313192069-1000
```

One important item to take note with this class is that without any filtering, it will return all domain accounts as well. So if you wanted a SID report of all local user accounts you would need something like this:

```
PS C:\> get-wmiobject win32_useraccount -filter "domain='$env:computername'" |
>> Select Caption,Name,SID
>>

Caption                Name          SID
-------                ----          ---
CLIENT1\Administrator Administrator S-1-5-21-4228342518-2946215861-1035086974-500
CLIENT1\Guest          Guest         S-1-5-21-4228342518-2946215861-1035086974-501
CLIENT1\HelpDesk       HelpDesk      S-1-5-21-4228342518-2946215861-1035086974-1002
CLIENT1\joe            joe           S-1-5-21-4228342518-2946215861-1035086974-1003
CLIENT1\LocalAdmin     LocalAdmin    S-1-5-21-4228342518-2946215861-1035086974-1000
CLIENT1\rgbiv          rgbiv         S-1-5-21-4228342518-2946215861-1035086974-1004
```

If you connect to a remote computer, adjust your filter accordingly.

Get Password Age

The **PasswordAge** property is the number of seconds elapsed since the password was last changed. Use ADSI to get this value and divide it by 86400 to get a value in days:

```
PS C:\> [ADSI]$user="WinNT://CLIENT01/HelpDesk,user"
PS C:\> $user.passwordage
12206223
PS C:\> ($user.passwordage).value/84600
141.275729166667
```

Because the password age is part of a property set, you need to use the **Value** property when you attempt to divide by 86400. The local account, HelpDesk on CLIENT01, last set a password over 141 days ago, as shown in the example. If you prefer a cleaner result, you can force the result as an integer:

```
PS C:\>($user.passwordage).value/86400 -as [int]
141
```

Change Password

Modifying the local user password is very easy:

```
PS C:\> [ADSI]$user="WinNT://FILE01/luser,user"
PS C:\> $user.setpassword("P@ssw0rd")
```

The change takes effect immediately without having to call the **SetInfo()** method.

Listing Local Group Membership

The .NET Framework shows some of its limitations here. While there is **MemberOf** property that works for domain user accounts, it does not work with local user accounts. To accomplish this for a local account, you need to evaluate all the local groups on the server and check for group membership of the specified user. Use my **Get-LocalGroupMembership** function to simplify this task:

Get-LocalGroupMembership.ps1

```
Function Get-LocalGroupMembership {
<#
.Synopsis
Display local group membership
.Description
List all the local groups that a user belongs to on a given
computer.
.Parameter Username
The name of a local user account.
.Parameter Computername
The name of the computer. The default is the localhost.
.Example
PS C:\> get-localmembership "rgbiv"
.Example
PS C:\> get-localmembership -user "jeff" -computer "CLIENT1"
.Inputs
None
.Outputs
Collection of strings representing local group names.
#>

[cmdletBinding()]
    Param(
        [Parameter(Position=0,Mandatory=$True,
        HelpMessage="Enter a local account name.")]
        [ValidateNotNullorEmpty()]
        [string]$username=$(Throw "You must enter a user name"),
        [string]$computername=$env:computername
    )
    Try {
        Write-Verbose "Checking group membership for WinNT://$computername/$Username,user"
        [ADSI]$LocalUser="WinNT://$computername/$Username,user"

        Write-Verbose "Processing groups"
        $groups=$Localuser.invoke("Groups") | ForEach-Object {
         $_.GetType().InvokeMember("Name", 'GetProperty', `
         $null, $_, $null)
        }
    } #close try
    Catch {
        Write-Warning "An error occurred getting group membership for $username on
$computername"
        Write-Warning $error[0].Exception.Message
        Break
    }

    #write result to pipeline
    write $groups
    Write-Verbose "Finished!"
} #end function
```

Assuming the function is loaded, here's how you might use it:

```
PS T:\>  get-localgroupmembership -username "HelpDesk" -computername "Client1"
Administrators
Users
```

With a single command you've identified the local groups that the account HelpDesk on Client1 belongs to. The function works by first connecting to the specified user on the specified computer:

```
[ADSI]$LocalUser="WinNT://$computer/$username,user"
```

There is a **Groups()** method, but you have to access the underlying psbase object to get to what you need:

```
$groups=$LocalUser.invoke("Groups") | ForEach-Object {
$_.GetType().InvokeMember("Name", 'GetProperty', $null, $_, $null)
}
```

The difficult part is getting the result of the **Groups()** method using the **Invoke()** method:

```
$LocalUser.invoke("Groups")
```

By itself, this doesn't return anything you can directly use. The result of the Invoke ("Groups") expression returns COM objects. Therefore, you need to pipe the results to a **ForEach-Object** cmdlet:

```
    $_.GetType().InvokeMember("Name", 'GetProperty', $null, $_, $null)}
```

This cmdlet will get the Name property by calling the **InvokeMember()** method, thus returning the name of each local group the user belongs to.

Modifying Local Group Membership

I will cover working with local groups shortly. However, you can use my **Add-UserToLocalGroup** function to add a local user to a local group. Membership is configured from the group perspective, not the user, as shown below:

Add-UserToLocalGroup.ps1

```
Function Add-UserLocalGroup {
<#
.Synopsis
Add a local user to a local group
.Description
Add a local user account to the specified local group on the
specified computer. The default computer is the local host.
computer.
.Parameter Group
The name of a local group on a member server.
.Parameter Username
The name of a local user account.
.Parameter Computername
The name of the computer. The default is the localhost.
.Example
PS C:\> add-usertolocalgroup "local administrators" "server01\rgbiv" "server01"
.Example
PS C:\> add-UserToLocalGroup -group "Power Users" -user "Jeff"

.Inputs
None
.Outputs
None
#>
```

```
[cmdletBinding(SupportsShouldProcess=$True)]

    Param(
        [Parameter(Position=0,Mandatory=$True,
        HelpMessage="Enter the name of a local group." )]
        [ValidateNotNullorEmpty()]
        [string]$group,
        [Parameter(Position=1,Mandatory=$True,
        HelpMessage="Enter the name of a local user account." )]
        [ValidateNotNullorEmpty()]
        [string]$username,
        [Parameter(Position=2,Mandatory=$False)]
        [string]$computername=$env:computername
        )

    Try {
        Write-Verbose "Connecting to WinNT://$computername/$group,group"
        if ($pscmdlet.ShouldProcess("\\$computername\$group")) {
            [ADSI]$LocalGroup="WinNT://$computername/$group,group"
            Write-Verbose "Adding WinNT://$username,user"
            $LocalGroup.Add("WinNT://$username,user")
            $LocalGroup.SetInfo()
        } #end if should process
    } #close Try

     Catch {
        Write-Warning "An error occurred setting group membership for $username on
$computername"
        Write-Warning $error[0].Exception.Message
        Break
    } #close Catch

    Write-Verbose "Finished!"
}
```

The function uses the [ADSI] type adapter for the specified group on the specified computer, and creates a directory entry object:

```
[ADSI]$LocalGroup="WinNT://$computername/$groupname,group"
```

To add a user to the group, call the **Add()** method passing the ADSI path of the user object:

```
$LocalGroup.Add("WinNT://$username,user")
```

Finally, call the **SetInfo()** method to commit the change:

```
$LocalGroup.SetInfo()
```

When you run this command:

```
PS C:\> Add-UserToLocalGroup -group "Administrators" -username "rgbiv"
```

The local user rgbiv will be added to the Administrators group on the local machine. You can also use this function to add a domain user to a local group. All you have to do is specify the user or group account as shown in the following example:

```
PS C:\> Add-UserToLocalGroup -group "Help Desk" -user "mycompany/HelpDeskTech"
```

Be sure to get your slash going the right way. In this example I've added the domain account HelpDeskTech from the MyCompany domain to the Help Desk group on the local computer.

Deleting Accounts

As you might expect, deleting a local user account is the opposite of creating a user account:

```
PS C:\> [ADSI]$server="WinNT://SERVER03"
PS C:\> $server.delete("user","TempAdmin")
```

You first must establish a reference to the parent object, in this case the computer SERVER03. To delete the local user TempAdmin, call the **Delete()** method. The action is immediate without any requirement for the **SetInfo()** method.

Managing the Masses

Often you need to work with multiple local user accounts, perhaps across multiple remote computers. This is where scripting and administrative automation come into play and let you go home at a decent hour. Even though you can work with PowerShell's console interactively to manage multiple local accounts or local accounts across a number of computers, you'll want to leverage the pipeline, user created functions, or scripts to do the really heavy lifting.

Creating and Deleting Accounts

If you need to create local user accounts on multiple computers, the best approach is to use ADSI:

```
PS C:\> $name="Tech"
PS C:\> $password="P@ssw0rd"
PS C:\> "Server1","Server2","Server3" | ForEach-Object {
>> [ADSI]$server="WinNT://$_"
>> $user=$server.Create("user",$name)
>> $user.SetPassword($password)
>> $user.SetInfo()
>> $user.Put("Description","Help Desk Support")
>> $user.SetInfo()
>> }
>>

PS C:\>
```

This code snippet connects to each server and creates a local user account called Tech for the help desk. You can easily set a few other properties as well. Remember that you have to call the **SetInfo()** method after creating the account before you can set any other properties. Or you might prefer to use the **New-LocalUser** function. Because it is an advanced function, it can accept pipelined input:

```
PS C:\> Get-Content "computers.txt" | new-localuser -Username "DevAdmin" `
>> -Description "Developer Account" -NoPasswordChangeAllowed -PasswordNeverExpires `
>> -Password "D3vP@$$246"
>>
```

```
distinguishedName :
Path              : WinNT://JDHLAB/CLIENT1/DevAdmin

distinguishedName :
Path              : WinNT://JDHLAB/MAIL/DevAdmin

...
```

This achieves essentially the same result as the first example, with a few more properties defined. Each computer name in the text file computers.txt is piped to the **New-LocalUser** function. The account DevAdmin is created on each computer with a non-expiring password that the user cannot change.

Do you need to delete a several accounts from several computers? Here's a simple solution that deletes the DevAdmin account you just created:

```
PS C:\> $username="DevAdmin"
PS C:\> Get-Content computers.txt | ForEach-Object {
>> [ADSI]$server="WinNT://$_"
>> $user=$server.delete("user",$username)
>> }
```

View All Local Accounts

Each user account is merely a child of the server ADSI object. Unfortunately, some user properties are buried in COM objects and it isn't intuitive to tease out this information. Lucky for you I've done all the hard work with this advanced **Get-LocalUserReport** function that will return all local user accounts for a specified computer:

Get-LocalUserReport.ps1

```
Function Get-LocalUserReport {

[cmdletBinding()]

    Param(
    [Parameter(Position=0,ValueFromPipeline=$True)]
    [ValidateNotNullorEmpty()]
    [ValidateScript({Test-Connection $_})]
    [string]$computername=$env:computername
    )

    Begin {
        write-verbose "Defining constants"
        New-Variable ADS_UF_ACCOUNTDISABLE 0x0002 -Option Constant
        New-Variable ADS_UF_PASSWD_CANT_CHANGE 0x0040 -Option Constant
        New-Variable ADS_UF_DONT_EXPIRE_PASSWD 0x10000 -Option Constant
    } #close begin

    Process {

        Try {
            Write-Verbose "Getting users from $computername"
            [ADSI]$server="WinNT://$computername"

            $users=$server.children | where {$_.schemaclassname -eq "user"}
        } #close Try
```

```
        Catch {
            Write-Warning "An error occurred setting group membership for $username on
$computername"
            Write-Warning $error[0].Exception.Message
            Break
        } #close Catch

        #continue if $users got defined
        if ($users) {
        $users | ForEach-Object {
        Write-Verbose "Processing $($_.name)"
            #password age in days
            [int]$pwdAge=$_.PasswordAge.value/86400

            if ($_.passwordexpired-eq 0) {
                $pwdExpired=$False
            }
            else {
                $pwdExpired=$True
            }

            if ($_.userflags.value -band $ADS_UF_ACCOUNTDISABLE) {
                $disabled=$True
             }
             else {
                $disabled=$False
             }

            if ($_.userflags.value -band $ADS_UF_DONT_EXPIRE_PASSWD) {
                $pwdNeverExpires=$True
             }
             else {
                $pwdNeverExpires=$False
             }

             if ($_.userflags.value -band $ADS_UF_PASSWD_CANT_CHANGE) {
                $pwdChangeAllowed=$False
             }
             else {
                $pwdChangeAllowed=$True
             }

            # Create a custom object
            New-Object -TypeName PSObject -Property @{
                "Computer" = $computername.ToUpper()
                "Name" = $_.name.value
                "FullName" = $_.fullname.value
                "Description" = $_.Description.value
                "AccountExpires" = $_.AccountExpirationDate.value
                "Disabled" = $disabled
                "PasswordAge" = $pwdage
                "PasswordExpired" = $pwdExpired
                "PasswordNeverExpires" = $pwdNeverExpires
                "PasswordChangeAllowed" = $pwdChangeAllowed
            } #property hash

         } #close ForEach
       } #if $users
     } #close Process

     End {
        Write-Verbose "Ending function"
     }
} #end function
```

The **Get-LocalUserReport** function uses the same ADSI techniques discussed earlier in this appendix for connecting to a server and managing user objects. This function writes a custom object with properties for each local user to the pipeline:

```
PS C:\> get-localuser


AccountExpires        :
FullName              :
PasswordNeverExpires  : True
Name                  : Administrator
Description           : Built-in account for administering the computer/domain
Disabled              : False
PasswordExpired       : True
PasswordAge           : 32
PasswordChangeAllowed : True
Computer              : CLIENT1

AccountExpires        :
FullName              :
PasswordNeverExpires  : True
Name                  : Guest
Description           : Built-in account for guest access to the computer/domain
Disabled              : True
PasswordExpired       : True
PasswordAge           : 0
PasswordChangeAllowed : False
Computer              : CLIENT1

AccountExpires        :
FullName              :
PasswordNeverExpires  : False
Name                  : HelpDesk
Description           : Helping Hands
Disabled              : False
PasswordExpired       : True
PasswordAge           : 32
PasswordChangeAllowed : True
Computer              : CLIENT1

AccountExpires        :
FullName              :
PasswordNeverExpires  : True
Name                  : LocalAdmin
Description           :
Disabled              : False
PasswordExpired       : True
PasswordAge           : 311
PasswordChangeAllowed : True
Computer              : CLIENT1

AccountExpires        : 6/28/2011 4:46:23 PM
FullName              : Roy G. Biv
PasswordNeverExpires  : False
Name                  : rgbiv
Description           :
Disabled              : False
PasswordExpired       : True
PasswordAge           : 0
PasswordChangeAllowed : True
Computer              : CLIENT1
```

Since the **Get-LocalUserReport** function accepts pipelined input and writes to the pipeline, you can run an expression like the one below:

```
PS C:\> Get-Content computers.txt | get-localuser | Where {-not ($_.Disabled)} |
>> Sort -property Computername,PasswordAge -descending |
>> Select -property Computer,Name,FullName,Description,AccountExpires,PasswordAge |
>> Export-CSV LocalUserReport.csv -NoTypeInformation
```

This expression goes through each computer in the text file, computers.txt. Each name is piped to the **Get-LocalUser** function returns all local user accounts. These objects are filtered by the **Where-Object** cmdlet to drop any disabled accounts. Each account object is sorted by its **computername** property, and then its **passwordage** property in descending order. The sorted objects are piped to the **Select-Object** cmdlet to grab a subset of properties. Finally everything is piped to the **Export-CSV** cmdlet to create a CSV file of the account name, fullname, description, account expiration date, and password age.

Suppose you want to check the password age of the local administrator account on a group of servers. If you have a list, this is as easy as using the code snippet below:

```
PS C:\> Get-Content "c:\servers.txt" | where {$_.length -gt 0} |
>> get-localuser | where {$_.name -eq "Administrator"}} |
>> Sort -property PasswordAge -descending | Format-Table Computer,Name,PasswordAge -autosize
>>

Computer   Name           PasswordAge
--------   ----           -----------
FILE01     Administrator          392
MAIL01     Administrator          258
PRINT01    Administrator           76
FILE02     Administrator           78
```

Changing Passwords

To change passwords in bulk, you can use the same technique as for creating accounts:

```
PS C:\> $username="administrator"
PS C:\> $password="AbC1@3DeF"
PS C:\> Get-Content c:\servers.txt | ForEach-Object {
>> [ADSI]$user="WinNT://$_/$username,user"
>> $user.SetPassword($password)
>> }
>>
PS C:\>
```

You connect to each user object and call the **SetPassword()** method with the new password. It's as easy as that. Although, if this is a recurring task using an advanced function like my **Set-LocalPassword** function is much easier:

Set-LocalPassword.ps1

```
Function Set-LocalPassword {

[cmdletBinding(SupportsShouldProcess=$True)]

Param(
```

```
        [Parameter(Position=0,ValueFromPipeline=$True,
        ValueFromPipelinebyPropertyName=$True)]
        [Alias("name")]
        [string]$computername=$env:computername,

        [Parameter(Position=1,HelpMessage="Enter the name of a local user account." )]
        [ValidateNotNullorEmpty()]
        [string]$username="Administrator",

        [Parameter(Position=2,Mandatory=$True,
        HelpMessage="Enter a new password")]
        [validateNotNullorEmpty()]
        [string]$password
        )

    Begin {
     Write-Verbose "Starting set password function."
     } #close Begin

     Process {
        #trim off $ from any computernames that might get piped in
         if ($computername.EndsWith("$")) {
            Write-Verbose "Trimming off trailing $"
            $computername=$computername.TrimEnd("$")
          }

        Try {
            Write-Verbose "Testing connection to $computername"
            if (-not (Test-Connection -ComputerName $computername -quiet)) {
                $Connected=$False
                Throw "Connection test failed to $computername"

            }
            else {
                $Connected=$True
            }
        } #close Try
        Catch {
            Write-Warning $error[0].Exception.Message
        } #close Catch

        #only continue if $Connected is true
        if ($Connected) {
            write-Verbose "Connecting to WinNT://$computername/$username"

            Try {
                [ADSI]$user="WinNT://$computername/$username"
                #verify you got an object
                if (-not $user.name) {
                    #if account not found throw an exception
                    Throw "Could not connect or find $username on $computername"
                }

                if ($pscmdlet.ShouldProcess("WinNT://$computername/$username")) {
                    write-verbose "Setting password"
                    $user.SetPassword($password)
                } #end ShouldProcess
            } #close Try

            Catch {
               Write-Warning "An error occurred seting a new password for
WinNT://$computername/$username "
                Write-Warning $error[0].Exception.Message
```

```
        }
    } #end if connected
  } #close Process

  End {
      Write-Verbose "Ending set password function."
  } #close End

} #end function
```

The **Set-LocalPassword** function defaults to the Administrator account on the local machine, so to set a new password all you need to do is specify it:

```
PS C:\> set-localpassword -password "$iM0nSay$"
```

The function is designed to take computer names as pipelined input. When the time comes to change the local administrator password on your member servers you can process a text list like this:

```
PS C:\> Get-Content computers.txt | set-localpassword -password "$iM0nSay$"
```

You can even combine this with AD cmdlets to get computers from organizational units or your domain:

```
PS C:\> Get-QADComputer -SearchRoot "OU=Servers,DC=jdhlab,DC=local" |
>> set-localpassword -password "P@$$w0rd1X3"
```

This will find all computer accounts in the Servers organizational unit and pipe each object to the **Set-LocalPassword** function. The **computername** parameter is configured to accept pipelined input. The computer object that the **Get-QADComputer** cmdlet from Quest Software writes to the pipeline includes a **computername** property, but that value is the computer's SAMAccountname which ends in a **$**. The **Set-LocalPassword** function strips that off if found. You can achieve similar results using the Microsoft **Get-ADComputer** cmdlet:

```
PS C:\> Get-ADComputer -filter * | Select name | set-localpassword -password "P@$$w0rd123"
```

To keep the pipeline simple and avoid using the **ForEach-Object** cmdlet, I pipe the results of the **Get-ADComputer** cmdlet to the **Select-Object** cmdlet since all I need is the name property.

Managing Local Groups

Working with local groups is very similar to working with local user accounts. Again, there are no cmdlets, but you can create your own tools with advanced functions that use the [ADSI] type adapter.

Creating Groups

The easiest approach to creating a new local group is like this:

```
PS C:\> [ADSI]$server="WinNT://$env:computername"
PS C:\> $newGroup=$server.Create("group","Local Admins")
PS C:\> $newGroup.SetInfo()
PS C:\> $newGroup.Description="users with local admin rights"
PS C:\> $newGroup.SetInfo()
```

In this example I've created a new local group called "Local Admins" on the local computer, but you could just as easily specify a remote computer name. In fact, you could very quickly create a new local group on many computers with a simple PowerShell expression:

```
$name="Local Admins"
Get-Content c:\servers.txt | ForEach-Object {
 [ADSI]$server="WinNT://$_"
 $newGroup=$server.Create("group",$name)
 $newGroup.SetInfo()
 $newgroup.Description="users with local admin rights"
 $newGroup.SetInfo()
}
```

Enumerating Groups

There are a few methods of enumerating local groups on a given server or desktop. Again, you rely on the [ADSI] type adapter:

```
PS C:\> [ADSI]$server="WinNT://$env:computername"
PS C:\> $server.children | where {$_.schemaclassname -eq "group"} |
>> Format-Table Name,Description -auto
>>

Name                                    Description
----                                    -----------
{Administrators}                        {Administrators have complete and unrestricted acc…
{Backup Operators}                      {Backup Operators can override security restricti…
{Cryptographic Operators}               {Members are authorized to perform cryptographic …
{Distributed COM Users}                 {Members are allowed to launch, activate and use Di…
{Event Log Readers}                     {Members of this group can read event logs from lo…
{Guests}                                {Guests have the same access as members of the Use…
{IIS_IUSRS}                             {Built-in group used by Internet Information Serv…
{Network Configuration Operators}       {Members in this group can have some administrativ…
{Performance Log Users}                 {Members of this group may schedule logging of pe…
{Performance Monitor Users}             {Members of this group can access performance coun…
{Power Users}                           {Power Users are included for backwards compatibil…
{Remote Desktop Users}                  {Members in this group are granted the right to l…
{Replicator}                            {Supports file replication in a domain}
{Users}                                 {Users are prevented from making accidental or in…
{Debugger Users}                        {Debugger Users are non administrators who are all…
{Demo Users}                            {ADSI Demo Users}
{Local Admins}                          {users with local admin rights}
{Test Users}                            {}
{__vmware__}                            {VMware User Group}
```

Each property you see in {} is technically a collection, which is OK to look at but doesn't work well if you wanted to do something else with this information such as export it to a CSV file. You need a slightly better approach. Additionally, you may want to inventory local groups on a number of computers. To meet these needs I came up with an advanced function, the **Get-LocalGroup** function, that will return a custom object with group information:

Get-LocalGroup.ps1

```
Function Get-LocalGroup {

[cmdletBinding()]

 Param(
        [Parameter(Position=0,ValueFromPipeline=$True,
        ValueFromPipelinebyPropertyName=$True)]
        [Alias("name")]
        [string]$computername=$env:computername,
        [Parameter(Position=1,ValueFromPipeline=$False)]
        [string]$group
        )

        Begin {
            Write-Verbose "Starting function"
        }
        Process {
             #trim off $ from any computernames that might get piped in
             if ($computername.EndsWith("$")) {
                Write-Verbose "Trimming off trailing $"
                $computername=$computername.TrimEnd("$")
              }

            Try {
                Write-Verbose "Testing connection to $computername"
                if (-not (Test-Connection -ComputerName $computername -quiet)) {
                    $Connected=$False
                    Throw "Connection test failed to $computername"
                }
                else {
                    $Connected=$True
                }
            } #close Try
            Catch {
                Write-Warning $error[0].Exception.Message
            } #close Catch

            if ($Connected) {
                write-Verbose "Connecting to WinNT://$computername"

             Try {

                [ADSI]$server="WinNT://$computername"
                #verify you got an object
                if (-not $server.name) {
                    #if account not found throw an exception
                    Throw "Could not connect $computername"
                }
                else {
                    if ($group) {
                        Write-Verbose "Getting group $group"
                        $groups=$server.children | where {
                          $_.schemaClassName -eq "group" -AND $_.name.value -eq $group
                          }
                    }
                    else {
                        #get all groups
                        Write-Verbose "Getting all groups"
                        $groups=$server.children | where {$_.schemaClassName -eq "group"}
                        Write-Verbose "Found $($groups.count) groups on $($server.name)"
                    }
```

```
                #write a custom object to the pipeline
                foreach ( $grp in $groups ) {
                  write-verbose $grp.name.value
                  New-Object -TypeName PSObject -Property @{
                    Computername=$server.name.value
                    Group=$group.Name.value
                    Description=$grp.Description.value
                    Path=$grp.path
                }
               } #foreach
            } #close Else

        } #close Try

         Catch {
            Write-Warning "An error occurred connecting to WinNT://$computername"
            Write-Warning $error[0].Exception.Message
        }

        } #end if $connected

    } #close Process

    end {
        Write-Verbose "Ending function"
    }
} #end function
```

The **Get-LocalGroup** function defaults to the local computer and writes a custom object for each local group. You can specify a group name like this:

```
PS C:\> get-localgroup -group "Administrators"

Description       Path                                     Computername     Group
-----------       ----                                     ------------     -----
                  WinNT://JDHLAB/CLIENT1/Administrators    CLIENT1          Administrators
```

If you don't specify a group name, then all local groups will be returned. You can easily build a report for all local groups from a list of computer names:

```
PS C:\> Get-Content computers.txt | get-localgroup | Export-Csv -Path LocalGroupReport.csv
```

An alternative is to use the **Get-Wmiobject** cmdlet and the Win32_Group class, which should give you the same results:

```
PS C:\> get-wmiobject win32_group -filter "localaccount='True'"|
>> Format-Table Name,Description -auto
>>

Name                          Description
----                          -----------
Administrators                Administrators have complete and unrestricted access to the compu
Backup Operators              Backup Operators can override security restrictions for the sole
Guests                        Guests have the same access as members of the Users group by defa
Network Configuration Operators Members in this group can have some administrative privileges to
Power Users                   Power Users possess most administrative powers with some restrict
Remote Desktop Users          Members in this group are granted the right to logon remotely
Replicator                    Supports file replication in a domain
```

```
Users                        Users are prevented from making accidental or intentional system-
HelpServicesGroup            Group for the Help and Support Center
```

You have to use the **–filter** parameter, or the Win32_Group class will also return all domain groups as well, even if you are querying a member desktop.

Deleting Groups

Deleting a local group uses almost the same steps as creating one:

```
PS C:\> [ADSI]$server="WinNT://APP02"
PS C:\> $server.Delete("group","Tech Users")
```

In this example, you connect to the server APP02 and call the **Delete()** method, specifying the object class and its name. The deletion takes effect immediately. There is no warning or prompt, so be careful.

Defining Group Properties

There isn't much to a local group you can change. All local groups are the same type. Nor can you rename a group with ADSI. The only thing you really can do is modify the description:

```
PS C:\> [ADSI]$group="WinNT://File02/local admins,group"
PS C:\> $group.description="Local Users with admin privileges"
PS C:\> $group.SetInfo()
```

You can't use WMI to modify properties either, but you can use it to rename a group:

```
PS C:\> $group=get-wmiobject win32_group -filter "name='Local Admins' AND localaccount='True'"
PS C:\> $group.Rename("Local Administrators")
```

Managing Group Membership

When it comes to managing membership of local groups, you can use either ADSI or WMI. Your choice of method depends on whether you need to specify alternate credentials.

Enumerating Members

Given the name of a local group and server, you can connect to it using the [ADSI] type adapter:

```
PS C:\> [ADSI]$admins="WinNT://$env:computername/administrators,group"
```

However, if you pipe $admins to the **Get-Member** cmdlet, you won't see any methods or properties to return group members. If you pipe $admins.psbase to **Get-Member**, you'll see more options, but again nothing here will work. You might think the **Children** property would work, but it doesn't for local groups. Although you don't see it, there is a **Members** property, but you need to use the **Invoke()** method to access it:

```
PS C:\> $members=$admins.invoke("Members")
```

$Members is now a COM object representing all members of the Administrators group. Manipulating $Members to give up its members requires a slightly more complicated PowerShell expression than you may be familiar with:

```
PS C:\> $members | ForEach-Object {
>>  $_.GetType().InvokeMember("Name", 'GetProperty',$null, $_, $null)
>> }
>>
Administrator
Domain Admins
LocalAdmins
HelpDeskPS C:\>
```

When you pipe $Members to the **ForEach-Object** cmdlet, you call the **InvokeMember()** method for each object. The expression essentially says "Get the **Name** property for the current COM object", which is then displayed. But since a local group is likely to have a combination of local and domain accounts, both users and groups, you might prefer to utilize a function, such as the **Get-LocalMembership** function below for enumerating group members:

Get-LocalMembership.ps1

```
Function Get-LocalMembership {

[cmdletBinding()]

    Param(
        [Parameter(Position=0,ValueFromPipeline=$True,
        ValueFromPipelineByPropertyName=$True)]
        [alias("name")]
        [string]$computername=$env:computername,
        [Parameter(Position=1,ValueFromPipeline=$False)]
        [string]$group="Administrators"
        )

    Begin {
        Write-Verbose "Starting function"
      }

    Process {
        #trim off $ from any computernames that might get piped in
             if ($computername.EndsWith("$")) {
                Write-Verbose "Trimming off trailing $"
                $computername=$computername.TrimEnd("$")
              }

            Try {
                Write-Verbose "Testing connection to $computername"
                if (-not (Test-Connection -ComputerName $computername -quiet)) {
                    $Connected=$False
                    Throw "Connection test failed to $computername"
                }
                else {
                    $Connected=$True
                }
            } #close Try
            Catch {
                Write-Warning $error[0].Exception.Message
            } #close Catch
```

```
if ($Connected) {
    write-Verbose "Connecting to WinNT://$computername/$group"

 Try {
     [ADSI]$LocalGroup="WinNT://$computername/$group,group"
    #verify you got an object
    if (-not $localgroup.name) {
        #if account not found throw an exception
        Throw "Could not connect to $group on $computername"
    }
    else {
        Write-Verbose "Enumerating group members"
        $LocalGroup.invoke("Members") | ForEach-Object {

        #get ADS Path of member
        Write-Verbose "Getting ADSPath"
        $ADSPath=$_.GetType().InvokeMember("ADSPath", 'GetProperty', `
        $null, $_, $null)

        #get the member class, ie user or group
        Write-Verbose "Getting class"
        $class=$_.GetType().InvokeMember("Class", 'GetProperty', `
        $null, $_, $null)

        #Get the name property
        Write-Verbose "Getting name"
        $name=$_.GetType().InvokeMember("Name", 'GetProperty', `
        $null, $_, $null)

        Write-Verbose "Parsing $ADSPath"
        #Domain members will have an ADSPath like
        #WinNT://MYDomain/Domain Users.  Local accounts will have
        #be like WinNT://MYDomain/Computername/Administrator

        #if computer name is found between two /, then assume
        #the ADSPath reflects a local object
        if ($ADSPath -match "/$computername/") {
            $local=$True
            $domain=$computername.toUpper()
            }
        else {
            $local=$False
             $domain=$ADSPath.Split("/")[2]
           }
        #create a custom object
        Write-Verbose "Creating new object"
        New-Object -TypeName PSObject -Property @{
            Computer =  $computername.toUpper()
            Path =  $ADSPath
            Domain = $domain
            IsLocal = $local
            Name = $name
            Class = $class
        }
    }  #foreach
   } #else
 } #close Try

 Catch {
    Write-Warning "An error occurred connecting to WinNT://$computername"
    Write-Warning $error[0].Exception.Message
    }
```

```
        } #end if $connected
    } #close Process

    End {
        Write-Verbose "Ending function"
    }
} #end function
```

The **Get-LocalMembership** function encapsulates the code explained previously, and takes it a step further to provide additional information such as the domain, class, and the full ADS path. The following example shows how you might use it with the default Administrator group:

```
PS C:\> "server01","client1" | get-localmembership


Name     : Administrator
Domain   : SERVER01
Class    : User
Path     : WinNT://JDHLAB/server01/Administrator
Computer : SERVER01
IsLocal  : True

Name     : Domain Admins
Domain   : JDHLAB
Class    : Group
Path     : WinNT://JDHLAB/Domain Admins
Computer : SERVER01
IsLocal  : False

Name     : Administrator
Domain   : CLIENT1
Class    : User
Path     : WinNT://JDHLAB/client1/Administrator
Computer : CLIENT1
IsLocal  : True

Name     : Domain Admins
Domain   : JDHLAB
Class    : Group
Path     : WinNT://JDHLAB/Domain Admins
Computer : CLIENT1
IsLocal  : False

Name     : LocalAdmins
Domain   : JDHLAB
Class    : Group
Path     : WinNT://JDHLAB/LocalAdmins
Computer : CLIENT1
IsLocal  : False

Name     : HelpDesk
Domain   : CLIENT1
Class    : User
Path     : WinNT://JDHLAB/client1/HelpDesk
Computer : CLIENT1
IsLocal  : True
PS C:\>
```

Because this function writes to the pipeline, you could use it in an expression like the one below:

```
PS C:\> Get-LocalMembership | where {-not $_.IsLocal} | Select Path,Name,Class,Computer,Domain |
>> Format-Table -autosize
>>

Path                        Name          Class Computer Domain
----                        ----          ----- -------- ------
WinNT://JDHLAB/Domain Admins Domain Admins Group CLIENT1  JDHLAB
WinNT://JDHLAB/LocalAdmins   LocalAdmins   Group CLIENT1  JDHLAB
WinNT://JDHLAB/jeff          jeff          User  CLIENT1  JDHLAB
```

This example gets all accounts that belong to the local Administrators group that are not local, but are domain members, and then displays a subset of useful properties.

If you want to enumerate the same group such as Administrators on multiple computers, you can use the **Get-LocalMembership** function in an expression such as the one shown below:

```
PS C:\> Get-Content computers.txt | get-localmembership | Sort Class |
>> Format-Table -GroupBy Computer Domain,Name,IsLocal,Class -AutoSize
```

Finally, suppose you want to query all groups on multiple servers, perhaps as part of a security audit. Let's combine some of the functions from earlier in this appendix. Here's one possibility:

```
$data=Get-Content computers.txt | get-localgroup -group "Administrators" | Foreach {
   write-host "Getting members for $($_.group) on $($_.computername)" -ForegroundColor Green
   $members=@()
   get-localmembership -computername $_.computername -group $_.group | Foreach {
    $members+=$_.Path
   }
   $_ | add-member -MemberType "NoteProperty" -name "Members" -value $members
   $_ | add-member -MemberType "NoteProperty" -name "MemberCount" -value $members.count `
-passthru } | ConvertTo-XML
$data.Save("c:\work\AdminAudit.xml")
```

What I've done here is: For every computer name in computers.txt, get the Administrators group. This group is then piped to the **ForEach-Object** cmdlet where I create a custom property of members using the **Get-LocalMembership** function and the number of members. All of the information is converted to XML. The last step is to save the XML data to a file.

Adding Members

Adding a member to a local group isn't too difficult:

```
PS C:\> [ADSI]$group="WinNT://Desk01/Power Users"
PS C:\> $group.Add("WinNT://Desk01/LocalJeff,user")
```

The **Add()** method requires the ADSI path to the object you want to add as a member. In this example, you are adding the local user account LocalJeff to the Power Users group on DESK01. The change takes effect immediately, and there is no need to call the **SetInfo()** method. Of course the user has to log off and back on before it applies to them. If you want to add a domain-based user or group you simply need to specify the correct ADSI path that includes the domain name:

```
PS C:\> [ADSI]$group="WinNT://Desk01/Power Users"
PS C:\> $group.Add("WinNT://Mycompany/Employees,group")
```

This snippet adds the Employees group from the Mycompany domain to the Power Users group on DESK01. Make sure you get the slashes going the right way!

Removing Members

To remove a group member, use the same technique as adding a member, except use the **Remove()** method. Here are some examples:

```
PS C:\> [ADSI]$group="WinNT://DESK01/Power Users"
PS C:\> $group.Remove("WinNT://MyCompany/Employees,group")
PS C:\> $group.Remove("WinNT://LocalJeff,user")
```

Again, the change is immediate.

Get the Code

All of these functions are part of a local user and group module that you can download from the SAPIEN Press website for this book. Almost all of the functions also include comment-based help, which I've omitted from listings in the appendix. Import the module into your Windows PowerShell session and you will have all of the advanced functions I've shown here.

Appendix B

Managing Active Directory with PowerShell and ADSI

Even though I hope you can use a cmdlet-based solution for managing Active Directory, there may be situations where you want to develop your own, or you may find a limitation in existing cmdlets. Because many PowerShell cmdlets rely on the directory service .NET classes, you can access these classes directly. In this Appendix, I want to provide an overview of how you might use them. If you've done any ADSI scripting using VBScript, much of this will look familiar.

Using the .NET Framework DirectoryService Classes

Let's start at the beginning. The parent .NET namespace you'll be using is System.DirectoryServices. However, you'll most likely be utilizing the System.DirectoryServices.DirectoryEntries and System.DirectoryServices.DirectoryEntry classes. The latter class will return, as the name suggests, an entry or object from a directory service. In this case, the directory service will be Active Directory, although the .NET directory service classes are designed for any LDAP-compliant directory service. In PowerShell, you use the **New-Object** cmdlet to create a new object. If you are running PowerShell with appropriate credentials, creating such an object is as easy as this:

```
PS C:\> New-Object DirectoryServices.DirectoryEntry "LDAP://mycompany.local"
distinguishedName
-----------------
{DC=mycompany,DC=local}
```

Be Patient

There are shortcuts for the information I'm presenting here, which I'll cover later in this appendix. But I wanted you to fully understand the mechanics and technology before getting to them. Still, if you want to jump ahead, skip to the section titled: "The ADSI Type Adapter".

All you need to do is specify the LDAP path of a specific Active Directory object. In the example above, I'm connecting to the root of the mycompany.local domain. You can also use the distinguished name format, as shown below:

```
PS C:\> New-Object DirectoryServices.DirectoryEntry "LDAP://dc=mycompany,dc=local"
distinguishedName
-----------------
{DC=mycompany,DC=local}
```

In fact, you need to use the distinguished name when you want to connect an organizational unit:

```
PS C:\> New-Object DirectoryServices.DirectoryEntry "LDAP://OU=Servers,DC=mycompany,dc=local"

distinguishedName
-----------------
{OU=Servers,DC=mycompany,DC=local}
```

If you need to authenticate with alternate credentials, you can add them as additional constructor parameters:

```
PS C:\> $admin="mycompany\da_jhicks"
PS C:\> $pwd=Read-Host "Enter the password for $admin"
Enter the password for mycompany\da_jhicks: P@ssw0rd
PS C:\> New-Object DirectoryServices.DirectoryEntry "LDAP://mycompany.local",$admin,$pwd

distinguishedName
-----------------
{DC=mycompany,DC=local}
```

Don't use the **-AsSecureString** parameter with the **Read-Host** cmdlet. The password that you use in this example can't be a secure-string. But don't fear—the password is not passed as clear text over the network. If you prefer, you can use a PSCredential as I do here:

```
PS C:\> $cred=Get-Credential mycompany\da_jhicks
PS C:\> New-Object DirectoryServices.DirectoryEntry `
>> "LDAP://mycompany.local",$cred.Username,$cred.GetNetworkCredential().Password
>>


distinguishedName
-----------------
{DC=mycompany,DC=local}
```

The $cred variable holds the PSCredential object. You can use its **Username** property to pass the string mycompany\da_jhicks to the **New-Object** cmdlet. To get the password as a string, call the **GetNetworkCredential()** method, which returns a System.Net.NetworkCredential object. The **Password** property of this object will be a string. This technique allows you to pass strings as necessary, but not directly expose them in the console.

Case Counts

As with the WinNT provider which you might be familiar with from VBScript, the LDAP provider is also case-sensitive and must be uppercase.

Now that you know how to create a directory service entry object, you can save it to a variable so you can explore it further:

```
PS C:\> $dsroot=New-Object DirectoryServices.DirectoryEntry "LDAP://mycompany.local",`
>> $cred.Username,$cred.GetnetworkCredential().Password
>>


PS C:\> $dsroot

distinguishedName
-----------------
{DC=mycompany,DC=local}
```

If you pipe the $DSRoot variable to the **Get-Member** cmdlet, you should see these properties for the domain root.

Table Appendix B-1 DirectoryEntry Properties

auditingPolicy	creationTime	dc
distinguishedName	dSASignature	forceLogoff
fSMORoleOwner	gPLink	instanceType
isCriticalSystemObject	lockoutDuration	lockOutObservationWindow
lockoutThreshold	masteredBy	maxPwdAge
minPwdAge	minPwdLength	modifiedCount
modifiedCountAtLastProm	ms-DS-MachineAccountQuota	msDS-AllUsersTrustQuota
msDS-Behavior-Version	msDs-masteredBy	msDS-PerUserTrustQuota
msDS-PerUserTrustTombstonesQuota	Name	nextRid
nTMixedDomain	nTSecurityDescriptor	objectCategory
objectClass	objectGUID	objectSid
pwdHistoryLength	pwdProperties	replUpToDateVector
rIDManagerReference	serverState	subRefs
systemFlags	uASCompat	uSNChanged
uSNCreated	wellKnownObjects	whenChanged
whenCreated		

Your list of properties may vary, depending on your Windows version or network configuration.

Get Domain Information

Once you know what properties are available, you can wrap things up in a function. For example, if you want to display some information about your domain, use an expression like this:

```
PS C:\> $DSRoot | Format-List @{label="DN";Expression={$_.DistinguishedName}},
>> @{label="Name";Expression={$_.Name}},`
>> @{label="Created";Expression={$_.WhenCreated}},`
>> @{label="Last Modified";Expression={$_.WhenChanged}},`
>> @{label="FSMO";Expression={$_.FSMORoleOwner}}
>>


DN            : DC=mycompany,DC=local
Name          : mycompany
Created       : 4/14/2008 10:52:27 PM
Last Modified : 2/4/2010 5:02:49 AM
FSMO          : CN=NTDS Settings,CN=MYDC01,CN=Servers,CN=Default-First-Site-Name...
```

In the example above, I created custom labels to make the output more user friendly.

Get Domain Account Policy Information

The domain's account policy information is stored in several properties such as the **minPwdAge** and **LockoutDuration** properties. However, getting these values is not an easy task. You might think you can use a PowerShell expression like this:

```
PS C:\> $dsroot | Select *pwd*,lock*
```

But if you run this, your output will be this:

```
maxPwdAge                  : {System.__ComObject}
minPwdAge                  : {System.__ComObject}
minPwdLength               : {7}
pwdProperties              : {1}
pwdHistoryLength           : {24}
lockoutDuration            : {System.__ComObject}
lockOutObservationWindow : {System.__ComObject}
lockoutThreshold           : {7}
```

The **length** and **threshold** properties are readable, but the rest are not. I'll discuss the **pwdProperties** value first.

The **pwdProperties** property is actually a bitmask flag representing different password properties. You can use constants:

```
New-Variable DOMAIN_PASSWORD_COMPLEX 1 -option constant
New-Variable DOMAIN_PASSWORD_NO_ANON_CHANGE 2 -option constant
New-Variable DOMAIN_PASSWORD_NO_CLEAR_CHANGE 4 -option constant
New-Variable DOMAIN_LOCKOUT_ADMINS 8 -option constant
New-Variable DOMAIN_PASSWORD_STORE_CLEARTEXT 16 -option constant
New-Variable DOMAIN_REFUSE_PASSWORD_CHANGE 32 -option constant
```

You can perform a binary AND operation using the **pwdProperties** value and each of these constants. I've created a function to simplify the process:

Get-PWDProperties.ps1

```
Function Get-PWDProperties {
    Param(
    [Parameter(Position=0,Mandatory=$True,HelpMessage="Enter a property flag value.")]
```

```
    [ValidateNotNullorEmpty()]
    [int]$flag
  )
    # constant values for pwdProperties bitmask flag
    New-Variable DOMAIN_PASSWORD_COMPLEX 1 -option constant
    New-Variable DOMAIN_PASSWORD_NO_ANON_CHANGE 2 -option constant
    New-Variable DOMAIN_PASSWORD_NO_CLEAR_CHANGE 4 -option constant
    New-Variable DOMAIN_LOCKOUT_ADMINS 8 -option constant
    New-Variable DOMAIN_PASSWORD_STORE_CLEARTEXT 16 -option constant
    New-Variable DOMAIN_REFUSE_PASSWORD_CHANGE 32 -option constant


    if ($flag -band $DOMAIN_PASSWORD_COMPLEX) {
         write "Complex passwords required"
        }

    if ($flag -band $DOMAIN_PASSWORD_NO_ANON_CHANGE) {
         write "Anonymous change not allowed"
        }

    if ($flag -band $DOMAIN_PASSWORD_NO_CLEAR_CHANGE) {
         write "No clear change allowed"
        }

    if ($flag -band $DOMAIN_LOCKOUT_ADMINS) {
         write "Admin lockout allowed"
        }

    if ($flag -band $DOMAIN_PASSWORD_STORE_CLEARTEXT) {
         write "Reversible encryption enabled"
        }

    if ($flag -band $DOMAIN_REFUSE_PASSWORD_CHANGE) {
         write "Refuse domain password change"
        }
    }
```

The function merely does a binary AND operation, with each possible flag value and the password property value. If the result is 1, then the function writes a message to the screen. If the function is loaded in your profile and the pwdProperties value is 7, you will see a result like this:

```
PS C:\get-pwdproperties 7
Complex passwords required
Anonymous change not allowed
No clear change allowed
```

Now, what about the other properties with a value of System.__ComObject? Without confusing you with .NET programming details, these objects are not readily discoverable. However, these property values are stored as large integers of 100 nanosecond intervals. ADSI, including the .NET directory service classes, split this 64- bit number into high and low parts. The formula for returning a 32-bit value is:

```
HighPart * 2^32 + LowPart
```

The easy solution is to use the .NET **ConvertLargeIntegerToInt64()** method. The method takes a value as a parameter. In this case, the **MaxPwdAge** property value. This value is actually the number of 100 nanosecond intervals between the time a password is set and the time it expires. To get a value in days, you need to divide the value by the number of 100 nanosecond intervals in a day:

```
((60 sec * 60 min*24 hours)* (1000000000/100)= 864000000000
```

Hence:

```
PS C:\> $dsroot.ConvertLargeIntegerToInt64($dsroot.MaxPwdAge.value) / -864000000000
60
```

Now you have a more meaningful number.

I put all of this together in a script that will return domain account policies:

Get-DomainAccountPolicy.ps1

```
Function Get-PWDProperties {

# returns a text list of password flag values

    Param([int]$flag=$(Throw "You must specify a property flag value."))

    # constant values for pwdProperties bitmask flag
    New-Variable DOMAIN_PASSWORD_COMPLEX 1 -option constant
    New-Variable DOMAIN_PASSWORD_NO_ANON_CHANGE 2 -option constant
    New-Variable DOMAIN_PASSWORD_NO_CLEAR_CHANGE 4 -option constant
    New-Variable DOMAIN_LOCKOUT_ADMINS 8 -option constant
    New-Variable DOMAIN_PASSWORD_STORE_CLEARTEXT 16 -option constant
    New-Variable DOMAIN_REFUSE_PASSWORD_CHANGE 32 -option constant

    New-Variable data
    if ($flag -band $DOMAIN_PASSWORD_COMPLEX) {
    #     write "Complex passwords required"
        $data=$data+"Complex passwords required"
        }

    if ($flag -band $DOMAIN_PASSWORD_NO_ANON_CHANGE) {
    #     write "Anonymous change not allowed"
        $data=$data+",'nAnonymous change not allowed"
        }

    if ($flag -band $DOMAIN_PASSWORD_NO_CLEAR_CHANGE) {
    #     write "No clear change allowed"
        $data=$data+",'nNo clear change allowed"
        }

    if ($flag -band $DOMAIN_LOCKOUT_ADMINS) {
    #     write "Admin lockout allowed"
        $data=$data+",'nAdmin lockout allowed"
        }

    if ($flag -band $DOMAIN_PASSWORD_STORE_CLEARTEXT) {
    #     write "Reversible encryption enabled"
        $data=$data+",'nReversible encryption enabled"
        }

    if ($flag -band $DOMAIN_REFUSE_PASSWORD_CHANGE) {
    #     write "Refuse domain password change"
        $data=$data+",'nRefuse domain password change"
```

```
        }

    write $data

}


#connection credentials are optional
#$admin="jdhlab\administrator"
#$pwd="P@ssw0rd!"

#the ADSI path to the domain root
$DN="LDAP://mycompany.local"

$DSRoot = New-Object DirectoryServices.DirectoryEntry $DN #,$admin,$pwd

$msg="Account Policies for {0}" -f ($DSRoot.DC.Value.ToUpper())

Write-Host $msg -ForegroundColor Cyan

$DSRoot | Format-List `
@{label="Minimum Password Length";Expression={$_.MinPwdLength}},
@{label="Password History";Expression={$_.PwdHistoryLength}},
@{label="Lockout Threshold";Expression={$_.LockoutThreshold}},
@{label="Lockout Duration (min)";Expression={
  $_.ConvertLargeIntegerToInt64($_.lockoutduration.value)/-600000000 }},
@{label="Lockout Window (min)";Expression={
  $_.ConvertLargeIntegerToInt64($_.lockoutobservationWindow.value)/-600000000 }},
@{label="Password Properties";Expression={Get-PWDProperties $_.PwdProperties.value}},
@{label="Max Password Age (days)";Expression={
  $_.ConvertLargeIntegerToInt64($_.maxpwdage.value) /-864000000000}},
@{label="Min Password Age (days)";Expression={
  $_.ConvertLargeIntegerToInt64($_.minpwdage.value) /-864000000000}}
```

I made a minor change to the original **Get-PWDProperties** function, so that a single value is returned, which is essentially a text list of password properties:

```
if ($flag -band $DOMAIN_REFUSE_PASSWORD_CHANGE) {
#      write "Refuse domain password change"
     $data=$data+",`nRefuse domain password change"
     }

write $data
```

The main part of the script is connecting to the domain. I'm using alternate credentials:

```
#the ADSI path to the domain root
$DN='LDAP://mycompany.local'

$DSRoot = New-Object DirectoryServices.DirectoryEntry $DN,$admin,$pwd
```

The script writes an informational header with the domain name in uppercase:

```
Write-Host "Account Policies for "$DSRoot.DC.Value.ToUpper()
```

Finally, I pipe the $DSRoot object to the **Format-Table** cmdlet and create custom labels:

```
$DSRoot | Format-List `
@{label="Minimum Password Length";Expression={$_.MinPwdLength}},
@{label="Password History";Expression={$_.PwdHistoryLength}},
@{label="Lockout Threshold";Expression={$_.LockoutThreshold}},
@{label="Lockout Duration (min)";Expression={
  $_.ConvertLargeIntegerToInt64($_.lockoutduration.value)/-600000000 }},
@{label="Lockout Window (min)";Expression={
  $_.ConvertLargeIntegerToInt64($_.lockoutobservationWindow.value)/-600000000 }},
@{label="Password Properties";Expression={Get-PWDProperties $_.PwdProperties.value}},
@{label="Max Password Age (days)";Expression={
  $_.ConvertLargeIntegerToInt64($_.maxpwdage.value) /-864000000000}},
@{label="Min Password Age (days)";Expression={
  $_.ConvertLargeIntegerToInt64($_.minpwdage.value) /-864000000000}}
```

You'll notice that I pass the large integer properties to the **ConvertLargeIntegerToInt64()** method and then divide the result by a number to give an appropriate value in minutes or days.

Here's the result when I run the script:

```
PS C:\> C:\scripts\Get-DomainaccountPolicy.ps1
Account Policies for  MYCOMPANY


Minimum Password Length : 7
Password History        : 24
Lockout Threshold       : 5
Lockout Duration (min)  : 30
Lockout Window (min)    : 30
Password Properties     : Complex passwords required,
                          Reversible encryption enabled
Max Password Age (days) : 60
Min Password Age (days) : 1
```

Get Child Items

It is very easy to view a list of child objects from a given directory services entry. Because of the way PowerShell adapts the .NET Framework classes, you'll need to access the underlying PSBase object:

```
PS C:\> $dsroot.children | Select distinguishedname

distinguishedName
-----------------
{OU=Admini,DC=mycompany,DC=local}
{CN=Builtin,DC=mycompany,DC=local}
{CN=Computers,DC=mycompany,DC=local}
{OU=Domain Controllers,DC=mycompany,DC=local}
{CN=ForeignSecurityPrincipals,DC=mycompany,DC=local}
{CN=Infrastructure,DC=mycompany,DC=local}
{CN=LostAndFound,DC=mycompany,DC=local}
{CN=NTDS Quotas,DC=mycompany,DC=local}
{CN=Program Data,DC=mycompany,DC=local}
{OU=Servers,DC=mycompany,DC=local}
{CN=System,DC=mycompany,DC=local}
{OU=Testing,DC=mycompany,DC=local}
{CN=Users,DC=mycompany,DC=local}
```

As you can see, the **Children** property returns a list of containers and organizational units from $DSRoot, which you created earlier in the chapter. Although this domain does not, it is possible to have user, computer, and group objects in the domain root. These objects would also be listed as child items. If you want to filter out these objects you can do this:

```
PS C\> $dsroot.children | where {$_.objectcategory -notmatch "Person" `
>> -AND $_.objectcategory -notmatch "Computer" -AND $_.objectcategory -notmatch "Group"}
```

I'll put all of this together in a script:

Get-ChildEntries.ps1

```
Param([string]$dn="LDAP://dc=mycompany,dc=local")

$dsroot = New-Object DirectoryServices.DirectoryEntry $DN

$children=$dsroot.children | where {$_.objectclass -match "container|organizationalunit"}

$children | Sort Name | Format-List `
@{Label="DN";Expression={$_.DistinguishedName}},
@{Label="Name";Expression={$_.Name}},
@{Label="Description";Expression={$_.Description}},
@{Label="Created";Expression={$_.WhenCreated}},
ObjectClass,objectCategory

Write-Host "There are $(($children | Measure-Object).count) child containers or OUs under
$($dsroot.distinguishedname.value)"
```

The script, which takes a distinguished name as a parameter, stores the child objects in $children, which are only containers or organizational units:

```
$children=$dsroot.children | where {$_.objectclass -match "container|organizationalunit"}
```

I pipe the $children object to the **Sort-Object** cmdlet to sort the containers and OUs by name and that output is piped to the **Format-List** cmdlet. As I did earlier, I use custom labels and expressions to return the property values.

When you run this script your output will look like this:

```
PS C:\> c:\scripts\get-childentries.ps1


DN             : CN=Builtin,DC=mycompany,DC=local
Name           : Builtin
Description    : {}
Created        : 2/24/2008 11:28:59 AM
ObjectClass    : {top, builtinDomain}
objectcategory : {CN=Builtin-Domain,CN=Schema,CN=Configuration,DC=mycompany,DC=local}

DN             : OU=Company Desktops,DC=mycompany,DC=local
Name           : Company Desktops
Description    : {}
Created        : 3/4/2008 5:23:07 PM
ObjectClass    : {top, organizationalUnit}
objectcategory : {CN=Organizational-Unit,CN=Schema,CN=Configuration,DC=bigcompany,DC=local}

DN             : OU=Company Shared Contacts,DC=mycompany,DC=local
Name           : Company Shared Contacts
Description    : company contact records
```

```
Created        : 3/26/2008 7:30:00 PM
ObjectClass    : {top, organizationalUnit}
objectcategory : {CN=Organizational-Unit,CN=Schema,CN=Configuration,DC=bigcompany,DC=local}

DN             : CN=Computers,DC=mycompany,DC=local
Name           : Computers
Description    : Default container for upgraded computer accounts
Created        : 2/24/2008 11:28:48 AM
ObjectClass    : {top, container}
objectcategory : {CN=Container,CN=Schema,CN=Configuration,DC=mycompany,DC=local}
...
```

The output above is truncated. Your results will vary depending on your domain. But what about a recursive search through the domain or any starting point for that matter? It's a little more complicated but achievable. Here's my solution:

Get-DSTree.ps1

```
Function Get-DSTree {
    Param([string]$container,[int]$i=0)

    [string]$rootDN="LDAP://$container"
    [string]$leader=" "
    [int]$pad=$leader.length+$i

    Write-Host ($leader.Padleft($pad)+$container)

    $dse=New-Object DirectoryServices.DirectoryEntry $rootDN

    $dse.children | where {$_.objectcategory -notmatch "Person" `
    -AND $_.objectcategory -notmatch "Computer" `
    -AND $_.objectcategory -notmatch "Group" `
    -AND $_.objectcategory -notmatch "Contact"} |

     ForEach-Object {
        [string]$dn=$_.distinguishedName
         Get-DSTree $dn ($pad+1)
     }
}
```

The **Get-DSTree** function takes a directory service distinguished name as a parameter. Because I want the output to visually represent a hierarchy, the second parameter is an integer used in formatting the output.

I created a variable, $leader, that is a single space:

```
[string]$leader=" "
```

Then I define a variable that is the length of $leader, plus the value of whatever was passed as $i:

```
[int]$pad=$leader.length+$i
```

Finally, I write the container name that is preceded by $leader and is padded by the number of spaces as specified by $pad:

```
Write-Host ($leader.Padleft($pad)+$container)
```

You'll see how this works at the end.

Now, I need to get the DirectoryServices.DirectoryEntry object:

```
$dse=New-Object DirectoryServices.DirectoryEntry $rootDN
```

I get the child objects and filter out everything except the containers and organizational units I want to display:

```
$dse.children | where {$_.objectcategory -notmatch "Person" `
-AND $_.objectcategory -notmatch "Computer" `
-AND $_.objectcategory -notmatch "Group" `
-AND $_.objectcategory -notmatch "Contact"}
```

That output is piped to the **ForEach-Object** construct, which recursively calls the **Get-DSTree** function, incrementing the pad value by 1:

```
ForEach-Object {
  [string]$dn=$_.distinguishedName
   Get-DSTree $dn ($pad+1)
}
```

Here's an excerpt of the output:

```
PS C:\> Get-DSTree "dc=mycompany,dc=local"
DC=mycompany,DC=local
   CN=Builtin,DC=mycompany,DC=local
   OU=Company Desktops,DC=mycompany,DC=local
     OU=Customer Service,OU=Company Desktops,DC=mycompany,DC=local
     OU=Finance,OU=Company Desktops,DC=mycompany,DC=local
     OU=IT Desktops,OU=Company Desktops,DC=mycompany,DC=local
     OU=Sales,OU=Company Desktops,DC=mycompany,DC=local
     OU=Training,OU=Company Desktops,DC=mycompany,DC=local
   OU=Company Shared Contacts,DC=mycompany,DC=local
   CN=Computers,DC=mycompany,DC=local
   OU=Divisions,DC=mycompany,DC=local
     OU=Boston,OU=Divisions,DC=mycompany,DC=local
     OU=LA,OU=Divisions,DC=mycompany,DC=local
   OU=Domain Controllers,DC=mycompany,DC=local
   OU=Employees,DC=mycompany,DC=local
     OU=Consumer Affairs,OU=Employees,DC=mycompany,DC=local
...
```

Please be aware that in a large Active Directory environment this script may take a while to complete. The filtering is done post processing, after the retrieval of the $dse object. There are better ways to search large volumes of data, which I discuss below.

Using the DirectorySearcher

By now you may be thinking to yourself: "That's a lot of work to find stuff in Active Directory." Fortunately, the .NET Framework provides a better solution, the DirectorySearcher class:

```
PS C:\> $searcher = New-Object DirectoryServices.DirectorySearcher
PS C:\> $searcher | Format-List *


CacheResults             : True
ClientTimeout            : -00:00:01
PropertyNamesOnly        : False
Filter                   : (objectClass=*)
PageSize                 : 0
PropertiesToLoad         : {}
ReferralChasing          : External
SearchScope              : Subtree
ServerPageTimeLimit      : -00:00:01
ServerTimeLimit          : -00:00:01
SizeLimit                : 0
SearchRoot               : System.DirectoryServices.DirectoryEntry
Sort                     : System.DirectoryServices.SortOption
Asynchronous             : False
Tombstone                : False
AttributeScopeQuery      :
DerefAlias               : Never
SecurityMasks            : None
ExtendedDN               : None
DirectorySynchronization :
VirtualListView          :
Site                     :
Container                :
```

By default, the DirectorySearcher class is configured to search for all objects:

```
Filter                   : (objectClass=*)
```

I'll show you how to change this a little later. The DirectorySearcher class begins its search from the **SearchRoot** property:

```
SearchRoot               : System.DirectoryServices.DirectoryEntry
```

You can see this property is a DirectoryEntry object like the one used earlier. In the current example, the SearchRoot is the domain root:

```
PS C:\> $searcher.searchroot

distinguishedName
-----------------
{DC=mycompany,DC=local}
```

[ADSISearcher]

Windows PowerShell includes another type accelerator called [ADSISearcher], which creates a searcher object with a minimum of steps. All you need to specify is an LDAP search filter:

```
PS C:\> [adsisearcher]$searcher="(&(objectcategory=person)(objectclass=user))"
PS C:\> $searcher
```

```
CacheResults               : True
ClientTimeout              : -00:00:01
PropertyNamesOnly          : False
Filter                     : (&(objectcategory=person)(objectclass=user))
PageSize                   : 0
PropertiesToLoad           : {}
ReferralChasing            : External
SearchScope                : Subtree
ServerPageTimeLimit        : -00:00:01
ServerTimeLimit            : -00:00:01
SizeLimit                  : 0
SearchRoot                 : System.DirectoryServices.DirectoryEntry
Sort                       : System.DirectoryServices.SortOption
Asynchronous               : False
Tombstone                  : False
AttributeScopeQuery        :
DerefAlias                 : Never
SecurityMasks              : None
ExtendedDN                 : None
DirectorySynchronization   :
VirtualListView            :
Site                       :
Container                  :
```

The searcher defaults to the current domain root:

```
PS C:\> $searcher.searchroot.path
LDAP://DC=mycompany,DC=local
```

The only difference between this approach and using the **New-Object** cmdlet is that this saves a little typing.

Finding Objects

Regardless of how you create the searcher, it has two primary methods: **FindOne()** and **FindAll()**. The first method will stop searching after the first object meeting the search criteria is found:

```
PS C:\> $searcher.findone() | Format-List


Path       : LDAP://DC=mycompany,DC=local
Properties : {fsmoroleowner, minpwdlength, adspath, msds-perusertrusttombstonesquota...}
```

The other method returns all objects in my Active Directory:

```
PS C:\> $searcher.findall() | Select path

Path
----
LDAP://DC=mycompany,DC=local
LDAP://CN=Users,DC=mycompany,DC=local
LDAP://CN=Computers,DC=mycompany,DC=local
LDAP://OU=Domain Controllers,DC=mycompany,DC=local
LDAP://CN=System,DC=mycompany,DC=local
LDAP://CN=LostAndFound,DC=mycompany,DC=local
LDAP://CN=Infrastructure,DC=mycompany,DC=local
LDAP://CN=ForeignSecurityPrincipals,DC=mycompany,DC=local
LDAP://CN=Program Data,DC=mycompany,DC=local
```

```
LDAP://CN=Microsoft,CN=Program Data,DC=mycompany,DC=local
LDAP://CN=NTDS Quotas,DC=mycompany,DC=local
LDAP://CN=WinsockServices,CN=System,DC=mycompany,DC=local
LDAP://CN=RpcServices,CN=System,DC=mycompany,DC=local
LDAP://CN=FileLinks,CN=System,DC=mycompany,DC=local
LDAP://CN=VolumeTable,CN=FileLinks,CN=System,DC=mycompany,DC=local
LDAP://CN=ObjectMoveTable,CN=FileLinks,CN=System,DC=mycompany,DC=local
LDAP://CN=Default Domain Policy,CN=System,DC=mycompany,DC=local
LDAP://CN=AppCategories,CN=Default Domain Policy,CN=System,DC=mycompany,DC=local
...
```

Of course, you may want a more limited search query. You can define the **Filter** property with any LDAP query:

```
PS C:\> $searcher.filter="(objectClass=organizationalunit)"
PS C:\> $searcher.findall() | Select Path

Path
----
LDAP://OU=Domain Controllers,DC=mycompany,DC=local
LDAP://OU=home,DC=mycompany,DC=local
LDAP://OU=Servers,DC=mycompany,DC=local
LDAP://OU=Testing,DC=mycompany,DC=local
LDAP://OU=omaha,DC=mycompany,DC=local
LDAP://OU=syracuse,DC=mycompany,DC=local
LDAP://OU=University,OU=syracuse,DC=mycompany,DC=local
LDAP://OU=Demo OU,OU=Testing,DC=mycompany,DC=local
LDAP://OU=sapien,DC=mycompany,DC=local
LDAP://OU=Demo,OU=Servers,DC=mycompany,DC=local
LDAP://OU=Admini,DC=mycompany,DC=local
```

The DirectorySearcher class is looking for all organizational unit objects and PowerShell is displaying just the **Path** property.

Here is a slightly more complicated example:

```
PS C:\> $searcher.Filter="(&(objectcategory=person)(objectclass=user))"
PS C:\> $searcher.findall() | Select Path

Path
----
LDAP://CN=Administrator,CN=Users,DC=mycompany,DC=local
LDAP://CN=Guest,CN=Users,DC=mycompany,DC=local
LDAP://CN=SUPPORT_388945a0,CN=Users,DC=mycompany,DC=local
LDAP://CN=krbtgt,CN=Users,DC=mycompany,DC=local
LDAP://CN=Jeffery Hicks,OU=home,DC=mycompany,DC=local
LDAP://CN=IUSR_MYDC01,CN=Users,DC=mycompany,DC=local
LDAP://CN=IWAM_MYDC01,CN=Users,DC=mycompany,DC=local
LDAP://CN=svcSharepoint,CN=Users,DC=mycompany,DC=local
LDAP://CN=Joe Hacker,OU=Testing,DC=mycompany,DC=local
LDAP://CN=ldog,OU=Testing,DC=mycompany,DC=local
LDAP://CN=test user1,OU=omaha,DC=mycompany,DC=local
LDAP://CN=Test User3,OU=Testing,DC=mycompany,DC=local
LDAP://CN=Test User4,OU=Testing,DC=mycompany,DC=local
LDAP://CN=da Hicks,CN=Users,DC=mycompany,DC=local
LDAP://CN=Bill Shakespeare,OU=Testing,DC=mycompany,DC=local
...
```

In this example, the search filter is a combination that should return all user objects in my domain. The output is truncated.

The search filters can get quite complicated. In fact, you can take any LDAP query that you create using the Saved Queries feature in Active Directory Users and Computers and use it in PowerShell:

```
PS C:\>$searcher.filter=`
>>"(&(objectCategory=person)(objectClass=user)(userAccountControl:1.2.840.113556.1.4.803:=2))"
>>
PS C:\> $searcher.findall() | Select Path

Path
----
LDAP://CN=Guest,CN=Users,DC=mycompany,DC=local
LDAP://CN=SUPPORT_388945a0,CN=Users,DC=mycompany,DC=local
LDAP://CN=krbtgt,CN=Users,DC=mycompany,DC=local
LDAP://CN=Joe Hacker,OU=Testing,DC=mycompany,DC=local
LDAP://CN=svcSonicAdmin,CN=Users,DC=mycompany,DC=local
LDAP://CN=test user1,OU=omaha,DC=mycompany,DC=local
LDAP://CN=Test User3,OU=Testing,DC=mycompany,DC=local
LDAP://CN=Test User4,OU=Testing,DC=mycompany,DC=local
LDAP://CN=azygot,OU=Testing,DC=mycompany,DC=local
LDAP://CN=Paul Jones,OU=Testing,DC=mycompany,DC=local
LDAP://CN=mapplebee,OU=Testing,DC=mycompany,DC=local
LDAP://CN=krogers,OU=Testing,DC=mycompany,DC=local
LDAP://CN=jjensen,OU=Testing,DC=mycompany,DC=local
LDAP://CN=stoobin,OU=Testing,DC=mycompany,DC=local
LDAP://CN=tsykes,OU=Testing,DC=mycompany,DC=local
LDAP://CN=amorales,OU=Testing,DC=mycompany,DC=local
```

I've taken the LDAP query to find all disabled users and used it as my search filter.

If you pipe the search results, you will see that you don't get the actual directory service entry, but rather a result object:

```
   TypeName: System.DirectoryServices.SearchResult

Name              MemberType Definition
----              ---------- ----------
Equals            Method     System.Boolean Equals(Object obj)
GetDirectoryEntry Method     System.DirectoryServices.DirectoryEntry GetDirectoryEntry()
GetHashCode       Method     System.Int32 GetHashCode()
GetType           Method     System.Type GetType()
get_Path          Method     System.String get_Path()
get_Properties    Method     System.DirectoryServices.ResultPropertyCollection
get_Properties()
ToString          Method     System.String ToString()
Path              Property   System.String Path {get;}
Properties        Property   System.DirectoryServices.ResultPropertyCollection Properties {get;}
```

This is important to know so you can understand how to get more information out of the search result. For instance, the example below shows how to find all the disabled accounts, and display more information about each user:

Get-DisabledUserReport.ps1

```
Function Get-PwdLastSetDate {

    Param([int64]$LastSet=0)
    if ($LastSet -eq 0) {
        write "Never Set or Re-Set"
```

```
    } else {
        [datetime]$utc="1/1/1601"
        $i=$LastSet/864000000000
        write ($utc.AddDays($i))
    }
}

$Searcher = New-Object DirectoryServices.DirectorySearcher

$searcher.filter=`
"(&(objectCategory=person)(objectClass=user)(userAccountControl:1.2.840.113556.1.4.803:=2))"

$searcher.findall() | Format-Table `
@{label="DN";expression={$_.properties.distinguishedname}},
@{label="Last Modified";expression={$_.properties.whenchanged}},
@{label="PWDLastSet";expression={
Get-PwdLastSetDate $_.properties.item("pwdlastset")[0]}} -autosize
```

You've seen most of this script already. One thing that is new is the function I wrote to convert the value of **PwdLastSet** to a more meaningful value:

```
Function Get-PwdLastSetDate {

    Param([int64]$LastSet=0)
    if ($LastSet -eq 0) {
        write "Never Set or Re-Set"
    } else {
        [datetime]$utc="1/1/1601"
        $i=$LastSet/864000000000
        write ($utc.AddDays($i))
    }
}
```

The function takes the **PwdLastSet** value, which is a 64-bit integer, as a parameter. This value is the number of 100 nanosecond intervals since January 1, 1601 when the user's password was last set. If the value is 0, then the password was never set or the account was flagged to force the user to change password at next logon. The function returns a message indicating that:

```
    if ($LastSet -eq 0) {
        write "Never Set or Re-Set"
```

Otherwise, I divide the PwdLastSet value by 864000000000 to get a value in days:

```
        $i=$LastSet/864000000000
```

To calculate what day that was, I use the value as a parameter for the **AddDays()** method from my [datetime] object:

```
        write ($utc.AddDays($i))
```

Something else you might notice is the syntax I used to get the **PwdLastSet** value:

```
Get-PwdLastSetDate $_.properties.item("pwdlastset")[0]
```

PowerShell is usually pretty forgiving and flexible. It will do what it can to properly format data, which is why this works:

```
@{label="DN";expression={$_.properties.distinguishedname}},`
```

However, because I need to pass the value to the **Get-PwdLastSetDate** function, something like this fails:

```
Get-PwdLastSetDate $_.properties.pwdlastset
```

Do you recall what type of object the DirectorySearcher class returned? It is a SearchResult object, not a user object, and the properties are stored as a collection. Therefore, I need more specific syntax to return a value that I can pass to the function. Even though there is only one value, the **PwdLastSet** property is treated as a collection, so I specify that I want the first item in the collection, [0].

Here's the end result:

```
PS C:\> C:\scripts\get-disableduserreport.ps1

DN                                                  Last Modified          PWDLastSet
--                                                  -------------          ----------
CN=Guest,CN=Users,DC=mycompany,DC=local             4/14/2010 10:52:30 PM Never Set or Re-Set
CN=SUPPORT_388945a0,CN=Users,DC=mycompany,DC=local 4/14/2010 10:52:30 PM 3/24/2010 10:41:04 P
CN=krbtgt,CN=Users,DC=mycompany,DC=local            4/14/2010 11:10:43 PM 4/14/2010 10:55:31 P
CN=Joe Hacker,OU=Testing,DC=mycompany,DC=local      6/18/2010 4:01:11 PM  11/12/2010 7:56:57 P
CN=jjensen,OU=Testing,DC=mycompany,DC=local         6/18/2010 4:01:10 PM  6/5/2010 11:45:47 PM
CN=stoobin,OU=Testing,DC=mycompany,DC=local         6/18/2010 4:01:11 PM  6/5/2010 11:45:47 PM
CN=tsykes,OU=Testing,DC=mycompany,DC=local          6/18/2010 4:01:11 PM  6/5/2010 11:45:47 PM
CN=amorales,OU=Testing,DC=mycompany,DC=local        6/18/2010 4:01:11 PM  6/5/2010 11:45:47 PM
...
```

I will show another search example that returns information about a user account, including when their password was last set and the password age in days:

Get-PasswordReport.ps1

```
#Get-PasswordReport.ps1
# This script writes a custom object for each non-disabled
# user account in your Active Directory domain to the pipeline

#nested functions
Function Get-PwdLastSetDate {
   Param([int64]$LastSet=0)
        if ($LastSet -eq 0) {
            write "Never Set or Re-Set"
        } else {
            [datetime]$utc="1/1/1601"
            $i=$LastSet/864000000000
            write ($utc.AddDays($i))
        }
} #Get-PwdLastSetDate

    Function Get-PwdAge {

        Param([int64]$LastSet=0)
```

```
        if ($LastSet -eq 0) {
            write "0"
        } else {
            [datetime]$ChangeDate=Get-PwdLastSetDate $LastSet
            [datetime]$RightNow=Get-Date

            write $RightNow.Subtract($ChangeDate).Days
        }
    } #end Get-PwdAge

$Searcher = New-Object DirectoryServices.DirectorySearcher

# find all non-disabled user objects
$searcher.filter="(&(objectCategory=person)(objectClass=user)
(!userAccountControl:1.2.840.113556.1.4.803:=2))"

$searcher.findall() | ForEach-Object {

    New-Object -TypeName PSObject -Property @{
    "Name"=$_.properties.item("name")[0]
    "DN" = $_.properties.item("distinguishedname")[0]
    "Description" = $_.properties.item("description")[0]
    "AccountCreated" = $_.properties.item("whencreated")[0]
    "AccountModified" = $_.properties.item("WhenChanged")[0]
    "LastChanged" = (Get-PwdLastSetDate $_.properties.item("pwdlastset")[0])
    "PasswordAge" = (Get-PwdAge $_.properties.item("pwdlastset")[0])
    }
 } #close foreach
```

This script uses much of the same code you've already seen. It uses a DirectorySearcher class that looks for all non-disabled user accounts:

```
$Searcher = New-Object DirectoryServices.DirectorySearcher

# find all non-disabled user objects
$searcher.filter=`
"(&(objectCategory=person)(objectClass=user)(!userAccountControl:1.2.840.113556.1.4.803:=2))"
```

The search results are piped to the **ForEach-Object** cmdlet. Instead of simply returning the search result values, I create a custom object using the **New-Object** cmdlet and a hash table of properties. The custom object has properties for the user's name, distinguished name, description, when the account was created, when it was last changed, when the password was last set, and the password age in days.

Because the **Get-PasswordReport** script returns an object, you can use it in a PowerShell expression like this:

```
PS C:\> c:\scripts\get-passwordreport.ps1 | where {$_.Passwordage -gt 365} |
>> sort PasswordAge -desc | Format-Table Name,LastChanged,PasswordAge -auto
>>

Name              LastChanged           PasswordAge
----              -----------           -----------
svcSharepoint     5/24/2010 5:36:37 PM         1359
Bill Shakespeare  10/27/2006 6:01:01 PM        1203
da Hicks          5/17/2008 1:11:09 AM          637
Jack Frost        10/22/2008 3:36:49 AM         479
Administrator     1/3/2010 10:35:06 PM          405
Jeffery Hicks     1/18/2010 4:38:04 PM          390
```

Here's one more DirectorySearcher class example that you might use on a regular basis:

Get-Computers.ps1

```
Function Get-Computers {
# This function writes a custom object for each computer
# object in your Active Directory domain to the pipeline

    Function Get-PwdLastSetDate {

        Param([int64]$LastSet=0)
        if ($LastSet -eq 0) {
            write "Never Set or Re-Set"
        } else {
            [datetime]$utc="1/1/1601"
            $i=$LastSet/864000000000
            write ($utc.AddDays($i))
        }
    } #Get-PwdLastSet

    Function Get-PwdAge {

        Param([int64]$LastSet=0)
        if ($LastSet -eq 0) {
            write "0"
        } else {
            [datetime]$ChangeDate=Get-PwdLastSetDate $LastSet
            [datetime]$RightNow=Get-Date

            write $RightNow.Subtract($ChangeDate).Days
        }
    } #Get-PwdAge

    $searcher=New-Object DirectoryServices.DirectorySearcher
    $searcher.Filter="(&(objectCategory=Computer)(objectClass=Computer))"

    $searcher.findall() | ForEach-Object {
        New-Object -TypeName PSObject -Property @{
            "Name" = $_.properties.item("name")[0];
            "DN" = $_.properties.item("distinguishedname")[0]
            "DNSName" = $_.properties.item("dnshostname")[0]
            "OS" = $_.properties.item("operatingsystem")[0]
            "ServicePack" = $_.properties.item("operatingsystemservicepack")[0]
            "OSVersion" = $_.properties.item("operatingsystemversion")[0]
            "AccountCreated" = $_.properties.item("whencreated")[0]
            "AccountModified" = $_.properties.item("WhenChanged")[0]
            "PasswordLastChanged" = (Get-PwdLastSetDate $_.properties.item("pwdlastset")[0])
            "PasswordAge" = (Get-PwdAge $_.properties.item("pwdlastset")[0])
            }
 } #foreach
}
```

The **Get-Computers** function is very similar to the previous example. It also creates a custom object, although as the name indicates, the searcher is looking for computer objects. The function returns a custom object with properties such as name, operating system, and service pack. Even though the function is returning all computer objects, you can use it to find a single computer object as well:

```
PS C:\> get-computers | Where {$_.name -match "dogtoy"}

Name                : DOGTOY
DN                  : CN=DOGTOY,CN=Computers,DC=mycompany,DC=local
DNSName             : dogtoy.mycompany.local
OS                  : Windows XP Professional
ServicePack         : Service Pack 2
OSVersion           : 5.1 (2600)
AccountCreated      : 6/24/2010 12:10:11 PM
AccountModified     : 2/13/2010 11:00:33 AM
PasswordLastChanged : 10/3/2010 3:15:21 AM
PasswordAge         : 10
```

Don't forget that you'll need to dot source the script file before you can use the Get-Computers function.

Here's another example. Perhaps you'd like to find the servers in your Active Directory domain:

```
PS C:\> get-computers | Where {$_.OS -match "server"} | Format-Table Name,OS,ServicePack -auto

Name       OS                    ServicePack
----       --                    -----------
MYDC01     Windows Server 2003   Service Pack 2
SWITCH     Windows Server 2003   Service Pack 1
PORTAL     Windows Server 2003   Service Pack 1
```

This function can also help you identify obsolete computer accounts by checking the computer's password age:

```
PS C:\> get-computers | Where {$_.passwordage -gt 45} | Sort PasswordAge -descending |
>> Format-Table DN,PasswordLastChanged,PasswordAge -auto
>>

DN                                                      PasswordLastChanged     PasswordAge
--                                                      -------------------     -----------
CN=GODOT,CN=Computers,DC=mycompany,DC=local             10/24/2004 5:43:09 PM          1206
CN=SWITCH,CN=Computers,DC=mycompany,DC=local            9/14/2005 9:07:27 PM            881
CN=PORTAL,OU=Servers,DC=mycompany,DC=local              10/14/2005 11:41:32 PM          851
CN=DemoServer01,OU=Demo,OU=Servers,DC=mycompany,DC=local 3/13/2009 4:11:53 AM           337
CN=TestSrv02,OU=Servers,DC=mycompany,DC=local           3/13/2009 4:11:29 AM            337
CN=TestSrv01,OU=Servers,DC=mycompany,DC=local           3/13/2009 4:11:11 AM            337
CN=TestSrv207,OU=Demo,OU=Servers,DC=mycompany,DC=local  3/13/2009 11:14:09 PM           336
CN=TestSrv206,OU=Demo,OU=Servers,DC=mycompany,DC=local  3/13/2009 11:14:09 PM           336
CN=TestSrv205,OU=Demo,OU=Servers,DC=mycompany,DC=local  3/13/2009 11:14:09 PM           336
CN=TestSrv210,OU=Demo,OU=Servers,DC=mycompany,DC=local  3/13/2009 11:14:10 PM           336
CN=TestSrv209,OU=Demo,OU=Servers,DC=mycompany,DC=local  3/13/2009 11:14:10 PM           336
CN=TestSrv208,OU=Demo,OU=Servers,DC=mycompany,DC=local  3/13/2009 11:14:10 PM           336
CN=TestSrv201,OU=Demo,OU=Servers,DC=mycompany,DC=local  3/13/2009 11:14:09 PM           336
CN=TestSrv200,OU=Demo,OU=Servers,DC=mycompany,DC=local  3/13/2009 11:14:09 PM           336
CN=test123,OU=Demo,OU=Servers,DC=mycompany,DC=local     3/13/2009 11:13:21 PM           336
CN=TestSrv204,OU=Demo,OU=Servers,DC=mycompany,DC=local  3/13/2009 11:14:09 PM           336
CN=TestSrv203,OU=Demo,OU=Servers,DC=mycompany,DC=local  3/13/2009 11:14:09 PM           336
CN=TestSrv202,OU=Demo,OU=Servers,DC=mycompany,DC=local  3/13/2009 11:14:09 PM           336
```

Fine Tuning the DirectorySearcher

My test domains are not very large, so I can usually get by with many of the DirectorySearcher class default properties. However, if you have a larger domain and want to control the performance of your domain controller queries, then there are a few properties you should set. This is especially true if your query will return more than 1000 objects, otherwise you will only get the first 1000 objects.

The first property to tweak is **PageSize**, which has a default of 0 and which uses a non-paged query. The domain controller returns the results in pages, which you can think of as a set. Non-paged queries are fine for small domains, but with large domains, performance will be better if you use a value such as this:

```
$searcher.pagesize=100
```

Now the searcher will return 100 results per paged query.

The **SizeLimit** property determines how many total results the server returns. The default is 0. In a non-paged query, this will effectively set the maximum number of returned objects to the default server limit of 1000. Of course, you can set it to a smaller number:

```
$searcher.sizelimit=500
```

Now only 500 objects will be returned. However, if you want to ensure you retrieve all objects, set a value for the **PageSize** property greater than 0, such as 100. The DirectorySearcher class will return all objects regardless of the value of the **SizeLimit** property as long as the **PageSize** value is equal or greater than the **SizeLimit**.

Most of the examples in this section are searched from the domain root, which is the default. However, you may prefer to search from a particular organizational unit. In that case, you can specify a new search root like this:

```
$root=New-Object DirectoryServices.DirectoryEntry 'LDAP://OU=Employees,DC=MyCompany,DC=Local'
$searcher.searchroot=$root
```

In addition to modifying the search root, you may need to modify the search scope. The default search scope is SubTree, and the DirectorySearcher class will search the root and all child objects. Your other search scope options are Base and OneLevel. A search scope of OneLevel will return child objects within the current root, but it won't search any deeper. It's like SubTree, but without recursion:

```
$searcher.SearchScope="OneLevel"
```

Use the Base search scope when you are searching within a specific object like a group and you want to search based on a certain attribute. This is known as an Attribute Scope Query. Set your search root to a base object and set the search scope to Base:

```
PS C:\> $searcher.searchroot=[ADSI]"LDAP://CN=Sales Staff,OU=Groups,DC=mycompany,DC=Local"
PS C:\> $searcher.searchscope="Base"
```

Now you can specify the attribute you want to search on. In this example, I want to search based on the group's **Member** property:

```
PS C:\> $searcher.AttributeScopeQuery="member"
```

The searcher will search within the group object on the **Member** property, and it should return user accounts. However, I'm going to suggest one more minor tweak. You may only want a subset of properties returned from the query. In that case, add those properties to the **PropertiesToLoad** property:

```
PS C:\> $searcher.PropertiesToLoad.Add("GivenName")
0
PS C:\> $searcher.PropertiesToLoad.Add("SN")
1
PS C:\> $searcher.PropertiesToLoad.Add("sAMAccountname")
2
```

All that's left is to set the filter and search:

```
PS C:\> $searcher.filter="(&(objectclass=user)(objectcategory=person))"
PS C:\> $searcher.findall() | Foreach {
>> $_ | Select @{Name="ADSPath";Expression={$_.properties.adspath[0]}},
>>         @{Name="SAM";Expression={$_.properties.samaccountname[0]}},
>>         @{Name="FirstName";Expression={$_.properties.givenname[0]}},
>>         @{Name="LastName";Expression={$_.properties.sn[0]}}
>> }
>>

ADSPath                          SAM              FirstName                    LastName
-------                          ---              ---------                    --------
LDAP://CN=Tom Sawyer,OU=Sa...    tsawyer          Tom                          Sawyer
LDAP://CN=Sales User,OU=Te...    salesuser        Sales                        User
LDAP://CN=Cass Ino,OU=Sale...    cino             Cass                         Ino
```

Finally, you may wish to sort results in a particular order. The **Sort** property is a System. DirectoryServices.SortOption object. With this object, you can specify the property name you wish to sort on and in what order. The default order is ascending:

```
$searcher.sort="Name"
```

Once you've fine tuned your searcher parameters, you can execute your searches using the **FindOne()** or **FindAll()** methods.

Before I leave this topic, I want to return to my earlier directory tree example. Although I like the output, if my domain had more than 1000 container objects, it's not very efficient. Here's a much more efficient approach using the DirectorySearcher class:

Get-DSTree2.ps1

```
Function Get-DSTree {
    Param([ADSI]$ADSPath="LDAP://DC=mycompany,DC=local",[int]$i=0)

    [string]$leader=" "
    [int]$pad=$leader.length+$i

    $searcher=New-Object directoryservices.directorysearcher
    $searcher.pagesize=100
    $searcher.filter="(&(!objectcategory=person)(!objectcategory=computer)" `
    +"(!objectcategory=group)(!objectcategory=contact)(!objectcategory=domain))"
    $searcher.searchScope="OneLevel"
    $searcher.searchRoot=$ADSPath
    $searcher.PropertiesToLoad.Add("DistinguishedName") | Out-Null
```

```
    $searcher.FindAll()  | Foreach {
        Write-Host ($leader.Padleft($pad)+$_.properties.distinguishedname[0])
        Get-DSTree $_.path ($pad+1)
    }
}
```

At first glance, this function appears similar in structure to the first, and it is. The function takes a directory path and an integer to calculate the padded spaces. This gives the output its visual appeal. The function uses the DirectorySearcher class and paging:

```
$searcher=New-Object directoryservices.directorysearcher
$searcher.pagesize=100
```

The filter is an LDAP version of my original filter to find container-like objects:

```
$searcher.filter="(&(!objectcategory=person)(!objectcategory=computer)" `
+"(!objectcategory=group)(!objectcategory=contact)(!objectcategory=domain))"
```

Because I want to look at each "level," I'm setting the search scope to OneLevel:

```
$searcher.searchScope="OneLevel"
```

The DirectorySearcher class will only find matches in the first level of the search root:

```
$searcher.searchRoot=$ADSPath
```

Since I'm only interested in the distinguished name, I'll take advantage of the **PropertiesToLoad** property and limit my search:

```
$searcher.PropertiesToLoad.Add("DistinguishedName") | Out-Null
```

All that's left is to start searching. Each result is piped to the **ForEach** construct, which writes a padded space plus the distinguished name of each object. The object's path is then passed back to the function to search for any child objects:

```
$searcher.FindAll()  | Foreach {
    Write-Host ($leader.Padleft($pad)+$_.properties.distinguishedname[0])
    Get-DSTree $_.path ($pad+1)
}
```

This recursive search provides me the same output as I had before. But there is one major difference: my original version took over 26 seconds to complete. This version, using the DirectorySearcher class is much more efficient. I get the same output in under five seconds! You probably noticed a new object type in the function as well, [ADSI].

The ADSI Type Adapter

When PowerShell was being developed, the product team realized ADSI support would be critical to PowerShell's adoption and deployment. Unfortunately, as PowerShell architect Jeffrey Snover is fond of saying: "To ship is to choose." The team couldn't meet everyone's expectations with v1.0, though they did add a new type adapter before the final release. This type adapter, [ADSI], gives PowerShell users a hint that you will be working with directory service objects. Now, you no longer need to explicitly create System.DirectoryServices.DirectoryEntry objects. To create an object representing your root domain, all you need is this:

```
PS C:\> [ADSI]$dsroot="LDAP://dc=mycompany,dc=local"
PS C:\> $dsroot.whencreated

Wednesday, April 14, 2009 10:52:27 PM
```

Pipe $DSRoot to the **Get-Member** cmdlet and you'll see that the underlying object isn't anything other than what you've been working with this chapter:

```
PS C:\> $dsroot | Get-Member


   TypeName: System.DirectoryServices.DirectoryEntry

Name                            MemberType Definition
----                            ---------- ----------
auditingPolicy                  Property   System.DirectoryServices.P
creationTime                    Property   System.DirectoryServices.P
dc                              Property   System.DirectoryServices.P
distinguishedName               Property   System.DirectoryServices.P
dSASignature                    Property   System.DirectoryServices.P
...
```

When using the [ADSI], you can't specify a connection credential as I did in the example for creating a new System.DirectoryServices.DirectoryEntry object.

The type adapter provides simplicity. You can create an ADSI object with a single line of code and access all of its properties:

```
PS C:\> [ADSI]$jeff="LDAP://CN=Jeffery Hicks,OU=home,DC=mycompany,DC=local"
PS C:\> $jeff.telephonenumber
555-1234
PS C:\> $jeff | Select Displayname,Department,Title,Company

displayName            department                     title                         company
-----------            ----------                     -----                         -------
{Jeffery Hicks}        {Projects,Training and Ser...  {SAPIEN Guru}                 {SAPIEN
```

The adaptation isn't perfect. For example, some properties like **pwdLastSet** are still stored as COM objects, so I need to use the functions I created earlier in the chapter to read the property:

```
PS C:\> get-pwdage (convert-adslargeinteger $jeff.pwdlastset.value)
391
PS C:\> get-pwdlastsetdate (convert-adslargeinteger $jeff.pwdlastset.value)

Thursday, January 18, 2010 4:38:04 PM
```

When you look at an object like $jeff piped to the **Get-Member** cmdlet, you'll see not every possible ADSI property and method is listed. However, if you know the property or method name, you can still call it. Here's an example:

```
PS C:\> [ADSI]$rgbiv="LDAP://CN=Roy G. Biv,OU=Employees,DC=SAPIEN,dc=local"
PS C:\> $rgbiv.SetPassword("N3wP@$$")
PS C:\> $rgbiv.SetInfo()
```

You'll never see a **SetInfo()** method, yet that is the method to call when setting a user's password. There are some things you are expected to already know.

Once you have the knowledge, you can use a type adapter like this to create a user account in a given organizational unit:

```
PS C:\> [ADSI]$ou="LDAP://OU=Employees,DC=MyCompany,dc=local"
PS C:\> $user=$ou.Create("user","CN=Jim Shortz")
PS C:\> $user.put("samaccountname","jshortz")
PS C:\> $user.setinfo()
PS C:\> $user.SetPassword("P@ssw0rd")
PS C:\> $user.put("title","Health Director")
PS C:\> $user.put("userprincipalname","jshortz@mycompany.com")
PS C:\> $user.put("givenname","Jim")
PS C:\> $user.put("sn","Shortz")
PS C:\> #enable the user account
PS C:\> $user.put("Useraccountcontrol",544)
PS C:\> $user.put("DisplayName","Jim Shortz")
PS C:\> $user.SetInfo()
```

The $ou variable will be a DirectoryServices.DirectoryEntry type which I already know has a **Create()** method for creating child objects:

```
PS C:\> $user=$ou.Create("user","CN=Jim Shortz")
```

The $user object will automatically be defined also as a DirectoryServices.DirectoryEntry object. I know that the **SAMAccountName** property must be defined and the object saved before I can make any other changes to it:

```
PS C:\> $user.put("samaccountname","jshortz")
PS C:\> $user.setinfo()
```

Once the object is committed to Active Directory I can go ahead and set the rest of the user properties. If I wasn't sure about property names, I could pipe $user to the **Get-Member** cmdlet to discover them.

If this chapter seems like a lot of work, well…it is. The .NET Framework classes PowerShell requires for directory service management aren't the easiest to work with for non-developers and PowerShell's abstraction, ostensibly to make life easier for you, isn't as complete as either you or I might like. If you read the rest of the book I trust you realized how much easier it is to use cmdlets. Although, even those cmdlets rely on the underlying .NET Framework classes so understanding them now will definitely help you out later.

Index

H

I

L

M

N

S

CPSIA information can be obtained at www.ICGtesting.com
Printed in the USA
LVOW11s2023250713

344556LV00005B/117/P

9 780982 131442